Birnbaum's

Walt Disney World

Expert Advice from the Inside Source

Wendy Lefkon EDITORIAL DIRECTOR

Jill Safro EDITOR

Frieda Christofides DESIGNER

Jody Revenson CONSULTING EDITOR

Alexandra Mayes Birnbaum CONSULTING EDITOR

Jessica Ward EDITORIAL ASSISTANT

Stephen Birnbaum FOUNDING EDITOR

Table of

Getting Ready to Go

7

Here is all the practical information you need to organize a Walt Disney World visit, down to the smallest detail: when to go; how to get there; how to save money and work within a budget; plus sample schedules; and hints for parents, travelers with disabilities, singles, and older visitors.

Transportation & Accommodations

55

Two big questions about Walt Disney World are where to stay and how to get around. Accommodations range from concierge suites to modest campsites, with thousands of rooms and villas in between. Our guide describes every Disney resort, with details presented in a handy chart. And we explain the World's vast transportation system, to boot.

Magic Kingdom

97

The enchantment of Walt Disney World is most apparent in the wealth of attractions and amusements that fill this, the most famous entertainment zone of all. Our land-by-land guide describes all there is to see and do, where to shop, and how to avoid the crowds, plus plenty of other insider tips.

Epcot

127

A gleaming silver geosphere introduces Walt Disney World's wonderland of discovery—an ambitious exploration of the world of the future as well as the present. Future World and World Showcase offer every visitor the opportunity to be a global and cerebral voyager, without setting foot outside Florida. Here's how to make the most of this uniquely fascinating destination.

Disney-MGM Studios

159

Now's your chance to be part of Hollywood's golden years. Everything from the magic of animation to the excitement of daring stunts and special effects is waiting to be enjoyed. There are also opportunities to go behind the scenes, create sound effects, and even experience a thrill ride or two. We've developed strategies for seeing this Tinseltown, ensuring the most fun and the least time standing around.

Disney's Animal Kingdom

175

This latest addition to Walt Disney World's theme park lineup celebrates the circle of life and all the wonders of the animal world. Amid nature's soothing majesty, you'll experience a stirring African safari, dodge dastardly dinosaurs, and ride raging rapids. Our detailed coverage guarantees a fun-filled trip to a place where humans are humbly reminded of their tenuous position in the food chain.

Contents

Everything Else in the World

Beyond the theme park boundaries lie countless acres full of just the sorts of wonders for which Disney is famous: state-of-the-art water parks, and a night-time entertainment, shopping, and dining district among them. So if you want to ride down watery slides, dance the night away, shop at elegant boutiques, pamper yourself at a spa, or even learn a few tricks of the trade by slipping behind the scenes, this chapter will help you find your way.

Sports

Walt Disney World has more tennis courts and golf greens than most posh resorts, plus plenty of places for boating, biking, horseback riding, swimming, and fishing. Here's how to combine these options with the rest of the fun at Walt Disney World.

Good Meals, Great Times

Restaurants around Disney World property run the gamut from simple snack shops to bastions of haute cuisine. Choices are nearly endless, so we've organized them into an area-by-area directory that lets you know where each restaurant is located and what specialties it offers, and a roundup of the dining spots we consider Birnbaum's Bests. We also tell you about the dinner shows, the best family fare, where to dine with Disney characters, and where to enjoy an after-dinner drink.

WHAT'S NEW?

To spotlight attractions making their Walt Disney World debut, some listings are marked with the special stamp shown here. Look for it throughout the book. Here are few highlights:

For Steve, who merely made all this possible

ISBN 1-4231-0051-4

Printed in the United States of America

Other 2007 Birnbaum's Official Disney Guides

Disney Cruise Line
Disneyland Resort
Walt Disney World Dining
Walt Disney World For Kids, By Kids
Walt Disney World Without Kids

A Word from the Editor

For some of us, our first Walt Disney World experience dates back to 1971, the year this new "Disneyland in Florida" made its debut. At that time, the Magic Kingdom was the only theme park, and it could be explored easily in a few days. Nonetheless, for those who came, it was love at first sight, and we've returned again and again.

This year, as Walt Disney World's second theme park, Epcot, marks its 25th anniversary (Where did the time go?!) there is as much incentive as ever to visit (and revisit) the memory-making capital of the world. The Living Seas, one of Epcot's original pavilions, has been revamped, revitalized, and renamed. The Seas with Nemo & Friends boasts a new undersea attraction and an innovative, interactive encounter

Editor Jill Safro consults with Mickey and Minnie, the ultimate Disney insiders.

with an animated turtle. The Land's high-flying Soarin' attraction continues to delight. And the Epcot International Food and Wine festival gets bigger and better each year. Of course, that's just the tip of the iceberg, as so much of Walt Disney World has grown and evolved since our last edition. We are both privileged and proud to provide readers with our extensively researched, insider look at some of the most cherished attractions, resorts, and restaurants on Earth.

When Steve Birnbaum launched this guide back in 1981, he made it clear what was expected of anyone who worked on it. The book would be meticulously revised each year, leaving no attraction untested, no snack or meal untasted, no hotel untried. First-hand experiences like these, accumulated over the years, make this book the most authoritative guide to the World. Our expertise, however, is not achieved by being escorted through back doors of attractions (although we would thoroughly enjoy that). Instead, we wait in lines with everyone else, always hoping to have a Disney experience like that of any other guest. Happily, logistical pickles are few and far between, leaving us time to investigate all the nooks and crannies of Walt's vast World.

After 35 fun-filled years, the World and the number of visitors have expanded—and so has our knowledge of the most popular vacation destination on the planet. On some occasions we've encountered sweltering weather and swelling crowds—times when even the happiest of travelers can turn into Grumpy for a moment or two. Had we known then what we know now, we could have spared ourselves some trying experiences. In one case, a staffer waited more than an hour to take a tour at the Studios. Standing in line with a notebook, she was asked by another guest if there was a quiz at the end. When she explained what she was doing, he expressed surprise to learn that she was waiting with the masses. But that's always been our strategy. We figure, the best way to gather useful advice for a Walt Disney World guest is to be one. Over and over again!

Take Our Advice

We've done our best to keep you from making any mistakes. We realize that even the most meticulous vacation planner needs *detailed, accurate, and objective information* to prepare a successful itinerary. To achieve that goal, we encourage the sharing of insight and information from Walt Disney World staffers—but the decision to use such information or not is entirely up to the discretion of the editor.

To that end, we have packaged handy bits of advice in the form of sample itineraries and "hot tips" throughout the book. This advice comes directly from the copious notes we've taken during our thousands of days spent in Walt Disney World. We've also used our "Birnbaum's Best" stamp of approval wherever we deemed it appropriate, highlighting our favorite attractions and restaurants—the crowd-pleasers we believe stand head, shoulders, and ears above the rest.

You, the reader, benefit from the combination of our many years of experience that, together with our access to current insider information, makes this guide unique. We like to think it's indispensable, but we'll let you be the judge of that a couple hundred pages from now.

Credit Where Credit Is Due

I hope I'm not omitting any names in thanking Debbie Mookini, Geoff Cook, Terri Alexandrou, Joe Schott, Karen Haynes, Mark Peters, Dara Trujillo, Barb Carroll, Sarah Morris, Cookie Abney, Carrie Matson, Amy Foster, Monica Griffin, Richard Gregory, Jen Rother, Mark Jaronski, Christi Erwin, Jason Laseki, Alison Mahoney, Christian Dhyne, Leigh Ann Thompson, Janice Hilliard, Bebee Frost, Irene Ferdinand, Rhonda Rosner, Stacey Cook, Pam Brandon, Darlene Papalini, Laura Simpson, and Jeff Titelius. Special thanks to Dave Herbst, who does so much to ensure the factual accuracy of the Birnbaum Guides.

Kudos to Michelle Olveira, for her outstanding fact-checking effort, to indexer William Feik, to proofreaders Sue Macy and Linda Verdon, and to Diane Hodges and Sharon Krinsky, copy editors extraordinaire. Heartfelt thanks, also, to Erika Warcholak, Nisha Panchal, Janet Castiglione, Sue Cole, Monica Mayper, and Guy Cunningham for their editorial support and production panache.

Hats off to those for whom doing Walt Disney World research is truly a labor of love. The "volunteer" class of 2007 includes Irene Safro, Roy Safro, Joy Safro, Amy Safro, Margaret Verdon, Linda Verdon, and Trace Schielzo.

Of course, no list of acknowledgments would be complete without mentioning our founding editor, Steve Birnbaum, whose spirit, wisdom, and humor still infuse these pages, as well as Alexandra Mayes Birnbaum, who continues to be a guiding light—to say nothing of being a careful reader of every word.

The Last Word

Finally, it's important to remember that every worthwhile travel guide is a living enterprise; the book you hold in your hands is our best effort at explaining how to enjoy Walt Disney World at this moment, but its text is in no way etched in stone. Disney is constantly changing and growing, and in each annual edition, we refine and expand our material to serve your needs even better. For this year's edition, though, this must be the final word.

Have a great visit!

Jill Safro

Don't Forget to Write

No contribution is of greater value to us in preparing the next edition of this book than your comments on what we have written and on your own experiences at Walt Disney World. Please share your insights with us by writing to:

Jill Safro, Editor
Birnbaum's Walt Disney World 2007
Disney Editions
114 Fifth Avenue, 14th Floor
New York, NY 10011

Getting Ready to Go

The key to a fabulous vacation at Walt Disney World is advance planning. This remarkably varied complex is too vast and diverse to allow a spontaneous visit to be undertaken with much success—especially when you consider the rapid rate at which the World has expanded. That does not mean that even the most casual visitors can't have some significant fun, but they are bound to have regrets about things they missed because of time pressures or a simple lack of information. The purpose of this guide is to eliminate potential frustration while getting the biggest bang for your vacation buck.

What follows, then, is meant to provide a sensible scheme for planning a satisfying visit to Walt Disney World, one that will offer the most fun and the least amount of disappointment. But how do you know which of the countless activities will be the most enjoyable for you and your family? Do your homework. The best strategy is to make sure you have a clear idea of all that is available long *before* you arrive in the Orlando area.

When to Go

When talk finally turns to the best time to make a trip to Walt Disney World, Christmas and Easter are often mentioned, as well as the traditional summer vacation period—especially if there are children in the family. But there is also good reason to avoid these periods, namely the tremendous crowds they attract. And when Disney World is crowded, it can be very crowded, indeed. On the busiest days, visitors may wait as much as two hours to experience the more popular attractions when waiting in lines. That's at least twice as long as during less busy times of the year. What's more, Fastpass assignments (see page 25) have a tendency to be maxed out early in the day.

Considering seasonal hours, weather, and the crowd patterns described in the charts that follow, optimal times to visit Walt Disney World are usually mid-January through early February, late April through late May, and September through December (except Thanksgiving and Christmas weeks).

Note that during some of the less crowded times of the year—particularly during the winter—some attractions are closed for renovations. In addition, water parks are often closed for refurbishment during cooler months. Call 407-824-4321 or check *www.disneyworld.com* for a current schedule, updated each season.

December is an especially festive time of year the world over, and Walt Disney World is no exception. All of the theme parks are decorated to the nines for the holiday season. The Magic Kingdom and Epcot hold nightly tree-lighting ceremonies. Many other special events are held during this period, including Mickey's Very Merry Christmas Party in the Magic

Kingdom (a separate admission ticket is required). The party brings a dusting of snow to Main Street from about 7 P.M. to midnight for several days between mid-November and the first three weeks of December. It also features holiday shows around the park, including Mickey's Very Merry Christmas Parade, plus a unique fireworks show: Holiday Wishes. Select performances from Mickey's Very Merry Christmas Party are also staged in the park during regular hours on the days leading up to, including, and following Christmas. Note that this event is extremely popular and usually sells out long ahead of time. Plan to purchase tickets in advance by calling 407-W-DIS-NEY (934-7639). It's usually easier to snag tickets for dates earlier in the season.

Epcot celebrates the season with Holidays Around the World, including the nightly Candlelight Processional, complete with 450-voice choir, 50-piece orchestra, and a reading of the story of Christmas by a celebrity narrator. Dinner packages are available for some World Showcase restaurants. (We recommend the dinner package: It guarantees seating for dinner as well as preferred seating at the Candlelight Processional. Without a package, you should arrive at least one hour before showtime or risk being shut out of your preferred performance.) The Disney-MGM Studios features a popular display of millions of lights depicting holiday scenes. Animal Kingdom offers Mickey's Jingle Jungle Parade. For updated information regarding the dates and location of this perennially popular, sparkly spectacular, visit *www.disneyworld.com*.

There are holiday decorations at each WDW hotel, too, including a Victorian Christmas at the Grand Floridian, a seaside party at the Yacht and Beach Club, and a Cajun holiday at Port Orleans Riverside.

For reservations, call a travel agent or 407-W-DISNEY (934-7639) or the Walt Disney Travel Company at 407-828-8101. Call 407-939-7630 or visit *www.disneyworld.com* for information. Special-event tickets are available separately.

Hot Tip!

The period between the end of Thanksgiving and the week before Christmas is one of the least crowded and most festive times of the year. It's a wonderful time to visit.

Crowd Patterns

Day-to-Day Trends

In general, the weekends tend to be among the most crowded days at Walt Disney World theme parks—most notably during the summer months and other peak periods. Monday is also a notoriously busy day, especially at the Magic Kingdom. Morning through early afternoon is a bustling time for the theme parks and their respective "E-ticket" attractions. Days that offer "Extra Magic Hours" tend to be more crowded at their respective theme parks (see page 21). When the weather's steamy, the water parks tend to pack them in—so be sure to get an early start if you're headed to Blizzard Beach or Typhoon Lagoon.

When the time comes to plot an itinerary, it's helpful to know about crowd patterns beyond the four theme parks as well. As a rule, Downtown Disney and Disney's water parks host their largest throngs on weekends. Of course, in these circles, a bigger crowd could possibly mean a better time. Golfers should note that weekend tee times are typically in the highest demand, while Monday and Tuesday tee times are the easiest to come by.

Seasonal Shifts

The chart below indicates the density of crowds in the theme parks throughout the year. Though it's tough to generalize about a property as vast and ever-changing as Walt Disney World—special events and package deals can swell park attendance during a period typically marked by smaller crowds—the chart highlights historic trends.

"Least Crowded" means that there will be lines, but most attractions can be visited without much waiting.

"Average Attendance" refers to times when there are lots of people around, but lines are relatively manageable.

"Most Crowded" reflects times when lines at popular attractions can mean a wait of as much as two hours. As a rule, when school is out, the crowds are most definitely in at Walt Disney World.

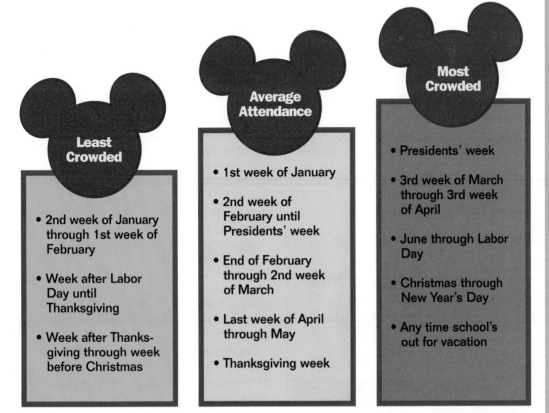

Least Crowded

- 2nd week of January through 1st week of February

- Week after Labor Day until Thanksgiving

- Week after Thanksgiving through week before Christmas

Average Attendance

- 1st week of January

- 2nd week of February until Presidents' week

- End of February through 2nd week of March

- Last week of April through May

- Thanksgiving week

Most Crowded

- Presidents' week

- 3rd week of March through 3rd week of April

- June through Labor Day

- Christmas through New Year's Day

- Any time school's out for vacation

Holidays and Special Events

Special affairs are staged throughout the year, not only to mark holidays but also to celebrate other interests. *The dates and details below are subject to change without notice;* call 407-824-4321 to confirm, or check out *www.disneyworld.com* for up-to-the-minute information about specific events.

JANUARY

Walt Disney World Marathon (January 7): Some 14,000 entrants run through several theme parks, Disney's Wide World of Sports complex, and many other areas of the World during this 26.2-mile race. Disney characters and cast members are on hand to inspire runners. Similar hoopla surrounds the half marathon (January 6). There's also a 5K run. (It's okay to walk this one.) Packages are available. Visit *www.disneyworldmarathon.com*, or call 407-939-7810 for information. Note that hotel rooms are in high demand for this event. Reserve yours as early as possible.

MARCH

Saint Patrick's Day (March 17): Everyone is Irish on Saint Patrick's Day—especially at Raglan Road, Pleasure *Ire*land's Irish Pub. Epcot's United Kingdom pavilion marks the day with Irish dining and dancing.

Atlanta Braves Spring Training (March): Play ball! Having weathered a long winter, giddy baseball fans flock to Disney's Wide World of Sports complex to enjoy a long overdue dose of America's Favorite Pastime.

APRIL

Easter (April 8): Most of the Disney theme parks stay open late during the two weeks straddling the Easter holiday. Keep in mind that this is an extremely busy time to visit.

Epcot International Flower and Garden Festival (mid-April through early June): Epcot is blooming with elaborate gardens (including more than 30 million fragrant blossoms) and topiary displays, behind-the-scenes tours, gardening workshops, concerts, and guest speakers. Learn from the experts how to create a beautiful garden of your own.

MAY – JUNE

Star Wars Weekends (May–June): Disney-MGM Studios salutes *Star Wars* with celebrities and characters from the movies, plus photo opportunities, trivia contests, and more.

JULY

Fourth of July Celebration: Double-size fireworks over the Magic Kingdom, Epcot, and the Disney-MGM Studios make for a very colorful night. This is an exceptionally busy time to visit Disney World.

SEPTEMBER

Night of Joy: Two nights of celebration highlight contemporary Christian music presented live in the Magic Kingdom. For dates and tickets, call 407-827-7200. Note that this very popular event attracts a bit of a rowdy crowd (of mostly teens and groups of young adults).

OCTOBER

WDW Golf Classic (October): Top PGA Tour players compete alongside amateurs in this big tourney, played on the Palm and Magnolia golf courses. Special packages are available. For more information, call 407-824-2250.

Epcot International Food and Wine Festival (October–mid-November): World Showcase celebrates the flavors of different countries (even those not usually represented around the lagoon) through tastings ($2 to $7 per sample), demos from top chefs, and wine and cooking seminars. It's a satisfying way in which to wander World Showcase.

Halloween (late October): Festivities vary from year to year. Past celebrations have included window displays and storytellers at Epcot.

Fort Wilderness Resort and Campground generally hosts a pumpkin-carving contest and a children's costume contest, followed by a screening of a scary movie.

Downtown Disney has hosted kids' costume contests and trick-or-treating. Grown-ups have been known to don costumes, too.

The Magic Kingdom will play host to its Halloween spectacular, **Mickey's Not-So-Scary Halloween Party**, mid-September through October. The special-ticket activities include a costume parade, dancing, appearances by Disney villains, trick-or-treating, and Halloween fireworks. This is an extremely popular Magic Kingdom event. Purchase your tickets as far in advance as possible. And don't forget to wear a costume!

As a spooky bonus, **Mickey's Boo to You Halloween Parade** makes its way through the Kingdom during the Halloween party. For information about specific dates on which the not-so-scary party will take place, call 407-824-4321.

NOVEMBER

ABC Super Soap Weekend: A celebration of ABC daytime dramas is held at the Disney-MGM Studios each year. Guests can meet soap stars; collect autographs; compete in trivia contests; and see sets, props, and costumes. For more information, call 407-397-6808.

Festival of the Masters (November): This three-day fine arts show draws more than 175 of the world's top artists to Downtown Disney.

DECEMBER

Disney's Magical Holidays: Decorations and festivities abound in Walt Disney World's parks and resorts. The Magic Kingdom hosts **Mickey's Very Merry Christmas Party** on several nights from mid-November through the first three weeks of December, complete with snow flurries on Main Street and hot cocoa. Entertainment for the special-ticket party includes **Mickey's Very Merry Christmas Parade** and a special edition of the Wishes fireworks show; select performances are staged during regular hours just before Christmas. Animal Kingdom presents the **Jingle Jungle Parade** during the holiday season, too.

Epcot's **Holidays Around the World** (November–December) features "The Lights of Winter" and a Christmas Candlelight Processional, including a choral concert, plus a celebrity narrator. The event is included with park admission, but seating is limited and it is extremely popular. Arrive at least an hour before showtime, or book a dinner package (which combines dinner at a World Showcase eatery with guaranteed Processional seating). For more information, call 407-824-4321.

The Osborne Family Spectacle of Lights (November–January) is back. This dazzling light display brightens the Disney-MGM Studios with millions of lights in the Streets of America area. For updates on this perennially popular holiday event, call 407-934-7639.

New Year's Eve Celebration (December 31): There are extra-large fireworks displays over the Magic Kingdom, Epcot, and the Disney-MGM Studios. These parks are usually open until about 1 A.M. (It varies from year to year.) Pleasure Island has also hosted special-ticket parties in the past. Many of the resort restaurants, as well as the nightspots at Downtown Disney West Side, also welcome the new year Disney style.

Keeping WDW Hours

Since operating hours fluctuate quite a bit, we strongly advise calling 407-824-4321 or visiting *www.disneyworld.com* for schedules—and confirm the information before you leave home.

THEME PARKS: Theme park hours vary seasonally. In May, September, October, parts of November and December, and all of January, the Magic Kingdom is usually open from 9 A.M. to 8 P.M.; Epcot is open from 9 A.M. to 9 P.M.; World Showcase opens at 11 A.M. and Future World closes at 7 P.M.; the Disney-MGM Studios is open from 9 A.M. until about dusk; and Animal Kingdom is open from 9 A.M. until about 5 P.M. The parks take turns offering "Extra Magic Hours" throughout the week. That is, on any given day, one of the parks may allow Disney World resort guests to enter an hour early or stay in the park for up to 3 hours after it closes to the public. For information and the Extra Magic Hours schedule, call 407-824-4321 or inquire at your resort's front desk when you check in.

The Magic Kingdom usually keeps later hours through summer and other busy periods, including Christmas and Easter. The parks may be open until 1 A.M. on New Year's Eve. The Disney-MGM Studios often stays open until 10 or 11 P.M. in the summer, too.

DOWNTOWN DISNEY MARKETPLACE: Shops are usually open from 9:30 A.M. until 11 P.M. daily. Restaurant hours vary.

DOWNTOWN DISNEY PLEASURE ISLAND: Clubs are open from about 8 P.M. to 1 or 2 A.M. nightly. At press time it was free to visit the island, but certain venues charged a cover.

DOWNTOWN DISNEY WEST SIDE: At the AMC Theatres cineplex, movies begin at about 1 P.M. Restaurants are generally open from about 11:30 A.M. to midnight. Shops are generally open from 11 A.M. to 11 P.M.

WATER PARKS: The water parks are open from about 10 A.M. to 5 P.M., with extended hours during summer months. An Extra Magic Hour is offered for most WDW resort guests on select mornings.

GETTING READY TO GO

WDW Weather

| | TEMPERATURE AVERAGE | | RAINFALL |
	High	Low	Average (inches)
January	71	49	2.3
February	73	50	3.0
March	78	55	3.2
April	83	59	1.8
May	88	66	3.6
June	91	72	7.3
July	92	73	7.2
August	92	73	6.8
September	90	72	6.0
October	85	65	2.4
November	79	58	2.3
December	73	51	2.2

How to Get There

By Car

While most visitors to the Orlando area fly in, some prefer to drive. If you opt for a road trip, pack lots of music and figure on logging no more than 350 to 400 miles a day—a reasonable distance that won't wear you down so much that you can't enjoy your trip.

Contact state tourist boards to inquire about the availability of free maps; for a Florida map and guide, call 888-735-2872, or pay a visit to *www.flausa.com*. Other map sources are the *Rand McNally Road Atlas* and the *AAA North American Road Atlas*; both are sold in bookstores. Driving directions from most cities are also available on the Internet. One site to try is *www.mapquest.com*.

From Orlando International Airport

By car: During rush hour, take the airport's South Exit to the Central Florida Greeneway (Route 417) to Route 536, which leads to Walt Disney World. The tolls run about $2.

For the shortest route, take the North Exit to Route 528 (now known as the "Beachline" Expressway), going west toward Tampa. Pick up I-4 west, and go to a WDW exit. The trip takes about half an hour, and tolls are $1.25. The route is heavily trafficked at all times, but manageable during non-rush periods of the day (with rush periods including weekday mornings and evenings and any time when a theme park is scheduled to open or close).

By Disney's Magical Express: Initiated in 2005, this tailor-made, complimentary transportation program is available to guests staying at select Walt Disney World resorts. For more information on the program, turn to page 15.

By car service: Reliable, friendly, towncar service is available from A Selective Limousine, Inc. Selective's drivers take guests directly to their resort. The company offers a special, round-trip rate for Birnbaum readers—mention this book and expect to pay about $95 for up to four passengers. Reservations are required and cancellations must be made at least 24 hours ahead. To make reservations, call 800-730-0211 or 407-854-7503.

Florida Towncar also offers efficient, congenial, direct service to Disney area resorts. And they offer our readers a special rate, too! Simply mention the Birnbaum guide when you book your ride and expect a round-trip rate of about $95 for up to 5 passengers. Call 407-277-5466 or 800-525-7246 up to 24 hours ahead, or visit *www.floridatowncar.com*. Online reservations should be made at least a week ahead.

By shuttle: At Orlando International Airport, Mears Motor Shuttle offers vans and buses 24 hours a day. It serves the Swan and Dolphin, Hotel Plaza Blvd. properties, and other non-Disney, area hotels. Shuttles make multiple stops; a trip can take an hour or more. On the return trip, Mears requires guests be picked up at least 3–4 hours prior to flight times. Reservations must be made 24 hours ahead.

The shuttle cost to most hotels is $18 one-way, $30 round-trip per adult; $14 one-way, $22 round-trip per child ages 4 through 11; free for children under 3. Fares to International Drive properties are a little lower. There may be a wait of up to three hours to get on a shuttle at the airport (it's happened to us on more than one occasion) and service is generally not direct. Call 407-423-5566 for information, or visit *www.mearstransportation.com*.

Cabs cost between $35 and $50 each way, depending on the destination. A taxi can accommodate up to 9 people and the trip is direct, so it's a good alternative to the shuttle. There's a taxi stand by baggage claim. Bell services can call for a cab at any WDW resort.

Gratuities are not included in any of the transfer rates. It is customary to tip for good service.

Reputable automobile clubs offer help with breakdowns; towing; insurance that covers personal injury, accidents, arrest, bail bond, and lawyers' fees for defense of contested traffic cases; and travel-planning services, including free maps and route mapping. Services vary from one club to the next, and membership fees range widely, from $36 to $85 a year.

By Air

When it comes to airfares, there is no real trick to unearthing the most economical ones: simply shop around. Call a travel agent, browse the Internet, and keep these tips in mind:

- Watch your local newspapers for ads announcing short-term promotional fares. When a deal presents itself, grab it.

- The more flexible you can be in your dates and duration of stay, the more money you're likely to save.

- Take advantage of advance-purchase fares (lower rates that apply if a ticket is bought at least two to three weeks prior to the scheduled departure).

- Keep in mind that the lowest airfares usually carry a penalty if you have to revise your flight schedule, and that certain discounted tickets are nonrefundable.

- When you call to make a reservation, ask about any fare restrictions, including an obligatory Saturday night stay-over.

- Fly when most people don't: For vacation destinations, that usually means leaving the ground midweek.

- If a fare comes down after you've purchased a ticket, you may be able to get a refund from the airline.

- Check out airline websites. They may e-mail information to you about discounted fares. Some sites even offer a discount for purchasing tickets online.

- As airlines go, we highly recommend JetBlue Airways. Their prices are usually reasonable and the service is second to none; visit *www.jetblue.com*.

By Train

Amtrak serves the Orlando area twice daily to and from New York City, with various stops made along the way. The trip takes approximately 22 hours and costs from about $208 to $456 round-trip, coach. (Book early for lower fares; discounts are often available, so be sure to ask.) If you're staying at Walt Disney World, plan to take a cab or shuttle to the area hotels. The cost varies, depending on the destination. Rental cars are also available by shuttle.

For reservations and information on this and other routes, call 800-USA-RAIL (872-7245), visit the Amtrak website at *www.amtrak.com*, or contact a travel agent.

By Bus

Greyhound provides frequent direct service to Orlando and Kissimmee (the latter is closer to Walt Disney World). From either destination, you can take a taxi to your hotel, but first check if your hotel offers shuttle service.

For more information, contact Greyhound at 800-231-2222 or visit *www.greyhound.com*.

Disney's Magical Express Service

Disney's Magical Express service is for guests planning a stay at a Walt Disney World-owned-and-operated resort and arriving at Orlando International Airport. Meant as a money-saver as well as a convenience, the service lets guests check luggage at their airport of origin, bypass baggage claim, and board a bus to their WDW resort. The luggage, which guests affix with special tags before leaving home, is usually delivered to the resort room within several hours of arrival. On the final day of a trip, prior to boarding the bus back to the airport, guests who fly participating airlines (at press time, that included JetBlue, American, Continental, Delta, United, and Ted), check their luggage at their resort and receive a boarding pass for their airline. Once at the airport, they can skip the airline check-in counter and proceed directly to the line for security. If you'd prefer to schlep your own bags, you can still hitch a free ride on the bus. Here are some specifics:

- Magical Express service is booked when you book your resort and must be done at least 10 days prior to arrival. (Have flight information handy when you make the call.) We recommend making the reservation as early as possible—preferably five to six weeks ahead.
- Reservations may be made via *www.disneyworld.com*, 407-W-DISNEY, or a travel agent.
- Tip the driver as you would had you paid for the trip: $1–$2 per bag is appropriate.
- Special luggage tags will be sent to the party that makes the reservation. These tags must be put on all bags that will be checked at the airport.
- Upon arrival at Orlando International Airport, follow signs to baggage claim (though you don't actually have to collect your luggage). Once you get to baggage claim, you'll find the Magical Express buses by following signs for GROUND TRANSPORTATION. Don't forget to have your transfer vouchers handy. Check in at the desk.
- On the return trip, expect to be picked up at least three hours before your scheduled flight departure time. Consider that when you make your air arrangements.
- Guests who require wheelchair accessible transportation should make their needs known when making the reservation. Confirm reservations before you leave home.
- Guests flying on "non-participating" airlines are entitled to the free shuttle service, too.

The good news? It is a money saver. In fact, a family of four can shave at least $80 off their total vacation cost by taking the Magical Express shuttle as opposed to other forms of transportation. It's also handy to bypass check-in at the airport on the return trip. The downside? Well, to call any service "magical" is to elevate expectations. It's not really "express," either—as most buses make multiple stops at Disney resorts. So if time is of the essence, it might not be the best choice. Same goes for the transportation of luggage. It may take an hour to arrive at your resort room, but it may also take three to six. So if you'll need anything right away—bathing suits, pajamas, sunscreen, medication, etc.—pack it in a day bag, carry it onto the plane, and transport it to the resort yourself.

Planning Ahead
Logistics

Organizing a trip properly takes time, but most travelers find the increased enjoyment well worth the effort. The fact is, planning can become a pleasant sort of "armchair" exercise, and kids will enjoy their visit to Disney all the more if they, too, are involved in the process.

To assist in that effort, we immodestly recommend *Birnbaum's Walt Disney World For Kids, By Kids*, a colorful look at the World from a young person's perspective, written for readers ages 7 through 14. For adults traveling *sans* children, *Birnbaum's Walt Disney World Without Kids* is the definitive source.

Information Sources

For information about Walt Disney World, call 407-824-4321. Lots of current specifics, such as park hours, ticket prices, refurbishment schedules, and directions are available through an automated system 24 hours a day. To speak with a representative, call 407-824-2222. For information by mail, write to Walt Disney World, Box 10000, Lake Buena Vista, FL 32830-1000.

Internet users can tap into updates about happenings in the World, get information on trip planning, reserve a room, order tickets, and get theme park hours and special-events listings by entering *www.disneyworld.com*. Disney Cruise Line vacation packages may be booked at *www.disneycruise.com*.

For information and discounts on area attractions, restaurants, and hotels, contact the Official Visitor Information Center, 8723 International Dr., Suite 101, Orlando, FL 32819; 407-363-5872 or 800-551-0181. Another resource for Orlando-area happenings is *www.orlandoinfo.com*.

For details about other Central Florida attractions, contact Visit Florida, 661 E. Jefferson St., Suite 300, Tallahassee, FL 32301; 888-735-2872 (to request a complimentary visitors guide and map) or 850-488-5607; *www.visitflorida.com*.

Disney Information Center: This full-service visitors center, located at the intersection of I-75 and S.R. 200 in Ocala, Florida, about 90 miles north of Orlando, can help WDW-bound vacationers plan their time, book (or confirm) hotel reservations, purchase park tickets, and even make restaurant reservations. For departing guests who didn't buy enough Mouse ears, it also stocks character merchandise.

On-site Resources: Those staying at Walt Disney World resorts should consider their hotel's Lobby Concierge desk the primary resource. Resort guests also receive WDW information via their room's television. Fort Wilderness campers are advised to stop at the Pioneer Hall Information and Ticket Window, call extension 2788, or touch 11 on a phone near any restroom.

What to Pack

While there is hardly a dress code at Walt Disney World, neat, casual clothing is the rule, with few exceptions. Most notably, jackets are required for men at Victoria & Albert's restaurant in the Grand Floridian resort. More generally, T-shirts and shorts are perfectly acceptable during the day. For evening, slacks, jeans, or Bermuda shorts are appropriate. Bathing suits are a must, along with the appropriate attire for any sport you want to pursue.

Lightweight sweaters are necessary even in summer—to wear indoors when the air-conditioning gets chilly. From November through March, warmer clothing is a must for evening. Pack for weather extremes so you'll be comfy should it become unseasonably warm or cool. Always bring plenty of sunscreen, and don't forget the bug spray. If possible, pack lightweight rain gear and a compact umbrella. The most important item of all? Comfortable walking shoes.

Guests at the resorts on Hotel Plaza Boulevard may access a tourist-information TV program of their own. Some other area hotels also show a version of the program, usually aiming to provide an overview of all Central Florida attractions.

For Day Visitors: When purchasing one-day admission to a given theme park, guests receive a complimentary guidemap and entertainment Times Guide for that park. Ticket holders may receive all four park guides upon request. Extra guidemaps are available at City Hall (in the Magic Kingdom) and at Guest Relations (in Epcot, the Disney-MGM Studios, and Animal Kingdom), as well as in many shops and restaurants throughout the park.

Package Pointers

The sheer number and diversity of packages offering vacations in Central Florida are enough to bewilder even the savviest traveler. Still, such plans are worth exploring. Most offer the convenience of a vacation that's completely organized in advance, and one that will generally cost less than the sum of the same transportation, accommodations, and admission elements purchased separately. In addition, since most package providers purchase blocks of Disney resort rooms, they are an excellent source for securing a room on Walt Disney World property when the hotel of your choice is booked.

American Airlines Vacations (800-321-2121), US Airways Vacations (800-455-0123), Southwest Vacations (800-243-8372), *www.expedia.com, www.travelocity.com,* and the Walt Disney Travel Company (407-934-7639 or *www.disneyworld.com*) offer packages that feature WDW on-site hotels, as well as choice off-property accommodations. Many packages include the added attraction of low-cost air transportation. The American Automobile Association (call 407-444-7000 or visit *www.aaa.com*) offers AAA Vacations and other travel packages, which include certain perks and discounts. For other possibilities, consider GOGO Worldwide Vacations (*www.gogowwv.com*), check the travel section of your local newspaper, or consult a travel agent.

Walt Disney Travel Company offers four different vacation plans. They are the "Magic Your Way" base package, the "Magic Your Way Package Plus Dining" package, the "Magic Your Way Premium" package, and the "Magic Your Way Platinum" package. These vacation plans are available year-round (see pages 18–19 for additional information).

Travel agents may design packages around a specific type of vacation: i.e., a golf getaway, honeymoon, or family reunion. They may include extra elements such as unlimited tee times or a carriage ride. Still others are tied to an annual event, such as the Walt Disney World marathon (see "Holidays and Special Events" on page 10 of this chapter). Finally, Disney's Sand and Castle package combines a Disney World vacation with a stay at Disney's Vero Beach Resort or other Florida beach resorts. (See page 81 in *Transportation & Accommodations* for more information about these options.) Air transportation, rental car, or airport transfers can be added to packages.

The value of a package depends on your needs. Before considering options, use this book to help determine which of the accommodations, activities, and attractions most appeal to you. There's real value in some package elements, such as airport transfers and meal discounts. Several packages also include meals with the Disney characters, tennis lessons, golf greens fees, spa treatments, boat rentals, and the like.

Never choose a package that includes elements you don't want or won't have time to enjoy. While extras such as welcoming cocktails may sound appealing, their cash value is negligible. Also beware of any packages that tout certain services as selling points that are available to every Walt Disney World guest.

Hot Tip!

When purchasing a Walt Disney World package, pay attention to the type of WDW ticket that's included—and make sure you are able to customize the ticket to meet your needs. See page 20.

"Magic Your Way" Packages

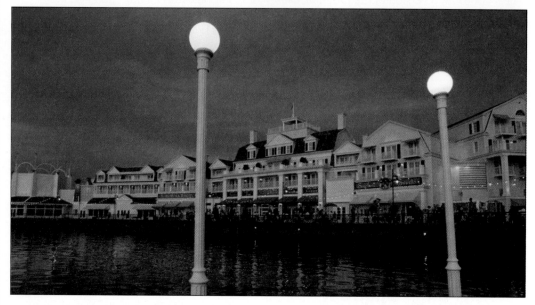

"Magic Your Way" is the name of the game when it comes to Disney World vacation planning. The phrase, meant to reflect each individual's freedom to customize his or her vacation, covers quite the gamut of options. Most of all, it covers vacation packages. There are four packages: Magic Your Way Base, Magic Your Way Plus Dining, Magic Your Way Premium, and Magic Your Way Platinum package. They can be booked through the Walt Disney Travel Company (407-939-7675), *www.disneyworld.com*, and travel agents.

The packages have some elements in common. For starters, they're all intended to be flexible and include a Walt Disney World resort stay and a theme park ticket of some kind. They must be paid for in full. All packages must be canceled at least 45 days before the trip to avoid a penalty. Everyone staying in the room must be in the same package and ticket options. Finally, they all come with the following:

• Extra Magic Hours benefit: WDW resort guests may enjoy exclusive access to theme parks select mornings and evenings. For details on Extra Magic Hours, see page 21.

• Disney's Magical Express service: complimentary transportation to and from Orlando International Airport, plus baggage delivery to your resort room. See page 15 for details.

• Complimentary use of the Walt Disney World transportation system (buses, boats, and the ever-popular monorail).

Magic Your Way Base Package: This "package" is, quite simply, a stay at any Walt Disney World-owned-and-operated resort paired with a theme park ticket. The big decisions to be made here are (1) which resort to reserve, (2) the number of days and add-ons you want on your park ticket. (For more on Walt Disney World theme park ticket structures and pricing, turn to pages 20–24.)

Magic Your Way Plus Dining Package: Take the above description of the Magic Your Way package, throw in a Disney dining plan, and you've got a vacation plan with the freedom to dine at over 100 different eateries—not to mention the potential to shave a few bucks off your dining budget. The package includes one quick-service meal, a snack, and one meal at a table-service restaurant per person, per night of your vacation. (For more information on the Dining Plan, see the box on page 19.) The package also includes a Magic Your Way base ticket. (See page 20 for ticket specifics.)

Magic Your Way Premium Package: It's called "premium" because it includes many of the World's most popular features:
• A stay at a Disney-owned-and-operated resort.
• Magic Your Way ticket with "add-ons." (See page 20 for details.)
• Premium Dining Plan: breakfast, lunch, and

dinner per person per night. For information on the WDW Dining Plan, see sidebar and visit *www.disneyworld.com*, or call 407-WDW-DINE (939-3463).

- Unlimited access to selected recreation opportunities including golf, guided fishing excursions, water sports, and more. (Restrictions apply and advance reservations may be required.)
- Admission to Cirque du Soleil's La Nouba show (one admission per person).
- Admission to a Disney Children's Activity Center at a selected Walt Disney World resort (ages 4–12).
- Unlimited admission to select Theme Park tours: Magic Kingdom's Family Magic Tour, "The Magic Behind Our Steam Trains," Keys to the Kingdom, and Mickey's Magical Milestones; Epcot's Gardens of the World, The Undiscovered Future World, and Hidden Treasures of World Showcase; and Animal Kingdom's Backstage Safari and Wild By Design. See pages 212–213 for details on tours.
- Admission to all Magical Gatherings "Grand Gathering" experiences, provided that you have 8 or more in your party.

Advance reservations are required. For more on Magical Gatherings, turn to page 38.

Note that the duration of the Magic Your Way ticket must equal the number of nights of your stay, plus one day.

Magic Your Way Platinum Package:

An upgrade from the Premium Package, the Platinum version features a stay at a deluxe Walt Disney World resort, plus additional options such as spa treatments and high-end dining opportunities.

Disney Dining Plan

The Disney Dining Plan sounds too good to be true: Forget the flexibility of dining at more than 100 different eateries for a moment and ponder the notion of saving up to 30 percent on rations for your trip. We're salivating at the prospect.

Each night of the plan—which starts at about $38 a day and is offered as part of the Magic Your Way Plus Dining package—includes:

- One table-service meal including appetizer, entrée, dessert (lunch or dinner), juice (breakfast) and non-alcoholic beverage.

- One quick-service meal including entrée, dessert, and nonalcoholic beverage.

- One snack, such as ice cream, popcorn, or a medium soft drink at select quick-service spots or snack carts.

- The option of exchanging two table-service meals for one meal at a high-end "signature restaurant" or a dinner show such as the Hoop-Dee-Doo Musical Revue.

To sum up: Say your family of four were to purchase a five-night package. Together you'd be entitled to 20 quick-service meals, 20 table-service meals, and 20 snacks. And you are free to use them in any way you want. That is, if you want to skip a meal one day or have five meals in a single day, by all means go for it. (Just remember that you have a finite number of meals allotted.) Usage is tracked electronically via your "Key to the World card" (aka your room key). Taxes are included, as are gratuities when appropriate (though you may always add to the tip for outstanding service). Hold onto your receipts, as they show your remaining meal balance.

In addition to the traditional table-service establishments, certain "character dining" experiences are available to Dining Plan participants, as are select Downtown Disney locations (though some items may carry a surcharge). Note that kids ages 3–9 are required to order from the children's menu where available. Some menu items carry an additional surcharge.

To find out which restaurants are participating, turn to our *Good Meals, Great Times* chapter. They are also indicated on all theme park guidemaps. For updates, call 407-939-3463 or go to *www.disneyworld.com*.

Finally, if you purchase the WDW Dining Plan, you still need to make reservations. Don't forget!

All About Theme Park Tickets

Buying a park ticket can be very simple. Plan on visiting one park on one day? Just pick up a "One-Day Base Ticket." Perhaps you are a frequent visitor, and expect to pass through theme park turnstiles dozens of times over the next calendar year. In that case, an Annual Pass is what you're looking for. Now, if your park-going plans lie somewhere in-between (and most do), you will have to be a little more strategic.

When it comes to selecting the perfect type of admission ticket, it pays to do some home-work. Study all the options, evaluate your priorities, and make no hasty decisions. For starters, there are four major factors to consider: (1) total number of days you'd like to visit theme parks, (2) to park-hop or not to park-hop, (3) whether you want to pre-pay (and

Hot Tip!

At the end of your visit, note the number of unused days on a multi-day ticket. Write it on the ticket itself. (Make sure you purchase the "no expiration" add-on within 14 days of first use.)

save a few bucks) for "extras" such as admission to water parks, Pleasure Island, Disney-Quest, etc., and (4) should you invest in the "no expiration" option for your ticket.

The following information was correct at press time and is meant to help you make wise choices. Keep in mind that *Disney ticket structures and prices are likely to change in 2007*, so call 407-824-4321 for up-to-the-minute information.

Did You Know?

The phrase "E-ticket ride" is American slang for "the ultimate in thrills." It comes from the early days of Disney parks, back when tickets were used for each attraction. E-tickets were reserved for the most exciting rides of all.

Magic Your Way Tickets

Base Tickets: Available for 1–10 days. Valid for admission to one park per day only—the Magic Kingdom, Epcot, the Disney-MGM Studios, or Disney's Animal Kingdom. (The base ticket does not allow for park-hopping.) Unused days expire 14 days after the ticket is

Extra Magic Hours

How'd you like to visit a Disney theme park *before* it opens to the public? Or stick around for hours *after* it's officially closed for the day? Well, if you're a guest staying at a Walt Disney World-owned-and-operated resort, the Swan, Dolphin, Shades of Green, or the Hilton on Hotel Plaza Boulevard, you can. It is one of the major perks that comes with staying on Disney property.

Here's how it works: One park opens its door an hour early or stays open three hours late on any given day. Basically, the park becomes something of a members-only private playground for Walt Disney World resort guests. So, provided that you have a WDW resort ID and a park ticket, you're in! No secret password necessary. Keep in mind that you will need park-hopping privileges if you plan to visit a park other than the one offering extra hours on any given day. If you don't plan to park-hop, you must visit the theme park offering Extra Magic Hours on that particular day. Note that Disney water parks offer an Extra Magic Hour on select mornings, too.

When a park opens early in the morning, guests are admitted starting exactly one hour prior to the official opening time. Transportation to the park starts about 30 minutes before that. For evenings, all guests taking advantage of Extra Magic Hours need to get a wristband. They are available at several locations in the park, about two hours before closing time. Present your resort ID and expect to receive a colorful paper bracelet. Wear it proudly. It allows you to visit some (but not all) attractions and mingle with Disney characters.

Ask the resort's Lobby Concierge for a schedule or visit *www.disneyworld.com*. At press time, this almost-too-good-to-be-true perk was free and was expected to stay that way.

activated, which is the first day a park is visited. (For pricing, see page 24.) The ticket is called a base ticket because, with the exception of Annual Passes, all other tickets begin as such. Guests may customize base tickets to fit their own vacation needs.

Park Hopper Option: This option lets guests visit more than one theme park on a single day. The privilege extends through the length of the ticket. It's available for $40 for all base tickets.

Water Park Fun & More Option: This option covers entry to Blizzard Beach and/or Typhoon Lagoon water parks, DisneyQuest (arcade), Downtown Disney Pleasure Island venues, or Disney's Wide World of Sports complex. For $50, you'll get between three and six visits to these spots. The number of visits depends on the number of days on your base ticket–the more days, the more visits.

Hot Tip!

Want to maximize your theme-park-ticket dollar? Buy more days than you plan to use and get the "no expiration" option. You can save unused days for a future trip and save a lot on your per-day admission price.

No Expiration Option: Remember when we used to say that Walt Disney World tickets don't expire until you do? Alas, that's no longer the case. Now, multi-day base tickets expire 14 days after the first day they are used. That's the bad news. The good? You can add the "no expiration" peace of mind for a fee: $10 for 2- and 3-day tickets; $20 for

4 days; $40 for 5 days; $50 for 6 days; $65 for 7-days; $110 for 8 days; $130 for 9 days; and $135 for 10 days.

Theme Park Annual Pass: This pass offers admission to the four theme parks for a year. It can be used in more than one park on the same day (also known as park-hopping), and includes use of Disney transportation, as well as free parking at the theme parks. Annual passes can be purchased at the entrance to any of the theme parks (they can be renewed there or by mail). A photo ID must be presented for purchase by adults and may be required for future use of the pass. Passes are non-transferable.

Annual pass-bearers (including those who have the Premium Annual Pass described at right) qualify for many Walt Disney World discounts and benefits, such as reduced rates at select Disney resorts at certain times of year. A special newsletter called the *Mickey Monitor* keeps passholders up to date regard-

ing discount offers. The pass expires one year after it is first used. A discounted renewal rate applies if the pass is renewed before expiration. (The old pass must be presented in order to receive the discounted renewal rate.) A pass may be renewed by mail or at the entrance to any theme park.

Premium Annual Pass: This pass has everything the Theme Park Annual Pass has to offer and more—namely, admission to the water parks, Disney's Wide World of Sports complex, DisneyQuest, and Pleasure Island for a year. Premium Annual Passholders are eligible for the same discounts and benefits as Theme Park Annual Passholders; Premium Annual Passes can be purchased at the entrance to any of the four theme parks (they can be renewed there or by mail). A photo ID must be presented for purchase by adults and may be required for future use. Premium Annual Passes are non-transferable. These passes expire one year after first use.

Deciding Factors

Choosing the Right Ticket: Before you make your decision, it helps to map out your vacation. Remember, all tickets start as "Base Tickets." They are a bare-bones, admission-

Ticket Tag System

As a means of enforcing the non-transferability aspect of all Walt Disney World tickets, Disney has devised a system to trace each ticket to its rightful owner. The procedure is as follows: Take your ticket (after signing the back of it) and slip it into the machine beside the turnstile at any park entrance. While the machine is crunching the data encrypted on the ticket's magnetic strip, make a "V" with your middle finger and forefinger. Gingerly place your finger-V into the little gizmo perched on the ticket-grabbing device. Remove your fingers and presto! Your ticket should pop out the other side, giving you the green light to enter. Grown-ups have to do this every time they use the ticket. Kids are spared the hassle. Though simple, the system tends to cause bottlenecks at the turnstiles. Be sure to allow extra time to get into the park.

to-one-theme-park-at-a-time deal. That's ideal for some folks—especially those planning a relatively short stay. Still, the first step for every potential guest is to decide just how many days they plan to spend in the theme parks. Keep in mind that as days are added, the average price per day drops a little. After four days, the daily rate drops significantly. Any unused days expire 14 days after the ticket is activated, unless the "no expiration" option is purchased. Once the length of stay is determined, it's time to customize the ticket. Do you want to park-hop? Add $40. Want to add the "Water Park Fun and More" package? For an extra $50, you can do so. Finally, if you're

Hot Tip!

To expedite your party's "ticket tag" experience, make sure each adult is holding his or her own ticket *before* getting on line at a theme park entrance.

not certain that you'll use all the days on your pass, you can add on a "no expiration" option. That starts at $10. It may seem like a lot to think about, but it makes for a very organized Walt Disney World vacation. And it can save you a chunk of change, too.

If you are planning a longer visit, or two trips in a year, we recommend an Annual Pass.

Advance Purchase Ticket Savings

A chance to save a few bucks always merits a little attention. So, even if a savings of $2 to $18 per ticket doesn't sound like much, it can add up once you start multiplying that by the number of people in your traveling party.

To net the discount, you'll have to buy 4- to 10-day Magic Your Way tickets with "Park Hopper" and/or "Water Park Fun & More" add-ons (see page 21) *outside* Florida and *before* you arrive at the Walt Disney World resort. (For information on advance purchasing, turn to page 25.)

In addition to unlimited admission to the parks, you'll get discounts on everything from dinner shows to room rates.

Note: Only one person per party need possess an annual pass to net a discount on a resort rate. This option is great for travelers with flexible vacation schedules, as the discounts do vary and are often announced just weeks before they go into effect.

Tickets with Unused Days: Prior to 2005, WDW tickets never expired. That is no longer the case. Remaining days on any multi-day admission tickets now expire 14 days after the ticket is first activated *unless* the "no expiration" option is purchased.

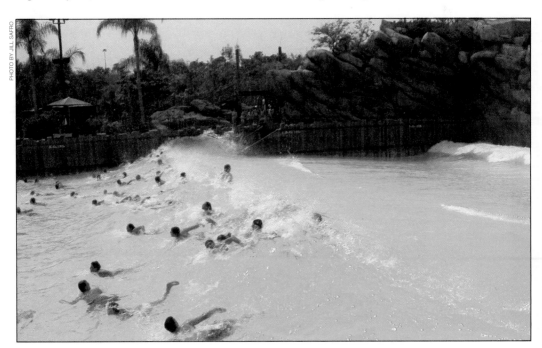

PHOTO BY JILL SAFFRO

Ticket Prices

		10-Day	9-Day	8-Day	7-Day	6-Day	5-Day	4-Day	3-Day	2-Day	1-Day
Base Ticket*	Ages 10 & up	$208 ($20.80/day)	$205 ($22.78/day)	$202 ($25.25/day)	$199 ($28.43/day)	$196 ($32.67/day)	$193 ($38.60/day)	$185 ($46.25/day)	$171 ($57/day)	$119 ($59.50/day)	$63
	Ages 3-9	$167 ($16.70/day)	$164 ($18.22/day)	$162 ($20.25/day)	$160 ($22.86/day)	$157 ($26.17/day)	$155 ($31/day)	$148 ($37/day)	$137 ($45.67/day)	$96 ($48/day)	$52
ADD: Park Hopper**		$40 ($4/day)	$40 ($4.44/day)	$40 ($5/day)	$40 ($5.71/day)	$40 ($6.66/day)	$40 ($8/day)	$40 ($10/day)	$40 ($13.30/day)	$40 ($20/day)	$40
ADD: Water Park Fun & More***		$50 6 visits	$50 6 visits	$50 6 visits	$50 6 visits	$50 6 visits	$50 5 visits	$50 4 visits	$50 3 visits	$50 3 visits	$50 3 visits
ADD: No Expiration****		$135	$130	$110	$65	$50	$40	$20	$10	$10	na
Advance Purchase Savings†	Ages 10 & up	$11	$11	$11	$11	$9	$7	na	na	na	na
	Ages 3-9	$9	$9	$9	$9	$7	$6	na	na	na	na

*Base Ticket admits guest to one theme park each day of use. Park choices are: Magic Kingdom, Epcot, Disney-MGM Studios, Disney's Animal Kingdom.

**Park Hopper option entitles guest to visit more than one theme park on each day of use. Park choices are any combination of Magic Kingdom, Epcot, Disney-MGM Studios, Disney's Animal Kingdom on each day of use.

***Water Parks & More option entitles guest to a specified number of visits (between 2 and 5) to a choice of entertainment and recreation venues. Choices are Disney's Blizzard Beach water park, Disney's Typhoon Lagoon water park, DisneyQuest, Pleasure Island, Disney's Wide World of Sports Complex.

****No Expiration means unused admissions on a ticket have no expiration date. All tickets expire 14 days after first use unless No Expiration is purchased.

†Advance Purchase Savings occur when 4-to-10-day tickets with Park Hopper and/or Water Parks & More are purchased domestically outside of Florida prior to arrival at WDW.

Save Time in Line!

For those of us who'd prefer not to waste time standing in line for theme park attractions, Disney's Fastpass is nothing short of a miracle. Basically, the system allows guests to forego the task of waiting in an actual line for a number of theme park attractions. How? Simply by walking up to the Fastpass booth (located near the entrance of participating attractions) and slipping their park ticket into the Fastpass machine. In return, guests get a slip of paper with a time period printed on it (in addition to the safe return of their park ticket). That time—for example 4:05 P.M. to 5:05 P.M.—represents the window in which guests are invited to return to the attraction and practically walk right in—without standing in a long line.

Once you use your Fastpass to enter an attraction (or the time on it has passed), you can get a new Fastpass time for another attraction. It may be possible to get another Fastpass within 45 minutes or sooner (depending on availability). To find out, read the fine print on your current Fastpass ticket. For example, if one pass was issued at 2 P.M., you can get a Fastpass for another attraction at 4 P.M. (possibly sooner). Sound confusing? It won't be once you've tried it.

At press time, Disney's Fastpass service was free and available to everyone bearing a valid theme park ticket. It should be available during peak times of the day and all peak seasons. Fastpass assignments are limited and tend to go quickly on busy days. Always start the day with your "must-see" attraction. We've placed the Fastpass logo (FP) beside the listing for all of the attractions that were participating at press time. However, since attractions may be added or dropped, check a park map for a complete listing of Fastpass attractions.

Note that all Disney attractions offer the option of standing in a traditional line. If you enjoy the standing-in-line experience, go for it. Otherwise, as long as it stays free, Fastpass is the way to go!

Purchasing Tickets

Admission tickets are sold at park entrances, WDW resorts, the resorts on Hotel Plaza Boulevard, Orlando International Airport, the Transportation and Ticket Center (TTC), and Downtown Disney Guest Relations. Cash, traveler's checks, personal checks (with ID), American Express, Visa, MasterCard, Discover, Diner's Club, JCB Card, and Disney's Visa card are accepted. Not all tickets are available at each location, so be sure to check. Call 407-824-4321 to confirm.

We recommend buying tickets in advance from a travel agent, or in one of these ways:

Tickets by Phone: All tickets can be purchased by phone; call 407-824-4321 or 407-934-7639. There is a $3 handling fee for home delivery. Allow two to three weeks. There is no fee for pickup at WDW.

Tickets Online: Tickets can be bought through *www.disneyworld.com*. There is a $3 handling fee. Allow at least 21 days for delivery.

Tickets at the Disney Store: Select multi-day theme park tickets are available for purchase at any local Disney Store.

Tickets by Mail (3- to 7-day Magic Your Way tickets only): Allow at least three to four weeks for processing, and include a return address. Send a check or money order (for the exact amount plus $3 for handling), payable to Walt Disney World Company, to: Walt Disney World, Box 10140, Lake Buena Vista, FL 32830-0030. Attention: Ticket Mail Order.

Hot Tip!

Prior to your visit, call 407-824-4321 or visit *www.disneyworld.com* for current ticket information. You may be able to save time and money by buying tickets before you arrive at Walt Disney World!

Money-Saving Tips

While there's no denying that a Walt Disney World vacation can be an exceptionally expensive undertaking, it is possible to keep costs down a bit. When budgeting for your trip, keep in mind that WDW prices are comparable to those in a large city. Here are a few tips to help you conserve cash.

Lodging

- When it comes to saving money on accommodations, timing is truly the key. While off-season dates tend to vary, depending on the hotel, value season for most Walt Disney World resorts generally means January through mid-February, late August through late September, and early November through late December.

- Consider how much time you will actually spend at your hotel, and don't pay for a place with perks you won't have time to enjoy. Hotels often allow kids to stay free in parents' rooms, but the cutoff age does vary. Budget chains are economical but usually offer few frills.

- When considering the cost-effectiveness of off-property lodging, factor in the time, money, and inconvenience of commuting to and from attractions.

- Realize, too, that the advantages of staying on-property (tops among them, the "Extra Magic Hours" perk, Disney's Magical Express, and access to Walt Disney World's transportation system) also apply to those staying in the least expensive rooms in Disney's hotels. The most important addresses for budget-watching Disney fans, the All-Star and Pop Century resorts, offer the lowest rates on Disney property. Rooms at Caribbean Beach, Port Orleans French Quarter and Riverside, and Coronado Springs are slightly higher priced. Also, note that the only difference between the least

Hot Tip!
Staying hydrated can get costly. Refill water bottles as often as possible—rather than buy new ones.

and most expensive rooms in a hotel is often the view. Consider how often you'll be looking out that window.

Food

- Visit costlier establishments at lunchtime (if you so desire) rather than at dinner; entrées often cost a bit less at the midday meal.

- Sometimes certain Epcot eateries have early-bird dinner deals; it pays to ask.

- Carry sandwich fixings and have lunches alfresco when possible (keeping in mind that outside food is not welcome inside Disney theme parks).

- Look for lodging with kitchen facilities: The savings on food, especially at breakfast time, may be more than the extra accommodations expense.

- Refrigerators are available for free at WDW deluxe and moderate resorts and for about $10 a day at value resorts.

- A souvenir mug can be purchased at most resorts, good for refills during your stay at the resort. (Similar mugs are sold in the parks, but don't come with free refills.)

- The Trail's End Restaurant at Fort Wilderness has an inexpensive yet satisfying, all-you-can-eat country breakfast buffet.

- Pack kid-friendly snacks, such as fruit, cereal, or even a lollipop. (Snack stands are plentiful, but not always handy or cost-efficient.)

- Don't plan on eating three big table-service meals a day. It gets expensive—and filling!

- The Magic Your Way vacation package with the Disney Dining Plan can control meal costs. It provides two meals and a snack per day. The fixed price (about $38 a day for guests ages 10 and up and $10 for kids between 3 and 9) includes tax and tip.

Satisfying Substitutes

Fewer frills rarely means less fun at Walt Disney World. Here are money-saving alternatives to two of Disney's higher-priced treats.

If you'd rather not spring for admission to Downtown Disney Pleasure Island venues, consider taking a trip to Disney's BoardWalk resort. Among other diversions, you'll find Jellyrolls (a sing-along piano bar with a cover of $10 or less), Atlantic Dance (a nightclub with no cover charge), and ESPN Club (a cover-free sports bar). A short walk will take you to the Swan hotel, home to the karaoke-friendly Kimonos Lounge.

If the Grand Floridian ($375–$845 a night) doesn't quite fit into your budget, consider staying in a Mansion room at Port Orleans Riverside ($145–$210 a night). Southern hospitality replaces Victorian splendor, and, though the guestrooms aren't quite as spacious, the understated elegance and air of sophistication make for a most satisfying stay.

Discounts

- Theme Park Annual and Premium Annual Passholders receive so many discounts on meals, dinner shows, tours, room rates, and more that it may be worth purchasing an annual pass for longer visits or if you plan to take more than one trip within a year.

- Walt Disney resorts that offer Annual Passholder discounts vary from month to month (with some periods devoid of special offers), and discounted rooms aren't always available for booking very far in advance. It's best to be flexible with travel dates. *At press time, there were rumors that a change in policy regarding Annual Pass discounts was afoot. For additional information, call 407-560-PASS (560-7277) or 407-824-4321.*

- Discounts on Disney World resort rates and theme park tickets are available to Florida residents, and seasonal promotions occur. Call 407-824-4321 for specifics.

- Several off-property hotels offer discounts to seniors and AAA or AARP members as well. Some AAA branches offer members ten percent off some park passes, as well as discounts on rooms and select packages with the AAA Disney Magic Moments

Savings Program. Contact your local branch for additional information.

- Web-based *travelocity.com* offers a variety of Disney vacation packages. Vacation Outlet also offers some packages at a reduced rate. Visit *www.vacationoutlet.com* or call 800-690-2210 for details.

- For a free copy of the Orlando Magicard (included in a complimentary packet of Orlando information and not to be confused with the Disney Visa Card), call 800-643-9492. Cardholders receive many discounts at Orlando-area hotels, restaurants, and shops, as well as on rental cars. Similar coupon offers can be found at the airport.

- Disney's Visa cardholders earn reward dollars when they use the card. These dollars can be redeemed at Walt Disney World, the Disney Cruise Line, and Disneyland. If you're not a Disney Visa cardholder, and would like to become one—flip to the back page of this book. Our coupon can help you get a $50 bonus gift card.

- It's possible to save a few bucks by purchasing some Magic Your Way tickets in advance (as in before you arrive at WDW). Qualifying tickets include those with all add-ons and a minimum of 4 days. Tickets can be purchased at *www.disneyworld.com*, or by calling 407-939-7639. Keep in mind that this policy may change at any time.

- When you call to make your resort reservation (407-939-7639), ask if any discounts apply. Hey, you've got nothing to lose.

Making a Budget

A stay at Disney's kingdom need not cost a king's ransom (though it easily can). In fact, with a well-planned budget, money at Disney World can stretch relatively far.

Vacation expenses tend to fall into five major categories: (1) transportation (which may include any combination of costs for airfare, airport transfers, train tickets, car rental, gas, parking, and taxi service); (2) lodging; (3) theme park tickets; (4) meals; and (5) miscellaneous (recreational activities, souvenirs, postcards, film, toiletries, and home expenses such as pet boarding, etc.).

When planning your budget, first consider what level of service suits your needs. Some people prefer to spend fewer days at Disney but stay at a deluxe hotel or dine at pricier restaurants, while others would rather make their money cover a longer vacation that includes a value-priced resort and less expensive meals. The choice is up to you. Once you've established your spending priorities, determine your price limit. Then make sure you don't exceed it when approximating your expenses—without a ballpark figure to work around, it's easy to get carried away.

Sample Budget

The following is an example of a low- to moderately priced budget designed for a family of four (two adults and two kids planning to stay at WDW for five nights and six days). Totals do not include tax.

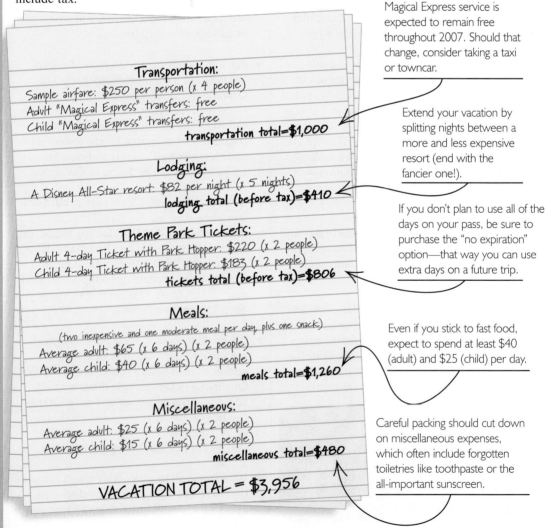

Transportation:

Sample airfare: $250 per person (x 4 people)
Adult "Magical Express" transfers: free
Child "Magical Express" transfers: free
transportation total=**$1,000**

Lodging:

A Disney All-Star resort: $82 per night (x 5 nights)
lodging total (before tax)=**$410**

Theme Park Tickets:

Adult 4-day Ticket with Park Hopper: $220 (x 2 people)
Child 4-day Ticket with Park Hopper: $183 (x 2 people)
tickets total (before tax)=**$806**

Meals:

(two inexpensive and one moderate meal per day, plus one snack)
Average adult: $65 (x 6 days) (x 2 people)
Average child: $40 (x 6 days) (x 2 people)
meals total=**$1,260**

Miscellaneous:

Average adult: $25 (x 6 days) (x 2 people)
Average child: $15 (x 6 days) (x 2 people)
miscellaneous total=**$480**

VACATION TOTAL = **$3,956**

Magical Express service is expected to remain free throughout 2007. Should that change, consider taking a taxi or towncar.

Extend your vacation by splitting nights between a more and less expensive resort (end with the fancier one!).

If you don't plan to use all of the days on your pass, be sure to purchase the "no expiration" option—that way you can use extra days on a future trip.

Even if you stick to fast food, expect to spend at least $40 (adult) and $25 (child) per day.

Careful packing should cut down on miscellaneous expenses, which often include forgotten toiletries like toothpaste or the all-important sunscreen.

Planning Your Itinerary A Time Line

First Things First

- Make hotel and transportation arrangements as far ahead as possible. Note that many Disney hotels fill up more than six months in advance. Call 407-W-DISNEY (934-7639) to book a room at a Disney hotel; your confirmation should arrive within two weeks. Log it and other pertinent information in your Birnbaum Trip Planner at the end of this book. (Don't forget to take the Trip Planner with you!)
- Create a day-by-day schedule, deciding which area of WDW to visit on each day of your vacation. This will help when it's time to make restaurant and recreation reservations.

6 Months

- Unless you purchased a package that includes theme park admission, it's time to order tickets. Refer to pages 20–25 for details, and call 407-824-4321; passes should arrive within four weeks. Keep in mind that you will save money by purchasing select tickets in advance.
- Choose dining spots from those listed in the *Good Meals, Great Times* chapter. Call 407-WDW-DINE to make restaurant reservations. *Guests with a confirmed reservation at a WDW-owned-and-operated resort may call 180 days before scheduled check-in date and book dining reservations for up to 10 days of their planned stay. Have your hotel confirmation number handy when you make the call.*
- Character meals such as those at Cinderella's Royal Table must be booked 180 days ahead. Call 407-WDW-DINE and have a credit card handy.
- Dinner-show reservations may be secured up to 180 days in advance. Consult page 260 for details, and call 407-WDW-DINE (939-3463) for reservations.
- Fishing excursions (see pages 220–221) may be booked by calling 407-WDW-BASS (939-2277).
- Specialty cruises (see page 211) may be booked by calling 407-WDW-PLAY (939-7529).

3 Months

- Find out park hours for your stay, and add them to your day-by-day schedule. Closing times will be particularly helpful when making evening plans. Call 407-824-4321, or consult Walt Disney World's website (*www.disneyworld.com*).
- If you have purchased a Magic Your Way Premium or Platinum package and plan to play golf, or will be staying at a WDW resort or a resort on Hotel Plaza Boulevard, you may book a tee time on one of WDW's golf courses now (see pages 216–217 for details on the courses). Golf lessons may also be reserved at this time. Call 407-WDW-GOLF (939-4653) for reservations. Those not staying on WDW property may make reservations 60 days ahead.
- Tennis lessons may be reserved by calling 407-WDW-PLAY. Turn to page 218 for information.
- Parasailing and waterskiing excursions (for details, see pages 219–220) may be booked by calling 407-939-0754.
- Trail-ride reservations may be made up to 90 days in advance. Call 407-WDW-PLAY.
- If you'd like to add a behind-the-scenes tour to your vacation, now is the time to make a reservation. See pages 212–213 for details, and call 407-WDW-TOUR (939-8687).
- Some attractions may be closed for refurbishment during your visit. An updated refurbishment schedule is released each season. Call 407-824-4321.

2 Weeks

- Airline confirmation and travel-package vouchers should have arrived by now. Contact your travel agent or the travel company if they have not.

1 Week

- Reconfirm all reservations. Finalize your day-by-day schedule, including all confirmation numbers. Make one copy for your suitcase and one to carry with you in the parks.

GETTING READY TO GO

Step-By-Step Sample Schedules

Many visitors have a deep desire to cover each and every inch of Walt Disney World in the span of a few short days. While we hesitate to discourage these most ambitious of travelers, we feel the need to enlighten them: Walt Disney World is a staggeringly large place. In fact, it's as big as San Francisco, and jam-packed with about as many diversions as you'd expect from a city that size. You could spend two full weeks on Disney property and still not have time to do it all. The theme parks alone require every bit of four days just to see the major attractions.

What's the best strategy for organizing a Walt Disney World visit? Make a list of the parks, attractions, and activities you *most* want to see and use it to create an itinerary. Don't forget to allow time for swimming, boating, or relaxing in a hammock. This is, after all, a vacation.

Assuming you've narrowed your "must-do" list to the barely manageable, we recommend a stay of at least four to five days. This allows for a visit to each of the theme parks and some time to enjoy many of the recreational activities at your resort. Longer stays can include water parks, Downtown Disney, a dinner show, and more. When planning your days (which you should do before leaving home), be sure to take into account theme park hours and seasonal temperatures in Central Florida.

The following sample schedules assume that you eat breakfast at your resort (unless otherwise stated) and arrive up to 20 minutes before the official opening time. These schedules, though tirelessly tested and proven successful by Birnbaum's editors, are not carved in stone. Use them as a guide, tailoring the itineraries to suit your family's individual tastes. Use them in conjunction with complimentary theme park Times Guides (available at park entrances).

Note that we have not included specific instructions with regard to Fastpass in our sample itineraries. It's not because we don't love the service. In fact, we highly recommend using Fastpass, even if working it into a daily schedule is still an inexact science. As more and more attractions are added to the program, it gets easier to breeze through the turnstiles in a highly organized manner. By all means, take advantage of the Fastpass opportunity every chance you get—not only will it make you feel like a VIP, but it will free up time in your schedule for things you otherwise might not have gotten to.

Magic Kingdom One-Day Schedule

- Begin the day with a brisk stroll down Main Street, U.S.A. Cut through Adventureland on your way to Splash Mountain and Big Thunder Mountain Railroad. Backtrack to Pirates of the Caribbean, Jungle Cruise, The Magic Carpets of Aladdin, or The Enchanted Tiki Room—Under New Management.

- Access Frontierland via the path near the Tiki Room. Consider lunching at Pecos Bill Cafe or Columbia Harbour House.

- If time allows, squeeze in The Haunted Mansion before the afternoon parade. Watch the parade and move on to Fantasyland. (But visit The Haunted Mansion first.)

- See as much of Fantasyland as possible, including Mickey's PhilharMagic, It's a Small World, Peter Pan's Flight, and The Many Adventures of Winnie the Pooh.

- Cool off at Ariel's Grotto in Fantasyland. If the timing's right, head to the front of the castle for a live stage show.

- Explore Mickey's Toontown Fair. Take daring kids on The Barnstormer. As a calmer alternative, hop on the railroad. Afterward, tour the country homes of Mickey and Minnie Mouse. Mickey greets guests in the Judge's Tent.

- If the evening parade is scheduled to run twice, explore Tomorrowland during the earlier showing. See The Laugh Floor Comedy Club, Space Mountain, Buzz Lightyear's Space Ranger Spin, Stitch's Great Escape!, and the race cars at the Speedway.

- View Wishes, a truly impressive fireworks display, from Main Street.

- Watch the nighttime parade from Frontierland.

- If there's time, revisit your favorite attraction (guests are usually admitted right up until closing time).

IF YOU HAVE YOUNG CHILDREN

Head directly to Fantasyland (walk right through the castle) and ride Dumbo, Peter Pan, Mickey's PhilharMagic, and The Many Adventures of Winnie the Pooh. Take fans to meet Ariel in her grotto and romp at Pooh's Playful Spot.

Go to Toontown Fair to meet Mickey in the Judge's Tent. Explore Toontown and stop for a spin in a teacup on the way to Frontierland. Meet Woody and friends at the Diamond Horseshoe.

Check the schedule for the Castle stage show before riding the carousel and It's a Small World.

Line up for the afternoon parade about 30 minutes early. Or skip the parade, finish up Fantasyland, and take a magic carpet ride in Adventureland.

Most little ones enjoy the Walt Disney World Railroad and the Tomorrowland Transit Authority, too.

LINE BUSTERS

Even when the park is packed, there are some attractions with shorter or faster-moving lines. Among them are: Tomorrowland Transit Authority, Walt Disney World Railroad, The Enchanted Tiki Room—Under New Management, Carousel of Progress, Country Bear Jamboree, It's a Small World, and Tom Sawyer Island.

Magic Kingdom Musts

Short on time? Here's a list of all the attractions that put the magic in the Magic Kingdom:

Splash Mountain • **Big Thunder Mountain Railroad**
Pirates of the Caribbean • **The Haunted Mansion**
Peter Pan's Flight • **It's a Small World**
Buzz Lightyear's Space Ranger Spin • **Space Mountain**
The Many Adventures of Winnie the Pooh • **Mickey's PhilharMagic**
The Laugh Floor Comedy Club • **Wishes (fireworks show)**

Epcot One-Day Schedule

• Start the day by making a beeline for Future World's Soarin' and Test Track. (If the Test Track line is long, consider jumping on the "single riders" line. It moves much faster.) If you have no health issues and no susceptibility to motion sickness whatsoever, experience the out-of-this-world adventure known as Mission: SPACE. (Otherwise ride "Mission SPACE-lite"—the "less intense," non-spinning version.) Follow it up with the Universe of Energy and The Seas with Nemo & Friends. Keep in mind that World Showcase doesn't open until about 11 A.M.

IF YOU HAVE YOUNG CHILDREN

Begin the day by thoroughly exploring The Seas with Nemo & Friends. Then head over to Imagination! to experience Journey Into Your Imagination with Figment and ImageWorks (skip Honey, I Shrunk the Audience—it scares little ones silly).

At World Showcase, head to Mexico's boat ride and, for braver tots, Norway's Maelstrom. Visit Kidcot Funstop at each country. Don't miss the koi pond in Japan and Germany's tiny village.

LINE BUSTERS

Tired of long lines? Go to: The Circle of Life movie in The Land, Universe of Energy, or The American Adventure. The Spaceship Earth line thins in the afternoon.

• Stop for lunch at The Land's Sunshine Seasons or Garden Grill or the Coral Reef restaurant in The Seas pavilion.

• After exploring The Land, be sure to see Honey, I Shrunk the Audience in the Imagination! pavilion (though it frightens small children). Save time to enjoy ImageWorks, a small, high-tech playground.

• If you're in the mood for some serious pin trading (or shopping), stop by Pin Central in Innoventions Plaza. (All Disney workers who are wearing pins are willing to trade.)

• Visit Spaceship Earth before heading to Innoventions.

• Make your way to World Showcase by early evening and start your circular tour of the world at Canada. Proceed counter-clockwise around the lagoon. Don't miss the *Impressions de France* movie in the France pavilion, the show in the American Adventure pavilion, and the Maelstrom attraction in Norway.

• After dinner, scope out a spot to watch IllumiNations: Reflections of Earth. (We enjoy the areas near Italy and Japan, but there are excellent viewing locations all around the World Showcase lagoon.)

Epcot Essentials

There is a lot to see and do at Disney's discovery park. Don't leave without investigating these outstanding attractions:

Universe of Energy • Honey, I Shrunk the Audience
Living with the Land • Test Track
Cranium Command • IllumiNations: Reflections of Earth
The American Adventure show • Impressions de France
Soarin' • Turtle Talk with Crush

Timing Tip: If you have reservations for dinner at World Showcase, give yourself 30 to 40 minutes to get there from the front gate. Taking a *FriendShip* water taxi can shave a few minutes off your trip (although it isn't much faster than brisk walking).

Disney-MGM Studios One-Day Schedule

- Some attractions open later in the morning: consult a park Times Guide for exact times. Also, many shows here run on a schedule; check for times throughout the day. Note that this park is not the easiest to navigate. You'll need a map to get your bearings in the region beyond the Chinese Theater.

- Daredevils should begin the day with Rock 'n' Roller Coaster, followed by some eye-opening drops at The Twilight Zone™ Tower of Terror.

- If Beauty and the Beast is playing soon, grab a seat. Otherwise, plan to come back later and go to The Magic of Disney Animation, Voyage of The Little Mermaid, and Walt Disney: One Man's Dream.

- Pause for lunch at the 50's Prime Time Cafe, Sci-Fi Dine-In Theater, or Hollywood & Vine.

- Line up 20 to 30 minutes early to watch the Disney Stars and Motor Cars parade. (Note that if you skip the parade, it is an excellent time to see The Magic of Disney Animation, Voyage of The Little Mermaid, or The Great Movie Ride.)

- Be sure to see (and hear) Sounds Dangerous, followed by the Disney-MGM Studios Backlot Tour, Star Tours, Muppet*Vision 3-D, Lights, Motors, Action! Extreme Stunt Show, and the Indiana Jones Epic Stunt Spectacular.

- Be sure to take tots to the Honey, I Shrunk the Kids Movie Set Adventure. (It's an elaborately themed playground.)

- If you missed Beauty and the Beast—Live on Stage, go now and, if you haven't hit it yet, The Great Movie Ride.

- Keep an eye on the clock: You want to get a spot for Fantasmic! *at least 60 minutes* before showtime. Note that if you choose to skip Fantasmic!, plan to exit the park before the last performance breaks. If you do stay for the show, know that you can meander through select shops while the throngs file through the turnstiles at the exit.

Studios Standouts

If you're short on time, be sure to catch as many of the following four-star attractions at the Disney-MGM Studios as possible:

The Twilight Zone™ Tower of Terror • Rock 'n' Roller Coaster

Beauty and the Beast—Live on Stage

The Great Movie Ride

Muppet*Vision 3-D • Star Tours

Fantasmic! • Stars and Motor Cars (parade)

Disney's Animal Kingdom One-Day Schedule

- Guests who arrive at park opening may enjoy a greeting by Disney characters. Many shows here run on a schedule, so check for times throughout the day. Make a point of seeing Festival of the Lion King and Finding Nemo—The Musical. They appeal to all ages. If you want to experience Expedition Everest (and you should!), now's the time to get the Fastpass.

- As you enter the park, pass through the Oasis and head toward DinoLand U.S.A. Ride Dinosaur before eating breakfast with Donald Duck at Restaurantosaurus (reservations are highly recommended). Explore DinoLand before catching Finding Nemo—The Musical.

IF YOU HAVE YOUNG CHILDREN

We recommend lingering a bit in the Oasis on your way into the park. Then make a sharp left and head straight to Camp Minnie-Mickey. Visit with some Disney characters, and watch Festival of the Lion King. (Warn sensitive youngsters that the music may be a bit loud.)

Stop by the Tree of Life to notice all of the animal carvings in its trunk. (Note that the show inside the tree, It's Tough to be a Bug!, is very intense and may frighten young children.)

Eat lunch at Pizzafari or head to DinoLand's Restaurantosaurus. Be sure to see The Boneyard playground, Finding Nemo—The Musical, and Chester and Hester's Dino-Rama!

In Asia, go to the Maharajah Jungle Trek. Consider riding Africa's bumpy Kilimanjaro Safaris. See the Pangani Forest Exploration Trail. Then take the train to Rafiki's Planet Watch.

LINE BUSTERS

When herds of guests mob Disney's Animal Kingdom attractions, there are a few places to escape the stampede: the Oasis, Pangani Forest Exploration Trail, Maharajah Jungle Trek, Discovery Island Trails, The Boneyard playground, and Rafiki's Planet Watch. (You'll need to take the Wildlife Express train to Rafiki's Planet Watch.)

- In Asia, tackle Expedition Everest, ride Kali River Rapids, then visit the tigers at the Maharajah Jungle Trek, and see Flights of Wonder at the Caravan Stage.

- Check a park Times Guide for the Festival of the Lion King schedule. Plan to arrive in Camp Minnie-Mickey at least 45 minutes before it starts (it's a wildly popular show). If possible, mingle with Disney characters before seeing Festival of the Lion King.

- Stop at Tusker House for lunch. Then jump aboard the Wildlife Express train to Rafiki's Planet Watch. Don't miss the Song of the Rainforest and Affection Section.

- After experiencing Africa's Kilimanjaro Safaris, take a relaxing hike on the animal-laden Pangani Forest Exploration Trail.

- Wander the Discovery Island Trails around the Tree of Life, taking time to search for animals carved into the tree and its roots.

- Finish off the day with a screening of It's Tough to be a Bug! and revisiting your favorite attractions.

Animal Kingdom Aces

An abbreviated visit to Disney's Animal Kingdom is enough to make anybody growl. The following attractions should help soothe the savage beast, er, guest:

Dinosaur • Kali River Rapids • **Kilimanjaro Safaris**
Festival of the Lion King • It's Tough to be a Bug!
Pangani Forest Exploration Trail • **Expedition Everest**
Finding Nemo—The Musical • Maharajah Jungle Trek

Hot Tip!

Many attractions are in the steamy outdoors. Bring a refillable water bottle when you visit.

Half-Day Schedules
Magic Kingdom

Morning at the Magic Kingdom

- Where to begin—Tomorrowland or Frontierland? It's a big decision. Know that the area you postpone may have long lines by the time you get there. We start with Tomorrowland.
- After Space Mountain, proceed to Buzz Lightyear's Space Ranger Spin, then The Laugh Floor Comedy Club.
- Cut across Main Street and head for Pirates of the Caribbean, Splash Mountain, and Big Thunder Mountain Railroad.
- Visit The Haunted Mansion and, if there's time before the parade, see the Country Bears.
- Watch the parade in Frontierland. Or skip the parade and see Fantasyland's Peter Pan's Flight, Winnie the Pooh, It's a Small World, and Mickey's PhilharMagic.

> **HALF DAY WITH YOUNG CHILDREN**
> Start at Mickey's Toontown Fair. (You can get there easily by boarding the Walt Disney World Railroad at Main Street Station.) Meet Mickey Mouse inside the Judge's Tent. After fully exploring Mickey's Toontown Fair, move on to Fantasyland. Then take in the Country Bear Jamboree. Finally, soar on a magic carpet in Adventureland before calling it a day.

The Magic Kingdom After Lunch

- Check a Times Guide and choose a time to take in the Castle stage show.
- Start in Adventureland. Ride the Jungle Cruise and Pirates of the Caribbean.
- Head to Frontierland. Do Splash Mountain and Big Thunder Mountain Railroad. Then see the Country Bears before taking the Walt Disney World Railroad to Mickey's Toontown Fair.
- Explore Toontown. If the wait to meet Mickey Mouse is more than 30 minutes, consider coming back in the late evening.
- Take a spin at the Mad Tea Party, and see the highlights of Fantasyland, including It's a Small World, Peter Pan, Mickey's PhilharMagic, and The Many Adventures of Winnie the Pooh.
- Pop in at The Haunted Mansion before dinner.
- Now it's time for Tomorrowland. (If you have the energy and the nighttime parade is running twice, plan to stay in Tomorrowland during the early run. See the parade later.) Go to Buzz Lightyear's Space Ranger Spin, The Laugh Floor Comedy Club, and Space Mountain.
- If it's offered, catch the nighttime parade. And don't miss the fireworks!
- Shop on Main Street, U.S.A., while the exiting throngs file out.

Epcot

Morning at Epcot

- Head right to Soarin' and Test Track. If you're up for the "less intense" Mission: SPACE, go for it. Then move to Honey, I Shrunk the Audience (inside Imagination) and The Land.
- See Universe of Energy and The Seas with Nemo & Friends before moving on to World Showcase—it opens at 11 A.M. (Note that Wonders of Life is only open during peak times and may be closed during your visit.) When hunger calls, stop for a light lunch. See the countries that interest you most, making sure to see the show inside the American Adventure and the boat ride in Norway.
- Finish up by seeing Future World's Spaceship Earth.

> **HALF DAY WITH YOUNG CHILDREN**
> Begin with a visit to Imagination!, taking time to fully explore the ImageWorks interactive play zone. Move to The Seas with Nemo & Friends to see Turtle Talk with Crush and search for Nemo and other sea creatures. If the Wonders of Life is open, head there. If not, check out the Kidcot Funstops throughout the park.

(Continued on page 36)

(Continued from page 35)

Epcot After Lunch

- If you don't have restaurant reservations and would like to have dinner at a World Showcase restaurant, stop by Guest Relations to make them. If not, consider dining at the nearby BoardWalk resort (it's a short stroll or boat ride away).
  - See as much of Future World as possible before going to World Showcase for dinner.
  - Spend the evening touring World Showcase. Keep an eye on the clock so you can secure a good spot around the Lagoon to watch the evening's presentation of IllumiNations.
- Avoid the crush of exiting crowds by browsing in Mouse Gear in Future World.

Disney-MGM Studios

Morning at the Disney-MGM Studios

- Kick-start the day with Rock 'n' Roller Coaster, followed by a trip to The Twilight Zone™ Tower of Terror. From there, move to Muppet*Vision 3-D and Star Tours.
- Before lining up for the parade, see The Magic of Disney Animation; Beauty and the Beast—Live on Stage; Lights, Motors, Action!; and The Great Movie Ride.

The Disney-MGM Studios After Lunch

HALF DAY WITH YOUNG CHILDREN
Start with Voyage of The Little Mermaid, followed by Playhouse Disney—Live on Stage, the Honey, I Shrunk the Audience Movie Set Adventure, and Beauty and the Beast—Live on Stage. Skip Fantasmic!—it is just too intense for most tykes.

- Begin with Tower of Terror, Rock 'n' Roller Coaster, Beauty and the Beast—Live on Stage, and The Magic of Disney Animation.
- See Voyage of The Little Mermaid, Star Tours, Muppet*Vision 3-D, The Great Movie Ride, Lights, Motors, Action!, and Disney-MGM Studios Backlot Tour.
- If there's time, see Walt Disney: One Man's Dream; Sounds Dangerous; and Indiana Jones before securing a spot for Fantasmic!

Disney's Animal Kingdom

HALF DAY WITH YOUNG CHILDREN
Scope out animal life in The Oasis before heading to Camp Minnie-Mickey. Meet Disney characters and see The Festival of the Lion King before visiting DinoLand U.S.A. Explore The Boneyard and ride TriceraTop Spin. If time allows, take the train to Rafiki's Planet Watch, where kids can bond with live animals (mostly goats) in the Affection Section.

Morning at Disney's Animal Kingdom

- Go to Asia for Expedition Everest, Kali River Rapids, and the Maharajah Jungle Trek.
- Experience the Kilimanjaro Safaris and the Pangani Forest Exploration Trail in Africa.
- Check a Times Guide for the next Festival of the Lion King show. Arrive at least 45 minutes ahead of time. (It's a very popular show.)
- Finish up with Finding Nemo—The Musical, Dinosaur, and It's Tough to be a Bug!

Disney's Animal Kingdom After Lunch

- Check a Times Guide for the Festival of the Lion King schedule. Arrive 45 minutes early during peak times of year. Then visit Disney characters in Camp Minnie-Mickey.
- If there is entertainment or a parade scheduled, stick around Discovery Island to enjoy it. Otherwise, head to the Kilimanjaro Safaris ride. Do the Pangani Forest Exploration Trail, and take the train to Rafiki's Planet Watch.
- Ride Expedition Everest and Kali River Rapids and experience the Maharajah Jungle Trek.
- Wander the Discovery Island Trails and see It's Tough to be a Bug!
- Before dinner, dodge dinos on Dinosaur and watch Finding Nemo—The Musical.

Making the Most of Longer Visits

Longer stays allow the chance to sample some of the World's myriad offerings. Spend another day in the one park you most enjoyed. Lounge by the pool, go biking, or play tennis or golf. Go shopping at Downtown Disney. Cool off at one of Disney's innovative water parks. Have lunch at a WDW resort, and try a special dinner at Victoria & Albert's in the Grand Floridian, or at California Grill in the Contemporary. Check out the clubs at Pleasure Island or Downtown Disney West Side, or spend the evening at the BoardWalk. Take golf or tennis lessons. Go fishing, waterskiing, or horseback riding. Visit a spa. Participate in a behind-the-scenes program. Play a round of miniature golf. See a game at Disney's Wide World of Sports complex. For even more ideas, see our *Sports*; *Everything Else in the World*; and *Good Meals, Great Times* chapters.

How to Save a Rainy Day

Florida rain showers come and go with such regularity that you could set your watch by them, especially during summer months. They're usually brief, though torrential. Of course, there are times when gray clouds linger longer. Here are some ways to make the most of a soggy day:

- Head for DisneyQuest, a huge interactive play zone at Downtown Disney West Side. It'll keep the whole family entertained (and dry) for hours.

- See a movie on one of AMC Theatres' 24 screens at Downtown Disney.

- Consider taking in an indoor event at Disney's Wide World of Sports complex. For information, call 407-939-1500.

- Don your rain gear and go to Epcot. The pavilions in Future World house a bounty of sheltered diversions. (Ponchos are sold throughout Walt Disney World for about $7 each.)

Magical Gatherings

You may have seen the ads. Perhaps you've heard friends talking about it. But just what is a Walt Disney World Magical Gathering? It's a special vacation package—a concept designed to help large travel groups organize their vacations *before* they get to Walt Disney World. The group may consist of family, friends, neighbors, colleagues, classmates—you name it. As long as there are at least eight of you (over the age of three) and everyone plans to stay at a Walt Disney World resort, the party qualifies for Grand Gathering experiences (more on that later).

It all starts with a phone call to 407-934-7639 or a visit to the magical gatherings area of *www.disneyworld.com/magicalgatherings.* Request a free vacation planning kit (including a DVD). It comes with a step-by-step guide on how to plan the trip.

Once the decision is made to plan a Magical Gathering—and you're certain you've got at least eight participants booking a stay at a WDW resort—you work with Magical Gatherings planning specialists. They will help reserve dining, recreation (including golf tee times), and special celebrations. Groups of eight or more may book "Grand Gathering" experiences. Those experiences, which include special dinner parties and fireworks voyages, do cost extra and must be reserved in advance.

They are communal experiences—bunches of smaller parties that come together to form one large, or "grand," one.

At press time, the following experiences were available to guests who book a Grand Gathering vacation (days, times, and prices may change):

Good Morning Gathering: A special breakfast at Tony's Town Square restaurant on the Magic Kingdom's Main Street, U.S.A., this experience takes dining with the characters to the next level. Here, the likes of Chip, Dale, and Donald Duck don't just mingle with guests, they wait on them! There may even be a chance to meet the big cheese, Mickey Mouse, one-on-one. The Good Morning Gathering is offered on Wednesdays and Saturdays at 9 A.M. Price (including tax and tip) is $39.99 for adults, and $19.99 for kids ages 3–9. Park admission is required but not included.

Safari Celebration Dinner: Guests enjoy an end-of-the-day safari at Animal Kingdom's Kilimanjaro Safaris attraction, followed by a dinner reception at the Tusker House restaurant in the Africa section of the park. Characters stop by for a meet-and-greet, as do some living creatures from nature's animal

Vacation Insurance

No one books a vacation expecting to cancel it at the last minute—yet sometimes life intervenes and it's simply unavoidable. So it may be worth working travel insurance into your vacation budget (we do). It may include coverage for trip cancellation and interruption, travel delay, loss of baggage, medical expenses, and more. Be sure to ask about travel insurance when you reserve your trip.

Now That's a Party!

While the adage "the more the merrier" certainly holds true at Walt Disney World, there is a limit to the size of a "Grand Gathering." If your group will require 10 or more resort rooms, call The Walt Disney World Group sales team. A group sales specialist will coordinate everything from resort accommodations and ticket packages to special-event planning—not to mention group benefits such as special resort rates and transportation. For additional information, call (800) 327-2989.

---

kingdom. The Safari Celebration Dinner is usually offered Sundays and Thursdays beginning in the late afternoon. The cost is $59.99 for adults and $24.99 for guests ages 3–9. Park admission is required but not included.

Hot Tip!

Guests under the age of three do not count toward the eight-person minimum required for a "Grand Gathering." Nor do they require a ticket for admission to any of the Grand Gathering experiences or Walt Disney World theme parks.

International Dinner and IllumiNations Dessert Reception: After enjoying a dinner with an international flair at an Epcot location, guests are treated to storytelling and an appearance by a Disney character. From there, the party moves over to a private area beside the World Showcase lagoon. Here guests enjoy VIP viewing of IllumiNations: Reflections of Earth, Epcot's popular nightly fireworks show.

The International Dinner experience is offered on select days (often Mondays and Fridays) at about 7:30 P.M. The price is $59.99 for adults and $24.99 for kids ages 3–9.

Magical Fireworks Voyage: An evening cruise on the Seven Seas Lagoon begins with walking the plank, er, dock behind the

Contemporary resort. Captain Hook and Mr. Smee are there to say hello and wave goodbye as you head out to sea and toward the Magic Kingdom.

The high seas journey is hosted by a silly swashbuckler named Patch, who helps navigate the ship while leading guests in singalongs and playing Disney trivia games. Once the vessel reaches Magic Kingdom waters, it's time to look up and enjoy Wishes—a dazzling fireworks show.

The return trip features a story about Peter Pan, who, coincidentally, is the very character who welcomes guests back to dry land.

The Magical Fireworks Voyage experience is offered several nights a week (during times when fireworks are presented). The price is $34.99 for grown-ups and $19.99 for for kids (ages 3–9).

Note: Availability for all Grand Gatherings experiences is limited. Reservations can (and should) be made up to 180 days in advance, and full payment for each experience is required 45 days prior to guest arrival. Reservation may not be made less than three days ahead of time. Cancellations are accepted up to six days prior to the scheduled Grand Gathering experience without penalty. Prices and specifics are subject to change. For updates, call 407-934-7639 or pay a visit to *www.disneyworld.com/magicalgatherings.*

Hot Tip!

When planning a Magical Gathering group vacation, it's best to appoint a group leader. The leader can act as a contact person for members of the group and as a liaison with the Walt Disney Travel Company. It makes for less confusion while the vacation is in its formative stages.

Customized Travel Tips
Traveling with Children

Tell youngsters that a Walt Disney World vacation is in the works and the response is apt to be overwhelming. Our guide *Birnbaum's Walt Disney World For Kids, By Kids*, written for children ages 7 through 14, can be a useful resource for getting them involved in the planning from the outset. Filled with information about the World from a kid's perspective, it can be used as a reference before and during the trip, and as a souvenir afterward.

Walt Disney World ranks among the easier spots on earth for families with children. Keep in mind, however, that kids under 7 must be accompanied by an adult to enter the theme parks; kids under 10 must be accompanied at the water parks. With most teens, however, it is enough to establish a meeting place and time inside the Magic Kingdom, Epcot, Disney-MGM Studios, or Animal Kingdom.

Child Care: In-room child-care service can be summoned to all Disney-owned resorts. The service is available 24 hours a day, seven days a week, though it is not run by Disney. For pricing and to make a reservation with Kid's Nite Out, visit *www.kidsniteout.com*, call 407-828-0920, or inquire at your resort's Lobby Concierge. Another outside company, All About Kids, offers this child-care service as well. To reach them, call 407-812-9300 or visit *www.all-about-kids.com*.

Children's Activity Centers: The Polynesian, Grand Floridian, Animal Kingdom Lodge, Wilderness Lodge, Yacht and Beach Club, and Dolphin resorts each have an on-site children's activity center. These centers accept (potty-trained) kids ages 4 through 12. For details and availability, phone 407-939-3463 for all but the Dolphin. For information on "Camp Dolphin," call 407-934-4000.

Baby Care Centers: Located in all four theme parks, these centers are for parents with young kids. They are not meant as day care. All children must be accompanied by a parent or guardian. There are rooms with rocking chairs and couches in feeding rooms for nursing mothers, and screenings of Disney films for young children. Centers have facilities for changing infants, preparing formula, warming bottles, and washing bottles. Diapers, bottles, formula, pacifiers, and baby food are among the supplies for sale. Baby Care Center locations are listed on theme park guidemaps. There are changing areas in most women's and in some men's restrooms.

Lost Children: Disney employees (aka "cast members") should know what to do if a child starts to call for his or her parents. If your child wanders off, stop in at the Baby Care Center or City Hall in the Magic Kingdom; at Guest Relations or the Baby Care Center in Epcot; at Guest Relations at the Disney-MGM Studios; or at Guest Relations in Animal Kingdom. A computerized system allows for a detailed description of the child and his or her status, helping to reunite families quickly. There are no paging systems, but in emergencies an all-points bulletin can be put out among cast members. The Guest Relations staff of each park can also help.

It helps to prepare your child for the possibility of an accidental separation. Direct him or her to contact an employee (anybody wearing a name tag) and ask for help.

Refrigerators: For parents of young children, an in-room fridge is not a mere luxury,

Parental Perk

Families with babies or small children should know about the "rider switch" policy (aka "baby swap") at the theme parks. At attractions with age or height restrictions, a parent who waits nearby with a young child while the other parent rides the attraction can go right on soon after the first parent comes off. Be sure to ask the attendant at the attraction's entrance. They'll tell you how to proceed.

it's a necessity. Disney's deluxe and moderate accommodations generally come equipped with a small refrigerator. (If your room does not have one, request it. And make sure you are not charged.) Guests in "value" resorts can rent one for about $10 per day. Request the fridge when you make your reservation, and be sure to confirm that request shortly before you arrive.

Baby Food: It's possible to purchase jars of baby food at most Disney resorts. However, the selection isn't huge. For a wider variety of foodstuffs to choose from, consider Gooding's grocery store. It's located at the Crossroads shopping center, near Hotel Plaza Boulevard. For directions, inquire at your resort's front desk, or ask a parking attendant.

Gooding's, as well as nearby convenience stores, is also within a reasonable cabbing distance. Be sure to hire an authorized cab for the trip (one with regulated rates). Your resort staff can make the arrangements and give you an estimate of the cost. Winn-Dixie is another good choice. It tends to be less expensive than other options, but it's a bit farther away. If you've got a car, this is the way to go.

If you have a milk (or other food-supply) emergency after hours, know that these resorts have 24-hour snack bars: Grand Floridian, Polynesian, Contemporary, Dolphin, and Buena Vista Palace.

Cribs: Most Walt Disney World resort rooms come with a small, playpen-like crib. (Look for it in the closet. If it's not there, call to request one.) They're free, but somewhat flimsy. If you'd like something a little bigger or sturdier, consider renting a crib from Children's Furniture Rentals (407-522-0233) or All About Kids (407-812-9300).

Diapers: Each Disney resort has at least one shop in which to pick up diapers. If you're brand loyal, pack your own. Be sure to throw a few waterproof diapers into your bag each morning. You never know when you'll run into an interactive fountain on Disney property. They're necessary for pool use, too.

Resort Fun: All Walt Disney World resorts have at least one arcade. Most of the hotels

Hot Tip!

Small children may become a bit anxious when dropped off at one of Disney's child activity centers. If that's the case, plan to stick around until the trepidation passes. And prepare your child ahead of time. Let him or her know they'll be playing with other kids—coloring, playing games, watching movies, and the like. Reassure kids that you'll be nearby and tell them what time you'll be coming back. That way, little minds can relax and have fun.

Tips for Tots

Walt Disney World is about as toddler-friendly as it gets. Here are a few pointers to make it even more so:

- Familiarize your child with Disney characters before your trip. That way they'll be more likely to enjoy meeting them and less likely to be frightened by them.

- Fireworks can scare little ones silly. If your tot is spooked by loud noises, be prepared to make a hasty exit once the booms begin. That said, most babies are enchanted by SpectroMagic, the Magic Kingdom's nighttime parade.

- Be sure to bring snacks when you head out for the day. It's tough to find toddler-friendly nibbles once you leave your resort.

- Don't forget sunscreen that's sensitive to toddler skin. Pack a hat for an infant.

- Pack a small, but treasured toy from home and keep it with you at all times.

- Don't underestimate the play value of a good splash. Take time to relax and enjoy the invaluable amenity that is the WDW resort pool.

- Remember that your little one can enter the parks for free until his or her third birthday.

Tips for Teens

When it comes to teens at Disney World, *The Little Mermaid*'s Ariel has plenty of company. Of course, be they of the fish or human variety, teenage guests have special needs all their own. Here are some tips, courtesy of Amy Newcomer, Birnbaum's WDW teen expert:

- Bring your own music. It's perfect for the trip to Disney World and for sitting poolside at your resort. But don't wear your earphones for your whole trip.

- Have some of your own money on hand. If it's your hard-earned cash, you won't spend it as fast as you would Mom and Dad's!

- Pack a hat. Why? It's much easier to throw a hat on than waste time doing your hair.

- Try to get along with your brothers and sisters—even if it isn't always easy. Don't bug them to do the things you want to do all the time. Offer to do things they want to do, too.

- One of the coolest things for teens to do is an "Extra Magic Hours" evening at a theme park. They let you stay in a park after hours and ride all the best rides with basically no wait! Another good thing to do at night is to go shopping, especially at Downtown Disney Marketplace.

- *Attention, parents!* Try to include your teens in planning your trip. If they get a say during planning, they will be much happier when they arrive at Walt Disney World. Also, don't make them get up every morning at 6 A.M. Try to give them a day or two to wake up late and lounge around the pool or a water park.

have little playgrounds as well as toddler-friendly pools. For information on specially tailored children's activities at Disney's Grand Floridian Resort & Spa, turn to page 210.

Strollers: Available for rent for $10 per day at stroller and wheelchair rental shops at each of the theme parks. (Strollers are not available for rent at the water parks.) Double strollers cost $18 a day. Note that deposits are no longer required for stroller rentals at the theme parks.

Keep in mind that strollers are not permitted inside the attractions (they can be parked

near each attraction entrance). If a stroller disappears while you're in an attraction, a replacement may be obtained. Ask a park worker for the nearest replacement location. Guests have to pay only once a day for a stroller. If you rent one in the morning and plan to spend the afternoon at another park, just present your receipt for a stroller there.

If you'll need a stroller for several days, consider purchasing the Length of Stay rental ticket. It'll save you two dollars off the daily price and it should cut down on time spent in the rental line. Simply buy the ticket on your first visit to a theme park and put your receipt in a safe place—that's what you'll need to show to get a stroller on the remaining days of your stay.

Downtown Disney Marketplace and West Side rent single strollers for $8 a day, with a $20 deposit (no doubles available).

You may also bring your own stroller into the parks, or rent one at your hotel by calling Children's Furniture Rentals (407-522-0233) or All About Kids (407-812-9300).

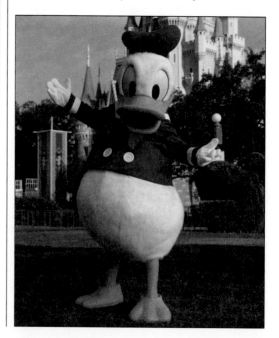

Traveling Without Children

Walt Disney World has become a popular destination for adults without children, appealing to singles, young couples, and empty nesters alike. Disney has responded to the demand with an entertainment complex and dining for grown-ups without kids in tow.

- Consider perusing *Birnbaum's Walt Disney World Without Kids*, our adult-oriented companion guide to this book.

- Crowds can be extremely heavy during traditional school-break times. Schedule your visits for off-peak seasons.

Older Travelers

Walt Disney World can sometimes be overwhelming for older travelers. The theme parks can be disorienting because of the crisscrossing pathways. And the heat, particularly in summer, can be hard to take. But with the proper planning and precautions, it's just as delightful for older visitors as for kids.

- Try to eat early or late to avoid the mealtime crowds. In the Magic Kingdom, select restaurants such as Tony's Town Square Restaurant and Columbia Harbor House. Or take the monorail to the peaceful Polynesian, Contemporary, or Grand Floridian resorts, where pleasant dining options abound (check ahead to find out which restaurants serve lunch). In Epcot, the Coral Reef restaurant and Le Cellier Steakhouse are pleasant spots. At the Disney-MGM Studios, the Hollywood Brown Derby offers a relaxing meal, as does Mama Melrose's Ristorante Italiano.

- The Florida sun tends to be brutal year-round. Always wear sunscreen!

- Don't underestimate distances at Epcot or Animal Kingdom; you may need to walk more than three miles in a day. If that's daunting, consider renting a wheelchair. (Epcot's *FriendShip* boats on the lagoon can also ease the burden on weary feet.)

- Pace yourself. It's smart to head back to your hotel for a swim or a nap in the afternoon and then return to the parks later on. The hotels connected by monorail are particularly convenient for this.

- Many Orlando-area hotels and attractions offer discounts to seniors and AARP members. Contact the Official Visitor Information Center (407-363-5872) for details.

Solo Travelers

Those who travel alone for the freedom and fun of it can have as memorable a time here as they would anywhere else.

- Solo travelers with extra time should consider taking a behind-the-scenes tour.

- Many of the finer restaurants now have counters to sit at—perfect for lone diners.

- Sometimes, being a solo traveler can mean shorter wait times at attractions. Test Track and Mission: SPACE are among those with "single rider" lines.

- Other opportunities for unencumbered travelers include parasailing and waterskiing (at the Contemporary), horseback riding (at Fort Wilderness), taking a spin in a racecar (at the Richard Petty Driving Experience), bass fishing (407-WDW-BASS; 939-2277), surfing lessons (407-939-7873), and watching a pro baseball game (at Wide World of Sports). Call 407-939-7529 for information.

- Downtown Disney's clubs and restaurants can prove to be fertile meeting places. The BoardWalk is another lively destination. Sports fans find its ESPN Club most inviting. And suds fans appreciate the home-brewed libations at Big River Grille & Brewing Works.

- The lounges at Walt Disney World hotels are relaxed and welcoming. The same atmosphere prevails at the Tune-In Lounge in the 50's Prime Time Cafe at the Disney-MGM Studios, and at the Rose & Crown Pub (in the United Kingdom pavilion) and the Matsu No Ma lounge (Japan), in Epcot.

Tips for International Travelers

Visitors from outside the U.S. need not feel like strangers in a strange land when they arrive at Walt Disney World—even if they speak a language other than English. Information is readily available in many different languages. These tips may also be helpful:

- Free park maps can be found in different languages at the entrance to all parks, as well as at Guest Relations.

- Free translation services are available at all four theme parks and include a specially designed translation device called Ears to the World, Disney's Show Translator. The units are lightweight headsets that use wireless technology to provide synchronized narration at several popular theme park attractions. They are available in French, German, Japanese, Portuguese, and Spanish. There is no charge to use the service, but a $100 refundable deposit is required to borrow the device.

- Several Disney resorts offer services for their international guests. Ask about them when you inquire about reservations.

- When making reservations through 407-WDW-DINE or WDW-PLAY, ask to speak with a foreign-language host or hostess.

- Most WDW restaurants offer menus in various languages. Some have picture menus.

- Foreign currency exchange is available at Guest Relations in each of the theme parks. Traveler's checks may be purchased at the SunTrust bank by Downtown Disney.

- Most Disney resort room keys can act as a charge card. Purchases made at WDW will be billed to a credit card that is presented at check-in (reducing the amount of currency that has to be exchanged).

- Many Disney employees are fluent in more than one language. Flags on their name tags symbolize which languages they speak.

- Guests traveling long distances and through time zones should conserve their energy. It might be wise to relax by the pool on the day of arrival, instead of trying to fit in a full day at a theme park—it's never beneficial to start a vacation exhausted!

- Phone cards good for international calls can be purchased at several Disney World shops. Look for a yellow star on the theme park map to locate one of the stores.

Telephone Dos and Don'ts

It's a common practice for hotels to assess a surcharge for phone calls, and Disney is no exception. To avoid whopping bills, charge calls to a phone card, and keep these tips in mind:

- A direct-dialed long-distance call will set you back the cost of the call at the AT&T operator-assisted day rate *plus a 55 percent surcharge*. (A recent one-minute call from a Disney resort to a New York City number cost $6.77.) The price-rate applies to both domestic and international long distance. Applicable taxes are included. Rates are subject to change.

- Prepaid phone cards are available for purchase in most WDW resort lobbies.

- Guests making credit card, prepaid phone card, or any type of operator-assisted call from a resort room phone will be charged a 75-cent fee per call.

- It costs 75 cents to call an 800 number from a WDW resort room.

- Calls made between most WDW resorts are toll calls.

- Directory assistance phone calls cost $1.40 each.

- There is no charge to call from room to room within a resort.

- If saving money is key, make calls from pay phones or cell phones when possible.

- All Disney-owned-and-operated resorts support mobile computing through a dataport connection on the guestroom telephone, with applicable charges.

Travelers with Disabilities

Disney tends to get high marks from travelers with disabilities because of attention paid to special needs. Here is an overview:

GETTING AROUND: Special parking is available for guests at the theme parks; ask for directions at the Auto Plazas upon entering. From the Transportation and Ticket Center (TTC), the Magic Kingdom is accessible by ferry or by monorail. All monorail stations are accessible to wheelchairs. The ramps are lengthy and a bit steep, but manageable.

Wheelchairs: Wheelchairs may be rented in theme parks for $10 per day ($8 per day with a "length of stay" rental). In the Magic Kingdom, they are available at the Stroller and Wheelchair Rental. Epcot's rental areas are inside the main turnstiles on the left and at the International Gateway entrance. Oscar's Super Service rents wheelchairs at Disney-MGM Studios. At Animal Kingdom, wheelchairs are available at Garden Gate Gifts.

If you plan to visit the parks for several days, consider getting a multi-day wheelchair rental. Called a "Length of Stay" ticket, it comes at a $2-per-day discount. You'll pay for the entire stay when you first visit a theme park. Simply show your receipt the next time you visit a rental location.

Guests who park in disability parking areas may use complimentary wheelchairs to help them get from the lot to the theme park wheelchair rental location. The chairs have blue seats and flags. They are not for park use.

The Disney water parks have a limited number of wheelchairs to rent. The cost is $10 per day. Downtown Disney Marketplace and West Side rent chairs for $10 a day, plus a $20 refundable deposit. The wheelchairs at Disney's Wide World of Sports may be borrowed for free.

Disney World resort guests may request a wheelchair at the front desk. It is advisable to request one in advance (do so when you reserve your room). It's free, but requires a $250 refundable deposit. Supplies are limited and wheelchairs are available on a first-come, first-served basis. Guests are always welcome to bring their own wheelchairs or Electronic Convenience Vehicles (aka ECVs or scooters).

> ## Hot Tip!
> Elderly, ill, or injured guests who do not ordinarily use a wheelchair may benefit by using one at Walt Disney World. There is a lot of ground to cover. And standing in line for attractions requires a certain amount of strength and stamina.

Resorts with zero-entry pools may have a small number of wheelchairs available to assist guests entering the pools.

Electric Convenience Vehicles (ECVs) are available for rent in every park. They cost $35 plus a $5 refundable deposit, per park per day. They usually sell out early. A word of advice for first-time users: Practice makes perfect. So, before you head into a thicket of park guests, take it for a test drive.

Equipment rented at a park *cannot leave that park*. If you'd like to hold onto yours for the whole trip, call a company that rents standard and electric wheelchairs, as well as scooters. It makes for a much less harried experience—but keep in mind that you will have to transport the wheelchair or scooter. (Monorails and buses are equipped to accommodate, boats are not.) Three companies from which to rent are LifeAire (800-417-9496), ScootAround (888-441-7575), and Walker Mobility (888-726-6837). Pick up and delivery (often for free or with a small surcharge) is available at all hotels in the WDW area (not just those on-property). Note that the Walt Disney Company is not affiliated with, nor does it endorse, these companies.

There are designated areas for guests in wheelchairs to view the fireworks at Epcot and to view the parades in each of the theme parks. Check a park guidemap for locations. Arrive early—the areas can fill up quickly.

Accessibility: It's relatively easy to get around the theme parks by wheelchair.

> ## Hot Tip!
> The theme park handicapped parking areas are quite a distance from the wheelchair rental areas—especially at the Magic Kingdom. If you require assistance, seek out a parking lot attendant and request a chair to get you to the rental location.

(Although, with its bumpier-than-the-other-parks terrain, Animal Kingdom does offer the occasional challenge.) Most attractions are accessible to guests who can be lifted from chairs with assistance from a member of their party, and many can accommodate guests who must remain in wheelchairs. Consult the *Guidebook for Guests with Disabilities* (for a free copy, write—well in advance—to Walt Disney World Guest Correspondence, Box 1000, Lake Buena Vista, FL 32830) for details about access, or check with the ride host or hostess. At the water parks, life jackets are available for travelers with disabilities.

All Walt Disney World hotels have accommodations equipped for guests with disabilities, including roll-in showers. Additional features—which vary, depending on the resort—include: wheelchair accessible bathrooms, bed accessories, strobe-light smoke detectors, in-room TTYs, and more. The following resorts have zero-depth entry pools: Animal Kingdom Lodge, Grand Floridian, Polynesian, and Saratoga Springs. For assistance in selecting the hotel that best fits your requirements, ask for the Special Reservations Department when you call Central Reservations (Voice: 407-939-7807; TTY: 407-939-7670).

RESOURCES: Visual Disabilities: Guests can get a tape recorder and a cassette that describes each park, as well as a Braille guidebook. Each requires a $25 refundable deposit.

Hearing Disabilities: Pay phones with Text Typewriters (TTYs) are available throughout Disney World. For more information, call 407-824-4321 (voice) or 407-827-5141 (TTY). Sign language is available for some shows. Call at least two weeks ahead for arrangements.

Listening devices that amplify attraction sound tracks are available at City Hall in the Magic Kingdom and at Guest Relations in Epcot, Animal Kingdom, and the Disney-MGM Studios. A $25 refundable deposit is required. Sites with assistive listening systems are listed on park guidemaps.

Ask about the availability of reflective and handheld captioning devices. The former project show dialogue onto panels in front

Attraction Access

Most park attractions are accessible to guests who are able to get out of their wheelchairs (with or without assistance). And a growing number have queues that can be navigated in a wheelchair or ECV. When that's the case, guests are urged to do so. If a wheelchair or ECV cannot be accommodated in the queue area, ask an attendant to direct you to an auxilliary entrance. Such entrances are intended for guests using wheelchairs or with service animals. For specifics on this policy, guests should visit any Guest Relations location.

of a guest; the latter provide captioning on personal devices at certain attractions. Scripts are available for some shows and attractions.

Note: *Service animals are welcome in all Disney parks.*

Booking the Trip: These organizations specialize in assisting disabled travelers:

• The Society for Accessible Travel & Hospitality (347 Fifth Ave., Suite 610, New York, NY 10016; 212-447-7284; *www.sath.org*)

• Accessible Journeys (Ridley Park, PA; *www.accessiblejourneys.com*; 610-521-0339 or 800-846-4537)

• Flying Wheels Travel (Owatonna, MN; 507-451-5005; *www.flyingwheelstravel.com*)

Vehicles: Wheelchair Getaways (*www.wheelchairgetaways.com*; 800-242-4990 or 407-281-8369), and Rainbow Wheels of Florida; (*www.rainbowwheels.com*; 800-910-8267) both rent wheelchair accessible vans and offer pick-up and delivery for most area hotels.

WDW Weddings & Honeymoons

Believe it or not, Walt Disney World is one of the most popular honeymoon destinations in the United States. Why the appeal? The resorts offer some romantic stretches of white-sand beaches for evening strolls, fine restaurants for candlelight dinners, and a host of activities to rival almost any European or Hawaiian destination. Add to that the fantasy of the Magic Kingdom, the wonder of Epcot, the glamour of the Disney-MGM Studios, and the majesty of Animal Kingdom, plus Downtown Disney and BoardWalk nightlife, water parks, and the Disney Cruise Line, and it's not hard to see why Walt Disney World is number one with newlyweds.

After years of fending for themselves, folks looking to honeymoon here now have help at hand. A variety of packages cater specifically to newly married couples. For information, call toll-free: 877-566-0969.

The folks at Walt Disney World have also received oodles of requests from couples who wanted to actually get married at one of the theme parks. Today, happy couples can tie the knot in evening ceremonies at some parks during seasons when they close early. (The area in front of Cinderella Castle in the Magic Kingdom is one of Walt Disney World's wedding hot spots, as are several Epcot sites.) Morning ceremonies are offered at Epcot's World Showcase.

The Yacht and Beach Club, BoardWalk, Animal Kingdom Lodge, Polynesian, and Wilderness Lodge resorts also host their share of weddings. The Wedding Pavilion, on the grounds of the Grand Floridian Resort and Spa, offers a Victorian-style indoor setting with a prime view of Cinderella Castle and the Seven Seas Lagoon. A combination of stained glass, sage green and soft pink florals, and benches with heart-shaped cutouts (seating around 250 guests) creates the romantic ambience. Couples can fill their wedding albums with photos taken at Picture Point, under a trellis of climbing white roses, with the faraway castle prominently in the background. Private ceremonies may also be performed at this scenic spot.

Weddings range from elegant affairs, without a hint of Disneyana, to ceremonies in which the bride arrives in Cinderella's coach and Mickey and Minnie Mouse are among the guests at the reception.

At Franck's Bridal Studio, Walt Disney World specialists work with couples to customize each wedding. Unique merchandise is available for purchase. Among the services offered are cakes, photography, hairstyling, flower arranging, and musical entertainment. Specialists can help secure accommodations, rehearsal dinners, bachelor parties, and more.

For information about planning a Walt Disney World wedding, call 407-828-3400, or visit *www.disneyweddings.com*; for honeymoon packages, call 877-566-0969, or visit *www.disneyhoneymoons.com*.

MAGICAL MILESTONES

Even frequent visitors have trouble keeping up with all the changes at Walt Disney World. The time line below will help you determine which major attractions have opened since your last visit.

1971–1982

1971
Magic Kingdom

1973
Pirates of the Caribbean, Tom Sawyer Island

1974
Star Jets (now Astro Orbiter)

1983–1990

1983
Journey into Imagination pavilion (now Imagination!)

1984
Morocco pavilion

1986
The Living Seas (Now The Seas with Nemo & Friends)

1991–1997

1991
Muppet*Vision 3-D, Beauty and the Beast—Live on Stage, SpectroMagic

1992
Splash Mountain, The Voyage of The Little Mermaid

1994
Legend of the Lion King, Innoventions (replaced Communicore), Honey, I Shrunk the Audience (replaced Captain EO), Food Rocks (replaced Kitchen Kabaret), The Twilight Zone™ Tower of Terror

1998–2006

1998
Disney's Animal Kingdom, Buzz Lightyear's Space Ranger Spin, Enchanted Tiki Room—Under New Management, Fantasmic!, DisneyQuest, Disney Cruise Line

1999
Sounds Dangerous starring Drew Carey, Kali River Rapids, Maharajah Jungle Trek, Test Track, Rock 'n' Roller Coaster, The Many Adventures of Winnie the Pooh, Cirque du Soleil

2001
The Magic Carpets of Aladdin

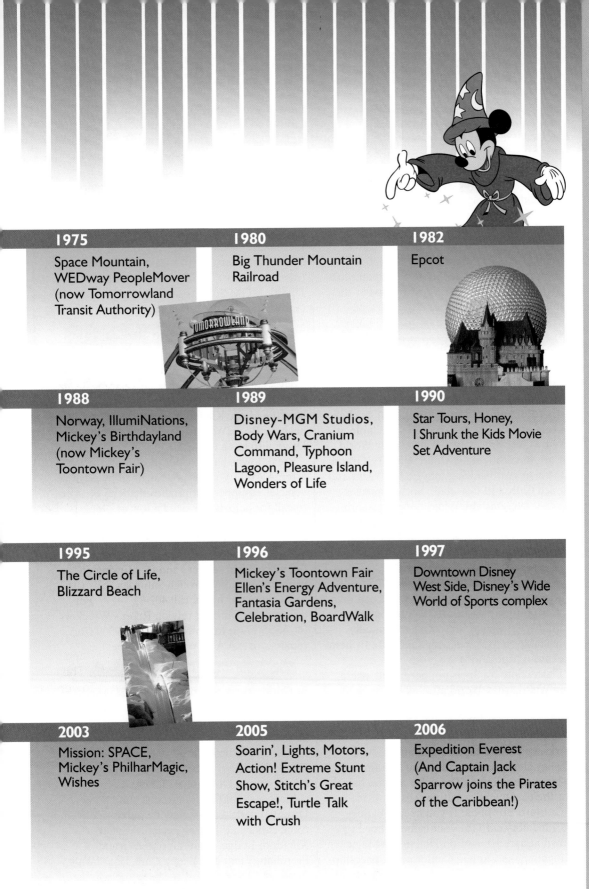

1975

Space Mountain, WEDway PeopleMover (now Tomorrowland Transit Authority)

1980

Big Thunder Mountain Railroad

1982

Epcot

1988

Norway, IllumiNations, Mickey's Birthdayland (now Mickey's Toontown Fair)

1989

Disney-MGM Studios, Body Wars, Cranium Command, Typhoon Lagoon, Pleasure Island, Wonders of Life

1990

Star Tours, Honey, I Shrunk the Kids Movie Set Adventure

1995

The Circle of Life, Blizzard Beach

1996

Mickey's Toontown Fair Ellen's Energy Adventure, Fantasia Gardens, Celebration, BoardWalk

1997

Downtown Disney West Side, Disney's Wide World of Sports complex

2003

Mission: SPACE, Mickey's PhilharMagic, Wishes

2005

Soarin', Lights, Motors, Action! Extreme Stunt Show, Stitch's Great Escape!, Turtle Talk with Crush

2006

Expedition Everest (And Captain Jack Sparrow joins the Pirates of the Caribbean!)

Fingertip Reference Guide

BARBERS AND SALONS

One of the most amusing places to get a haircut is the Magic Kingdom's old-fashioned Harmony Barber Shop. It's located beside the Car Barn in the Town Square section of Main Street.

Haircuts, coloring, manicures, and other services are available at the American Beauty Shoppe/Captain's Chair in the Contemporary (407-824-3411), Periwig Beauty and Barber Shop at the Yacht and Beach Club (407-934-3260), Ivy Trellis at the Grand Floridian (407-824-3000, ext. 2581), the Mandara Spa at the Dolphin (407-934-4250), and the Casa de Belleza at Coronado Springs (407-939-3965).

BUSINESS SERVICES

Disney provides a range of services for those who simply must mix business with pleasure. Photocopiers, fax machines (also found at Guest Relations in the theme parks), pocket pagers, and FedEx materials are available at Lobby Concierge at any Walt Disney World resort. In addition, the Contemporary, Grand Floridian, Animal Kingdom Lodge, Yacht and Beach Club, and Coronado Springs resorts provide secretarial services, computers, printers, and Internet access for a fee. A videoconferencing center is located near Downtown Disney. For information, call 407-827-2000.

CAMERA NEEDS

Photo spots around the theme parks can help you capture the best shots. To photograph fireworks, your camera must have a manually adjustable shutter speed and aperture (it helps to have a tripod, too).

Flash photography is not permitted inside any Walt Disney World attraction. Film and disposable cameras are available at many shops throughout the World. The best selection can be found at the camera shops in each park. Also, when capturing moments with Disney characters on videotape, refrain from using camera lights. (The lights are too bright for the characters' sensitive eyes.)

Camera Supplies: If you need a battery or a memory card for your camera, head to Town Square Exposition Hall in the Magic Kingdom; the Camera Center near Spaceship Earth, Cameras and Film at the Imagination! pavilion, or World Traveler at International Gateway in Epcot; The Darkroom on Hollywood Blvd. in the Disney-MGM Studios; or Garden Gate Gifts in Animal Kingdom. Film is no longer processed on-property. If you're traveling by plane, pack film in a carry-on bag. (Checked baggage screening equipment will damage film.)

Digital Camera Services: Guests can transfer photos onto CDs in camera centers at these park locations: Exposition Hall in the Magic Kingdom, Epcot's Camera Center (main entrance), The Darkroom at the Disney-MGM Studios, and Animal Kingdom's Garden Gate Gifts (entrance plaza).

CAR CARE

Three gas stations with convenience stores are on the property, all of which are open 24 hours a day. One is on Buena Vista Drive across from Pleasure Island; another is on Floridian Way near the Magic Kingdom Auto Plaza. The third, near the BoardWalk resort on Buena Vista Drive, also has a car wash.

Breakdowns happen, but they don't spell disaster. All WDW roads are patrolled by security vehicles equipped with radios that can be used to call for help. If you need a tow or other services, call the AAA Car Care Center (407-824-0976). Located in the Magic Kingdom Auto Plaza, the AAA Car Care Center offers full mechanical services and free towing on property, Monday through Saturday, 7:30 A.M. to 10 P.M. After hours, call 407-827-4777. For off-property car care, rely on Riker's Wreckers (407-855-7776) for towing; 407-238-9800 (for repairs), or AAA (if you're a member).

DRINKING LAWS

In Florida, the legal drinking age is 21. Minors are permitted to accompany their parents to WDW lounges and bars, but may not sit or stand at the bar. No alcohol is served in the Magic Kingdom, but alcoholic beverages are sold in Epcot, the Disney-MGM Studios, Animal Kingdom, and Downtown Disney.

Alcohol is sold in at least one shop at most Disney resorts. Liquor may be purchased from room service at the Polynesian, Animal Kingdom Lodge, Contemporary, Grand Floridian, Yacht and Beach Club, BoardWalk, Swan, and Dolphin resorts; beer and wine are usually available for delivery at other resorts.

LOCKERS

Attended lockers can be found in the following theme park locations: to the right, just inside the Magic Kingdom entrance, beside Spaceship Earth in Epcot, next to Oscar's Super Service inside the main entrance at the Disney-MGM Studios, and just inside the entrance and to the left at Animal Kingdom. Lockers are also available at the Transportation and Ticket Center (TTC).

Items too big to fit can be checked with the locker attendant at the Magic Kingdom, at Package Pickup in Epcot, and at Guest Relations at the Disney-MGM Studios and Animal Kingdom. Cost is about $5 per day (plus a $2 deposit) for unlimited use. Items may not be stored overnight. Lockers are cleaned out after the park closes.

Note: Be sure to save your rental receipt; it can be used again that day to secure a locker in any of the four theme parks.

LOST & FOUND

The extensive indexing system maintained by Walt Disney World's Lost and Found department is impressive, especially when a prized possession turns up missing, whether it's false teeth or a camera. (Both have been lost in the past; the dentures were never claimed.)

If you lose (or find) something, report it at any one of these Lost and Found locations: the Transportation and Ticket Center (TTC), City Hall in the Magic Kingdom, the Guest Relations lobby in Innoventions East at Epcot, Oscar's Super Service just inside the Disney-MGM Studios, Guest Relations near the Animal Kingdom entrance, or Guest Services at any WDW resort. At Fort Wilderness, dial 7-2726 from a comfort station telephone; from outside the campground, phone 407-824-2726; and from Downtown Disney, phone 407-828-3058.

Items lost in a theme park may be claimed on the day of the loss at the park's Lost and Found, and thereafter at the Transportation and Ticket Center (TTC) Lost and Found station. To report lost items after your visit, call 407-824-4245. Hats, strollers, sunglasses, and WDW merchandise are kept for one month; everything else is kept three months.

MAIL

Postage stamps can be purchased at all WDW resorts; at City Hall in the Magic Kingdom; at shops near the lockers in Epcot, the Studios, and Animal Kingdom; and at Guest Services in the Downtown Disney Marketplace.

The old-fashioned mailboxes in the theme parks are not official U.S. mailboxes, but letters (with postage) can be mailed from them. Postmarks read "Lake Buena Vista," not "Walt Disney World."

A post office at 10450 Turkey Lake Road in Orlando is open from 8 A.M. to 7 P.M. weekdays and 9 A.M. to 5 P.M. on Saturday. Call 407-351-2492 for more information.

Mail may be addressed to guests care of their hotel. The address for all WDW resorts is Walt Disney World, Box 10000, Lake Buena Vista, FL 32830.

MEDICAL MATTERS

Travelers with chronic health problems should carry copies of all prescriptions and get names of local doctors from hometown physicians. However, Walt Disney World is equipped to deal with many types of medical emergencies. In the Magic Kingdom, next to the Crystal Palace, there is a First Aid Center staffed by a registered nurse; there is another such facility at Epcot in the Odyssey Center complex. At the Disney-MGM Studios, the First Aid Center is inside the Guest Relations building at the main entrance, accessible from both inside and outside the park. The Animal Kingdom First Aid Center is located on Discovery Island near the back side of Creature Comforts.

Walt Disney World resort guests and those staying at other area hotels have access to services providing nonemergency medical care. Centra Care Walk-In Medical Care, owned and operated by Florida Hospital, has fourteen area locations, most adjacent to pharmacies and with X-ray facilities.

The main facility is at 12500 South Apopka-Vineland Road (407-239-6463; near Disney resorts) and is open 8 A.M. to midnight weekdays and 8 A.M. to 8 P.M. weekends. The facility at 6001 Vineland Road (407-351-6682; near the resorts at Universal Studios Orlando) is open 7 A.M. to 7 P.M. weekdays and 8 A.M. to 6 P.M. on weekends. One location in Kissimmee is at 7848 W. Irlo Bronson Highway (407-397-7032). It's open 8 A.M. to 8 P.M. weekdays and 8 A.M. to 5 P.M. weekends.

Courtesy transportation is available from most area hotels to Centra Care clinics, and there is a no-tipping policy. Waits in walk-in clinics can be lengthy, but Centra Care drivers call ahead to learn which has the shorter wait. For patients who prefer to have the doctor come to them, a 24-hour house-call-only medical service, Doctors On Call Service, can be reached at 407-399-DOCS (399-3627).

The most common maladies reported by Walt Disney World guests? Sunburn (Don't forget to wear your sunscreen!), blisters, colds, fevers, earaches, and injuries from falls. For emergencies, dial 911, or call nearby Orlando Regional Sand Lake Hospital (407-351-8500) or Celebration Health (407-303-4000).

For Diabetics: All Walt Disney World resorts can provide refrigeration services for insulin. All "deluxe" and "moderate" accommodations have their own refrigerators, and small refrigerators are available for rent at other resorts for about $10 a night.

Prescriptions: Turner Drugs (407-828-8125) delivers medications to many area resorts, including those on Disney property.

MONEY

Cash, traveler's checks, American Express, MasterCard, Visa, Discover Card, Diner's Club, JCB Card, Disney's Visa card, and Disney gift cards are accepted as payment for most charges at Disney. Personal checks may be used to book vacation packages, purchase tickets at Walt Disney World, and for resort account settlements (at the end of your stay). Checks must bear your name and address, be drawn on a U.S. bank, and be accompanied by a government-issued photo ID and a major credit card. Some snack stands only accept cash.

A Disney resort guest perk: Leave a credit card imprint at check-in and the hotel IDs may be used to cover purchases in shops, lounge and restaurant charges, and recreational fees incurred inside Walt Disney World. A bill will be sent to your home for all charges made past check-out time.

ATMs: Automated teller machines are scattered throughout Walt Disney World. Theme park locations include the Magic Kingdom (near the locker rental just inside the entrance, in City Hall on Main Street, U.S.A., in Frontierland near the Shootin' Gallery, and in the Tomorrowland arcade), Epcot (near the main entrance, on the pathway between Future World and World Showcase, and in Germany), the Disney-MGM Studios (at the entrance, and inside Toy Story Pizza Planet), and Animal Kingdom (at the entrance), plus the Transportation and Ticket Center (TTC). Most Disney resorts have ATMs in the lobby; the Fort Wilderness ATM is outside Pioneer Hall. Three can be found in Downtown Disney: near the Rock 'n' Roll Beach Club at Pleasure Island, next to Guest Services in the Marketplace, and by the West Side's Forty Thirst Street. Most bank cards and credit cards are accepted; the fees range from $2 to $2.50.

Banking: SunTrust, located across from Downtown Disney Marketplace, offers a variety of services. Guests can get cash advances on MasterCard, Discover, and Visa credit cards; receive incoming wire transfers up to $3,000 (for a $50 fee); and cash, replace, or purchase American Express traveler's checks. This branch is open from 9 A.M. to 4 P.M. weekdays, until 5:30 P.M. Thursdays (407-828-6103 or 800-786-8787). The drive-thru is open until 5 P.M. Monday through Friday, but you must have a SunTrust account to use it.

Disney Dollars: Money bearing the image of Mickey, Goofy, or Minnie is available for purchase at City Hall (Magic Kingdom) and Guest Relations (Epcot, the Disney-MGM Studios, and Animal Kingdom) in $1, $5, and $10 denominations. (The exchange rate is always a buck for a buck.) Disney Dollars are accepted as cash throughout the World.

Traveler's Checks: Even the most careful of vacationers occasionally loses a wallet. Traveler's checks can take the sting out of that loss. Look for promotions by banks at home in the months preceding a vacation to see if one of the major brands—American Express, MasterCard, Visa, Citibank, and Bank of America—is available free. Stash the receipt bearing the check numbers in a place separate from the checks themselves, along with a piece of identification such as a duplicate driver's license or a spare credit card to speed the refund process should your checks get lost.

To purchase, cash, or replace American Express traveler's checks, go to the SunTrust bank across from the Downtown Disney Marketplace. (If you do not have a record of the check numbers, first contact the place where you purchased the travelers checks. Then, an American Express referral number is required; call 800-221-7282.)

AAA members can visit the AAA Travel Center in the Magic Kingdom for traveler's check assistance.

Foreign Currency Exchange: Up to $50 per person in foreign currency may be exchanged daily at Guest Relations in the theme parks, and up to $500 at the Guest Services desk at WDW resorts. Foreign currency exchange is also available at the Gooding's grocery (407-827-1200) at the Crossroads shopping center near Hotel Plaza Boulevard.

PETS

No pets (other than service animals) are allowed in the theme parks or the Walt Disney World resorts, except at certain campsites at Fort Wilderness (request a pet site for $5 extra per day). Travelers who bring pets along can lodge them in one of the five air-conditioned Pet Care Kennels: near the Transportation and Ticket Center (TTC), left of Epcot Entrance Plaza, at the Disney-MGM Studios entrance, at the Disney's Animal Kingdom entrance, and at the Fort Wilderness campground entrance. (The last one is next to a field where owners can take their pets out for a run.)

During busy seasons, it is best to arrive before the 9 A.M. rush. Kennels close one hour after the closest theme park closes. In case of emergency, a vet will be called on your pet's behalf.

Owners must put more unusual animals into the kennels' cages. Rabbits, birds, turtles, hamsters, nonpoisonous snakes, and other animals unsuited (because of their size) to cat- and dog-size cages must have their own escape-proof carriers.

Guests may board pets overnight in any of the kennels on-property. While there are no staffers on duty overnight, it just takes a phone call to gain access to your pet after hours (guests receive the number when they check their pet in). Cost is $15, including Friskies dry food (Walt Disney World resort guests pay $13 per night to leave pets

overnight); a day stay is $10, with one feeding. Guests are urged to visit their animals at least three times each day throughout their stay, as animals are not otherwise sprung from their cages. Pets will be fed special food, if provided by the owner. For information, call 407-824-6568. Reservations are not accepted (there's always availability).

Be sure to bring along your pet's certificate of vaccinations, since Florida law requires proof of immunization for animals involved in biting incidents. It's always a good idea to pack your pet's favorite blanket, pillow, or toy, too. Never leave a pet in your car. It is extremely dangerous for the animal and is against the law.

Outside Walt Disney World: A few hotels in the Orlando area, including the Quality Inn Plaza (for $10 plus tax per night; 407-996-8585), let pets stay with guests. Call the Orlando/Orange County Convention & Visitors Bureau (407-363-5871 or 800-551-0181; the latter is a recording).

POCKET PAGERS

Two types of devices are available to signal a phone call or message. They can be rented at nearly all WDW hotels; ask at the front desk.

RELIGIOUS SERVICES

Note that religious services are no longer offered on Disney property, though one need not venture far to find them.

Protestant: Sundays at 9 A.M. and 10:30 A.M. at River of Life Presbyterian, 8323 W. Sand Lake Rd. Call 407-351-4333. Also, Sundays at 10:15 A.M. at Lake Buena Vista Baptist Church, 11551 County Rd. 535; 407-239-6030.

Muslim: Prayer takes place five times a day at Jama Masijid, 11543 Ruby Lake Rd. Call 407-238-2700 for more information.

Catholic: The closest Catholic church is Mary, Queen of the Universe Shrine, 2½ miles south of Lake Buena Vista, at 8300 Vineland Ave. This church seats 2,000 people. Call 407-239-6600 for mass times.

Jewish: Reform services are held at the Congregation of Reform Judaism (928 Malone Dr., Orlando; 407-645-0444), near Winter Park, about 20 miles from Walt Disney World. Conservative services are held at Temple Ohalei Rivka, also known as the Southwest Orlando Jewish Congregation (11200 S. Apopka-Vineland Rd.; 407-239-5444), less than two miles from the Downtown Disney district.

SHOPPING FOR NECESSITIES

Almost any everyday item can be purchased right on the property. At least one shop in every Disney resort stocks a small selection of toiletries. In addition, over-the-counter health aids, plus many other useful items, can be purchased at the Emporium on Main Street in the Magic Kingdom; they're kept behind the counter, so ask for what you want.

Aspirin and sunscreen are also available at Island Supply in Adventureland and Mickey's Star Traders in Tomorrowland. In Epcot, sundries are sold in at least one shop in each World Showcase pavilion and at all Future World stores. At the Disney-MGM Studios, stop by the Crossroads of the World and Movieland Memorabilia shops. At Animal Kingdom, you can pick up bare necessities at Island Mercantile.

Local supermarkets include Winn-Dixie and Gooding's (which are close to the resorts on Hotel Plaza Boulevard), and Publix (a bit farther afield, but still worth considering). Gooding's, at the Crossroads at Lake Buena Vista, is convenient, but pricey.

SMOKING

Walt Disney World's strict nonsmoking policy became even stricter with the adoption of the Florida Clean Air Act. Smoking is prohibited in all indoor and outdoor spaces, unless specifically designated as "smoking areas." These areas are marked on park guide-maps. All dining establishments are smoke-free, as are clubs and lounges. Tobacco products are not sold in the theme parks. Guests may purchase tobacco products at Walt Disney World resorts and Downtown Disney.

All Disney resorts have rooms for smokers and nonsmokers alike. Be sure to request the room type of your choice as you check in.

Remember, this is a statewide smoking policy, so if you venture off Disney property, the same rules apply.

Lost Adults

Occasionally, traveling companions get separated in the crush of the crowds, or someone may fail to show up at a meeting spot. When this happens, it's good to know that messages can be left for fellow travelers at Guest Relations in any of the four theme parks.

TELEPHONE CALLS

It takes more than the traditional seven digits to make a local call in this neck of the woods. Every time a local call is placed in Central Florida, callers must dial the area code and the seven-digit number. The rule applies to calls made within the same area code as well as for those that connect with other area codes. For local calls, it is not necessary to dial a 1 before the ten-digit number.

Local calls made from pay phones cost 50 cents each. Rates charged by local resorts can vary quite a bit (for local and long-distance calls alike). Ask about rates and fees *before* you make calls beyond your resort. See page 44 for more telephone tips.

Hot Tip!

The point is to escape the real world, so turn off that cell phone! That way you'll ensure that the magic—for you and those around you—will be uninterrupted. If you *have* to make a call, do so by the nearest public phone station.

If you plan to connect to the Internet via personal computer, don't forget to bring a list of local access numbers for dial-up service. And know that even if the area code is 407, it doesn't guarantee that the number is a local one.

TIPPING

Tips are no less valued at Disney resorts than at any other hotel—$1 per bag is appropriate for lugging luggage; $1 to $3 per person, per night for housekeeping services (include a note to avoid confusion). Gratuities of 15 to 20 percent (excluding tax) are customary at full-service restaurants. (If service is exceptional or otherwise, adjust accordingly.) Gratuity is included in the room service bill at WDW resorts and some off-property hotels. Check before you tip twice. Note that a 10 percent gratuity is added at the Pepper Market at Coronado Springs (despite the self-serve set-up).

Give cab drivers a 15 percent tip for good service. Baggage handlers at the train station and airport expect about $1 per bag.

WEATHER

Call Walt Disney World Weather Information (407-824-4104), or check The Weather Channel website (*www.weather.com*).

Transportation & Accommodations

The popularity of Walt Disney World has made the region around Orlando one of the world's major tourism and commercial centers, and transportation facilities, from a state-of-the-art airport to an efficient network of highways, bring visitors to the area by the millions.

There's no doubt that getting to and around the Walt Disney World region can be very confusing. The only more perplexing dilemma may be choosing the best accommodations for your family from the huge assortment of hotels and motels.

The accommodations owned-and-operated by Disney itself range from futuristic towers to cabins buried deep in piney woods. In between are resorts that evoke striking images of Africa, the South Pacific, historic Florida, the Pacific Northwest, the Caribbean, New England, early Atlantic City, New Orleans, the Southwest, Mexico, and the sports, movie, and music worlds, plus a sprawling, well-maintained campground. And that list doesn't include the many villas or the studios and homes with one, two, and three bedrooms that can be "purchased" through a special vacation-ownership system. What follows should help travelers sort out the broad range of lodging options within the borders of Walt Disney World. Regardless of where you plan to stay, we offer this advice: Book your room as far in advance as possible. You won't regret it.

Getting Oriented

Orlando, the Central Florida city of more than one million residents, is the municipality with which Walt Disney World is most closely associated. Walt Disney World, however, is in a far smaller community called Lake Buena Vista, 15 miles from Orlando's business center. A number of hotels and restaurants are located in Lake Buena Vista, though there are many more in Orlando.

Hot Tip!

Parking spaces are cleverly labeled throughout Walt Disney World. Yet many drivers still misplace their vehicles. Avoid being dopey: Always write down your parking location!

ORLANDO-AREA HIGHWAYS: The most important Orlando traffic artery is I-4, which runs diagonally through the area from southwest up to northeast, cutting through the southern half of Walt Disney World. It then angles on toward Orlando and Winter Park, ending near Daytona Beach at I-95, which runs north and south along the coast.

All the city's other important highways intersect I-4, and each has a name as well as a number. From south to north, they include U.S. 192 (aka Irlo Bronson Memorial Highway), which takes an east-west course that crosses the Walt Disney World entrance road and leads into downtown Kissimmee on the east; S.R. 528 (aka the Beach Line Expressway), which shoots eastward from I-4; S.R. 435 (aka Kirkman Road), which runs north and south and intersects International Drive, where many motels catering to WDW visitors are located; U.S. 17-92-441 (aka Orange Blossom Trail), which runs north and south, paralleling Kirkman Road on the east; and S.R. 50 (aka Colonial Drive), which runs east and west.

WALT DISNEY WORLD EXITS: The 47-square-mile tract that is Walt Disney World is roughly rectangular. I-4 runs through its southern half from southwest to northeast. The major Disney destinations are most efficiently reached by taking the I-4 exits suggested in the paragraphs that follow; off the highway, clear signage makes it easy for

Did You Know?

When it comes to fashion, Walt Disney World is the biggest clotheshorse of them all. There are more than 2.5 million garments in its corporate costume closet, making it the largest working wardrobe in the world.

visitors to get anywhere in the World. This road is congested more often than not. Keep in mind that construction work and special events will often require rerouting of traffic patterns on I-4, so it's best to follow signs as directed:

- **Exit 64,** marked "192/Magic Kingdom," leads to the Magic Kingdom, Disney-MGM Studios, Fort Wilderness, Palm and Magnolia golf courses, and Pop Century, Contemporary, Polynesian, Grand Floridian, and Wilderness Lodge resorts.
- **Exit 65,** leads to Disney's Wide World of Sports complex, Disney's Animal Kingdom, Blizzard Beach, Coronado Springs, All-Star Music, Sports, and Movies, and Disney's Animal Kingdom Lodge. It is also a good alternate route to the Disney-MGM Studios park.
- **Exit 67,** marked "Epcot/Downtown Disney," leads to Epcot, Typhoon Lagoon, Downtown Disney, Lake Buena Vista golf course, Disney's Saratoga Springs Resort & Spa, Bonnet Creek Golf Club, the BoardWalk, Caribbean Beach, Swan, Dolphin, Yacht and Beach Club, Port Orleans, and Old Key West resorts.
- **Exit 68,** marked "S.R. 535/Lake Buena Vista," is the best route to the resorts on Hotel Plaza Boulevard and the Crossroads of Lake Buena Vista shopping center. It can serve as an alternate route to Epcot.

Hot Tip!

The cost to valet park a vehicle at any Walt Disney World–owned-and-operated resort is $7 per day (not including gratuity). There is no charge for self-parking for guests at any of the resorts.

WDW Transportation

Walt Disney World transportation is extensive, with boats, buses, and the monorail all doing their part to shuttle guests around. Visitors staying at WDW hotels should receive a detailed brochure about transportation options at check-in. (If you don't, just ask.) For transportation information, call 407-824-4321.

One of the system's hubs is called the Transportation and Ticket Center (TTC), located near the Magic Kingdom. Monorail, bus, and ferry service connect the TTC to points throughout the World. Day visitors must park here before taking a monorail or ferry to the Magic Kingdom. (Most Disney resort guests can bypass the TTC via direct buses.)

The monorail runs along a circular route near the Magic Kingdom, stopping at the TTC, Polynesian, Grand Floridian, Magic Kingdom, and Contemporary. A separate extension of the monorail system connects the TTC to Epcot. Bus service is the cornerstone of the WDW transportation system. It is efficient, if occasionally confusing. With a few exceptions, buses arrive every 15 to 20 minutes, from one hour before park opening until about an hour after closing; bus stops are clearly marked. Travel times vary, depending on the route.

Although Disney resort guests are provided with complimentary transportation to all sites on-property, that transportation is not always direct. *Build in extra time for travel*, especially if you have made reservations at a restaurant. Also, know that traveling between resorts can

Should You Rent a Car?

If you plan to spend all of your time on WDW turf, you can spare yourself the hefty expense. Towncar service from the airport to all area hotels is available around the clock, and taxis are in good supply. Within the World, an exhaustive network of transportation brings guests from point to point (if not always directly). Most area hotels offer their own bus service to and from Disney theme parks (inquire in advance about schedules and costs, if any).

However, for those planning to visit Orlando-area restaurants and any attractions outside Walt Disney World, a rental car is a must. Also, certain routes are more convenient by car. It is easiest to rent from one of the companies at the airport: National (800-227-7368), Avis (800-331-1212), Budget (800-527-0700), or Dollar (800-800-4000). Other rental agencies provide shuttles from the airport, so it may be worth the extra time if you get a good deal. For day trips, consider Alamo or National at the Magic Kingdom Auto Plaza (407-824-3470) or one of the rental agencies that have desks at the resorts on Hotel Plaza Boulevard, or simply inquire about car rental at the front desk of your resort.

be time consuming and usually requires at least one transfer.

From several Walt Disney World locales, water launches usher guests to the Magic Kingdom, Epcot, the Disney-MGM Studios, Downtown Disney, or between resorts. Boats generally depart every 20 to 30 minutes.

TRANSPORTATION ID REQUIREMENTS:
Guests who wish to use the Disney transportation system may be asked for proof of riding privileges. Accepted IDs afford different degrees of access. WDW resort ID cards, Magic Your Way tickets with Park Hopper options or Water Parks & More options, and Annual Passes let guests use all Disney buses, monorails, and boats. Valid one-day theme park tickets permit guests to use monorails and the ferries running between the TTC and the Magic Kingdom, but do not allow use of buses.

TAXI SERVICE: Taxi cabs are available for about $3.50 for the first mile, $2.50 per extra mile (though it may vary, depending on the number of passengers). Stick with authorized cab services. Many independent taxi services charge outrageous rates. When we travel between resorts that aren't joined by boat or monorail and find ourselves pressed for time, we splurge and take a cab. Inquire at the bell services desk at your resort's front entrance. They'll direct you to the nearest authorized taxi or order one on your behalf.

THE MONORAIL: The Disney World monorail system is an efficient (and to many, downright exciting) way to travel. There are two main loops, which converge at the Transportation and Ticket Center (TTC) stop. One loop connects the Contemporary, Polynesian, and Grand Floridian resorts with the Magic Kingdom and the TTC. The other loop links Epcot with the TTC, making the monorail a park hopper's dream come true. Note that guests staying in the aforementioned resorts have a private track on the Magic Kingdom loop, making for a hastier exit at closing time. Monorails run from about 7 A.M. until about two hours after park closing.

Did You Know?
The Walt Disney World monorail system—a 14.7-mile highway in the sky—has carried more than a billion passengers since 1971.

Timing Tip: It takes about three to five minutes to get from stop to stop on the Magic Kingdom's resort monorail loop, making for a grand circle total of about 12 to 25 minutes.

Transportation Tips

• If you are staying at a Disney resort, be sure you get the "Handy Guide to All the Magic" brochure at check-in.

• Most buses are equipped with wheelchair lifts. Such buses have a blue emblem on the windshield and rear door.

• When using the WDW transportation system to travel between your resort and a theme park, or from one park to another, allow an extra 30 minutes to get to your destination.

• The interval between the arrivals of most Disney buses is about 20 minutes.

• Be forewarned: It takes a long time to travel by bus from resort to resort. Plan on a trip of up to 90 minutes and at least one transfer (at a park or at Downtown Disney).

• Monorails usually run until two hours after the latest park closing time (one hour after Magic Kingdom "Extra Magic Hours").

• Note that there is no direct transportation between Disney's BoardWalk and most other resorts. You must first travel to Downtown Disney or a park and transfer to the appropriate bus. (Or take a cab.)

• Never attempt to vacate a theme park just as a park closes. Instead, plan to linger a bit in a shopping area, or grab a seat and watch the crowds crawl toward their respective buses, boats, cars, and monorails.

• It is not uncommon, especially at park opening and closing times, for guests to be asked to stand on the bus or monorail.

• Keep in mind that the most obvious mode of transportation may not be the quickest. For example, it is much faster to walk to the Magic Kingdom from the Contemporary resort than it is to take the monorail.

• It's possible to rent a car from any Disney resort. For details, inquire at the Lobby Concierge desk, or contact the front desk.

• WDW resort guests who arrive with a car receive a complimentary parking permit upon check-in. The permit, good for the length of your stay, allows you to park most places on property for free.

WDW Accommodations

With hundreds of resorts in the Orlando area to choose from, it's definitely a challenge to select a hotel. Here's our advice.

Weigh the Options: First decide whether to stay on or off Disney property. Many opt for a Disney resort because the conveniences and perks offered to resort guests are appealing (see page 60). Given that, there are still two major factors that tend to lure guests off property: budget and schedule.

Travelers on a tight budget will find some off-property options that are quite reasonable. Remember, however, that Disney offers rooms as low as $82 per night, so choose off-property accommodations only if the difference in price is substantial.

Guests who will spend only part of their trip exploring Disney may also prefer an off-property hotel—one that's closer to the other attractions on their itinerary.

There's also the issue of what one may or may not consider deluxe. Disney-owned-and-operated "deluxe" resorts do tend to provide more amenities and service than their "moderate" and "value" counterparts, but do not always rival comparably priced accommodations in the real world.

Deciding Factors: Once the on- or off-property decision has been made, it's time to look at hotels. The big differences among on-property accommodations are in the size of the rooms and bathrooms, attention to decor, level of service, dining options, transportation options, recreational facilities, landscaping, location, and, of course, cost.

Consider how much time you'll spend in the room, whether you'd like to return to the hotel during the day, and if you'll have time to use all the amenities that are included in the price. Parties with five or more members have an additional concern: how best to accommodate their group. It may be less expensive to reserve adjoining, value-priced rooms instead of one luxury room or villa. Kids under 17 stay free at Disney resorts, but there is a fee for each additional adult over two staying in a room.

Ask the Right Questions: Once a hotel that meets all basic criteria is selected, it's best to do one last round of research, so there will be no surprises at check-in.

For example, ask about any possible hidden costs, like shuttle service to and from Walt Disney World (which can be more than $20 per person, round-trip) or taxes that may not be included in the quoted price. Though most off-property hotels offer transportation to WDW, the frequency and number of buses vary significantly. Find out the exact schedule and the number of stops made. Ask where the bus picks up and drops off, too. Try to avoid those that stop in busy parking lots.

Some hotels advertise a misleading proximity to Disney. While a hotel may be only a short distance from the border, the actual commute to the theme parks may be considerable. Get specifics. (Distance from your favorite theme park is also a factor to consider when staying on-property.)

Reserve a Room: Found the perfect hotel? Book it before someone else does, and don't forget to ask about any special discounts or seasonal promotions.

A Room with a View

There's a lot to be said for throwing back the curtains and gazing at a breathtaking view, provided you have the time to appreciate it and your view is within your price range. The following is a breakdown of different "views" you may select from at the various WDW resorts. It will help you determine the best view for your budget.

Although the categories vary, depending on the resort type, the "standard view" is always the lowest rate available.

Value Resorts

Standard View = Parking lot, pool, garden, and everything else

Moderate Resorts

Standard View = Parking lot or landscaping

Water View = Pool, marina, lake, river

Deluxe Resorts

Standard View = Parking lot

Garden View = Landscaping

Water View = Pool, lake, or other water

Lagoon View = Seven Seas Lagoon

Savanna View = Animal pastures (at Animal Kingdom Lodge)

Walt Disney World Resorts

Walt Disney World hotels fall into two categories: Disney-owned-and-operated and non-Disney-owned resorts. Of all the WDW properties, the Swan and Dolphin and the resorts on Hotel Plaza Boulevard don't belong to Disney. Expect services and benefits in the non-Disney resorts to be slightly modified (see pages 77 and 93).

On-Property Perks: WDW resorts offer guaranteed admission (with ticket) to the theme parks—even when they're filled to capacity and closed to the general public; use of the WDW transportation system; the convenience of charging most purchases to their hotel bill. Guests who stay at a Disney-owned-and-operated resort and arrive via air at Orlando International Airport are entitled to Disney's Magical Express service (see page 15) and the "Extra Magic Hours" benefit which allows extra time in a select park on select days.

Room Amenities: Disney rooms have alarm clocks; shampoo; a safe (not big enough to fit a laptop); voicemail; TVs with local and national channels, including the Disney Channel and ESPN. There are hair dryers, irons, small refrigerators (in deluxe and moderate resorts), and coffeemakers in many rooms. Laundry facilities, dry cleaning, and room service are provided in most resorts (for a fee).

Resort Primer

Payment Methods: Hotel bills and room deposits may be paid by credit card, Disney gift cards, traveler's check, cashier's check, money order, cash, or personal check. Checks must bear the guest's name and address, be drawn on a U.S. bank, and be accompanied by proper ID (a valid driver's license or government-issued passport will do).

Room Deposit Requirements: When booked through Central Reservations, a deposit equal to one night's lodging (or campsite rental) is required *within 14 days* of the time that a reservation is made. Reservations are automatically canceled if deposits are not received by the 14-day deadline. (Reservations booked less than 30 days prior to arrival will receive special instructions for deposits.) Reservations booked through the Walt Disney World Travel Company are subject to a substantial cancellation fee. Ask about the cancellation policy when you book your room.

When booking by phone, guests may pay the deposit with a major credit card. Those who wish to use another payment method may do so by mailing it with the payment stub that comes with the reservation confirmation.

Cancellation Policy: With the exception of "Magic Your Way" packages, deposits for resort stays will be fully refunded if the reservation is canceled at least five days before the scheduled arrival. Magic Your Way packages must be canceled at least 45 days ahead.

Additional Charges: When more than two adults (age 17 and up) occupy a standard room, the added per-day fee for each extra adult is $2 at Fort Wilderness campsites; $5 at Fort Wilderness Cabins; $10 at the Pop Century and All-Star resorts; $15 at Caribbean Beach, Port Orleans French Quarter and Riverside, and Coronado Springs; and $25 at all other WDW resorts. Note that in some resorts, an additional bed may be required to sleep an extra adult. If so, the cost is $15.

Check-in and Check-out: The early check-out time (11 A.M. at all WDW lodgings) and the late check-in times (1 P.M. at the campsites, 3 P.M. in most hotels, 4 P.M. at BoardWalk, Saratoga Springs, Wilderness Lodge, and Beach Club, plus All-Star resorts, and Old Key West) often come as a surprise. Guests who arrive before check-in time can preregister, store luggage at Guest Services (without fee), and head to the parks or relax by the pool.

WDW ID Cards: Issued on guests' arrival at Disney resorts, the cards (which double as room keys) entitle guests to use of WDW transportation (through the last day of your stay) and charge privileges (provided you leave a credit card imprint with the hotel) to cover purchases in shops and restaurants, as well as recreational fees incurred in the World.

Note: Charges incurred on a hotel ID after check-out will be reflected in a revised bill, which will be sent by Disney. Swan and Dolphin guests may use their IDs to charge meals inside the two hotels only.

WALT DISNEY WORLD RESORT FINDER

DELUXE

Name & Location	Setting/ Theme	Favored By	Romantic Hideaways	Kids Adore	Dining Tip	Resort Category & Amenities
Animal Kingdom Lodge Animal Kingdom area (page 87)	African wildlife preserve	Animal lovers—nearly every room affords a view of wandering wildlife. Art aficionados—authentic African artwork abounds	Private balconies by moonlight. Sunset lounge overlooking the savanna	The kopje, a rocky outcropping from which to spy on critters. Story time beside the lobby fireplace. Rustic bunk beds (on request)	Sample the exotic eats and atmosphere of Boma while savoring the sights of the savanna.	Full-service restaurants, fast-food spots, room service
BoardWalk* Epcot area (page 79)	Turn-of-the-century Atlantic City	Night owls—the entertainment options are numerous and right in the backyard. Epcot lovers, who will appreciate the short commute. Disney Vacation Club members	Moonlight strolls along the boardwalk. A special fireworks cruise	The Keister Coaster, a 200-foot waterslide at the main pool. The face-painting booth on the boardwalk at night	Snack on saltwater taffy, cotton candy, or old-fashioned sticky buns while strolling along the boards.	Luggage service — Valet parking — Swimming pools
Contemporary Magic Kingdom area (page 66)	Retro-futuristic	Families—the monorail whisks through it, and the Magic Kingdom is a short walk away. Professionals, who can take advantage of the hotel's many business services	The rooftop lookout (available only to California Grill patrons) helps make up for the resort's otherwise less-than-romantic atmosphere and decor.	The "party" held every 45 minutes at Chef Mickey's fabulously fun character meals. Watching the monorail whoosh through the resort	Reserve California Grill for a time that's likely to coincide with the Magic Kingdom's Wishes fireworks show. The view is amazing.	Beach access‡ — On-site recreation, such as boat rentals‡ — On-site kids' activities
Grand Floridian Magic Kingdom area (page 69)	Victorian seaside resort	Honeymooners—who will love spending much of their vacation basking in the resort's unebbing romantic atmosphere. Magic Kingdom and monorail fans	Manicured rose gardens. Honeymoon suites. The Grand Lobby for a cocktail while an orchestra performs on the balcony	The "zero-entry" swimming pool. Having dinner with Cinderella and her princess friends at 1900 Park Fare	Have a spot of traditional afternoon tea, accompanied by a scone, at the Garden View Lounge.	Most rooms sleep five guests — Monorail, bus, or boat transport to all parks ($215–$845)
Polynesian Magic Kingdom area (page 67)	South Pacific	Romantics—the white-sand beaches and lush, tropical setting may make you swoon. Vacationers looking for a hotel with a real resort feel. Magic Kingdom and monorail fans	Beach coves for two. Sunset Pointe	The weekend torch-lighting ceremony in the Great Ceremonial Hall. The slide- and waterfall-endowed pool	The Polynesian Luau is favored by many for its entertainment and revamped menu.	‡Except Disney's Animal Kingdom Lodge

* Beach Club, BoardWalk, and Wilderness Lodge also have Vacation Club accommodations.

❦ This resort hosts character meals.

61

Name & Location	Setting/ Theme	Favored By	Romantic Hideaways	Kids Adore	Dining Tip	Resort Category & Amenities
DELUXE						($215–$845)
Swan & Dolphin Epcot area (page 77)	Beachfront whimsy	Conventioneers—the services are excellent / Guests who want many of the Disney perks but not necessarily the Disney hotel / Serious swimmers—the only WDW lap pools are here	A secluded area behind the grotto pool waterfall	The swan-shaped pedal boats / The giant swan and dolphin statues perched atop their respective resorts	The Swan's Kimonos Lounge serves scrumptious sushi with a side of karaoke.	Full-service restaurants, fast-food spots, room service / Luggage service / Valet parking / Swimming pools
Wilderness Lodge* Magic Kingdom area (page 71)	America's grandest national parks	Sweethearts—love is always in the air at this resort / Winter visitors—the warm, cozy atmosphere is even more inviting when the many fireplaces are roaring / Disney Vacation Club members	Steamy, bubbling "hot springs" whirlpools / The cozy alcoves hidden on each floor of the main building	Totem poles, an erupting geyser, and countless Hidden Mickeys—there's even a free tour to help guests find them	Sample berry cobbler or the cedar plank salmon, Artist Point signature dishes. / Savor morning coffee from a fireside rocking chair.	Beach access‡ / On-site recreation, such as boat rentals‡ / On-site kids' activities / Most rooms sleep five guests
Yacht & Beach Club* Epcot area (page 75)	Martha's Vineyard and Nantucket Island	Ambitious guests—those who plan to see and do everything Disney has to offer will like the central location / Everyone—deluxe atmosphere and amenities appeal to all Disney Vacation Club members	The Yacht Club's peaceful gazebo / Secluded whirlpools / The beach—perfect for twilight strolls	Stormalong Bay—the sand-bottomed, three-acre pool, with a waterslide and a shipwreck to play on	Cape May Cafe's bountiful nighttime clambake has many a surf-and-turf fan lining up for more.	Monorail, bus, or boat transport to all parks / ‡Except Disney's Animal Kingdom Lodge
DISNEY VACATION CLUB						($279–$1,850)
Disney's Old Key West Downtown Disney area (page 85)	Key West	Guests looking for a homey, village atmosphere / Disney Vacation Club members / Those who appreciate roomy rooms	Private whirlpool tubs—they come with all accommodations but the studios	The weekly Tiny Tot Tea Parties and Un-Birthday Parties with snacks, games, and treats, held at Community Hall / One super pool slide	Good's Food To Go can box up any item from Olivia's (the table-service restaurant next door)	Kitchens, restaurants, pizza delivery / Luggage service / Swimming pools / On-site recreation, such as boat rentals / Front-door parking / Villas sleep 4–12
Disney's Saratoga Springs Resort & Spa Downtown Disney area (page 84)	Historic Saratoga Springs, New York	Peace seekers—the atmosphere is meant to soothe / Disney Vacation Club members / Space seekers. The accommodations are generally more spacious than at other resorts.	Pretty gardens and meandering pathways / Private whirlpool tubs—they come with all accommodations but the studios	The kids-only water-spray area near the pool / Kid-oriented activities at Community Hall	Downtown Disney's tempting array of eateries is a mere stone's throw away.	Bus or boat transport to all parks / Washers and dryers / Boat to Downtown Disney

MODERATE · VALUE · CAMPGROUND

Resort	Theme	Ideal for	A special touch	Kids will love	Insider tip	Amenities & price
Caribbean Beach Epcot area (page 74)	Tropical islands	Families—while all Disney resorts have kid appeal, the colorful design, themed pool, and beach setting make this hotel ideal for families with kids of any age	Aruba beach—the hotel's longest, most secluded strip of sand	The fortress pool and Parrot Cay Island; The coconut postcards sold at the Calypso shop (real coconuts!)	Try a food court kids meal—it's served in a sand bucket with a shovel (and keep an ear out for the talking trash cans!).	**MODERATE:** Restaurant, food court, limited room service; Luggage service; Swimming pools with slides; On-site recreation, such as bikes and boat rentals; Rooms sleep four guests; Bus transport to all parks ($145–$210)
Coronado Springs Animal Kingdom area (page 88)	Mexico and Southwest USA	Conventioneers—which means more business services (and a health club), higher food prices, and slightly less family entertainment than at the other moderate resorts	The waterfront in the peaceful Casitas area; The gazebo-style boat-rental dock at twilight	The Dig Site—which encompasses the resort's playground and main pool with its Mayan temple waterslide	Carry-out items at the Pepper Market food court are spared the 10 percent gratuity charge.	
Port Orleans French Quarter and Riverside Downtown Disney area (pages 82–83)	Antebellum South and New Orleans French Quarter, respectively	Lovebirds on a budget—the Riverside decor is like many of Disney's deluxe hotels, as is the romance factor; but the price is considerably less. The French Quarter provides a peaceful, urban alternative	Any room in Magnolia Bend's stately mansions; The peaceful gardens scattered about the Riverside quarters	The pool, fishing hole, and playground at the Riverside's Ol' Man Island; The French Quarter's Doubloon Lagoon—a sea-serpent-themed family pool	Sample the fresh beignets from the food court. You'll think you're in Jackson Square.	
All-Star Movies, Music, & Sports Animal Kingdom area (page 86)	Comic book	Penny-savers of all ages—these resorts offer fun, colorful theming, plus all the WDW perks, at a much lower price than at other Disney resorts. Space-cravers adore the Family Suites at All-Star Music	All-Star Music's Jazz and Broadway areas (note that Music tends to attract more couples without kids than the other two themes)	Awe-inspiring, super-size icons—the movie and sports themes score the highest points; Extra-large arcades	Pick up a pizza at the pickup window in the food court and have a pizza party.	**VALUE:** Food court, pizza delivery; Luggage service; Swimming pools; Bus transport to all parks ($82–$265)
Pop Century Animal Kingdom area (page 89)	American pop culture	Budget watchers and nostalgia buffs—this sprawling resort celebrates pop history with bright colors and big icons; Young athletes and their families—Disney's Wide World of Sports is located nearby	Sipping specialty cocktails poolside	The state-of-the-art arcade; Wildly oversize cell phones, yo-yos, bowling pins, and more; The interactive water fountain near the playground	The refillable mug, good for use at the resort throughout your stay, definitely scores points as far as bargains go.	
Fort Wilderness Resort and Campground Magic Kingdom area (page 73)	Rustic woods	Motor-home mavens—Disney's hookups are considered top-notch; Families—who appreciate the kitchen and extra space of the cabins, which fit six	The Fort Wilderness beach at night—perfect for viewing the Electrical Water Pageant on Bay Lake	Pony rides, wagon rides, a blacksmith's shop, and free campfire marshmallow roasts	Join the nightly campfire circle and roast marshmallows with Chip and Dale.	**CAMPGROUND:** Recipient of perfect ratings from *Trailer Life* and *Woodall's* magazines; Bus transport to all parks ($41–$329)

* Beach Club, BoardWalk, and Wilderness Lodge also have Vacation Club accommodations.

❤ This resort hosts character meals.

Rates at WDW Properties

	Value	Regular	Peak*
DELUXE‡			
Animal Kingdom Lodge			
Rooms (sleep 4 to 5)	$215–$265	$265–$395	$325–$460
Rooms–Club Level (5)	$325	$380	$455
BoardWalk Inn			
Rooms (5)	$315–$390	$345–$435	$429–$510
Rooms–Club Level (5 to 6)	$445–$540	$505–$600	$565–$645
Contemporary			
Rooms–Garden Buildings (5)	$259–$330	$299–$375	$339–$425
Rooms–Tower (5)	$365–$395	$410–$445	$470–$515
Rooms–Club Level (4)	$535	$600	$680
Grand Floridian Resort & Spa			
Rooms (5)	$375–$455	$425–$520	$495–$615
Rooms–Club Level (5)	$490–$650	$565–$740	$665–$845
Polynesian			
Rooms (5)	$329–$455	$385–$515	$449–$600
Rooms–Club Level (5)	$465–$675	$530–$650	$620–$875
Swan & Dolphin (Rates were accurate at press time, but are likely to change. Call 800-227-1500 for current prices.)			
Rooms (5)	$339–$375	not applicable	$379–$445
Rooms–Club Level (5)	$459	not applicable	$495
Suites (5 to 10)	$639		$665
Wilderness Lodge			
Rooms (4)	$215–$270	$265–$320	$325–$385
Rooms–Club Level (4)	$375	$425	$490
Yacht & Beach Club			
Rooms (5)	$315–$385	$359–$440	$429–$500
Rooms–Club Level (5)	$435–$515	$490–$575	$565–$650
‡ For information about suites, call 407-934-7639.			
DISNEY VACATION CLUB			
Disney's Beach Club Villas			
Studios (4)	$315	$359	$429
1-BR Villas (4)	$425	$480	$560
2-BR Villas (8)	$595	$770	$975
Disney's BoardWalk Villas			
Studios (5)	$315	$359	$429
1-BR Villas (4)	$425	$480	$560
2-BR Villas (8)	$595	$770	$975
Grand Villas (12)	$1,440	$1,645	$1,850
Disney's Old Key West			
Studios (4)	$279	$309	$359
1-BR Vacation Homes (4)	$370	$420	$485
2-BR Vacation Homes (8)	$515	$610	$745
3-BR Grand Villas (12)	$1,135	$1,265	$1,430
Saratoga Springs Resort & Spa			
Studios (4)	$279	$309	$359
1-BR Villas (4)	$370	$420	$485
2-BR Villas (8)	$515	$610	$745
Grand Villas (12)	$1,135	$1,265	$1,430

	Value	Regular	Peak*
DISNEY VACATION CLUB (continued)			
The Villas at Wilderness Lodge			
Studios (4)	$305	$349	$415
1-BR Villas (4)	$425	$470	$570
2-BR Villas (8)	$590	$765	$920
MODERATE			
Caribbean Beach			
Rooms (4)	$145–$160	$165–$185	$185–$210
Coronado Springs			
Rooms (4)	$145–$160	$165–$185	$185–$210
Port Orleans French Quarter and Riverside			
Rooms (4)	$145–$160	$165–$185	$185–$210
VALUE			
All-Star Movies, All-Star Music, and All-Star Sports			
Rooms (4)	$82–$94	$99–$111	$119–$131
Pop Century			
Rooms (4)	$82–$94	$99–$111	$119–$131
CAMPGROUND			
Fort Wilderness Campsites			
Sites w/partial hookup (10)	$41	$58	$67
Sites w/full hookup (10)	$46	$69	$79
Preferred sites (10)	$55	$75	$85
Fort Wilderness Cabins			
Cabins (6)	$249	$289	$329

Check-in time: 3 P.M. except at the Beach Club Villas, BoardWalk Villas, Wilderness Lodge Villas, Saratoga Springs, All-Star resorts, and Old Key West, where check-in is at 4 P.M., and at Fort Wilderness Resort and Campground, where it's 1 P.M. **Check-out time:** 11 A.M. for Fort Wilderness and all hotels.

2007 Value rates apply: January 1 to February 14, August 5 to October 3, and November 25 to December 19 for all Value and Moderate resorts; January 1 to February 14 and July 29 to November 15 for the Campground; January 1 to February 14, July 7 to October 3, and November 25 to December 19 for all other WDW properties. **2007 Regular rates apply:** April 15 to May 23 and October 4 to November 23 for all Value and Moderate resorts; April 15 to July 28 for the Campground; April 15 to July 7 and October 4 to November 24 for all other WDW properties (except Swan and Dolphin). **2007 Peak rates apply:** February 15 to April 14 for all WDW properties (except Swan and Dolphin). **2007 Pre-holiday rates apply:** November 16 to December 19 (Fort Wilderness cabins only). **2007 Holiday rates apply:** December 20–31. **2007 Summer rates apply:** May 24 to August 4 (Value and Moderate resorts only). For Swan and Dolphin resort rates, call 800-527-1500.

Room capacity: Numbers in parentheses reflect maximum occupancy based on existing beds. A trundle bed (for one) can be rented at some properties for $15 a day. Playpen-like cribs can be requested for free in most resorts. Rates include up to two adults. There is an additional charge for each extra adult in a room.

CALL 407-934-7639 FOR RESERVATIONS

Note: The prices provided here were correct at press time, but rates do change, so be sure to double check with the hotels before setting your final budget. Charge is for one-day, single or double occupancy.

*During holiday seasons, rates are higher.

TRANSPORTATION & ACCOMMODATIONS

Magic Kingdom Area

Contemporary

Watching the monorail trains disappear into this hotel's enormous 15-story A-frame tower never fails to impress first-timers. The sleek trains look like long spaceships docking as they slide inside.

Passengers, for their part, are impressed by the cavernous lobby, with its tiers of balconies and, at its center, the soaring 90-foot-high, floor-to-ceiling tile mural depicting scenes from the Southwest. (Look carefully and you may spot the five-legged goat.)

This imposing structure has 1,008 rooms in its tower and the garden buildings that flank it on either side. There are shops, restaurants, snack bars, lounges, a marina, beach (with hammocks), health club, and more. The pool area incorporates two whirlpools and a waterslide. The convention center offers business services. Perhaps the resort's most notable feature is its 15th-floor observation deck. From here guests dining at the resort's California Grill restaurant can enjoy a bird's-eye view of the Magic Kingdom. Another bonus: the walking path to the Magic Kingdom (it's a mere 5- to 10-minute stroll away).

A club level package is available for guests who stay in the hotel's 14th-floor suites. Amenities include express check-in and check-out, complimentary continental breakfast, evening refreshments, and nightly turndown service. The 12th floor also provides guests with special club level privileges. To contact the Contemporary, call 407-824-1000.

ROOMS: Boasting a new, sleek, and truly contemporary design, the rooms here are evenly apportioned among the main tower and two garden buildings. All rooms located in the tower have private balconies and views of Bay Lake or the Magic Kingdom. Most rooms can accommodate five guests (plus a child under 3). Typical units have a daybed and two queen-size beds; some rooms have a king-size bed and a daybed. The bedding is a cut above most Disney resorts. And every room has a flat-screen TV (to which you can connect your own DVD player). Business-minded folks rejoice over the desk space and high-speed Internet connection (for a fee). While the ceiling fans have gone away, room temperature may be set as low as 65 degrees. Note that the bathrooms here, though elegant in design, are a bit baffling. There's not much shelf or counter space, the side-by-side flat sinks tend to stay damp, and the sliding doors don't lock.

Connecting rooms may be requested, though not guaranteed. A variety of suites, consisting of a living room and one or two bedrooms, can accommodate 4 to 8 people. There is free, weekday newspaper delivery.

Warning: Pop music sometimes blares from the pool area on the Bay Lake side. The monorail can be heard from lower tower rooms, too. For maximum quiet, request a park view on a higher floor, or stay in a garden wing. Of course, all rooms get serenaded by the nightly fireworks at the nearby Magic Kingdom park.

WHERE TO EAT: In addition to the many restaurants and snack spots, 24-hour room service provides a wide range of offerings.

California Grill: On the 15th floor. The specialty is California fare—flatbread pizza, grilled meats, seafood, and market vegetables. An added treat: the spectacular view of the Magic Kingdom fireworks for dining guests.

Chef Mickey's: Located on the fourth-floor concourse. Mickey and his friends host daily buffets. Breakfast features Mickey Mouse pancakes as well as more traditional items. Dinner offers carved meats, prime rib, nightly specials, a variety of entrées, plus a sundae and dessert bar. A true crowd-pleaser.

WHERE TO DRINK: The Magic Kingdom's no-alcohol policy doesn't trickle over to its nearest neighbor.

California Grill Lounge: On the resort's 15th floor, adjoining the California Grill. Picture windows provide a dramatic backdrop for sipping California wines and other drinks, and nibbling on appetizers. Seating is limited.

Contemporary Grounds: A lobby coffee bar, near the escalators. Serves cappuccino, espresso, latte, and other gourmet coffees, as well as biscotti.

Outer Rim: On the fourth-floor concourse, overlooking Bay Lake. Serves appetizers, cocktails, and specialty drinks.

Sand Bar: This poolside spot offers drinks, fruit plates, and light snacks from the grill.

WHAT TO DO: Volleyball nets are set up on the beach, and a basketball court is nearby. Waterskiing, parasailing, and fishing excursions may be arranged (see *Sports* for details).

Boating: Sea Raycer motorboats and other boats may be rented at the resort's marina.

Health Club: The Olympiad health club has stair-climbers, bicycles, a sauna, treadmills, lockers, and massage (by appointment). Equipment use is free to WDW resort guests.

Parasailing: Supervised excursions are offered at the marina. Cost is about $90 per person, or $140 for two to ride tandem. Reservations are necessary; call 407-939-0754.

Salon: Contemporary Resort Salon on the third floor of the tower provides haircuts, facials, manicures, and other services.

Shopping: The fourth-floor concourse is home to several shops. Fantasia sells character merchandise, including plush animals and clothing for kids. Concourse Sundries & Spirits has newspapers, magazines, books, snacks, and liquor—just what's needed for a cocktail party on the terrace. Bay View Gifts (BVG) carries character merchandise and apparel for adults, items with the Contemporary Resort logo, jewelry, souvenirs, home decor items, kitchenware, and candy.

Swimming: In addition to a round, lakeside pool, the free-form pool features a 17-foot-high curving slide. Two whirlpools have been added (one is located in the center of the pool, the other is tucked off to the side).

Video Arcade: Slated to move from the first floor to the fourth, this fun-zone may not be open in 2007. If that turns out to be the case, know that guests are welcome to enjoy the arcade at any neighboring WDW resort.

Waterskiing, Wakeboarding, Tubing: Ski boats with instructors may be rented for $140 per hour at the marina. Call 407-939-0754 for reservations and pricing information.

TRANSPORTATION: The Contemporary resort is connected to the Transportation and Ticket Center (TTC) and the Magic Kingdom by monorail. From the TTC, Epcot can be reached by transferring to another monorail. Buses take guests to the Disney-MGM Studios, Animal Kingdom, and Blizzard Beach, Typhoon Lagoon, and Downtown Disney. Watercraft travel from the marina to Fort Wilderness and Wilderness Lodge.

Polynesian

The Polynesian resort is as close an approximation of the real thing as Walt Disney World's designers could create. The vegetation is lush, and the architecture summons the tropics. The mood is set by a three-story garden that occupies most of the lobby. Water cascades over craggy volcanic rocks, while coconut palms tower over about 75 different species of tropical and subtropical plants.

The structure that contains this mass of greenery, the Great Ceremonial House, is the central building in the Polynesian complex. The front desk, shops, and most of the restaurants are located here. Flanking the Ceremonial House on either side are 11 two- and three-story village longhouses named for various Pacific islands. These structures house the resort's 853 rooms. The monorail stops at this hotel, making it a convenient place to stay; in fact, it's just a short ride to the Magic Kingdom.

Club level service offers such amenities as express check-in, continental breakfast, cookies and soft drinks every afternoon, hors d'oeuvres and desserts in the evening, and a lounge with a prime view of the Seven Seas Lagoon and Cinderella Castle (not to mention the nightly fireworks displays in the Magic Kingdom). Club level rooms and suites are located in the Tonga and Hawaii buildings. The telephone number for the Polynesian is 407-824-2000.

ROOMS: Many of the rooms have balconies, and most have a view of the gardens, Seven Seas Lagoon, or one of the resort's swimming pools; rooms in the Tokelau, Tahiti, and Rapa Nui buildings are the largest. Most rooms have two queen-size beds and a daybed, and can accommodate five guests (plus a child under

---

Did You Know?

The white sand on the beaches near the Polynesian and Grand Floridian resorts and along the Seven Seas Lagoon actually came from the bottom of Bay Lake, located behind the Contemporary resort.

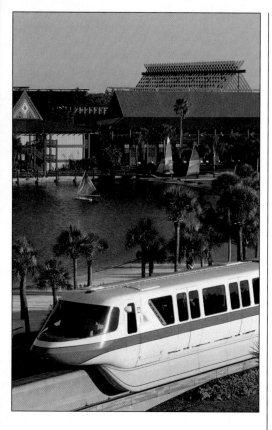

age 3). Adjoining rooms may be requested. The resort's suites—located exclusively in the Tonga building—can accommodate four to nine guests. Some have a king-size bed in the bedroom and one queen-size bed in the parlor.

WHERE TO EAT: A variety of specialties are available from room service between 6:30 A.M. and midnight. Also, some interesting eating spots are located here.

Captain Cook's Snack Company: On the lobby level of the Great Ceremonial House. This is a good spot for continental breakfast. Snacks are available 24 hours a day. At press time, Captain Cook's nook was scheduled for refurbishment and a possible name change.

Kona Cafe: On the second floor of the Great Ceremonial House. This family restaurant serves lunch and dinner with an Asian flair, while the breakfast menu is filled with traditional American selections. A coffee bar provides the perfect capper to any meal. (This is one of the best cups of coffee you'll get at Walt Disney World.) The coffee bar is usually open until about 11 A.M.

'Ohana: On the second floor of the Great Ceremonial House. 'Ohana serves family-style dinners roasted in a large fire pit. Disney characters host a breakfast every morning.

WHERE TO DRINK: The Polynesian theme has inspired a whole raft of deceptively potent potables. As might be expected, both the drink offerings and the settings in which they are served are as tropical as they come.

Barefoot Bar: Adjoining the Swimming Pool Lagoon, and open seasonally.

Tambu: There's a tropical air about this lounge adjoining 'Ohana. The bar serves appetizers and exotic specialty drinks. Sporting events are shown on a large TV.

WHAT TO DO: A wide range of activities is available at the Polynesian, including a jogging path. Morning fishing excursions can also be arranged.

Boating: Several types of sailboats, Sea Raycer boats, canopy boats, and pontoon boats are available for rent at the marina.

Children's Program: The Never Land Club is a supervised activity program for (potty-trained) kids ages 4 through 12. It's offered between 4:30 P.M. and midnight. The cost is $10 per hour. Reservations are necessary; call 407-824-3463.

Shopping: Boutiki is the place for swimwear, resort wear, souvenirs and more. Trader Jack's sells Disney souvenirs, toys, newspapers, magazines, and fashions. It's also stocked with food, spirits, soft drinks, snacks, and other fixings for an impromptu room party. Wyland Galleries of Florida features art with a sea theme.

Swimming: There are two pools here: the unguarded elliptical East Pool, in the shadow of the Tokelau, Hawaii, Tuvalu, Rapa Nui, and Tahiti buildings, and the larger free-form Swimming Pool Lagoon, found closer to the marina and main beach. The latter boasts a popular volcano-themed watering hole, complete with slide. It appeals to swimmers of all ages. Guests often get water-logged into the wee hours of the morning (though the lifeguards go home at night). Toddlers have their own sprinkler area nearby. The beaches are strictly for sunbathing, sandcastle- building, and snoozing. There is a sprinkler area for toddlers, too.

Video Arcade: Moana Mickey's has an assortment of current video games. It is located next to the Never Land Club.

TRANSPORTATION: The Polynesian resort is on the monorail line to the Magic Kingdom and the Transportation and Ticket Center (TTC). From the TTC, Epcot can be reached

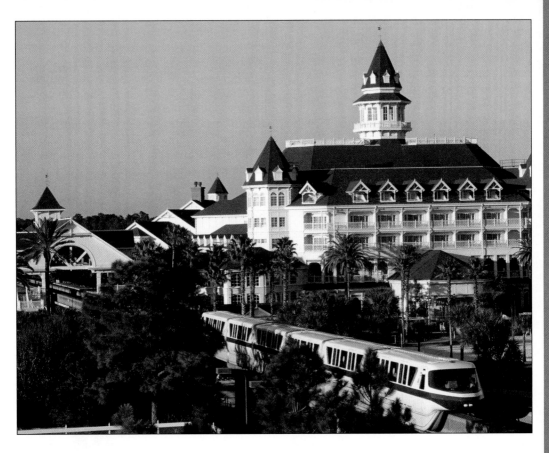

by transferring to another monorail. Buses take guests to the Disney-MGM Studios, Animal Kingdom, Blizzard Beach, Typhoon Lagoon, and Downtown Disney. Watercraft travel from the marina to Fort Wilderness and Wilderness Lodge.

Grand Floridian Resort & Spa

At the turn of the century, Standard Oil magnate Henry M. Flagler saw the realization of his dream: The railroad he had built to "civilize" Florida had spawned along its right-of-way an empire of grand hotels, lavish estates, prominent families, and opulent lifestyles. High society blossomed in winter, as the likes of John D. Rockefeller and Teddy Roosevelt checked into the Royal Poinciana, in Palm Beach, enjoying the sea breezes from the oceanside suites.

The hotel later burned to the ground, and Florida's golden era faded with the Depression. But nearly a century after Flagler first made Florida a fashionable resort destination, Walt Disney World opened a grand hotel—an 867-room Victorian structure with gabled roofs and carved moldings—on 40 acres of Seven Seas

Lagoon shorefront, between the Magic Kingdom and the Polynesian.

Like its late-19th-century predecessors, the Grand Floridian resort boasts abundant verandas, ceiling fans, intricate latticework and balustrades, turrets, towers, and red-shingle roofs. And yet, it offers all the advantages of modern living, including monorail service. With five restaurants, two lounges, five shops, and an arcade, plus a children's activity center, convention center, swimming pool, marina, and full-service health club and spa, the Grand Floridian is not only a grand hotel but a complete resort.

The main building houses the Grand Lobby, a palatial space soaring five stories to a ceiling of stained-glass domes and glittering chandeliers. Palms and an aviary decorate the sitting area; an open-cage elevator carries guests to the shops and restaurants on the second floor. The turn-of-the-century theme is everywhere, from the costumes worn by the employees to the shop displays, restaurants, and room decor. The telephone number for the Grand Floridian resort is 407-824-3000.

ROOMS: The rooms are decorated as they might have been a century ago—with printed

Did You Know?

Movie buffs may find the Grand Floridian strangely familiar. Its design is based, in part, on that of the Hotel Del Coronado, in California. Scenes from the classic film *Some Like It Hot* were shot there.

wall coverings, marble-topped sinks, ceiling fans, and Victorian woodwork. Amenities include hair dryers, bathrobes, mini-bars, nightly turndown service, and daily newspaper delivery.

The main building houses club level rooms and suites; lodge buildings, each four and five stories high, contain standard rooms, slightly smaller "attic" chambers, and suites. Most rooms measure about 400 square feet and include two queen-size beds, plus a daybed, to accommodate up to five people. Many rooms have terraces. Suites include a parlor, plus one, two, or three bedrooms; there are king-size or queen-size beds in the bedrooms. Most of the 15 honeymoon rooms, located on the second, third, fourth, and fifth floors, enjoy wonderful views. In the main building, access to the upper three club-level suite floors is restricted by private elevator.

On the third floor, the club level desks offer such services as reservations and information. The fourth floor features a quiet seating area where continental breakfast and evening refreshments are served. Club level service is also available in the Sugar Loaf building.

WHERE TO EAT: Most restaurants and lounges are located on the first two floors of the main building. Room service offers a wide assortment of items 24 hours a day.

Cítricos: The largest of the hotel's restaurants is also the newest. It features market-fresh cuisine from southern Europe. Open for dinner, on select days. Some seating affords excellent views of the nightly fireworks presentation at the Magic Kingdom. Closed Monday and Tuesday.

Gasparilla Grill & Games: This 24-hour snack bar offers light items for all-day dining and snacking, plus a selection of video games.

Grand Floridian Cafe: Its peaches-and-cream color scheme and veranda-like feel make this a great place for a quick sit-down meal. All meals are served.

Narcoossee's: This casual restaurant and bar has a romantic shoreline location. The ever-changing menu includes such staples as roast lamb chops and seafood. The partially open kitchen is the focal point of the restaurant. Guests may sip cocktails on the veranda.

1900 Park Fare: A buffet restaurant decorated with carousel horses, plants, and Big Bertha, the carnival organ. Characters host breakfast and dinner daily.

Victoria & Albert's: The eatery is named after the former queen and prince consort of England. Meals are served to no more than 60 guests. Jackets are required for men, and reservations are a must.

WHERE TO DRINK: Guests will find the refined lounges here to be especially nice escapes. Cocktail service is provided in the lobby from 4 P.M. to 11 P.M. daily. Cítricos and Narcoossee's both have lounges, complete with scenic views of the Magic Kingdom.

Garden View Lounge: This pretty spot on the first floor offers a view of the hotel's lush, landscaped garden and pool area. Afternoon tea is served (as are finger sandwiches and small desserts).

Shades of Green

This 228-room resort is near the Grand Floridian but is not linked with the monorail system. Shades of Green is a recreational retreat for active and retired military personnel and their families, members of the reserves and the National Guard, and Department of Defense employees.

The resort features two tennis courts, two pools, a small health club, restaurant, bar and lounge, gift shop, arcade, laundry facilities, and free transportation around WDW.

Room rates are based on military or civilian grade. Select multi-day tickets are offered at a discount. The property's three golf courses—the Palm, the Magnolia, and Oak Trail—are open to all WDW guests (see *Sports* for details). All other activities are for hotel guests and their families only.

"Magical Express" service is not available to guests at this resort. The number for Shades of Green is 407-824-3400. For reservations, call 407-824-3600.

Mizner's Lounge: Named after the eccentric, wildly prolific architect who defined much of the flavor of Palm Beach County, this bar is on the second floor.

Pool Bar: The place for pool and beachside refreshments, this spot features a variety of snacks and beverages.

WHAT TO DO: The Grand Floridian offers all the recreational facilities of a beach resort. Fishing excursions can be arranged (refer to the *Sports* chapter for details).

Boating: Sailboats, canopy boats, pontoon boats, and Sea Raycer speedboats are available for rent (by the hour or half-hour) at Captain's Shipyard Marina. The *Grand 1* yacht (complete with a captain and first mate) can be rented for $400 an hour.

Children's Programs: The Mouseketeer Club is a supervised program for kids ages 4 through 12. It's open from 4:30 P.M. to midnight; the cost is $10 per hour for each child. Reservations are required; call 407-WDW-DINE (939-3463). Kids ages 4 to 10 may also embark on a special Pirate Adventure and search for treasure near the Magic Kingdom. The 90-minute trip costs $30 per child. Refer to page 210 for details. For additional information and to make reservations, call 407-WDW-DINE (939-3463).

Health Club: The health club has exercise machines, saunas, whirlpools, and steam rooms.

Salon: The Ivy Trellis salon offers a full line of hair-care services.

Shopping: On the first floor of the main building is Summer Lace, specializing in women's resortwear and swimwear, and Sandy Cove, for gifts, sundries, and home decor. One level up is the M. Mouse Mercantile character shop, a Bally leather-goods store, and Commander Porter's, a men's shop.

Spa: The spa offers more than a dozen treatment rooms for massage, herbal wraps, and aromatherapy. There are some spa programs for children.

Swimming: There are two pools and a kiddie pool for guests to splash in. The pool nearest the spa is a "zero-entry" pool and features a 120-foot slide.

Tennis: There are two clay courts. There is no charge to play; available on a first-come, first-served basis.

Video Arcade: Gasparilla Grill & Games is on the first floor of the main building.

TRANSPORTATION: The Grand Floridian is connected to the Transportation and Ticket Center (TTC) and Magic Kingdom by monorail. From the TTC, Epcot can be reached by transferring to another monorail. Buses take guests to the Disney-MGM Studios, Animal Kingdom, Blizzard Beach, Typhoon Lagoon, and Downtown Disney. Watercraft travel from the marina to Fort Wilderness and Wilderness Lodge.

Wilderness Lodge & Villas

This resort recalls the spirit of the early American West and the feeling of the National Park Service lodges built during the early 1900s. These grand structures architecturally unified the elements of the unspoiled wilderness parks, kept harmony with nature, and incorporated the culture of Native Americans. The Wilderness Lodge artfully recaptures this rustic charm.

The resort is located between the Contemporary resort and Fort Wilderness on Bay Lake. The lobby, which is shared by the lodge and villas, is in an eight-story, log-structured building. Massive bundled log columns support a series of trusses, while two Pacific Northwest totem poles soar 55 feet into the air. Four levels of corridors surround the lobby, providing access to guestrooms, sitting nooks, and terraces. The monorail does not stop here. Concierge service is available on the top floor. The telephone number for the Wilderness Lodge and Villas is 407-824-3200.

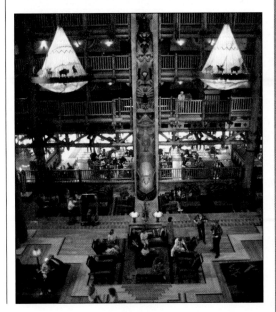

ROOMS: Most of the 727 guestrooms have two queen-size beds, a table and chairs, and a balcony. Some have a queen-size bed and a bunk bed. The bathrooms have separate vanity areas with double sinks. The wallpaper has a Native American–motif border, and the colorful bedspreads and plaid curtains add to the decor. Images of wildlife complete the theme. Suite rooms include an iron (with board), hair dryer, and weekday newspaper delivery.

The 181 deluxe villas are housed in a five-story tower adjoining Disney's Wilderness Lodge. This tribute to turn-of-the-twentieth-century design is also one of the Disney Vacation Club properties. The style of the villas building was inspired by the grandeur of Rocky Mountain geyser country. Villas are available to all guests when not occupied by Disney Vacation Club members.

Each studio has a queen-size bed and a double sleeper sofa, plus a kitchenette with microwave, coffeemaker, and mini refrigerator. Larger (one- and two-bedroom) villas sleep four to eight and have dining areas, kitchens, laundry facilities, master baths with whirlpool tubs, and VCRs. They include a king-size bed in the master bedroom, a living room with a queen sleeper sofa, and either two queen-size beds or a queen-size bed and a double sleeper sofa in extra bedrooms. All rooms come with an iron (and board), folding crib, and hair dryer. Rooms in the Wilderness Lodge have weekday newspaper delivery.

WHERE TO EAT: The Northwest theme is carried out with flair in the hotel's eateries. Room service runs from 7 A.M. to 11 A.M. and 4 P.M. to midnight.

Artist Point: Decorated with art representing painters who first chronicled the Northwest landscape, this fine dining spot features salmon, game, steak, seafood, and wines from the Pacific Northwest.

Roaring Fork Snacks: Fast food and light munchables are available at this snack bar.

Whispering Canyon Cafe: A boisterous, family-style restaurant with all-day dining.

WHERE TO DRINK: Two spots are available for a relaxing break.

Territory: This lounge honors the survey parties who led the move westward. In addition to specialty drinks, microbrewed beer, espresso, and snacks are served.

Trout Pass: The poolside bar features a variety of specialty drinks and snacks.

WHAT TO DO: The resort offers many recreational activities. Teton Boat & Bike Rental is in the Colonel's Cabin by the lake. Fishing excursions may be arranged (refer to the *Sports* chapter for details).

Biking: Bikes may be rented for scenic rides around the resort. A three-quarter-mile path leads to Fort Wilderness.

Boating: Sea Raycer boats, Boston Whaler Montauks, sailboats, and pontoon boats may be rented for trips around Bay Lake and the Seven Seas Lagoon.

Children's Program: The Cubs Den is a supervised dining and entertainment club for (potty-trained) kids ages 4 through 12. Supervised activities, including Disney movies and Western-themed arts and crafts, keep kids entertained from 4:30 P.M. to midnight. Cost is $10 per hour per child. Dinner and a snack are included. Call 407-939-3463 for reservations, which are required.

Health Club: The only thing rustic about the Sturdy Branches health club is the structure it's housed in. It features modern equipment, stair-climbers, bicycles, sauna, and more. Massage therapy is available for a fee.

Iron Spike Room: A fireplace and railroad memorabilia add atmosphere to this relaxing room, equipped with comfy seating, tables, and games. It is located in the Wilderness Lodge Villas building.

Shopping: Wilderness Lodge Mercantile stocks necessities and sundries as well as a line of clothing with the Wilderness Lodge logo and Disney character merchandise. There's also a pin-trading cart in the lobby.

Swimming: The main pool looks as if it were carved from the rockscape. A beach, a kiddie pool, two whirlpools, and a geyser complete the design. Fire Rock Geyser erupts on the hour from early morning until 10 P.M. The Hidden Springs pool and whirlpool spa near the Villas provide a quieter alternative.

Video Arcade: The Buttons and Bells Arcade has about 30 games to keep kids (and grown-ups) busy.

TRANSPORTATION: Boats go to the Magic Kingdom, Contemporary, and Fort Wilderness. Buses go to Epcot, the Disney-MGM Studios, Animal Kingdom, Blizzard Beach, and the Transportation and Ticket Center (TTC). Buses go directly to Typhoon Lagoon and Downtown Disney. (Don't make the mistake of boarding a Fort Wilderness bus—it does not stop here.)

Fort Wilderness Resort & Campground

The very existence of this canal-crossed expanse—with more than 700 acres of cypress and pine—always surprises visitors who come to Walt Disney World expecting to find nothing more than theme parks.

Tucked among the campsites are hundreds of air-conditioned Wilderness Cabins for rent, complete with housekeeping service. The cost is comparable to that of some of the more expensive rooms at Disney resorts. The phone number for the Fort Wilderness resort and campground is 407-824-2900.

CAMPSITES: Fort Wilderness has 784 traditional sites. They feature electricity hookups (30/50-amp), water, sanitary disposal, and cable television. (Note that some loops, including pet loops, are not wired for cable.) Partial-hookup campsites supply electricity and water hookups only. All campsites feature a paved driveway pad, picnic table, and charcoal grill. Most loops have at least one air-conditioned comfort station with restrooms, private showers, an ice machine, phones, and a laundry room. A site allows for occupancy by up to ten. Each site has room for one car (in addition to the camping vehicle). Other cars may be parked in the main lot.

The various campground areas are designated by numbers. The 100–500 loops are closest to the beach, the Settlement Trading Post, and Pioneer Hall. The 1500–2000 loops are farthest away from the beach and many other Fort Wilderness activities, but they are quieter and more private. Pets are welcome at certain campsites for a nightly charge of $5.

WILDERNESS CABINS: These woodland dwellings offer a rustic escape. The interiors of the six-person, log-cabin-like buildings are decorated with wilderness accents. Each one is shaded by a pine canopy. Cabins include a television, a VCR (your own videos), full bath, hair dryer, iron, a deck, picnic table, and charcoal grill.

Note: No extra camping equipment allowed; all guests must be accommodated in a cabin.

WHERE TO EAT: There are a couple of dining options, but many people cook here. A small selection of supplies is sold at the Meadow Trading Post and the Settlement Trading Post.

Gooding's supermarket is located at the Crossroads of Lake Buena Vista. Ask about nearby grocery stores when you check in.

Trail's End Buffet: This log-walled spot in Pioneer Hall serves home-style buffet fare three meals a day. Pizza is an option from 4:30 P.M. to 10 P.M. Spirits are available. The breakfast buffet delivers a hefty bang for the buck.

WHERE TO DRINK: Cocktails are served at Crockett's Tavern in Pioneer Hall.

FAMILY ENTERTAINMENT AFTER DARK: The Hoop-Dee-Doo Musical Revue is quite popular with families. Reservations should be made in advance; call 407-939-3463. There's also a free nightly campfire program held near the Meadow Trading Post. (For details, see the *Everything Else in the World* and *Good Meals, Great Times* chapters.)

WHAT TO DO: There's a plethora of free activities to choose from, including two pools, tennis courts, and campfire sing-alongs. For a fee, guests can enjoy wagon rides, pony rides, carriage rides, boat and bike rentals, and more. Activities are described in *Everything Else in the World* and *Sports*.

TRANSPORTATION: Buses circulating at 10- to 30-minute intervals provide transportation within the campground, while buses and boats connect Fort Wilderness to the rest of the World. The Magic Kingdom, Contemporary, and Wilderness Lodge are best reached via watercraft that depart from the marina. Buses to Wilderness Lodge, Disney-MGM Studio, and the TTC depart from the Settlement stop only. Buses to Epcot, Animal Kingdom, Blizzard Beach, Typhoon Lagoon, and Downtown Disney leave from the Outpost stop.

Electric golf carts and bikes may be rented at the Bike Barn as an alternative means of getting around within the campground. Call 407-824-2742 for reservations.

Epcot Area

Caribbean Beach

This colorful hotel is set on 200 acres south-east of Epcot and near the Disney-MGM Studios. It is composed of five brightly colored "villages" surrounding a 45-acre lake called Barefoot Bay. Each village is identified with a different Caribbean island—Martinique, Barbados, Trinidad, Aruba, and Jamaica—and features pastel walls, white railings, and vividly colored metal roofs. There are 2,112 rooms in all, making Caribbean Beach one of the largest hotels in the United States.

The villages consist of a cluster of two-story buildings, a swimming pool, a guest laundry, and a lakefront stretch of white-sand beach. Guests check in at the Custom House, a reception building that projects the feeling of a tropical resort. Decor, furnishings, and staff costumes all reflect the Caribbean theme. Old Port Royale, a complex located near the center of the property, evokes images of an island market. Stone walls, pirates' cannons, and tropical birds and flowers add to the atmosphere. The area houses the resort's food court, restaurant and lounge, arcade, and two shops.

The lakeside recreation area includes a pool with waterfalls and a slide; the main beach; the Barefoot Bay Boat Yard and Bike Works, where boats and bicycles may be rented; and a 1.4-mile promenade around the lake that's perfect for biking, walking, or jogging. It should come as no surprise that kids love it here. The telephone number for the Caribbean Beach resort is 407-934-3400.

ROOMS: Rooms are located in two-story buildings in each island village. A typical 340-square-foot room has two double beds and can sleep up to four. The rooms here are a bit larger than standard rooms at Disney's other moderate resorts. Rooms are decorated in tones softer than the colors found on the exterior. Each room has a refrigerater and coffee-maker. A note for the budget-conscious: All rooms here are identical in terms of size and comfort, and the only difference between the most and least expensive is the view. To minimize time spent walking, request a room nearest the lobby or bus stop when you check in.

WHERE TO EAT: A full-service eatery called Shutters and the Market Street food court are located in Old Port Royale. Limited room service is available from 4 P.M. to 11:30 P.M.

Bridgetown Broiler: Omelets, biscuits, and French toast are offered for breakfast. Dinner brings rotisserie chicken and other items.

Grab-N-Go Market: Open from early morning until about 11 P.M., this spot sells sandwiches and salads, plus an assortment of pastries, bagels, cheesecake, pies, and more.

Montego's Deli: Breakfast items such as pancakes, sausage, and oatmeal are served in the morning. Salads and deli sandwiches are offered for dinner.

Old Port Royale Hamburger Shop: Hot sandwiches and burgers are on the menu.

Royale Pizza & Pasta Shop: Pizza is available in individual portions, along with pasta dishes and salads.

Shutters at Old Port Royale: This full-service Old Port Royale restaurant features items such as prime rib and a catch of the day. Cocktails are served.

WHERE TO DRINK: The tropical theme is carried out in the specialty drinks found at Banana Cabana. Light snacks are also available at this poolside spot.

WHAT TO DO: There are many recreational opportunities here. The promenade around the lake is ideal for walking, biking, or a jog.

Biking: Bikes may be rented at the Barefoot Bay Boat Yard and Bike Works.

Boating: Sailboats, Sea Raycer boats, Boston Whaler Montauks, canoes, pedal boats, and pontoon boats are available for rent at the Barefoot Bay Boat Yard and Bike Works for use on the resort's scenic 45-acre lake.

Fishing: At press time, pole fishing and fishing excursions were planned for Barefoot Bay. Call 407-WDW-BASS for updates.

Playgrounds: Playgrounds are located on Parrot Cay Island, as well as on the Barbados, Jamaica, and Trinidad beaches.

Shopping: At Old Port Royale, there's the Calypso Straw Market, which carries a slew of items with the resort logo and swimwear. Calypso Trading Post stocks Disney character merchandise and sundries.

Swimming: Each village has its own pool, and one of the pools has a waterfall and a slide in a Caribbean-themed setting, conjuring up images of swashbuckling adventures. Kids adore it.

Video Arcade: Goombay Games at Old Port Royale offers a selection of amusements.

TRANSPORTATION: Buses go to the Magic Kingdom, Epcot, the Studios, Animal Kingdom, and Blizzard Beach. Other bus routes lead to Downtown Disney and Typhoon Lagoon. Getting around within the resort is done via buses bearing an "Internal Shuttle Resort" sign.

Yacht & Beach Club and Beach Club Villas

The New England seaside exists at Disney World in the form of the Yacht and Beach Club, and the Beach Club Villas. Situated beside Epcot, the resorts, designed by noted architect Robert A. M. Stern, are set around a 25-acre lake. The adjacent properties share most facilities—including a convention center offering access to business services—and transportation options.

The Yacht Club's design evokes images of the New England seashore hotels of the 1880s. Guests enter the five-story beige clapboard building along a wooden-planked bridge. Hardwood floors and brass enhance the nautical theme. A lighthouse on the pier serves as a beacon to welcome guests back to the hotel from WDW attractions. To reach the Yacht Club by telephone, call 407-934-7000.

Distance from the ocean is irrelevant over at the sand-and-surf-focused Beach Club resort, approached along an entrance drive flanked by oak trees. A walkway leads past a croquet

Meetings & Conventions

Convention centers at Walt Disney World range in size from 20,000 to 200,000 square feet. The Dolphin's center, featuring an exhibit hall and an executive boardroom, is the largest; the Swan provides additional space. The Contemporary has three ballrooms and a spacious pre-function area with lots of natural light. The convention center at the Yacht and Beach Club is reminiscent of a grand turn-of-the-century New England town-meeting hall. The Grand Floridian Resort and Spa has a lavish center with silk brocade walls. The BoardWalk offers a smaller conference area with a lakeside gazebo for outdoor events. And Coronado Springs, the first moderately priced Disney resort to offer convention facilities, boasts the largest hotel ballroom in the U.S.

Among the unique services available to Disney conventioneers is the use of Disney characters and performers for events. Special events can even be held in the parks. Resort business centers have clerical staffs and computers, in addition to faxing and photocopying equipment. (These services are available to all resort guests.)

Those interested in scheduling a convention should call 321-939-7221. Organizers are advised to book their events six months in advance, especially for large groups.

court to beachside cabanas on the white-sand shore. Guests are met by hosts and hostesses dressed in colorful beach resort costumes of the 1870s. The telephone number for the Beach Club resort is 407-934-8000.

ROOMS: The rooms at the Yacht Club are decorated in a nautical motif. The Beach Club's rooms are also amply sized and, naturally, reflect a beach motif. In each room the furniture is white, and (at the Yacht Club) the headboard design on the one king-size bed or two queen-size beds incorporates small ship's wheels. Some rooms have daybeds. Most of the suites have a king-size bed as well as two sleeper sofas. In the bathrooms there is a separate vanity with double sinks. Each room has a ceiling fan, iron (with board), hair dryer, newspaper delivery, mini-bar, wall-mounted make-up mirror, small table (complete with a checkerboard top), and two chairs. Chess and checkers sets may be requested. Club level rooms are available.

A five-story building beside the Beach Club is home to 282 Beach Club villas. The villas are available to Disney Vacation Club members. (They are available to all guests when not occupied by Vacation Club members.) Each studio has a queen-size bed and a double-sleeper sofa, plus a kitchenette with a microwave, coffeemaker, and mini fridge. Larger villas sleep four to eight, and all have a dining area, kitchen, laundry room, master bath with whirlpool tub, and a DVD player. They include a king-size bed in the master bedroom, living room with queen sleeper sofa, and either two queen-size beds or a queen-size bed and a double sleeper sofa.

WHERE TO EAT: The themes of yachting and the sea play an important role in the restaurants that are found at their respective resorts. A wide variety of menu items is available from room service 24 hours a day.

Beach Club Marketplace: Stop here for hot and cold breakfast items, salads, sandwiches, and snacks selections. Among the dessert options is homemade gelato.

Beaches and Cream Soda Shop: A small, classic soda fountain where shakes, malts, and sundaes are the prime lure. The shop is located between the two resorts.

Cape May Cafe: An indoor clambake is held here at the Beach Club each night. The varied and bountiful buffet features several types of clams and mussels, plus beef ribs and chicken.

Hot Tip!

Playpen-like cribs that accommodate one child under age 3 are available at all Disney resorts. Ask about them when you call to reserve your room. They're free. (If you'd like a more substantial sleeping apparatus for your toddler, refer to page 41 of the *Getting Ready to Go* chapter.)

A character breakfast is presented daily.

Hurricane Hanna's Grill: Burgers, hot dogs, sausages, and other snacks are served at this spot. A full bar is also located here, and poolside beverage service is available.

Yacht Club Galley: There is a breakfast buffet, as well as à la carte menu for breakfast, lunch, and dinner.

Yachtsman Steakhouse: Select cuts of aged beef are the specialty of the house. Fresh seafood and poultry are also offered.

WHERE TO DRINK: The lounges in both resorts offer a variety of specialty drinks in relaxing seaside settings.

Ale and Compass: This Yacht Club lobby lounge, featuring specialty coffees and drinks, provides a nice respite after a long day.

Crew's Cup: The place to try beer shipped in from the world's seaports before dining at Yachtsman Steakhouse next door.

Martha's Vineyard: This quiet lounge at the Beach Club offers selections from American and international vineyards, served in sample sizes and by the glass or bottle, as well as a full bar.

WHAT TO DO: There is enough to do here to fill an entire vacation. A sand volleyball court may be found on the Beach Club side of the property. Equipment is available at no cost at the Ship Shape health club. Bikes and boats may be rented.

The Fantasia Gardens Miniature Golf complex is close at hand, and guided two-hour fishing excursions may be arranged (see *Sports* for details). Free garden tours are available throughout the week. And last but not least, the BoardWalk entertainment district is a short walk around the lake.

Boating: Pedal, pontoon, Sea Raycers, and other boats are available for rent at the Bayside Marina.

Children's Program: The Sandcastle Club, for potty-trained kids ages 4 through 12, is available from 4:30 P.M. to midnight. Cost is

Special Room Requests

Central Reservations accepts requests for rooms with particular views or in certain locations. Agents will do their best to accommodate such requests, but cannot guarantee they will be able to fulfill every wish. Call 407-W-DISNEY (934-7639).

$10 per hour for each child. Reservations are required; call 407-939-3463. Toys, videos, games, and computers are on hand to keep children entertained. Dinner and a snack are included.

Health Club: The Ship Shape health club has exercise machines, sauna, whirlpool, steam room, and massage (by appointment). The health club is open to resort guests ages 14 and older.

Salon: The Periwig salon for men and women is located in the central area.

Shopping: At the Yacht Club, Fittings & Fairings Clothes and Notions is an all-purpose shop offering character merchandise and sundries. At the Beach Club, the Beach Club Marketplace has a similar selection of goods.

Swimming: Between the marina and the beach is the centerpiece of the dual resort—Stormalong Bay, a three-acre pool that's like a mini water park. There is a lagoon expressly for relaxed bathing, and another with currents, jets, and sand-bottomed areas. Several whirlpools are scattered throughout the area. Adjacent to the main pool is a shipwreck, where guests can enjoy a waterslide. There is one unguarded pool and whirlpool at the far end of each hotel. There is also an unguarded pool by the Beach Club villas. Guests may also opt to sunbathe on the beach.

Tennis: There is one lighted tennis court on the Yacht Club side of the property. Rental equipment is available at the Bayside marina.

Video Arcade: Lafferty Place Arcade has about 60 video games and pinball machines.

TRANSPORTATION: Guests travel to Epcot and the Disney-MGM Studios via ferryboats or walkways. Buses go to the Magic Kingdom, Animal Kingdom, Downtown Disney, Typhoon Lagoon, and Blizzard Beach.

Swan & Dolphin

These sister resorts, situated on the shores of Crescent Lake, can easily be distinguished by the 47-foot swan and 56-foot dolphin statues that top them. The waterfalls, rows of palm trees, and beachfront location all reflect the tropical Florida landscape that was their inspiration. Both hotels were designed by noted architect Michael Graves as examples of "entertainment architecture." The turquoise waves on the colored facade of the Swan's 12-story main building and two 7-story wings are clearly evidence of this design, as is the Dolphin's exterior mural, which features a banana-leaf pattern. The soaring 27-story triangular tower at the center of the Dolphin is flanked by four 9-story guestroom wings.

Hot Tip!

The Swan and Dolphin resorts run seasonal promotions throughout the year. For information, call 800-227-1500 or visit www.swandolphin.com.

The resorts share extensive convention facilities, many recreational options, and a host of restaurants. The Swan and Dolphin are operated by Westin and Sheraton, respectively, but are treated as Walt Disney World resorts; guests here enjoy most WDW resort benefits. One notable difference involves room-key charging privileges: guests cannot use their room keys to charge purchases on Walt Disney World property, with the exception of within the Swan and Dolphin resorts themselves. The telephone number for the Swan is 407-934-3000; for the Dolphin, it's 407-934-4000. Reservations for either resort may be made by calling 800-227-1500 or by visiting *www.swandolphin.com*.

Be aware that there is an automatic room charge assessed per day to cover services such as newspaper delivery, local phone calls (up to 60 minutes per call), high-speed Internet access, coffee, use of the health club, etc. Valet parking costs $14 per day. Self-parking costs $8 per day.

ROOMS: The corridors outside the Swan guest-rooms feature patterned carpets and murals on the walls that extend the wave theme from its exterior design. Inside, the rooms sport a contemporary look with soft colors. Each room has one king-size or two queen-size beds; safes and mini-bars are among the amenities. There are 54 club level rooms on the 11th and 12th floors, and 55 suites.

The 1,509 rooms at the Dolphin, including 136 suites, were recently redecorated. All rooms feature two double beds or a king-size bed, as well as mini-bars, vanity dressing area, irons and boards, and coffeemakers. Concierge rooms are located on the 12th and the 14th floors. There are rooms equipped for guests with disabilities, and nonsmoking rooms are available at both resorts. Rooms here do not have ceiling fans.

WHERE TO EAT: In addition to many restaurant choices, 24-hour room service provides an extensive all-day dining menu. (The room service here is the best at Walt Disney World.)

Cabana Bar & Grill: This full-service pool-side spot near the Dolphin serves burgers, sandwiches, yogurt, and fruit. The full bar serves specialty drinks.

The Fountain: Homemade ice cream is the specialty at this Dolphin eatery. Huge sundaes, shakes, malts, and burgers are also offered.

Fresh Mediterranean Market: Designed to resemble a cheerful marketplace, this Dolphin spot serves breakfast and lunch. Items may be chosen from a menu or made to order. Breakfast and lunch only.

Garden Grove Cafe: This Swan eatery, which features a greenhouse atmosphere, serves breakfast and lunch daily. At dinner, the restaurant transforms into Gulliver's Grill.

A buffet breakfast with the characters is held on Saturdays and Sundays, while a character dinner takes place several nights a week.

Palio: An upscale Italian eatery, located at the Swan, featuring veal specialties, home-made pasta, and brick-oven pizza. There are daily specials and strolling musicians.

Picabu: A cafeteria with a bit of flair. The 24-hour convenience store here sells snacks and sundries. It has Starbucks coffee, too.

Shula's Steak House: An upscale celebration of two American favorites: steak and football. It's a bit pricey, but the steaks are superb and the side orders are big enough to share.

Splash Grill: A poolside cafe near the Swan serving lunch and snacks. A full-service bar is also located here.

Todd English's bluezoo: This eatery features coastal cuisine, beef, and chicken dishes with international and domestic influences. There is a café menu offering lighter fare.

WHERE TO DRINK: It's easy to find a nice cocktail spot in this neck of the woods.

Kimonos: The Asian decor makes this Swan lounge an inviting place for sake, sushi, and other Japanese selections. Karaoke is a house specialty. This place is generally hopping later than most other WDW resort lounges.

Lobby Court: This spot at the Swan offers a respite from the hubbub. Enjoy gourmet coffees with pastries in the morning and wine and specialty drinks at night.

Lobby Lounge: A cozy Dolphin area featuring wine and specialty drinks.

Shula's Steak House Lounge: Settle into a comfy chair, light up a stogie, and sip a drink in this lounge adjacent to Shula's dining room.

WHAT TO DO: The Swan and Dolphin share many recreation options. Volleyball nets and hammocks are set up on the beach. The Fantasia Gardens Miniature Golf complex and BoardWalk are nearby (the proximity to BoardWalk and Epcot is a big plus). The Disney-MGM Studios is a boat ride (or about a 20-minute walk) away.

Boating: Pedal boats are available for rent on the beach between the Swan and Dolphin.

Children's Program: Camp Dolphin welcomes children (potty-trained) ages 4 through 12 and has supervised activities from 5:30 P.M. to midnight. The cost is $10 per child per hour.

Health Clubs: There is a fitness center near the pool area at the Dolphin. State-of-the-art equipment is available, as are personal trainers. There is a sauna, steam room, large whirlpool, and massage therapists. There's also a smaller health club with basic exercise equipment near Splash Grill at the Swan.

Playground: A play area with a slide, swings, chain bridge, sandbox, and several jungle gyms is located next to the Swan lap pool.

Spa and Salon: The Mandara Spa features full-service body treatments, plus hairstyling, manicures, pedicures, and more.

Shopping: Disney Cabanas, located in the lobby of the Swan, features character merchandise and sundries. Four shops are located at the Dolphin. Sugar3 allows chocolate lovers the chance to sample some tasty concoctions. LaMonts offers resortwear for men and women. Daisy's Garden is the place to find character goods at the Dolphin. Galleria Sottil is the Dolphin's new art gallery. Expect to find paintings, sculptures, and other assorted works of art.

Swimming: In addition to a shared children's wading pool, there are two lap pools, and a themed grotto pool with slides between the Swan and Dolphin. Several whirlpools are scattered around the area.

Tennis: Hard-surface tennis courts are located behind the pool area closest to the Dolphin resort. They are lighted for night play and are open 24 hours a day.

Video Arcades: A room full of video games is located near Picabu at the Dolphin. Another can be found in Splash Grill at the Swan. Sony PlayStations are available in-room.

TRANSPORTATION: Guests travel to Epcot and the Disney-MGM Studios via ferryboats or walkways. Buses go directly to the Magic Kingdom, Animal Kingdom, Downtown Disney, Typhoon Lagoon, and Blizzard Beach.

BoardWalk Inn & Villas

The enchantment of a bygone era is recaptured in the BoardWalk. The resort combines a waterside entertainment complex with deluxe hotel accommodations and vacation villas. Dining, recreation, shopping, and entertainment venues line the boardwalk, and twinkling lights trim the buildings. The ambience continues throughout, with detailed architecture featuring sherbet-colored facades, flagged turrets, and striped awnings, all reminiscent of the turn of the twentieth century. The BoardWalk resort is adjacent to

Resort Roundup

What's the best place to stay at Walt Disney World? It's a tough question—and one that Birnbaum editors are asked all the time. The answer? Well, it depends. Do you have a favorite park? What's your price range? Will a clown's tongue that doubles as a pool slide make your day? All factors to consider. That said, here are our favorites in each of Disney's price categories:

BIRNBAUM'S BEST **DELUXE**
Yacht and Beach Club: In addition to a picturesque setting, these sister resorts are all about location. For starters, you can walk to Epcot (and the Studios if you're feeling ambitious). Of course, you can always take a water taxi. You're a stone's throw from the excitement of the bustling BoardWalk entertainment district, but get to enjoy the relative peace of life on the quieter side of Crescent Lake. Excellent dining options abound. And the pool area's to die for. We prefer to stay at the Yacht Club. *Very honorable mentions: Grand Floridian and Polynesian*

BIRNBAUM'S BEST **MODERATE**
Port Orleans Riverside: One need not be a Southern aristocrat to live like one. Many of the guest buildings at this resort, formerly known as Dixie Landings, were designed to look like historic mansions. Even the food court has a certain Southern ambience. There's a table service restaurant and a cozy lounge (which occasionally offers up live entertainment). Kids enjoy dropping their hooks in the fishing hole (strictly catch-and-release) and splashing in the free-form pool on Ol' Man Island. Pretty gardens and a relatively reasonable price add to the appeal. *Honorable mention: Caribbean Beach*

BIRNBAUM'S BEST **VALUE**
All-Star Movies: This, the newest of the All-Star properties, has some of the best theming around (i.e., *Toy Story* and *101 Dalmatians*), but what really sets it apart is the food court. It's bigger and brighter than its All-Star counterparts, and as such, makes for a more pleasant and efficient dining experience. *Honorable mention: Pop Century (The '60s)*

Epcot's International Gateway and connected to it via walkway. The phone number for BoardWalk is 407-939-5100.

ROOMS: Accommodations here evoke the charm of early Eastern seaboard inns. Most have private balconies or patios. The Board-Walk Inn has 371 deluxe hotel rooms decorated with cherry-wood furniture, boardwalk post-card-print curtains, and light green accents. Guestrooms at the Inn sleep up to five, and feature two queen-size beds (or one king-size bed) and a child's daybed. Romantic two-story garden suites each have a private garden enclosed by a white picket fence. They sleep four, and have a living room on the first floor and a king-size bed in the bedroom loft. The Inn also has club level rooms and suites.

The 532 vacation villas are collectively called Disney's BoardWalk Villas. These are Disney Vacation Club villas, available when not occupied by members. Each studio has a queen-size bed and double sleeper sofa, plus a kitchenette with microwave, coffeemaker, and small refrigerator. Larger (one-, two-, and three-bedroom) villas sleep 4 to 12 people, and feature dining areas, fully equipped kitchens, laundry facilities, master baths with whirlpool tubs, and VCR/DVD players. They also include a king-size bed in the master bedroom, living room with a queen sleeper sofa, and a queen-size bed plus a double sleeper sofa in any additional bedrooms. Rooms at the BoardWalk Inn include free newspaper delivery. All rooms have an iron (with board) and a hair dryer.

WHERE TO EAT: This resort has a wealth of dining and snacking options. A variety of

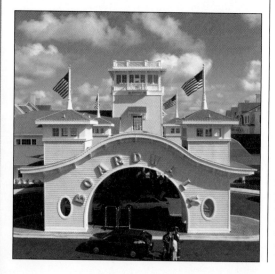

vendors along the boardwalk tempt with hot dogs, crêpes on a stick, gourmet coffee, and more. For those looking to eat in, 24-hour room service is available.

Big River Grille & Brewing Works: This working brewpub features a full menu, complemented by fresh specialty ales. View the on-site brewmaster through floor-to-ceiling glass walls.

BoardWalk Bakery: A popular stop that offers fresh baked goods, sandwiches, espresso, and cappuccino. Huge display windows allow passersby to watch bakers at work. "Bun rises" are held here every morning. Note that the line moves slowly.

BoardWalk Carts: Stands along the boardwalk offer snacks and coffee.

ESPN Club: A serious sports bar for serious sports fans, it provides interactive sports video entertainment and all-day dining.

Flying Fish Cafe: This restaurant has a show kitchen, and its dinner menu emphasizes seafood, steak, and fresh seasonal items.

Seashore Sweets': An old-fashioned sweetshop that serves candies, saltwater taffy, ice cream, frozen yogurt, and specialty coffees.

Spoodles: Mediterranean cuisine is the focus of this establishment geared toward families; the appetizers are meant for sharing.

WHERE TO DRINK: Guests have a multitude of options right in their backyard, with the BoardWalk's clubs and lounges on hand.

Atlantic Dance: This waterfront club is an elegantly designed dance spot. You must be at least 21 to enter. There usually isn't a cover charge, but that may change.

Belle Vue Room: Listen to old-time tunes on antique radios and play board games in this cocktail lounge near the lobby.

Jellyrolls: Dueling pianos provide live entertainment in a casual warehouse atmosphere. The cover charge is generally about $5 to $10 nightly. You must be at least 21 to enter.

Leaping Horse Libations: The carousel-themed pool bar at Luna Park serves a variety of cocktails, as well as snacks.

WHAT TO DO: The three-quarter-mile pathway encircling Crescent Lake (en route to Epcot) provides a ready venue for walkers and joggers. BoardWalk guests may rent boats from Yacht & Beach Club's Bayside marina. The Fantasia Gardens Miniature Golf complex is nearby. At the resort itself, Ferris W. Eahlers Community Hall rents out equipment for many recreational pursuits, including croquet, shuffleboard, table tennis, badminton—even books and videos. Fishing excursions can be arranged.

Biking: Community Hall offers a variety of bicycles for rental. Surreys (canopied quadra-cycles for four) may also be rented.

Health Club: Muscles & Bustles health club has steam rooms, modern exercise machines, and circuit-training equipment, as well as massages (by appointment). Fees apply.

Midway Games: This area on the BoardWalk's WildWood Landing features games of luck and skill similar to those found along traditional boardwalks.

Shopping: Dundy's Sundries in the lobby is the source for basic necessities. Character Carnival on the boardwalk has children's apparel as well as character merchandise. Screen Door General Store stocks groceries, dry goods, snacks, and beverages. Thimbles & Threads, also on the boardwalk, carries apparel for men and women. Wyland Galleries features marine and environmental art.

Surrey Bike Ride: A trip around the lake in a pedal-powered surrey is available for a fee.

Swimming: The BoardWalk's swimming area, Luna Park, features a large pool with a 200-foot waterslide, "Keister Coaster," patterned after a wooden roller coaster. (The pool slide is a clown's tongue.) A family of elephants is found posed throughout the area; their trunks act as a shower for adults on the pool deck or children in the wading pool. The resort has two unguarded pools. There are three whirlpools, one in each pool area.

Tennis: Two lighted tennis courts are available for play.

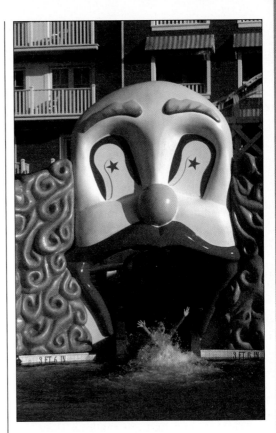

Video Arcades: Side Show Games Arcade has video games, and a sports-themed arcade entertains at the ESPN Club.

TRANSPORTATION: Guests may travel to Epcot and the Disney-MGM Studios via ferryboats or walkways. Buses transport guests to the Magic Kingdom, Animal Kingdom, Typhoon Lagoon, Blizzard Beach, and Downtown Disney.

Disney Vacation Club

Disney Vacation Club grants members the convenience of flexible vacations from year to year, with the ability to choose when and where to visit, how long to stay, and the type of accommodations. It starts with the purchase of a real estate interest in a Disney Vacation Club property. For a one-time purchase price and annual dues, members can enjoy vacation stays at Old Key West Resort, the Beach Club Villas, BoardWalk Villas Resort, the Villas at Disney's Wilderness Lodge, and Saratoga Springs Resort & Spa at Walt Disney World; Disney's Vero Beach Resort in Florida; and Disney's Hilton Head Island Resort in South Carolina; plus access to additional destinations around the globe. Through "Member Getaways," members may also elect to stay at their choice of more than 500 resorts worldwide, including most Disney resorts and the Disney Cruise Line.

Disney's Vero Beach Resort is a two-hour drive from Walt Disney World. It has villa-type accommodations comparable to those at Disney's Old Key West Resort—with lush surroundings, the beach, and local sights. The proximity makes it easy to tack a beach vacation onto a WDW visit.

Disney Vacation Club information centers may be found at each of the Walt Disney World hotels and theme parks. For more information, call 800-800-9100, or visit *www.disneyvacationclub.com*.

Downtown Disney Area

TRANSPORTATION & ACCOMMODATIONS

Port Orleans French Quarter

This 1,008-room resort invites comparisons to the historic French Quarter of New Orleans. (Although Port Orleans French Quarter and Port Orleans Riverside [formerly known as Dixie Landings] technically function as one resort, we give them individual attention, to provide guests with the information necessary to select the area that works best for them.)

Starting at the entrance gate, with its wrought-iron portal and overgrown landscape, the appeal of the Delta City surrounds arriving guests. The entry drive leads to the heart of the city, which is Port Orleans Square. The central building was based on a turn-of-the-twentieth-century mint. The Mint houses check-in facilities (for Port Orleans French Quarter *only*), a shop, food court, and arcade. It has a vaulted ceiling, and the check-in desks are designed as bank-teller windows. The musical notes in the mural are the notes to "When the Saints Go Marching In."

The phone number for Port Orleans French Quarter is 407-934-5000.

ROOMS: The guestrooms are located in seven 3-story buildings (with elevators). Each room has two double beds; some king-size beds are available. The rooms are a bit smaller than the standard rooms at the more expensive Disney hotels, but they are comfortable for a family of four. (The photos on the walls were donated by Disney employees.)

The buildings are painted cream, pink, blue, purple, and yellow, and feature wrought-iron railings of varying designs. Connecting rooms may be requested but can't be guaranteed. The least expensive rooms overlook gardens or parking areas, and the most expensive rooms offer water views.

WHERE TO EAT: A counter-service food court has a variety of dining options.

Sassagoula Floatworks & Food Factory: A variety of specialty foods is available in this food court, including gumbo, chicken with red beans and rice, fresh-baked beignets, and other traditional Creole dishes. Burgers, pizza, ice cream, and baked goods are also on the menu.

WHERE TO DRINK: A pool bar operates seasonally, and guests on a quest for a cocktail may head to Port Orleans Riverside—it's a short bus ride away. Of course, there's always Downtown Disney or any theme park other than the Magic Kingdom.

WHAT TO DO: A themed pool is the highlight of the recreational opportunities here.

Biking: Bicycles are available for rent at Port Orleans Riverside.

Boating: Pedal boats, kayaks, canoes, motorboats, and pontoon boats are available for rent at nearby Port Orleans Riverside.

Carriage Rides: Refer to page 83 for details.

Shopping: Jackson Square Gifts & Desires, located at Port Orleans Square, features Disney character merchandise, clothing bearing the Port Orleans resort logo, and sundries.

Swimming: Doubloon Lagoon is a free-form pool built around a bright blue sea serpent. The waterslide is actually the creature's tongue. A shower at the pool features an alligator's head, and there is a large clamshell where an all-gator band serves as the centerpiece of a fountain. There is a large whirlpool nearby. Port Orleans French Quarter guests are also invited to swim in the pool at Ol' Man Island at Port Orleans Riverside.

Video Arcade: South Quarter Games is located at Port Orleans Square. It features state-of-the-art video and arcade games.

TRANSPORTATION: Buses go to the Magic Kingdom, Epcot, Disney-MGM Studios, Animal Kingdom, Typhoon Lagoon, Blizzard Beach, and Downtown Disney. Small water ferries transport guests to Downtown Disney, too.

Port Orleans Riverside

Here, the city feel of the French Quarter gives way to the rural South. The resort is divided into "parishes." Closest to the "city," guestrooms are found in Mansion homes; farther upriver are the Bayou guestrooms, with a more rustic feel. The phone number for the Port Orleans Riverside resort is 407-934-6000. This resort area used to be known as Dixie Landings.

ROOMS: The 2,048 Mansion and Bayou guestrooms are of the same size, and each room features two double beds (some king-size beds are available); 963 of the Bayou rooms have trundle beds (designed to sleep one child) as well. There is an additional fee of $15 per night for a trundle bed. The Magnolia Bend Mansion rooms, appointed with tapestries and cherry-wood furniture, are situated in sprawling, elegant manor homes with stately columns and grand staircases. The Alligator Bayou rooms are in rustic, weathered-wood buildings that are tucked among flora native to the area. Although all buildings have two to three floors, only the Magnolia Bend Mansions have elevators.

The Bayou rooms surround Ol' Man Island, a 3½-acre recreational area with a pool, playground, and fishing hole. Decorative touches in the rooms include wood and tin armoires and pedestal sinks with brass fittings. The beds have hickory bedposts. As is common with Disney's non-deluxe resorts, the closet space is not enclosed. The rooms are a bit on the small side, but they can accommodate a family of four.

WHERE TO EAT: In addition to a restaurant and food court, the hotel offers limited room service via Sassagoula Pizza Express, which delivers from 4 P.M. until midnight.

Boatright's Dining Hall: This 200-seat table-service eatery, next to Riverside Mill, serves Cajun specialties and American fare for dinner. Breakfast is also served.

Riverside Mill: This food court resembles an old-fashioned cotton mill with a working waterwheel that powers the cotton press inside.

The five counter-service stands here offer all sorts of choices. The basic selections are available for breakfast. **Acadian Pizza 'n' Pasta** has pasta dishes, pizza, and calzone. **Bleu Bayou Burgers and Chicken** offers fried and grilled chicken and burgers. **Filé Cajun Broiler** serves spit-roasted chicken and barbecued ribs. **Riverside Market and Deli** is a store that stocks snack foods, soda, salads, sandwiches, beer, and wine. **Southern Trace Bakery** serves pastries, pies, and sticky buns. Soft drinks may be refilled on a meal-by-meal basis.

WHERE TO DRINK: Two lounges possess an enticing degree of charm.

Muddy Rivers: The poolside bar serves cocktails, plus hot dogs, popcorn, and ice cream during pool hours. Seasonal.

River Roost: Situated in a room designed as a cotton exchange, this lounge features specialty drinks and light hors d'oeuvres.

WHAT TO DO: Many of the resort activities are at Ol' Man Island, a recreation center featuring a pool, whirlpool, wading pool, interactive fountains, playground, and fishing hole stocked with fish for catch-and-release.

Biking: Bicycles of all types can be rented.

Boating: Pedal boats, canoes, kayaks, motorboats, and pontoon boats are available for rent.

Carriage Rides: Horse-drawn carriages take guests for 25-minute rides throughout the grounds of the resort. Carriages hold up to 4 adults or 2 adults and 3 small kids. Tickets are sold by the driver. Each trip costs $35 and departs from the marina. Call 407-939-7529 for reservations.

Fishing: Two-hour guided fishing excursions are available (see *Sports*), and guests may fish on their own at the Ol' Fishin' Hole.

Playground: An elaborate play area is located on Ol' Man Island next to the pool.

Shopping: Fulton's General Store in the Riverside building stocks Disney character merchandise, clothing, and sundries.

Swimming: In addition to the main pool and kiddie pool at Ol' Man Island, there are five unguarded pools at the resort. Guests may also swim in the French Quarter pool.

Video Arcade: The Medicine Show Arcade features a small selection of games.

TRANSPORTATION: Buses go to the Magic Kingdom, Transportation and Ticket Center (TTC), Epcot, the Disney-MGM Studios, Animal Kingdom, Typhoon Lagoon, Blizzard Beach, and Downtown Disney.

Disney's Saratoga Springs Resort & Spa

Just across the lake from the hustle and bustle of Downtown Disney, this new resort is a peaceful complement to its nearest neighbor. From the colorful Victorian architecture to the historic influence of horse racing, Disney's Saratoga Springs Resort & Spa aspires to recapture the heyday of upstate New York country retreats of the late 1800s. The resort— which covers 65 acres formerly occupied by the Disney Institute—is the newest and largest addition to Disney Vacation Club. To contact the resort, call 407-827-1100.

ROOMS: There are studios and villas with one, two, and three bedrooms. A studio consists of a room with a queen-size bed and a full-size sofa bed, bathroom, kitchenette with wet bar, mini fridge, microwave, and coffeemaker. All units have a porch or balcony and access to complimentary laundry facilities.

One-bedroom villas have a king-size bed in the master suite and a queen-size sleeper sofa in the living room. The one bathroom has a whirlpool tub. The full kitchen includes a fridge, stove, microwave, toaster, coffeemaker, blender, dinnerware, and dishwasher. Each unit has a porch or balcony and a washer and dryer. Two-bedroom villas have an additional bathroom and bedroom, with either one queen-size bed and a double sleeper sofa or two queen-size beds. The three-bedroom Grand Villa is similar to the two-bedroom models, but is about twice the size and has four bathrooms.

WHERE TO EAT: There is one source of sustenance at the resort and dozens across the lake. There are two barbecue areas available to guests who want to have a cookout.

The Artist's Palette: Set in a converted artist's loft, this spot offers breakfast, lunch, and dinner. Among the selections are fresh tossed salads, made-to-order sandwiches, pizza, baked goods, and more.

Groceries: In these parts, in-room grocery delivery is available from Artist's Palette, and many guests cook their own meals. If you've got a car, ask for directions to a grocery store.

WHERE TO DRINK: In addition to the on-site bars, guests imbibe at nearby Downtown Disney.

On the Rocks: A pool bar serving the usual battery of cocktails.

Turf Club: This lounge and billiard room serves cocktails and light fare in the evening.

WHAT TO DO: In addition to the ever-popular spa, guests here rent bikes, swim, walk, swat some tennis balls, or just sit back and enjoy the view of Downtown Disney.

Biking: Bicycles may be rented from Horsing Around Recreational Rentals.

Boating: Boats may be rented at nearby Downtown Disney.

Golf: The resort is adjacent to the Lake Buena Vista golf course.

Health Club: The fitness center features cardiovascular and weightlifting equipment.

Playground: A kids' play area is located by the resort's themed pool.

Shopping: The Artist's Palette stocks souvenirs and sundries.

Spa: The award-winning spa has treatment rooms for massage, manicures, facials, aromatherapy, and more.

Swimming: High Rock Spring cascades down rugged rockwork and feeds into a free-form, heated "zero-entry" pool. The splash zone features a waterslide, two whirlpools, and an interactive play area for kids.

Video Arcade: Expect to find the usual bells and whistles at "Win, Place, or Show."

TRANSPORTATION: Buses go to all theme and water parks. Boats ferry guests to Downtown Disney.

Disney's Old Key West Resort

Escape to the spirit of the Florida Keys. Disney's Old Key West Resort is the original Disney Vacation Club property, but villas not occupied by members are available for nightly rental. It has the laid-back feel of a resort community and all the amenities that go with resort life. The homey accommodations have lots of space and the convenience of kitchen facilities, making the resort especially comfortable for longer stays. The villas are designed in a Key West theme, with soothing color schemes. The telephone number for Disney's Old Key West resort is 407-827-7700.

VILLAS: There are 761 studios and villas with one, two, or three bedrooms. A studio consists of a large room with two queen-size beds, a table and chairs, and a small fridge, coffeemaker, microwave, and sink. Bathrooms are spacious. Each of the one-bedroom villas has a king-size bed in the master bedroom and a queen-size sleeper sofa in the living room; the master bath has a whirlpool tub, sink, and shower.

The two-bedroom villa features a king-size bed in the master bedroom, two queen-size beds in the second bedroom, a living room with a queen-size sleeper sofa and a DVD player, a dining room, and a kitchen with a refrigerator, dishwasher, toaster, and coffeemaker, plus dishes, flatware, cooking utensils, and more.

The master bathroom is divided into two rooms with an extra-large whirlpool tub and a sink in one and an oversize shower, sink and vanity, and toilet in the other. There's a porch or balcony off the living room and bedroom and ceiling fans in each room. The configuration of the two-story, three-bedroom Grand Villas is similar to that of the two-bedroom models, but adds a third bedroom with two double beds. As for capacity, the studios and one-bedroom villas sleep 4 people, the two-bedroom villas sleep 8 guests, and two-story, three-bedroom villas accommodate 12.

WHERE TO EAT: In addition to the restaurant here, there are grills and picnic tables.

Good's Food to Go: The perfect place to pick up fixin's for a continental breakfast, this place also offers burgers, conch fritters, salads, sandwiches, and simple snacks.

Olivia's Cafe: This full-service restaurant serves Key West favorites, plus more traditional items, for breakfast, lunch, and dinner. Menus change seasonally.

WHERE TO DRINK: The watering holes at Old Key West are as laid-back as they come.

Gurgling Suitcase: This tiny bar serves specialty drinks, wine, beer, and soft drinks.

Turtle Shack: This poolside spot serves pizza, salads, sandwiches, and snacks. Open seasonally.

WHAT TO DO: At Conch Flats Community Hall, table tennis, board games, a large-screen television, DVD rentals, and planned activities are offered. There are basketball, shuffleboard, and volleyball courts, and equipment is available at Hank's Rent 'N Return.

Biking: Bikes may be rented from Hank's.

Boating: Pedal boats, motorboats, and pontoon boats are available for rent at Hank's.

Health Club: The Fitness Center at R.E.S.T. Beach features exercise equipment, a sauna, and massage (by appointment).

Playground: A kids' play area is located by each of the resort's swimming pools.

Shopping: Conch Flats General Store has groceries, books, sundries, and more.

Swimming: The sprawling main pool, with a large whirlpool nearby, is located behind the Hospitality House. The children's pool and play area looks like a big sandcastle and features a 120-foot slide. Additional pools are found around the resort.

Tennis: There are three courts.

Video Arcade: The Electric Eel Game Room is in the Hospitality House; the Flying Fish Game Room, by Turtle Shack snack bar.

TRANSPORTATION: Buses go to the theme parks, water parks, and Downtown Disney. Water launches also make the trip between the resort and Downtown Disney.

Animal Kingdom Area

All-Star Movies, Music & Sports

The All-Star resorts are among the most brightly and boldly themed at Walt Disney World. Each resort has 1,500 to 1,920 rooms housed in ten buildings devoted to five Disney movies, types of music, and sports.

Sports fans will find themselves in a world of baseball, football, tennis, surfing, or basketball at the All-Star Sports resort. Brightly colored, larger-than-life football helmets, surfboards, tennis balls, basketball hoops, and baseball bats adorn the buildings.

At the All-Star Music resort, Broadway, country, jazz, rock, and calypso are the themes. A walk-through, neon-lit jukebox, a three-story pair of cowboy boots, and a Broadway theater marquee are among the giant icons.

The All-Star Movies resort celebrates five classic Disney films: *Toy Story*, *The Mighty Ducks*, *Fantasia*, *101 Dalmatians*, and *The Love Bug*. Buildings are adorned with such icons as 40-foot Dalmatians and wildly oversize versions of Buzz Lightyear and Woody.

As value resorts, the All-Star properties offer few frills, but the service and whimsical atmosphere are pure Disney.

Guests check in at Cinema Hall for All-Star Movies, Melody Hall for All-Star Music, or Stadium Hall for All-Star Sports. Each has a food court, arcade, shop, and Guest Services. To reach All-Star Movies, call 407-939-7000; to phone All-Star Music, call 407-939-6000; to contact All-Star Sports, call 407-939-5000.

ROOMS: The guestrooms, measuring 260 square feet, are rather small compared with those at Port Orleans, which are 314 square feet. Each room has two double beds (with the exception of rooms designed for travelers with disabilities, which have one king-size bed), a vanity area with a sink, a separate bathroom, a small dresser, and a small table with chairs.

In 2006, All-Star Music converted 400 guest rooms into Family Suites. Each of the 192 suites sleeps up to six guests and has two bathrooms, a "master" bedroom with its own flat-screen TV, a kitchenette with counter space, sink, microwave, coffeemaker, and under-counter refrigerater.

WHERE TO EAT: Three food courts—**World Premiere** in Cinema Hall, **Intermission** in Melody Hall, and **End Zone** in Stadium Hall. Each features a bakery, convenience market, and several stands geared to barbecue, pizza and pasta, and burgers. Each food court has a seating area with a beverage bar. The All-Star resorts all deliver pizza, salads, beer, and wine to rooms from 4 P.M. to midnight.

WHERE TO DRINK: There are no lounges at the All-Star resorts; however, the **Silver Screen Spirits, Singing Spirits**, and **Team Spirits** pool bars serve drinks throughout the day and evening. The bars are in the main pool areas.

WHAT TO DO: Guests may swim in any of the resort's pools. All-Star guests may rent boating equipment at any WDW resort marina.

Playground: A playground is located in each hotel's courtyard area.

Shopping: Maestro Mickey's in Melody Hall, Sport Goofy's Gifts and Sundries in Stadium Hall, and Donald's Double Feature in Cinema Hall all have magazines, books, character merchandise, and sundries.

Swimming: Each hotel has two pools and one kiddie pool. The main pool at All-Star Movies has a *Fantasia* theme (look for Sorcerer Mickey). The smaller Duck Pond Pool is based on *The Mighty Ducks*. At the All-Star Music resort, the Calypso Pool is in the form of a giant guitar, while the Piano Pool bears a striking resemblance to a grand piano. At All-Star Sports, Surfboard Bay has a soothing ocean motif. The smaller Grand Slam Pool pays tribute to our national pastime—it's shaped like a baseball diamond (Goofy is on the mound).

Video Arcades: Each of the All-Star resorts boasts one video arcade.

TRANSPORTATION: Buses make pickups at Cinema Hall, Melody Hall, and Stadium Hall for trips to each of the four theme parks, Blizzard Beach, Typhoon Lagoon, and Downtown Disney. Each resort has its own bus stops.

A word about All-Star resort transportation: The bus service at these "value" resorts tends to be slightly more efficient than at other locations. The combination of fewer stops and connections is a bonus for guests staying here.

Disney's Animal Kingdom Lodge

At first glance, Disney's Animal Kingdom Lodge evokes images of a sleepy, little, thatched-roof game lodge in the wilds of southern Africa. Upon closer examination, however, it's clear that the only things sleepy or little about this place are the small creatures that live in its shadow. Those animals, along with their more sizable cousins, inhabit the 33 acres of meticulously re-created African savanna that practically surround this 1,293-room resort. In all, more than 100 birds and hoofed animals, including giraffes, zebras, ostriches, and Thompson's gazelles, call Disney's newest wildlife reserve home. With the freedom to wander within a dozen or so yards of the lodge itself, these critters allow guests to go on safari without leaving their balconies.

The resort, located about a mile from Disney's Animal Kingdom park, opened in April 2001. The lobby is a huge, high-ceilinged room, richly appointed—as is the rest of the property—with colorful African artwork and artifacts. The biggest draw here is neither the large mud fireplace nor the suspension bridge spanning this cavernous chamber, but the four-story observation window overlooking the savanna. It's one of many portals through which to gaze upon meandering wildlife.

Like the African game lodges on which it is based, Disney's Animal Kingdom Lodge was constructed using a semicircular design. From overhead, it looks a bit like a horseshoe. This allows for maximum animal-viewing potential. Indeed, many of the resort's guestrooms have direct views of the savanna areas. Be sure to specify your viewing preference when you book a room. The telephone number for Disney's Animal Kingdom Lodge is 407-938-3000.

ROOMS: The 1,293 rooms, all finished in tapestries and vibrant colors, feature handcrafted dark-wood furniture, sand-colored walls, and earth-tone-patterned carpets. Deluxe rooms are a bit more spacious than their standard counterparts. Most rooms have two queen beds (some king-size beds are available), plus a daybed to accommodate up to five people; bunk beds are available in many rooms. All rooms have balconies. Suites include a parlor, plus one or two bedrooms; there are king-size or queen-size beds in the bedrooms. Bathrooms have a separate vanity area with double sink. All rooms include an iron (with board), hair dryer, refrigerator, and newspaper delivery. Like at real African game lodges, some beds come draped with mosquito netting. Unlike in Africa, however, the nets here are purely decorative. Concierge service is available.

WHERE TO EAT: In addition to its restaurants, the hotel offers round-the-clock room service.

Boma—Flavors of Africa: Boma is modeled after a bustling African marketplace. This sprawling, popular family restaurant boasts many different types of cuisine in what chefs describe as a "global fusion" style. The cuisine, served buffet style, is a blend of French, Malaysian, Indian, Chinese, and English.

Jiko—The Cooking Place: The colors of sunset are the backdrop for this sublime eatery with an African flair. Wines from South Africa are featured.

The Mara: A spacious fast-food restaurant serving such kid-pleasers as pizza, burgers, and chicken fingers.

WHERE TO DRINK: The lounges here are rustic and inviting. Some even offer the opportunity to sip cocktails while observing animals on the savanna.

Cape Town Lounge and Wine Bar: Adjacent to Jiko—The Cooking Place, this spot features wines imported from South Africa.

Uzima Springs: The resort's poolside bar serves specialty and traditional drinks during regular pool hours.

Victoria Falls: Set alongside a soothing waterfall, this mezzanine-level lounge features coffee, tea, South African wines, and assorted cocktails.

WHAT TO DO: Spying on wildlife is the main event in these parts. However, if you can manage to pry yourself away from those hoofed exhibitionists for a bit, there are plenty of other diversions available. Note that guests are welcome to partake in activities offered at other Walt Disney World resorts.

Children's Programs: The Simba's Cubhouse play area, for (potty-trained) kids ages 4 through 12, is open in the evenings starting at 4:30 P.M. Reservations are required. Kids can learn about the wildlife surrounding the resort through nature-themed activities. For pricing information or to make reservations, call 407-939-3463.

Health Club: The Zahanati Massage and Fitness Center has exercise equipment and a sauna, plus spa services including massage (by appointment).

Playground: The Hakuna Matata playground is located near the pool.

Shopping: Zawadi Marketplace stocks Africa-themed gifts, Disney character merchandise, clothing with the Animal Kingdom Lodge logo, and sundries.

Swimming: The resort has just one swimming pool, but it is huge. More impressive than its size, however, is the view from the pool deck. In addition to a kiddie pool, there are two whirlpools nearby.

Video Arcade: Pumbaa's Fun & Games features a selection of video games.

TRANSPORTATION: Buses go to the Magic Kingdom, Epcot, the Disney-MGM Studios, Animal Kingdom, Typhoon Lagoon, Blizzard Beach, and Downtown Disney.

Coronado Springs

This resort reveals its Southwestern U.S.-Mexican theme in such elements as a tiled stucco lobby with a fountain and a pyramid with water tumbling down from it that appears to have created the Mayan ruin-themed pool. The hotel's 1,921 rooms are found in three guest areas that stretch around Lago Dorado, a 22-acre lake. (It can take five minutes or more to walk to the farthest

rooms.) The food court, restaurant, and lounge are all near the lobby. A convention center offers access to business services. The telephone number for Coronado Springs is 407-939-1000.

ROOMS: Standard rooms are smaller than those at Disney's deluxe hotels, but adequate for a family of four; each has two double beds (some king-size beds are available). In-room amenities include a coffeemaker, refrigerator, hair dryer, and dataport. Decor varies in each section but is characterized by yellow, blue, and scarlet accents. In the Casitas area, where most suites are located, terra-cotta guest buildings occupy a citylike landscape. In the pueblo-style Ranchos, scattered along a dry streambed, rooms have a rustic feel. Cabanas, located along the rocky palm-lined beach, reflect the casual feel of their namesake.

WHERE TO EAT: In addition to a full-service restaurant and food court, limited room service is available for breakfast and dinner.

Maya Grill: Open for breakfast and dinner, this spot offers seafood, steak, lamb, and pork cooked over an open-pit, wood-fired grill.

Pepper Market: High ceilings make this nontraditional food court feel like an open-air market. The fare includes tacos, tostadas, pizza, pasta, and omelets made to order. Note that there is an automatic 10 percent gratuity for dining in the Pepper Market.

WHERE TO DRINK: There are two places to wet your whistle at Coronado Springs.

Francisco's: This colorful lounge provides cocktails and evening entertainment and is located in the main building.

Siesta's: In the Dig Site area, this poolside bar lets swimmers and archaeologists enjoy a variety of cocktails and light snacks.

WHAT TO DO: There is an array of water sports in which to participate, as well as volleyball and a short nature trail.

Biking: Bikes may be rented at La Marina.

Boating: A variety of boating equipment is available for rent at La Marina.

Fishing: Two-hour, guided fishing excursions are offered on the 22-acre Lago Dorado. Call 407-WDW-BASS.

Health Club: La Vida health club offers a full range of fitness equipment.

Playground: The Explorer's Playground is part of the Dig Site play area and includes a huge sandbox, complete with Mayan carvings waiting to be excavated.

Salon: The Casa de Belleza salon, located near La Vida Fitness Center, offers a variety of spa services.

Shopping: Panchito's Gifts & Sundries is where to find items with a Southwestern flavor, Disney merchandise, film, and necessities.

Swimming: The main pool can be found in the Dig Site area. It surrounds a Mayan pyramid and features a towering waterslide. There is a 22-person whirlpool and a kiddie pool nearby. Each of the guestroom areas features an unguarded quiet pool.

Video Arcades: The Jumping Beans Arcade is found in the main building, and the Iguana Arcade is in the Dig Site area.

TRANSPORTATION: Buses go to the Magic Kingdom, Epcot, the Disney-MGM Studios, Animal Kingdom, Typhoon Lagoon, Blizzard Beach, and Downtown Disney.

Pop Century

What do you get when you mix decades of American pop culture with a sprawling Disney resort? Pop Century! Like the All-Star Resorts, Pop Century is a vivid celebration of Americana. The 2,880-room resort represents the second half of the twentieth century. The resort's larger-than-life "time capsules" commemorate the toys, fads, dance crazes, and catchphrases that swept the nation during the 1950s through the 1990s. It's meant to be groovy . . . you dig?

As a value resort, the Pop Century property offers few frills, but the service is good, the atmosphere's colorful, and the transportation is efficient. Guests check in at Classic Hall, which also features a food-and-merchandise location, arcade, and guest services desk. To reach Pop Century resort, call 407-938-4000.

ROOMS: The guestrooms, measuring 260 square feet, are a bit on the small side compared with those at Port Orleans, which are 314 square feet. Each room has two double beds (with the exception of guestrooms designed for travelers with disabilities, which have one king-size bed), a vanity area with a sink, a separate bathroom, a small dresser, a small table with chairs, voice mail, and a dataport.

WHERE TO EAT: The food court features a bakery, convenience market, plus several stands geared to pizza and pasta, and burgers. The Pop Century resort delivers pizza to guestrooms from about 4 P.M. to midnight.

WHERE TO DRINK: There is a bar located poolside and a lounge integrated into the Classic Hall food and merchandise area.

WHAT TO DO: Guests may swim in any of the Pop Century resort pools. They may rent boating equipment at any WDW resorts.

Playground: There is a soft-surface playground with, among other compelling features, an interactive water fountain.

Shopping: The Everything Pop! shop has a selection of books, character merchandise, sundries, and snacks.

Swimming: Each section of the hotel has three pools and a kiddie pool.

Video Arcade: Revisit classic video games or discover some new ones in this arcade.

TRANSPORTATION: Buses stop at Classic Hall for trips to each of the four theme parks, Blizzard Beach, Typhoon Lagoon, and Downtown Disney.

Disney Cruise Line

The *Disney Wonder* and its sister ship, the *Disney Magic*, rank among the world's finest oceangoing vessels. The onboard experience is essentially the same on both ships, but some restaurant names, entertainment, and theming differ. As do the length of the cruises, as well as the destinations. A *Disney Magic* voyage takes guests on a 7-night cruise to the Caribbean (there is an eastern and two western itineraries) or a 10- or 11-night cruise to the Mediterranean, while the *Wonder* journeys to the Bahamas (typically for three or four nights).

A three- or four-night cruise may be paired with a stay at a WDW resort. After spending three or four nights at Walt Disney World, guests (except those at the Swan and Dolphin) retain the same room keys for their staterooms aboard the *Disney Wonder*. There is no second check-in on the ship. Staterooms closely match the category of the resort accommodations, from moderate to deluxe. Guests may also opt for a seven-night cruise. This package does not include a stay at a WDW resort. All seven-night cruises take place on the *Disney Magic*.

When transfers are purchased, guests travel by bus to Port Canaveral, the departure point for all cruises. They then board a 2,700-passenger ship for their journey. From the ship design to entertainment options, families, teens, and adults all have their own comfort zones—without ever having to say good-bye to Mickey. (In addition to the Mouse, the usual cast of characters is onboard.) Three-

and four-night cruises include a stop at Nassau in the Bahamas. The seven-night Eastern Caribbean cruise takes guests to St. Thomas (including excursions to St. John) and St. Maarten. The 7-night Western itinerary stops at Key West, Grand Cayman, and Cozumel. Each voyage includes a day at Castaway Cay. The Mediterranean itinerary includes visits to Spain, Italy, and France. A valid passport is required for everyone planning to sail on a Disney Cruise—no exceptions.

The ships' classic exteriors recall the majesty of early ocean liners. For example, *Disney Magic* guests enter a three-story atrium, where traditional definitions of elegance expand to include a bronze statue of Mickey as helmsman and subtle cutout Disney character silhouettes along the grand staircase. There's even a 15-foot, topsy-turvy statue of a "goofy" painter hanging off the *Disney Magic's* stern.

Vacations can be booked through a travel agent or by calling 800-910-3659 or visiting *www.disneycruise.com*.

ROOMS: All 877 staterooms aboard both ships are a cut above the standard cruising cabin. On average, staterooms offer about 25 percent more space, most have a bath and a half, and 73 percent are outside rooms with ocean vistas—many with verandas. All feature telephones with "land lines," TVs, hair dryers, and safes. There are rooms equipped for guests with disabilities. All staterooms are nonsmoking.

There are 12 stateroom categories that correspond to WDW resorts with comparable room rates. The seven-night vacations start at about $799 for adults per person, double occupancy. (Packages for kids ages 3 through 12 who are the third or fourth person in a stateroom start at $399.) The seven-night land-sea package price includes Walt Disney World accommodations, admission to the theme parks, shipboard meals, cruise and port charges, and more. Depending on availability, guests may opt for a three- or four-night cruise.

Note: Some names and theming differ from ship to ship, but the experiences are comparable.

WHERE TO EAT: There are three themed dining rooms (and one adults-only alternative), in addition to 24-hour room service, on each ship; guests dine in each of the three main rooms, enjoying a different culinary experience each night.

Animator's Palate: Here, the restaurant and the food are works of art. As in the movie *The Wizard of Oz*, everything begins in black and white—from the floors to the waiters' attire to the food (to a degree). As the meal progresses, color creeps into the picture. When dessert arrives, the room is awash in brilliant hues.

Lumière's: Continental food, chandeliers, and *Beauty and the Beast* trompe l'oeil effects characterize this casually elegant dining room. An abundance of roses completes the theme. On the *Magic* only.

Palo: A dining room reserved for adults, Palo is a romantic restaurant perched atop the vessel. Chefs prepare Italian cuisine in an exhibition kitchen. Reservations are required, and there is an additional fee. Make arrangements ahead of time at *www.disneycruise.com* or as soon as possible after boarding the ship. It's a popular spot.

Parrot Cay: In a colorful Caribbean setting complete with Sebastian wall sconces, this restaurant features tasty tropical cuisine.

Topsider Buffet: The *Magic*'s indoor-outdoor cafe serving breakfast, lunch, snacks, and a buffet dinner for kids. On the *Wonder*, it's Beach Blanket Buffet.

Triton's: An elegant setting in which guests enjoy seafood and an "under the sea" theme. On the *Wonder* only.

WHERE TO DRINK: Among the options are several lounges, including Diversions sports bar the Promenade Lounge. Beat Street is a colorful, adults-only cluster of nighttime entertainment venues located on the *Magic*. The *Wonder* equivalent is known as Route 66.

Rockin' Bar D and Wavebands: Dance club with a live band and deejay (the former is on the *Magic*, the latter on the *Wonder*).

Sessions and Cadillac Lounge: Piano bars on the *Magic* and *Wonder*, respectively.

WHAT TO DO: Recreational areas on each ship, as well as at its ports of call, are strategically located to attract families, teens, and adults to different areas, with nearly an entire deck devoted to kids. A cruise director keeps guests apprised of the options. Shore excursions may be booked ahead at *www.disneycruise.com* or once aboard.

Adult Activities: Adults-only activities range from wine tasting to guest lectures. There is an adults-only pool onboard and a secluded beach for grown-ups at Castaway Cay.

Biking: Bikes may be rented by the hour at Castaway Cay.

Buena Vista Theater: A 270-seat cinema, this movie theater offers feature films.

Children's Programs: A huge area dedicated exclusively to kids offers supervised, age-specific programs for kids ages 3 through 12 from 9 A.M. until midnight. The Oceaneer Club provides engaging activities for the 3- through 7-year-old set. The Oceaneer Lab, designed for children 8 through 12, is a science-based interactive play area. Teens can enjoy special programs at The Stack (*Magic*) and Aloft (*Wonder*). Ocean Quest is a new kids' area that lets young sailors experience a scaled replica of the ship's bridge.

Deck Parties: Guests may dance to live music, sip cocktails, and nibble snacks at informal, swinging shindigs at sea. The pirate-themed party—with fireworks!—is a standout.

Internet Access: On the *Magic*, there are Internet stations in the Promenade Lounge, The Stack (teens only), and in Cove Cafe (adults only). On the *Wonder*, access the Internet in the Promenade Lounge, Cove Cafe (adults only), and Aloft (teens only). The cost is 75 cents per minute, with a five-minute minimum. Packages are also available. (We always opt for a package. It's usually the most cost-efficient way to go.) Wi-Fi is available at select locations on both ships.

Shopping: In addition to the colorful shipboard shops—Mickey's Mates, Treasure Ketch, and Shutters—guests may indulge their shopping fantasies while exploring the various ports of call. Shops on the ship are duty free.

Sports: Guests play volleyball and basketball on the sports deck and at Castaway Cay.

Swimming: There are several whirlpools and three swimming pools on each ship: a family pool, a kids' pool, and an adults-only pool. Guests may also swim off the sandy shores and lagoon of Castaway Cay.

Teen Entertainment: On the *Magic*, a place called The Stack is where teens (and teens only) may hang out, watch movies, and listen to music. On the *Wonder*, it's at Aloft. There are also teen-oriented activities on the ship, as well as on Castaway Cay. Activities are for teens ages 13–17.

Vista Spa and Salon: Adult guests get in shipshape at this newly expanded modern facility, which offers exercise equipment and spa treatments (with indoor and outdoor treatment rooms), educational and enrichment programs, sauna, steam room, whirlpool, and massage. The salon offers many services, including haircuts, manicures, and pedicures (for a fee). Note that appointments fill up fast—book in advance at *www.disneycruise.com* or as soon as possible once aboard the ship.

Walt Disney Theater: A tribute to the grand theatrical palaces of long ago. Guests see an original live production each night.

Castaway Cay

Every Disney Cruise Line trip wraps up with a visit to Castaway Cay (pronounced *key*). Disney has maintained the island's natural beauty while providing a host of outdoor activities, including snorkeling, biking, and boating. The island has a beach for families, a beach for teens, and a mile-long stretch of sand—complete with massage cabanas—for adults seeking less action and more privacy.

As guests awaken at the island, they find their ship docked at Castaway Cay's private pier. The pier allows for easy access to and from the ship.

Castaway Cay, a 1,000-acre tropical island, is in the Bahamas, east of Fort Lauderdale. Trams are available for guests who wish to explore the island. All of the architecture, including a bar, restaurant, market, and even a post office, is in traditional Bahamian style.

Resorts on Hotel Plaza Blvd.

These seven hotels—Best Western Lake Buena Vista, DoubleTree Guest Suites, Grosvenor, Hilton, Royal Plaza, Buena Vista Palace, and Holiday Inn (currently closed for renovations)—though inside Walt Disney World boundaries, are neither owned nor operated by Disney. However, many have been here since the park opened in 1971 or soon thereafter (sometimes under different names), accommodating Mickey enthusiasts from the beginning. The hotels are not themed, but the three largest (the Hilton, Buena Vista Palace, and Grosvenor) do have meals hosted by Disney characters.

Often referred to as the Downtown Disney Resort Area Hotels, they line the mile-long Hotel Plaza Boulevard. The Hilton, Buena Vista Palace, and Grosvenor are across the street from the Marketplace, with its shops, restaurants, and nightlife. The other four properties are a 10- to 25-minute stroll away. They are also close to the Crossroads at Lake Buena Vista shopping center, home to inexpensive eateries and a 24-hour grocery. Privileges of staying in one of these hotels include:

• Car rental on the premises (at all but the Best Western Lake Buena Vista resort).

• Free bus service to the four theme parks, with limited service to Downtown Disney, Typhoon Lagoon, and Blizzard Beach. The buses, which are not part of the Disney transportation network, make up to two trips every hour; be sure to allow extra time for bus travel. One bus serves the Hilton and Buena Vista Palace; another, the other hotels (it takes at least ten minutes to stop at all five). Note that buses load and unload in the middle of the parking lot at some parks.

• Flexibility to book tickets for both on- and off-WDW-property attractions.

• Preferred access to Disney golf courses.

• A "Passport to Savings" coupon book with exclusive discounts and specials on dining, shopping, and entertainment.

• Reservations for Disney dinner shows and theme park restaurants.

Note that guests staying in the resorts on Hotel Plaza Boulevard do have to pay for parking at Disney parks and other Walt Disney World attractions, and they cannot charge purchases made at Disney World shops and restaurants with a resort ID.

To book a room, call the individual hotel's toll-free number or WDW Central Reservations at 407-W-DISNEY (934-7639). The resorts on Hotel Plaza Blvd. are included in several Walt Disney Travel Company packages. Internet users can get information via *www.downtowndisneyhotels.com.*

All of the hotels offer nonsmoking rooms and accommodations for travelers with disabilities. To get to the hotels from the airport, take Exit 68 off I-4.

BEST WESTERN LAKE BUENA VISTA:

This mostly leisure-oriented, 18-story hotel is surrounded by pines and has an entry lined with oaks draped in Spanish moss. Each of the 325

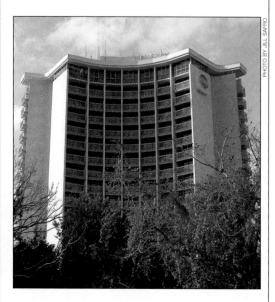

spacious rooms and suites has either one king-size bed and a queen sofa bed or two queen-size beds, as well as a balcony. Rooms also come with voice mail, free coffee, safe, hair dryer, and iron with board. Baths have one sink and plenty of counter space. Small refrigerators may be rented for $10 a day.

Each of the four suites occupies a corner of the 18th floor and features a wet bar, two phones, two TVs, a whirlpool tub, and an impressive glassed-in porch with skylights and a ceiling fan; they offer fine views of the other resorts on Hotel Plaza Boulevard and, from some of the nonsmoking rooms, the (distant) fireworks at Disney theme parks.

The hotel also has a fitness center, business center, an arcade, a heated pool, small kiddie pool, playground, sundries shop, and guest laundry facilities. Other amenities include room service. Traders Island Grill serves breakfast, lunch, and dinner, as well as assorted snacks and pizza.

The hotel's lobby and restaurant area features the Flamingo Cove cocktail lounge and a game room. Rates range from $89 to $199 for guestrooms; $199 to $399 for suites. Best Western Lake Buena Vista Resort, 2000 Hotel Plaza Blvd., Box 22205, Lake Buena Vista, FL 32830; 407-828-2424 or 800-348-3765; *www.orlandoresorthotel.com.*

DOUBLETREE GUEST SUITES:

This 229-unit property has a stellar staff, homey atmosphere, low-slung facade reminiscent of WDW's Contemporary hotel, bright colors and whimsical patterns throughout, and an aviary in the lobby, where a child's check-in desk adjoins the one for grown-ups. Kids get a bag of goodies, and everyone gets cookies. The only all-suite hotel at Walt Disney World, it has roomy (625 square feet) units, each with a living room and sleeper sofa, dressing area, and separate bedroom. The one-bedroom suites sleep up to six; there are five two-bedroom suites. Most of the bedrooms have two double beds; a few king beds are available.

The decor features vibrant blues, greens, and oranges, with plaid chairs and sofas. (More subdued surroundings are available.) Room amenities include two TVs, pay-per-view movies, wet bar, refrigerator, coffeemaker, microwave oven, hair dryer, high-speed Internet access, a desk, and safe (for a daily charge). The bathroom has a small TV.

Recreational facilities include a large heated pool and a whirlpool in a landscaped area, as well as a fitness room, sand volleyball court, two lighted tennis courts, and small playground. The Kids' Theater (children's playroom) has a big-screen TV, toys, games, popcorn, and seasonal activities. Streamers restaurant features American classics and a breakfast buffet; it's also the source for more of those cookies. Streamers Market sells snack items and groceries. There is a Budget Rental Car desk by the lobby.

Rates range from $119 to $299. DoubleTree Guest Suites, 2305 Hotel Plaza Blvd., Lake Buena Vista, FL 32830; 407-934-1000 or 800-222-8733; *www.doubletreeguestsuites.com.*

GROSVENOR: The name is pronounced *GROVE*-nor, and this hotel attracts many international guests. The 626 rooms are in a 19-story tower and two wings framing two large courtyards with griffin centerpieces. An automatic daily resort fee covers WebTV, in-room video games for kids, free local calls, Internet access, and a Dining Rewards Card (good for free beverages at Baskervilles restaurant).

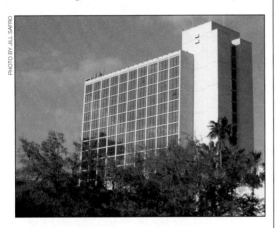

There is wireless high-speed Internet access in the resort's public spaces. Most rooms have two double beds, though some 35 king-bed rooms are available; 65 rooms also have daybeds and can sleep up to five. Bathrooms are small but stocked with toiletries.

Extensive recreational facilities—the hotel's appeal—include an exercise room, two lighted tennis courts, shuffleboard, basketball, volleyball, two heated pools, children's pool, play area, and arcade. Changing rooms with showers accommodate guests who check in or out early. Baskervilles restaurant incorporates a replica of Sherlock Holmes's office, and serves breakfast and dinner buffets; Disney characters come for breakfast three days a week; the popular Murder Watch Mystery Theatre takes place on Saturday at 6 P.M.

Crumpets Cafe, open 24 hours a day, serves snacks and light fare. For cocktails, there's Crickets lounge and Moriarty's pub. Rates range from $69 to $149 for two guests, year-round; suites are $345 to $480. Grosvenor, 1850 Hotel Plaza Blvd., Lake Buena Vista, FL 32830; 407-828-4444 or 800-624-4109; *www.grosvenorresort.com.*

HILTON: This hotel gets high marks for its 23 well-groomed acres, laid-back ambience, pool area, and upscale shops. The 814 rooms, all of which recently underwent extensive refurbishment, have mini-bars, voice mail, safes, and high-speed Internet access.

Among the resort's restaurants and lounges, Andiamo Italian Bistro & Grille offers grilled steaks and chicken (dinner only); Cape Cod–themed Covington Mill serves breakfast (with Disney characters in attendance on Sunday) and lunch only; Rum Largo Poolside Cafe serves burgers, sandwiches, salads, and tropical drinks alfresco; Mainstreet Market, open 24 hours, is part deli, part country store (serving Starbucks coffee). For light meals, snacks, or cocktails, drop by John T's Lounge (off the lobby); after-dinner drinks, specialty coffees, beer, and wines by the glass are served at Mugs Coffee & Wine Bar.

Recreational facilities include two whirlpools, two heated swimming pools, a kiddie pool, fitness room, and large gameroom. There is an Avis Rental Car desk in the lobby. Rates range from $109 to $299; suites are $149 to $659. Hilton in the Walt Disney World Resort, 1751 Hotel Plaza Blvd., Lake Buena Vista, FL 32830; 407-827-4000 or 800-782-4414; *www.hilton-wdwv.com.*

Note: This is the *only* hotel on Hotel Plaza Boulevard to offer the "Extra Magic Hours." For details about this program (which, on select days, lets guests enter a theme park an hour before it officially opens or stay up to three hours after it closes), ask at the front desk.

HOLIDAY INN: At press time, this hotel was closed for renovation and was tentatively scheduled to re-open some time in 2007. For information, call 800-223-9930. Holiday Inn, Box 22204, 1805 Hotel Plaza Blvd., Lake Buena Vista, FL 32830; *www.holidayinnwdw.com.*

ROYAL PLAZA: A subtle pineapple motif, a symbol of hospitality, permeates this property. The 394 guest units, including 22 suites, are divided between a 17-story main tower, with a glass-enclosed elevator scaling the facade, and two-story lanai wings with standard and superior rooms, and gated patios or small balconies. Each guestroom has a sitting area set off by shuttered partitions, a desk, dresser, double armoire with closet space, oversize bathtub, safe, and mini-bar. Baths have marble counters and corner tubs (whirlpools on the concierge level); baths in the spacious rooms with king-size beds have a separate glass-enclosed shower. All rooms are decorated in shades of coral, teal, and green; they have either two double beds or a king-size bed, ceiling fans, sofa beds, hair dryers, safes, mini-bars, and free coffee and tea.

Recreational facilities include a large heated pool, a whirlpool, fitness room (for guests 16 and older), gamerooms for adults and kids, and four lighted tennis courts. There is also a business center and a Disney merchandise shop.

The Giraffe Cafe offers all meals, including an ample breakfast buffet; the Marketessen is open until 2 A.M. Rates range from $69 to $179 for up to five in a room; suites, $209 to $699. Royal Plaza, 1905 Hotel Plaza Blvd., Lake Buena Vista, FL 32830; 407-828-2828 or 800-248-7890; *www.royalplaza.com*.

BUENA VISTA PALACE: The tallest resort in the Downtown Disney resort area and the largest of the resorts on Hotel Plaza Boulevard (it's actually at the intersection of Hotel Plaza Boulevard and Buena Vista Drive) is a cluster of towers set on 27 acres beside Lake Buena Vista. Each of the 1,012 rooms has a ceiling fan, two phones, including one cordless (with voice mail, speaker-phone, and high-speed Internet access), two queen beds or a king, a coffeemaker, Sony PlayStation, and weekday newspaper delivery. Most rooms have a balcony or patio. There are also one- and two-bedroom suites (with

coffeemakers, microwaves, refrigerators, mini-bars, and living rooms with queen sofas), and two-story penthouses. Safes are available free of charge.

The resort's European-style spa features myriad treatments and services, a full-service salon, fitness center, and private lap pool with a resistance jet stream. Recreation Island accommodates two swimming pools, a kiddie pool, whirlpool, lighted tennis court, sand volleyball court, and children's playground and arcade.

The hotel also provides 24-hour room service, and it has boutiques and a guest laundry. Dining spots include the lakeside Watercress Cafe, which serves breakfast and lunch only (Disney characters are in attendance Sunday morning); the Watercress Mini Market, open from 6 A.M. to midnight, for baked goods and sandwiches; and the Outback restaurant (not part of the chain) for seafood and steak.

Conventions and other big groups may book the Laughing Kookaburra Good Time Bar, referred to by locals as "The Kook." The elegant Top of the Palace lounge—which is open to everyone—provides the perfect perch to gaze at the sunset or fireworks over a glass of fine wine. Rates for rooms range from $99 to $259 per night (no charge for kids under 18); suites, which sleep up to six, are $159 to $339. Rollaways cost $15 per night, cribs are free. Buena Vista Palace, 1900 Buena Vista Dr., Lake Buena Vista, FL 32830; *www.buenavistapalace.com;* 407-827-2727 or 866-397-6516.

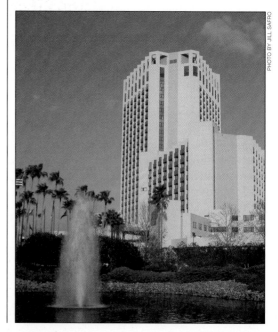

Magic Kingdom

The Magic Kingdom is the most enchanting part of the World. Few who visit it are disappointed, and even the most blasé travelers manage a smile. The sight of the soaring spires of Cinderella Castle, the gleaming woodwork of the Main Street shops, and the crescendo of music that follows the parades never fails to have its effect. Even when the crowds are large and the weather is hot, a visitor who has toured this wonderland dozens of times can still look around and think how satisfying this place is for the spirit.

What makes the Magic Kingdom timeless is its combination of the classic and the futuristic. Both childhood favorites and space-age creatures have a home here. Every "land" has a theme, carried through from the costumes worn by the hosts and hostesses and the food served in the restaurants to the merchandise sold in the shops, and even the design of the trash cans. Thousands of details contribute to the overall effect, and recognizing these touches makes any visit more enjoyable.

But the delight most guests experience upon first glimpse of the Magic Kingdom can disappear when disorientation sets in. There are so many bends to every pathway, so many sights and sounds clamoring for attention, it's too easy to wander aimlessly and miss the best the Magic Kingdom has to offer. So we earnestly suggest that you study this chapter before your visit.

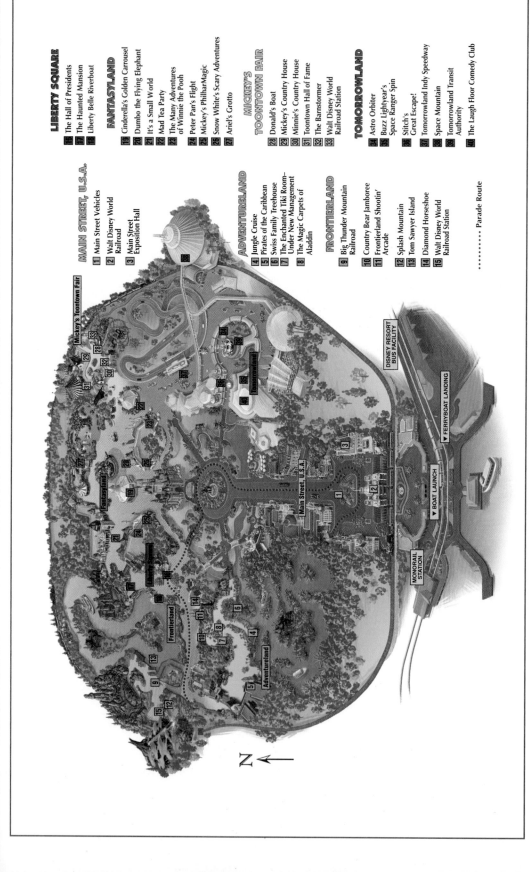

MAIN STREET, U.S.A.

1 Main Street Vehicles
2 Walt Disney World Railroad
3 Main Street Exposition Hall

ADVENTURELAND

4 Jungle Cruise
5 Pirates of the Caribbean
6 Swiss Family Treehouse
7 The Enchanted Tiki Room— Under New Management
8 The Magic Carpets of Aladdin

FRONTIERLAND

9 Big Thunder Mountain Railroad
10 Country Bear Jamboree
11 Frontierland Shootin' Arcade
12 Splash Mountain
13 Tom Sawyer Island
14 Diamond Horseshoe
15 Walt Disney World Railroad Station

········· Parade Route

LIBERTY SQUARE

16 The Hall of Presidents
17 The Haunted Mansion
18 Liberty Belle Riverboat

FANTASYLAND

19 Cinderella's Golden Carrousel
20 Dumbo the Flying Elephant
21 It's a Small World
22 Mad Tea Party
23 The Many Adventures of Winnie the Pooh
24 Peter Pan's Flight
25 Mickey's PhilharMagic
26 Snow White's Scary Adventures
27 Ariel's Grotto

MICKEY'S TOONTOWN FAIR

28 Donald's Boat
29 Mickey's Country House
30 Minnie's Country House
31 Toontown Hall of Fame
32 The Barnstormer
33 Walt Disney World Railroad Station

TOMORROWLAND

34 Astro Orbiter
35 Buzz Lightyear's Space Ranger Spin
36 Stitch's Great Escape!
37 Tomorrowland Indy Speedway
38 Space Mountain
39 Tomorrowland Transit Authority
40 The Laugh Floor Comedy Club

Getting Oriented

When you visit Walt Disney World's original theme park, it's vital to know the lay of the "lands." The Magic Kingdom has seven lands—Main Street, U.S.A.; Adventureland; Frontierland; Liberty Square; Fantasyland; Mickey's Toontown Fair; and Tomorrowland. Main Street begins at Town Square, located just inside the park gates, and runs directly to Cinderella Castle. The area in front of the castle is known as the Central Plaza or, more aptly, the Hub. Bridges over the narrow waterways here serve as passages to each of the lands.

As you enter the park, the first bridge on your left goes to Adventureland; the next, to Liberty Square and Frontierland. On your right, the first bridge heads to Tomorrowland, the second to Fantasyland and Mickey's Toontown Fair. The end points of the pathways leading to the lands are linked by a street that is roughly circular, so that the layout of the Magic Kingdom resembles a wheel. All attractions, restaurants, and shops are found along the wheel's rim and spokes.

Guidemaps and Times Guides are available at the turnstiles, at City Hall in Town Square, and at many shops. Be sure to pick them up as soon as possible. You'll find them to be valuable navigational and scheduling resources.

HOW TO GET THERE

Take Exit 64B off I-4. Continue about four miles to the Auto Plaza and park; walk or take a tram to the main entrance complex, known as the Transportation and Ticket Center (TTC). Choose a seven-minute ferry ride or a slightly shorter trip by monorail for the last leg of an anticipation-filled journey.

By WDW Transportation: From the Grand Floridian and Polynesian: monorail or boat. From the Contemporary, monorail or walkway. (It is about a 10- to 15-minute stroll.) From Epcot: monorail to the Transportation and Ticket Center (TTC), then transfer to the Magic Kingdom monorail or ferry. From the Disney-MGM Studios, Animal Kingdom, and the resorts on Hotel Plaza Blvd.: buses to the TTC, then transfer to ferry or monorail. From Fort Wilderness, boat or bus. From Disney's Wilderness Lodge, boat or bus. From Downtown Disney, bus to any Disney resort and transfer to the Magic Kingdom bus (or monorail). From all other Disney resorts: buses.

PARKING

All-day parking at the Magic Kingdom is $9 for day visitors (free to Walt Disney World resort guests with a valid resort ID or an annual pass). Simply bear left after passing through the Auto Plaza; attendants will direct you into one of a dozen lots, all named after Disney characters. Minnie, Sleepy, and Dopey are within walking distance of the TTC; other lots are served by trams.

Note the section and aisle in which you park. The parking ticket allows for re-entry to the parking area throughout the day.

HOURS

The Magic Kingdom is generally open from 9 A.M. to 8 P.M. However, during busy seasons, it's open later. It's best to reach the park entrance about a half hour before the opening time. To avoid the morning crush, consider postponing your visit until 1 P.M. or later.

Note that on select days, the Magic Kingdom opens early or stays open late for WDW resort guests only (this is known as "Extra Magic Hours"). Call 407-824-4321 or visit *www.disneyworld.com* for details and current schedules. The park tends to be more crowded on such days, so consider starting here and "hopping" elsewhere later in the day.

GETTING AROUND

Walt Disney World Railroad steam trains make a 20-minute loop of the park, stopping to pick up and drop off passengers at stations on Main Street, Frontierland, and Mickey's Toontown Fair. (It's an efficient way to travel when parades are being run or there's a lot of foot traffic.) Horseless carriages, a fire engine, and horse-drawn trolleys take turns offering one-way trips down Main Street.

Park Primer

BABY FACILITIES

The best place in the Magic Kingdom to take care of little ones' needs is the Baby Care Center. This cheery site, equipped with changing tables and facilities for nursing mothers, is located next to the Crystal Palace restaurant. Disposable diapers are for sale at many Magic Kingdom shops (they're kept behind the counter, just ask). All park restrooms are equipped with changing facilities.

CAMERA NEEDS

The Camera Center in the Town Square Exposition Hall proffers memory cards and disposable cameras, plus film and batteries. It's also possible to make 4-by-6-inch prints and transfer images from your media card to a CD. Film is sold in many Magic Kingdom shops, but cannot be developed in the park.

DISABILITY INFORMATION

Most Magic Kingdom shops and restaurants, and many attractions, are accessible to guests using wheelchairs. Additional services are available for guests with visual or hearing disabilities. The *Guidebook for Guests with Disabilities* provides an overview of all services available, including transportation, parking, and attraction access. For more information, see the "Travelers with Disabilities" section of the *Getting Ready to Go* chapter.

FERRY VERSUS MONORAIL

For guests arriving by car or bus, it's necessary to decide whether to travel to the Magic Kingdom by ferry or monorail. The monorail makes the trip from the Transportation and Ticket Center (TTC) in about five minutes while the ferry takes about seven. During busy seasons, the ferry will often get you there faster (long lines can form at the monorail, and most people don't make the short walk to the

ferry landing). Vacationers who use wheelchairs should note that while the monorail platforms are accessible, the ramp leading to the boarding area is a bit on the steep side.

FIRST AID

A registered nurse tends to minor medical problems at the First Aid Center, located near the Crystal Palace restaurant.

INFORMATION

City Hall, just inside the park entrance, serves as the Magic Kingdom's information headquarters. Guest Relations representatives can answer questions. Guidemaps and Times Guides, updated weekly (including details about entertainment, as well as character greeting times and locations), are available here, and all kinds of arrangements can be made, including reservations for restaurants. Should you have problems with your ticket or a question about the number of unused days remaining on a ticket, City Hall is the place to go.

LOCKERS

Attended lockers are located just inside the park entrance, all the way to the right. Lockers are also available at the Transportation and Ticket Center (TTC). Cost is $5 per day (plus a $2 refundable deposit) for unlimited use. If you "hop" to another park on the same day, you don't have to pay to get another locker. Simply present your receipt to the attendant and you're all set.

LOST & FOUND

On the day of your visit, report lost articles at City Hall or at the TTC. Recovered items can also be claimed at these locations. After your visit, call 407-824-4245.

Hot Tip!

Certain attractions keep shorter hours than the Magic Kingdom itself (i.e., The Hall of Presidents and Tom Sawyer Island). To make sure you catch all your favorites, check a Times Guide when you enter the park.

Pal Mickey

He may look like just another plush toy, but Pal Mickey is a bit out of the ordinary. He's actually a high-tech theme park tour guide and companion. As guests stroll through the parks, Mickey shares helpful park-related advice, tells jokes and Disney fun facts, and plays games.

He can be purchased in select shops at all four Disney theme parks, at Walt Disney World–owned-and-operated resorts, and at the Once Upon a Toy shop at the Downtown Disney Marketplace.

LOST CHILDREN

Report lost children at City Hall or the Baby Care Center, and alert the nearest Disney employee to the problem.

MONEY MATTERS

The Magic Kingdom has four Automated Teller machines (ATMs): near the locker rental site just inside the entrance, inside City Hall on Main Street, U.S.A., near the Frontier Shootin' Arcade, and at the Tomorrowland Light & Power Co. arcade (next to Space Mountain). Most foreign currency can be exchanged at City Hall.

Credit cards (American Express, Visa, MasterCard, JCB, Discover Card, Diner's Club, Disney gift cards, and the Disney Visa card) are accepted as payment for admission, merchandise, and meals at all full-service restaurants and fast-food locations. Traveler's checks and Walt Disney World resort ID cards are also accepted in most places. Some food and souvenir carts accept cash only.

Disney Dollars are available at City Hall (as well as all Disney Stores) in $1, $5, and $10 denominations. They are accepted for dining and merchandise throughout Walt Disney World and can be exchanged at any time for U.S. currency.

PACKAGE PICKUP

Individual shops can arrange for purchases of any size to be transported to The Gallery, on Main Street, next to City Hall, for pickup between noon and park closing time (at least three hours after purchase). Packages may be sent to Disney resorts, too. The delivery service is free.

SAME-DAY RE-ENTRY

Be sure to retain your ticket if you plan to return later the same day. A hand stamp is no longer required for re-entry.

STROLLERS & WHEELCHAIRS

Wheelchair Rental, located just inside the turnstiles, all the way to the right, offers wheelchairs (some oversized) and Electric Convenience Vehicles (ECVs). Strollers are available under the Main Street Train Station. The cost for strollers and wheelchairs is $10 per day; $35 for ECVs, with a $5 refundable deposit. Quantities are limited. Hold onto your receipt; it can be used on the same day to get a replacement stroller or wheelchair at any of the theme parks. Multi-day rentals, called Length of Stay tickets, save you two dollars off the daily price. Keep your receipt handy.

Note that during busy times, the park may offer "stroller express" service. Guests prepay for a stroller before passing through the turnstiles and bypass the line once inside.

To prevent your stroller from getting lost in a sea of stroller clones, consider personalizing it with an item such as a ribbon or a balloon.

SECURITY CHECK

Guests entering Disney theme parks are subject to a security check. Backpacks, parcels, purses, etc., will be searched by Disney security personnel before guests are permitted to pass through the turnstiles.

TIP BOARDS

Located at the end of Main Street, U.S.A., closest to Cinderella Castle, the Tip Board is an excellent source of information on waiting times for attractions, as well as showtimes and other entertainment information. The board is often overseen by a park-savvy employee, ready and willing to answer guest questions.

Admission Prices

ONE-DAY BASE TICKET
(Restricted to use only in the Magic Kingdom. **Prices do not include sales tax and are likely to change in 2007.**)
Adult $63
Child* $52
*3 through 9 years of age; children under 3 free

Main Street, U.S.A.

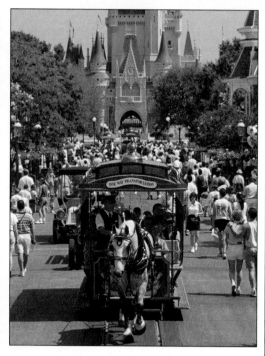

Stepping onto Main Street, U.S.A., is like jumping through a time portal. Welcome to turn-of-the-20th-century America! Horse-drawn trolleys are the transportation of choice, peppy patriotic music underscores the bustle of merry, moving masses, and the tantalizing aroma of fresh-baked cookies constantly perfumes the air.

A rose-colored retrospective? Maybe. But this is Disney's version of a small-town Main Street—and the charm of this nostalgic land is lost on no one. Anchored by an old-fashioned train station at one end and a fairy-tale castle at the other, Main Street, U.S.A., whisks you from reality to fantasy in a few short blocks.

All of the addresses here feature just-dried coats of paint, curlicued gingerbread moldings, and pretty details. Add to that the baskets of hanging plants and genuine-looking gaslights, and Main Street, U.S.A., becomes a true showplace—both in the bright light of high noon and after nightfall, when the tiny lights edging all of the rooflines are flicked on.

The street represents an ideal American town. Although such a town never really existed, many claim to have served as the inspiration for it. Chances are Walt Disney got the idea from Marceline, Missouri, the tiny rural town that was his boyhood home.

Most of the structures along the thoroughfare are given over to shops, and each one is different. Some emporiums are big and bustling, others are relatively quiet and orderly; some are spacious and airy, others are cozy and dark. Inside and out, maintenance and housekeeping are superb.

Hot Tip!

Plan to do your shopping in the early afternoon, rather than at day's end when the Main Street shops are normally jammed.

White-suited sanitation workers patrol the street to pick up litter and quickly shovel up any evidence of the horses that pull the trolley cars from Town Square to the Hub. As in the rest of the Magic Kingdom, the pavement here is washed down every night with hoses. There's one crew of maintenance workers whose sole job is to change the little white lights around the roofs; another crew devotes itself to keeping the woodwork painted. As soon as these people have worked their way as far as the Hub, they start all over again at Town Square. The greenish, horse-shaped, cast-iron hitching posts are repainted 20 times a year on average—and totally scraped down each time.

The "attractions" along Main Street, U.S.A., are relatively minor compared to the really big deals such as Tomorrowland's Space Mountain, Frontierland's Splash Mountain, or The Haunted Mansion in Liberty Square. But each and every shop has its own quota of merchandise that is meant as much for show as for sale. It's almost as entertaining to watch the cooks stir up gooey batches of fudge or peanut brittle at the Main Street Confectionery as it is to actually savor a sweet sample. The shop windows, particularly at the Emporium, are also worth a look.

Once you start to meander along Main Street, be sure to notice the names on the second-story windows. Above the Uptown Jewelers store (near the Confectionery) is that of Walt's nephew, Roy E. Disney. And you'll see Walt's name above the ice cream parlor. Other names are those of people connected with The Walt Disney Company.

Note: Attractions in Main Street, U.S.A., are described in the order in which they are encountered upon entering the park.

WALT DISNEY WORLD RAILROAD: The best introduction to the Magic Kingdom, the 1½-mile journey on this rail line is as much a must for the first-time visitor as it is for railroad buffs. It offers an excellent orientation as it passes by most of the park's major lands.

The 1928 steam engine happens to be exactly the same age as Mickey Mouse. Walt Disney himself was a railroad aficionado. During the early years of television, viewers watched films of him circling his own backyard in a one-eighth-scale train, the *Lilly Belle* (named for his wife).

The Walt Disney World Railroad also has a *Lilly Belle* among its quartet of locomotives. The others are named *Roy O. Disney*, *Walter E. Disney*, and *Roger E. Broggie* (a Disney Imagineer who shared Walt Disney's enthusiasm for antique trains). All of them were built in the U.S. around the turn of the century and later taken to Mexico to haul freight and passengers in the Yucatán, where Disney scouts found them in 1969. The United Railways of Yucatán was using them to carry sugarcane. Brought north once again, they were completely overhauled, and even the smallest of parts were reworked or replaced.

The train circles the park in 20 minutes, making stops in Frontierland, Mickey's Toontown Fair, and Main Street, U.S.A. Trains arrive in each station every 4 to 10 minutes. The line is usually shortest in Toontown, but there's rarely a long wait at any of the stations. The train is the most efficient way to reach the exit when parades take over Main Street, U.S.A.

Note: The Walt Disney World Railroad does not run during fireworks presentations.

MAIN STREET VEHICLES: A number of these can be seen traveling up and down Main Street—horseless carriages and jitneys patterned after turn-of-the-century vehicles (but fitted with Jeep transmissions and special mufflers that make a putt-putt-putting sound); a spiffy scarlet fire engine; and a troop of trolleys drawn by Belgians and Percherons, two strong breeds of horse that once pulled plows in Europe. These animals—weighing in at about a ton each and shod with plastic (easier on their hooves)—pull the trolley the length of Main Street about two dozen times during each of their working days. Between shifts, they can be seen resting inside Main Street's Car Barn. Feel free to stop by and say hello. At day's end they go home to their barn at Fort Wilderness (where you can also visit them). The horses are sometimes hosed down next to the Main Street firehouse. Youngsters love to watch.

TOWN SQUARE EXPOSITION HALL: A veritable shrine to photography, Town Square Exposition Hall does double duty as a museum and camera-supply shop. Exhibits take guests on a voyage through time, connecting the high-tech cameras of today with their primitive cousins of yesteryear. The humble beginnings of Mickey Mouse are celebrated here, too. *Steamboat Willie* and other classic Mickey toons (previously shown at the Main Street Cinema) are screened throughout the day.

Be sure to take your own camera to the Exposition Hall—photo opportunities abound. You can also pay to have your image superimposed on a Disney background. Don't forget to say "cheese."

Adventureland

ADVENTURELAND

Adventureland seems to have even more atmosphere than the other lands. That may be a result of its neat separation from the rest of the Magic Kingdom by the bridge over Main Street on one end and by a gallery-like structure (where it merges with Frontierland) on the other, or, possibly, it's because of the abundance of landscaping.

The centrally located attraction, The Magic Carpets of Aladdin, sets the tone for this corner of the Kingdom. Still surrounded by tropical splendor, the area has the look and feel of a bustling marketplace—the likes of which one might stumble upon in Agrabah. The shops here offer imports from around the globe.

As guests stroll away from Main Street, U.S.A., they just may hear the sound of beating drums, the squawks of parrots, and the regular boom of a cannon. Paces quicken. And the wonders soon to be encountered do not disappoint.

SWISS FAMILY TREEHOUSE: "Everything we need is right at our fingertips," said the father in Disney's 1960 rendition of the classic story *Swiss Family Robinson*. He was describing the treehouse that he and his kids built for the family after their ship was wrecked in a storm. When given a chance—several adventures later—to leave the island, all but one son decided to stay on. That decision is not hard to understand after a tour of the Magic Kingdom's version of the Robinsons' banyan-tree home. This is everybody's idea of the perfect treehouse, with its many levels and comforts—patchwork quilts, lovely mahogany furniture, candles stuck in abalone shells, even running water in every room. (The system is rather ingenious.)

The Spanish moss draping the branches is real; the tree itself—unofficially christened *Disneyodendron eximus*, a genus that is translated roughly as "out-of-the-ordinary Disney tree"—was constructed entirely by the props department. Some statistics: The roots, which are made of concrete, poke 42 feet into the ground, and about 300,000 lifelike polyethylene leaves "grow" on the tree's 1,400 individual branches.

JUNGLE CRUISE: [FP] Inspired in part by the 1955 documentary film *The African Lion*, this ten-minute adventure is one of the crowning achievements of Magic Kingdom landscape artists for the way it takes guests through

> ## Hot Tip!
> During non-peak seasons, Jungle Cruise may open one hour *after* the rest of the Magic Kingdom opens for the day.

surroundings as diverse as a Southeast Asian jungle, the Nile Valley, and an Amazon rain forest. Along the way, passengers encounter zebras, giraffes, lions, headhunters, and more (all of the Audio-Animatronics variety); they also see elephants bathing and tour a temple—while listening to an amusing, though corny, spiel delivered by the skipper. (Bet you didn't know that Schweitzer Falls was named after the famous doctor Albert . . . Falls.)

This adventure, which is best enjoyed by daylight, is one of the park's slower-moving attractions, and tends to be quite crowded from late morning until late afternoon.

THE ENCHANTED TIKI ROOM—UNDER NEW MANAGEMENT: Though cherished for its historical significance (the Tiki Birds starred in the first Audio-Animatronics attraction ever), the Tiki show was growing a bit tiresome. Now, thanks to clever new costars and zippy new tunes, the Tiki Room is rockin' once again.

The nine-minute show still features Michael, Pierre, Fritz, and José (who is pining for his beloved Rosita)—plus some 200 birds, flowers, and tiki statues singing up a tropical storm. But before long, their sweet serenade is interrupted by an unimpressed Iago (Jafar's partner in crime from *Aladdin*).

It seems that Iago, along with Zazu from *The Lion King*, is a new owner of the Tiki Room—and he has big changes in store for the show. In a fractured version of "Friend Like Me," the bratty Iago warns the Tiki Birds that they'd "better get hip, or the audience will disappear." In a welcome twist, it is Iago who disappears, leaving the Tikis to prove just how hip they are. While it helps to have seen the old show to appreciate all of the silly humor, even first-time guests manage to get at least a mild kick out of The Enchanted Tiki Room—Under New Management.

THE MAGIC CARPETS OF ALADDIN: Welcome to Agrabah! Adventureland's newest attraction is conveniently situated in the center of the action. It features not one, but 16 carpets that fly through the air in a fashion similar to those airborne elephants over in Fantasyland. Each flying carpet

accommodates four guests at a time. Depending on where you sit, you'll have control of the carpet's vertical movement (the controls are in the front). Be prepared to dodge the occasional stream of liquid, courtesy of an expectorating camel.

PIRATES OF THE CARIBBEAN: Quite simply, this is one of the very best of the Magic Kingdom's classic adventures. The beloved ten-minute cruise is a Disneyland original, added to Walt Disney World's Magic Kingdom (in slightly revised form) due to popular demand. Here, guests board a small boat and set sail for a series of scenes showing a pirate raid on a Caribbean island town, dodging cannon fire and weathering one small, though legitimate, watery dip along the way. There are singing marauders, plastered pigs, and wily wenches; the observant may note a couple of new rapscallion residents. Yep, that beloved scallywag Captain Jack Sparrow has dropped anchor here, as has his nefarious nemesis Captain Barbossa.

While it's by no means the most politically correct attraction on-property (far from it, actually), the rendition of "Yo Ho, Yo Ho, a Pirate's Life for Me"—the attraction's theme song—makes what is actually a rather brutal scenario into something that comes across as good fun.

Before entering the queue area, stop and give a nod to the parrot dressed as a pirate, near the Pirates of the Caribbean sign. And, yes, this is the attraction that inspired the movie.

Frontierland

With the Rivers of America lapping at its borders and Big Thunder Mountain rising up in the rear, this re-creation of the American Frontier encompasses the area from New England to the Southwest, from the 1770s to the 1880s. In these parts, shops, restaurants, and attractions have unpainted barn siding or stone or clapboard walls, and outside there are several wooden sidewalks of the sort Marshal Matt Dillon used to stride along. The Walt Disney World Railroad makes a stop here.

FRONTIERLAND SHOOTIN' ARCADE: This modest arcade is set in an 1850s town in the Southwest Territory. Positions overlook Boothill, a town complete with bank, jail, hotel, and cemetery.

Genuine Hawkins .54-caliber buffalo rifles have been refitted, and when the infrared beam strikes any of the targets, an interesting result is triggered. Struck tombstones rise, sink, spin, or change their epitaphs; hit a cloud and a ghost rider gallops across the sky; a bull's-eye on a grave digger's shovel causes a skull to pop out of the grave. Sound effects—howling coyotes, creaking bridges, and shooting guns—are created by a digital audio system.

There is an additional charge to play here (Usually about 50 cents).

COUNTRY BEAR JAMBOREE: The Country Bears may never make it to Broadway, but they don't seem to mind. Disney's brood of banjo-strummin' bruins has been playing to packed houses in Grizzly Hall for more than a quarter century. Judging by all the toe tappin' and hand clappin' that accompany each performance, the show remains a countrified crowd-pleaser. As for the few folks who aren't charmed by the backwoods ballads and down-home humor, well, they just have to grin and *bear* it.

As guests are settling into their seats (all of which provide a decent view), Buff, Max, and Melvin are beginning to grumble. Despite their status as permanent fixtures in the theater, the mounted animal heads would rather not "hang around all day" waiting for the show to get going. The 17-minute review opens with a rousing ditty by the Five Bear Rugs. The wheels set in motion, the remaining songs come fast and furious. Together, they capture the spirit of a genre that has a tendency to celebrate and lampoon itself simultaneously.

For example, Bunny, Bubbles, and Beulah bemoan "All the Guys That Turn Me On Turn Me Down"; Henry, the easy-going emcee who sports a coonskin cap (still attached to the 'coon), belts out "The Ballad of Davy Crockett"; and Big Al, the oversize tone-deaf fan-favorite, woefully croons "Blood on the Saddle," much to the delight of the giggle-prone audience.

The bears present a special Christmas concert during the holiday season.

Timing Tip: This attraction opens at 10 A.M. each day, even when the rest of the park opens earlier in the morning.

TOM SAWYER ISLAND: This patch of land in the middle of the Rivers of America has hills to scramble up; a working windmill, Harper's Mill, with an owl in the rafters and a perpetually creaky waterwheel; and a few pitch-black caves. To reach the island, guests take a raft across the river. (It's the only way to get there and back.)

Paths wind this way and that, and it's easy to get disoriented. Keep an eye out for mounted maps scattered about the island.

There are two bridges here—a suspension bridge and a barrel bridge, which floats atop some lashed-together wooden barrels. When one person bounces, everybody lurches—and all but the most chickenhearted laugh. Both of the bridges are easy to miss, so be sure to keep your eyes peeled.

Across the suspension bridge is Fort Langhorn. Poke around and you'll discover a twisting, dark, and occasionally scary escape tunnel. Walk along the pathway on the banks of the Rivers of America and you'll find your way back to the bridges.

The whole island seems as rugged as backwoods Missouri, and probably as a result, it actually feels a lot more remote than it is—enough to be able to provide some welcome respite from the bustle.

One particularly pleasant way to relax here is at a waterside table. It's sometimes possible to buy a snack—and you are always welcome to bring your own. Restrooms are beside the main raft landing and inside Fort Langhorn.

Timing Tip: This attraction closes at dusk.

BIRNBAUM'S BEST **SPLASH MOUNTAIN:** FP On the day this attraction made its official 1992 Walt Disney World debut, *everyone* got soaked—thanks in part to a particularly potent Florida rain cloud. But the rain wasn't entirely responsible for the sea of soggy Magic Kingdom guests. The five-story drop into an aqueous briar patch was. And a steady stream of thrill seekers has been taking the plunge ever since.

In this guaranteed smile inducer, guests enjoy a waterborne journey through brightly colored swamps and bayous, and down waterfalls, and are finally hurtled from the peak of the mountain to a briar-laced pond five stories below.

Hot Tip!
If you'd like to get soaked on Splash Mountain, request a seat up front.

Splash Mountain is based on the animated sequences in Walt Disney's 1946 film *Song of the South*. The scenery entertains as the story line follows Br'er Rabbit as he tries to reach his "laughin' place." It's tough for a first-time rider to take in all the details, since the tension of waiting for the big drop is all-consuming.

It is a bit terrifying at the top, but once back on the ground, it seems most riders can't wait

for another trip—even though they may get drenched. (Water-wary guests are often seen wearing rain ponchos on this attraction. On the other hand, if you *want* to get wet, try to sit up front or on the right; seats in the back receive a smaller splash.)

By the second or third time around, it's possible to relax a bit, enjoy the interior scenes, and take in the spectacular views of the Magic Kingdom from the top of the mountain. At this point you may even manage to keep your eyes open for the duration of the final fall—or at least part of it.

Splash Mountain's designers not only borrowed characters and color-saturated settings from *Song of the South*, but also used quite a bit of the film's Academy Award–winning music in this attraction. As a matter of fact, the song in Splash Mountain's final scene, "Zip-a-Dee-Doo-Dah," has become something of a Disney anthem over the years.

Note: You must be at least 40 inches tall to ride Splash Mountain. (There is a small play area nearby to keep little ones occupied while older kids ride.) If you'd like to absorb as little precipitation as possible, sit on the left side of the log.

 BIG THUNDER MOUNTAIN RAILROAD: FP It's certainly not hard to spot Big Thunder, the lone red rock formation this side of the Mississippi. Even newcomers to the Magic Kingdom will be able to distinguish the landmark from its famed counterparts—Splash and Space mountains—because it's the only one that actually looks like a mountain range. The designers took Utah's Bryce Canyon as inspiration, and the resemblance is remarkable.

According to Disney legend, the 2.5-acre mountain is chock-full of gold. Unfortunately for the residents of Tumbleweed, the local mining town, a flood has ruined any chance of uncovering the remaining gold. Before these prospectors find drier land, they are having one last party at the saloon to celebrate their riches. Even though in danger of washing away, they don't seem too worried, and guests who decide to take a trip on the Big Thunder Mountain Railroad have nothing to worry about either.

As passengers board the 15-row train, they are advised to "hang on to your hats and glasses 'cause this here's the wildest ride in the wilderness." Do heed the warning, but don't despair. The ride, though thrilling, is relatively tame, so relax and enjoy the sights.

Note that passengers seated nearest the caboose experience more turbulence than those up front.

A bleating billy goat atop a peak, a family of opossums hanging overhead, and a dark cavern full of bats, not to mention chickens, donkeys, and washed-up miners, can be spotted along the way. Be sure to keep an eye out for the not-yet-sunken saloon—it's easy to miss the first time around.

A continuous string of curves and dips around Big Thunder's pinnacles and caverns is sure to please thrill seekers of all ages, but the adrenaline surge is caused by more than just the speed of the trip. The added sound of a rickety track, a steam whistle that blows right before the train accelerates into a curve, and an unexpected earthquake all compound the passengers' anticipation, making this attraction one of the Magic Kingdom's most popular. Note that you must be at least 40 inches tall and immune to motion sickness to experience the Big Thunder Mountain Railroad attraction.

Timing Tip: Plan to visit early in the morning, during a parade, or just before closing time. Of course, you can always plan ahead and get a Fastpass. If you will be visiting during a parade, consider taking the Walt Disney World Railroad to the Frontierland station. The train circumvents much of the parade congestion.

Liberty Square

The transition between Frontierland on one side and Fantasyland on the other is so smooth that it's hard to say just when you arrive at Liberty Square, yet ultimately there's no mistaking the location. The small buildings are clapboard or brick and topped with weather vanes; the decorative moldings are Federal or Georgian in style; the glass is sometimes wavy, and there are flower boxes in shop windows, brightly colored gardens, neatly trimmed borders of Japanese yew, and masses of azaleas in a number of varieties and shades of white, pink, and red. There's a bounty of shops; plus two of the park's most famous attractions, The Haunted Mansion and The Hall of Presidents; and the Liberty Tree Tavern, one of the few full-service restaurants in the Magic Kingdom.

THE HALL OF PRESIDENTS: This classic is long on patriotism and short on silliness. But the detail of this classic 20-minute show is fascinating. After a film (which is presented on a sweeping 70-mm screen) discusses the importance of the Constitution from the time of its framing through the dawn of the space age, the curtain goes up, revealing a cast of American leaders. All of the chief executives are represented by Audio-Animatronics likenesses. (A small portion of the show was held over from the Disney-designed Illinois Pavilion's exhibition Great Moments with Mr. Lincoln, from New York's 1964–65 World's Fair.)

All of the chief executives are announced in a roll call, and each President responds with a nod; careful observers will note the others swaying and nodding, fidgeting, and whispering to each other during the proceedings.

Costumes were created by two famous film tailors coaxed out of retirement. Not only are the styles those of the period in which each president lived but so are the tailoring techniques and the fabrics. Some had to be specially woven for the show. Each of the Audio-Animatronics figures has at least one change of clothes—jewelry, shoes, hair texture, and even George Washington's chair are re-created exactly as indicated by careful research of paintings, diaries, newspapers, and government archives. Perceptive viewers should be able to see the braces on Franklin Delano Roosevelt's legs. The effect is so lifelike that the figures look almost real, even at very close range.

Timing Tip: Planning to visit the Presidents? This attraction opens at 10 A.M., even when the rest of the park opens earlier. The show usually starts on the hour and half hour.

LIBERTY SQUARE RIVERBOAT: The *Liberty Square*, built in dry dock at Walt Disney World, is a real steamboat. Its boiler turns water into steam, which is then piped to the engine, which drives the paddle wheel that propels the boat. It is not the real article in one respect, however: It moves through the nine-foot-deep

Rivers of America on an underwater rail.

The pleasant ride, with narration by an actor playing Mark Twain, is a good way to beat the heat on steamy afternoons. En route, a variety of props create a sort of Wild West effect: moose, deer, a burning cabin, and the like. The tour is completed within 17 minutes.

BIRNBAUM'S ★BEST **THE HAUNTED MANSION:** FP This eight-minute experience is among the Magic Kingdom's most enjoyable. However, guests who expect to be scared silly when they enter the big old house, modeled after those built in New York's Hudson River Valley in the 18th century, will be just a tad unfulfilled. This haunted house steers clear of anything too terrifying, and a good-spirited voice-over keeps the mood light.

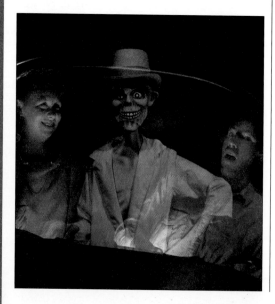

Once you're inside the portrait hall, entered after passing through the front doors, it's amusing to speculate: Is the ceiling moving up, or is the floor dropping? It's also where you meet your "Ghost Host" and learn how he met his untimely demise.

The spooky journey through the mansion takes place in a "Doom Buggy." The attraction is full of tricks and treats for the eyes; just when you think you've seen it all, there's something new: bats' eyes on the wallpaper, a suit of armor that comes alive, a terrified cemetery watchman and his mangy mutt, and the image of a creepy lady in a crystal ball.

One of the biggest jobs of the maintenance crews here is not cleaning up, but keeping things dirty. The mansion is littered with some 200 trunks, chairs, dress forms, harps, rugs, and assorted knickknacks and requires a lot of dust. Local legend has it that enough dust has been used since the park's 1971 opening to bury the mansion. (Which begs the questions: Where did it all go? And where did it all come from?) Cobwebs are bought in liquid form and strung up by a secret process.

When waiting to enter, take note of the amusing inscriptions on the tombstones in the overgrown cemetery. On the way out, take a moment to pay your respects at the pet cemetery.

WOODY & FRIENDS AT THE DIAMOND HORSESHOE: The Diamond Horseshoe Saloon is now the site of the rootin-tootin-est character greeting the Wild West has to offer. Stop here to interact with Disney characters such as Woody, Jessie, Bullseye, and others. Don't forget your cameras and autograph books. Yee-ha!

Fantasyland

Walt Disney called this a "timeless land of enchantment," and his successors termed it "the happiest land of all"—and it is, for some. It is the home of a number of rides that are particularly well liked by children.

CINDERELLA CASTLE: Just as Mickey stands for all the merriment in Walt Disney World, this storybook castle represents the hopes and dreams of childhood—a time in life when anything is possible.

At a height of about 190 feet, Cinderella Castle is nearly twice the height of Disneyland's Sleeping Beauty Castle. For inspiration, Disney Imagineers looked to the famous palaces of Charles Perrault's France, still showplaces of Europe. Their design took the form of a romanticized composite of such courts as Fontainbleu, Versailles, and a dozen famed chateaux of the Loire valley. Of course, they also turned to the original designs for the fairy tale castle in Disney's 1950 classic, *Cinderella*.

Unlike real European castles, this one is made of steel and fiberglass; in lieu of dungeons, it has service tunnels. Its upper reaches contain security rooms; there's even an apartment originally meant for the Disney family (but never occupied). From any

vantage point, Cinderella Castle looks as if it came straight from the land of make-believe.

Mosaic Murals: The elaborate murals beneath the castle's archway rank among the true wonders of the World. They tell the story of the little cinder girl and one of childhood's happiest happily-ever-afters, using a million bits of glass in some 500 different colors, plus real silver and 14-karat gold.

Cinderella Wishing Well: This pleasant alcove, nestled along a path to Tomorrowland, is a nice spot from which to gaze at the castle. Any coins tossed into the water are donated to children's charities. Don't forget to make a wish as you part with your penny.

CINDERELLA'S GOLDEN CARROUSEL: Not everything in the Magic Kingdom is a Disney version of the real article. This carrousel, discovered at the now-defunct Olympic Park in Maplewood, New Jersey, was built back in 1917. That was the end of the golden century of carousel building, which began around 1825. During the Disney refurbishing, many of the original horses were replaced with horses made of fiberglass.

FAIRYTALE GARDEN: This special little corner of the Kingdom is tucked beside Cinderella Castle. Several times a day, Belle (from *Beauty and the Beast*) stops by to read a story and, afterward, mingle with guests. There is seating for about 20 at a time. Check a park Times Guide for showtimes.

BIRNBAUM'S ★BEST★ MICKEY'S PHILHARMAGIC: FP Mickey Mouse and a panoply of his pals (including Donald, Simba, and Ariel) strut their musical stuff in this ear- and eye-popping production.

The show, which marked its debut in late 2003, is an ambitious amalgam of music, special effects, and animated film. Of course, this being Fantasyland, the film is by no means ordinary. It's crisp, colorful, and to the delight of many a goggle-wearing guest, three-dimensional. The 3-D experience unfolds on a 150-foot-wide canvas, which is one of the largest screens ever created for a film of this kind. Special effects and surprises take place off-screen, too. Overall, the experience is intended to engage guests of any age.

MAGIC KINGDOM

The show is presented in the PhilharMagic Concert Hall, the venue that once hosted the Mickey Mouse Revue (a musical romp that ran from 1971 through 1980) and, more recently, The Legend of the Lion King. (*Lion King* devotees can get their fill by taking in the Festival of the Lion King stage show at Disney's Animal Kingdom park.)

As with many attractions, there may be occasional moments of darkness. If you're unsure as to whether your child might find this (or any attraction) unsettling, express your concern to an attendant. They'll help you make the right decision.

BIRNBAUM'S ★BEST★

PETER PAN'S FLIGHT: FP "Come on, everybody, here we go!" So says Peter Pan at the start of this nonstop flight to Never Land. The three-minute adventure, which takes you soaring in a pirate ship, fancifully retells the story of Peter Pan—a boy with a knack for flying and an immunity to maturity. The effects in this classic Fantasyland attraction are simple, but enchanting.

The journey starts in the Darling family nursery—which siblings Wendy, Michael, and John quickly abandon to follow Peter Pan on a trip to his homeland. As in Disney's animated feature, one of the most beautiful scenes—and one that makes this attraction a treat for grown-ups as well as smaller folk—is the sight of nighttime London, dark blue and speckled with twinkling lights. Keep your eyes peeled for Big Ben and London Bridge.

By the time you spot your first mermaid, you're deep in the heart of Never Land. Alas, something is terribly wrong—Captain Hook and his buccaneer buddies have taken the Darling kids captive. It's all really a trap for Peter (Hook is still peeved at Pan for serving his hand to a hungry crocodile). Does everyone live happily ever after? We'll *never* tell.

Timing Tip: The slow-moving lines for this popular attraction can be somewhat daunting. Take advantage of the Fastpass option. Or plan to arrive close to when the park opens, late in the evening, or during any of the parades throughout the day.

Hot Tip!

Toddlers love to splash in the fountains near Ariel's Grotto (in Fantasyland) and Donald's Boat (in Toontown). Waterproof diapers are an absolute must.

IT'S A SMALL WORLD: *Hola! Guten Tag! Hello!* No matter what language you speak, what you look like, or where you live, you still have a lot in common with folks the world over (including an especially high tolerance for a singsong melody that repeatedly reminds us that it's a small world, after all). That's the message driving this ten-minute boat ride around the world.

Originally created for New York's 1964–65 World's Fair, the attraction is an oldie-but-goodie (and is quite popular with young children). The ride moves at slightly swifter than snail's pace, drifting past hundreds of colorfully costumed dolls from around the world—all of whom know all the words to the ride's infectious theme song.

PHOTO BY JILL SAFRO

A showcase of diversity, the attraction is a simple celebration of human similarities. It's also a relaxing alternative to many of the park's higher-tech, longer-line attractions. (This attraction underwent a massive refurbishment in 2005. Even if you've done it to death, it's worth revisiting!)

DUMBO THE FLYING ELEPHANT: This is purely and simply a kiddie ride, though children of all ages have admitted to loving it. A beloved symbol of Fantasyland, the ride is most popular with the 2-to-7-year-old set. Inspired by the 1941 film classic *Dumbo*, the attraction lasts two memorable minutes. Consider stopping here first thing in the morning, or during the afternoon parade, when the line—which is often prohibitively long—thins a bit. Incidentally, the rodent in the center of the circle of flying elephants is Dumbo's faithful sidekick, Timothy Mouse.

MAD TEA PARTY: The theme of this two-minute ride—in a group of oversize pastel-colored teacups that whirl and spin wildly—

Hot Tip!

Many of the Fantasyland attractions are dark, and in some cases, special effects may be too intense for small children.

was inspired by a scene in the Disney Studios' 1951 movie production of Lewis Carroll's novel *Alice in Wonderland*. During the sequence in question, the Mad Hatter hosts a tea party for his un-birthday.

Unlike many rides in Fantasyland, this is not just for younger kids; the 9-to-20 crowd seems to like it best. Keep in mind that when the cups stop spinning, your head may continue to do so. Skip this ride if you suffer from motion sickness or if you've recently enjoyed a snack. Don't miss the woozy mouse that pops out of the teapot at the center of the platform—he ignored our advice.

BIRNBAUM'S BEST

THE MANY ADVENTURES OF WINNIE THE POOH: FP Perhaps as a tribute to the mischievous Mr. Toad, the host of the attraction previously housed here, everyone's favorite honey-lovin' cub treats Magic Kingdom guests to a wild and whimsical 3½-minute tour of his home turf.

The attraction features a most unlikely form of transportation: honey pots! They whisk (and bounce) guests through the pages of a giant storybook and into the Hundred Acre Wood, where the weather's most blustery. The wind is really ruffling the feathers of one of the locals. It seems Owl's treehouse has been shaken loose and just may topple to the ground—and onto the honey pots below. Similar sight gags abound, from a bubble-blowing Heffalump (hey, this is Fantasyland) to a treacherous flood that threatens to sweep Tigger, Piglet, and the rest of the gang away.

When Pooh saves the day, it's time to cele-brate—and everyone is invited to the party.

Note that, like other Fantasyland attractions, some parts of The Many Adventures of Winnie the Pooh take place in the dark. Timid youngsters may find the dark a bit unsettling.

POOH'S PLAYFUL SPOT: A patch of the Hundred Acre Wood has sprung up in Fantasyland, just across the way from The Many Adventures of Winnie the Pooh. Geared toward young guests, this soft-surface play zone has logs to climb on, a treehouse to explore, plus honey pots, a slide, and more.

SNOW WHITE'S SCARY ADVENTURES: This three-minute attraction takes guests on a twisting, turning journey through a few happy moments and several scary scenes from the Grimm brothers' fairy tale, which Walt Disney made into the world's first full-length animated feature in 1937. Snow White makes several appearances, as do the seven Audio-Animatronics dwarfs. But the wicked witch—evil, long-nosed, and practically toothless—shows up more than once with a suddenness that startles some youngsters (particularly those under the age of 5).

Ariel's Grotto

The Little Mermaid's Ariel doesn't greet Magic Kingdom guests in the traditional way, since mermaids, like most fish, find it difficult to walk around theme parks. Instead, she invites folks of all ages to stop by her Fantasyland home away from home—a colorful grotto surrounded by starfish, coral, and waterfalls. Here, guests can meet and pose for a picture with the ever-popular Disney heroine (don't forget to take your camera). The area, which is very popular with little ones, also features a soft-surface play zone filled with squirting fountains. Note that the line to meet Ariel is often long enough to scare Ursula herself.

"Hooray!"

Mickey's Toontown Fair

The newest neighborhood in the Magic Kingdom was built with little visitors in mind. Not only do Mickey, Minnie, and their pals keep homes here, but the county fair is always in town. Tucked away behind Fantasyland, the area can be reached by a path from the Mad Tea Party or Space Mountain and via the Walt Disney World Railroad. Guests who arrive by stroller are advised to park their vehicles in the lot across from Pete's Garage. Keep in mind that traffic here is heaviest early in the day.

THE BARNSTORMER AT GOOFY'S WISEACRE FARM: At this mini-coaster attraction, guests of most sizes climb into crop dusters and follow the same fluky flight path taken by the Goof himself. The planes zip through the farm and crash through a barn, causing quite a ruckus among the chickens. Don't let the size fool you. This roller coaster proves that big thrills come in small packages. Although guests as young as three are allowed to ride, it may be too turbulent for some.

Explore Goofy's Wiseacre Farm before lining up for the ride. Cotton, tomatoes, and

other real crops have been spotted growing here. The observant may notice the unconventional parking spot that Goofy found for his plane. (Hint: Look up.) Guests must be at least 35 inches tall to ride.

DONALD'S BOAT: If you want to cool off a bit, stop at Donald Duck's boat, the *Miss Daisy*. The vessel has sprung so many leaks, it looks like a fountain. It's almost impossible to walk across the "duck pond" without getting squirted. The ship's sparse interior includes a captain's wheel and a whistle—pull it and water shoots out the top. Tykes love it.

MICKEY'S COUNTRY HOUSE: Don't bother knocking—the door is always open. Guests are welcome to peer inside each of the cottage's rooms: bedroom, living room, kitchen, and game room. The kitchen is being remodeled, but it's worth a peek (after which you'll vow never to hire Donald Duck and Goofy to redecorate your own home). As the game-room shows, the Mouse is quite an accomplished sportsman, dabbling in everything from Ping-Pong to football. (Is that a Heisman trophy on the shelf?!)

Despite all there is to see, one thing is conspicuously missing from Mickey Mouse's house . . . Mickey himself. Don't despair. The head judge of the county fair is in the Judge's Tent, where he greets guests all day long. (It's the best place to meet Mickey in all of Walt Disney

Hot Tip!

Toontown bustles with the most activity during the first half of the day. To avoid the biggest crowds, visit Mickey's country hideaway in the late afternoon or in the evening.

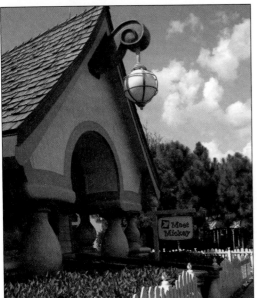

World.) To get there, slip out the back door of the house and follow the path toward the tent. (Others can exit through the garage, which packs some surprises of its own.) It's fun to check out the backyard, where Mickey's award-winning garden is bursting with giant vegetables, many of which have mouse ears. This is also the spot to look at Pluto's doghouse.

JUDGE'S TENT: A must for fans of the Mouse, this place is all Mickey all the time. The waiting area (and there is always a significant wait) features a pre-show video that highlights all of his county fair successes. All guests are treated to a private meeting with the star, so have those cameras ready! To get to the Judge's Tent, take a trip through Mickey's Country House. The line is usually shortest late in the day or during a parade.

TOONTOWN HALL OF FAME: Just beyond Cornelius Coot Commons and across from Goofy's Wiseacre Farm is the Toontown Hall of Fame. The big tent is stocked with Disney souvenirs as well as some of the prize-winning entries from the Toontown Fair. (Only the former are for sale.) Beyond this area, three different rooms offer guests the opportunity to meet Disney characters.

Hot Tip!
The line to meet Mickey in the Judge's Tent can be quite lengthy. It's usually shorter late in the day and during parades.

There is a separate line for each room, and characters vary throughout the day. One of the rooms is dedicated to Disney princesses, so fans can meet princesses whenever Mickey's Toontown Fair is open. Signs indicate which characters are on hand at any given moment. It's best to have cameras (and autograph books) ready before entering the area.

MINNIE'S COUNTRY HOUSE: Since Minnie and Mickey are neighbors here in the country, Minnie's house is merely a hop, skip, and a jump from Mickey's. Young kids love it here because the special toon furniture is meant for climbing. As they explore, guests may push a button to listen to her answering-machine messages, open the refrigerator (Minnie has cheese-chip ice cream in the freezer, which is actually chilly inside), and try in vain to snatch some chocolate chip cookies (it's a mirror trick, courtesy of Minnie herself).

The screen porch is full of some very special plants. Don't miss the palm tree (it's made of hands), the Tiger Lilies (feline faces), and the Twolips (no explanation necessary).

PETE'S GARAGE: This cleverly disguised restroom is the place to make a pit stop in Toontown. The toon vehicle, which is parked out front, makes for an excellent photo op.

TOON PARK: Centrally located, this covered green provides a nice respite from the sun (or the rain). There are shaded benches surrounding a spongy, toddler-friendly play area.

Tomorrowland

The original Tomorrowland attempted a serious look at the future. But as Disney planners discovered, it isn't easy to portray a future that persists in becoming the present. So the old Tomorrowland has given way to a friendlier, space-age town whose neighborhood atmosphere is more in keeping with the other lands in the Magic Kingdom. This is the future that never was, the fantasy world imagined by the science-fiction writers and moviemakers of the 1920s and '30s. It's a land of sky-piercing beacons and glistening metal, where shiny robots do the work, whisper-quiet cars glide along an elevated highway, and even time travel is possible.

Note: Tomorrowland attractions are described in the order that they are encountered upon entering the land from the Hub and heading (counterclockwise) away from Cinderella Castle.

STITCH'S GREAT ESCAPE!: **FP** Like its predecessor, the ExtraTERRORestrial Alien Encounter, this attraction features the adventures of a renegade alien. In this case, however, said extraterrestrial is more of a menace than a threat—not so much scary as ill-mannered and mischievous. The 20-minute show is a prequel to Lilo & Stitch, but one need not be familiar with the drooling, intergalactic imp to

Hot Tip!

Parents take note: This attraction is much less scary than The ExtraTERRORestrial Alien Encounter. Still, there are moments of darkness and Stitch's madcap shenanigans may be daunting to little ones.

follow the attraction's story line.

The action begins with a short pre-show, followed by the crowd spilling into a circular theater-type room. All chairs face center, where there's a mysterious tube. (Sit up straight when the shoulder harness is lowered—this will enhance the the effects and make for a less restraining experience.)

What's all the fuss about? Bad-boy Stitch, aka Experiment 626, is being moved to a prison processing center and you have been recruited to keep an eye on him. Up to the task? Chances are you're not: The little blue rascal manages to escape every time. And when he does, chaos ensues. This attraction tends to be best appreciated by younger park-goers.

Note: Some youngsters may be frightened by dark moments and loud noises. Also, shoulder restraints may spook claustrophobes. You must be at least 40 inches tall to enter.

BIRNBAUM'S BEST

BUZZ LIGHTYEAR'S SPACE RANGER SPIN: FP The Evil Emperor Zurg is up to no good. As soon as he swipes enough batteries to power his ultimate weapon of destruction—KERPLOOEY!—it's curtains for the toy universe as we know it. It's up to that Space Ranger extraordinaire Buzz Lightyear and his Junior Space Rangers (that means you) to save the day.

So goes the story line of Tomorrowland's video-game-inspired spin through toyland. The adventure is experienced from a toy's point of view. Guests begin their 4½-minute tour of duty as Space Rangers at Star Command Action Center. This is where Buzz gives his team a briefing on the mission that lies ahead. Then it's off to the Launch Bay to board the ride vehicles. The ships feature dual laser cannons, glowing lights, and a piloting joystick.

Once Junior Space Rangers blast off, they find themselves surrounded by Zurg's robots, who are mercilessly ripping batteries from toys. As Rangers fire at targets, beams of light fill the air. For every target hit, you will be rewarded with sight gags, sound effects, and points. The points, which are tallied automatically, are accumulated throughout the journey. Although the vehicles follow a rigid "flight" path (they're on a track), the joystick allows riders to maneuver the ships, arcing from side to side or spinning in circles while taking aim at your surroundings.

When the star cruiser arrives at Zurg's spaceship, it's showdown time. Will good prevail over evil? Or has time run out for the toy universe? And will you score enough points to be a Galactic Hero? Most people improve their scores with a little practice.

THE LAUGH FLOOR COMEDY CLUB: That Mike Wazowski is one enterprising eyeball. It seems the fuzzy fellow from *Monsters, Inc.* has plans to open a comedy club in early 2007. Why? Well, it seems his hometown is experiencing a bit of an energy crisis. Mike's plan is to tap into a decidedly alternative (not to mention free) fuel source to provide power for Monstropolis . . . laughter. But where can he gather enough giggles to fuel a whole city? In a 400-seat theater in Tomorrowland, that's where. To accomplish his goal, Monster of Ceremonies Mike has recruited a couple of cornball comedians. Their job is to make you laugh yourself silly. And they are not too proud to resort to slapstick while doing so. Expect to grin, grimace, and occasionally guffaw.

PHOTO BY JILL SAFRO

TOMORROWLAND TRANSIT AUTHORITY: Boarded near Astro Orbiter, these trains (known to purists as the WEDway PeopleMover) move at a speed of about seven miles per hour along almost a mile of track, beside or through most of the attractions in Tomorrowland. They are operated by a linear induction motor that has no moving parts, uses little power, and emits no pollution.

The peaceful, breezy excursion through Tomorrowland takes about ten minutes. There's rarely a wait to board. It's one of our favorites.

ASTRO ORBITER: Here, passengers fly around for two minutes in machine-age rockets designed to look more like oversize Buck Rogers toys than 21st-century space shuttles. Riders are surrounded by vibrantly colored, whirling planets as they get an astronaut's-eye view of Tomorrowland.

BIRNBAUM'S ★BEST★ SPACE MOUNTAIN: **FP** This attraction, which blasted onto the Magic Kingdom scene in 1975, is a can't-miss crowd-pleaser for throngs of thrill seekers. Rising to a height of more than 180 feet, this gleaming steel-and-concrete cone houses an attraction that most people call a roller coaster. It's the Disney version—a roller coaster and then some.

The 2-minute, 38-second ride takes place in an outer-space-like darkness that gets inkier and scarier as the journey progresses.

The rockets that roar through this blackness attain a maximum speed of just over 28 miles per hour—but somehow it feels much faster.

The Space Mountain experience is wild enough to send glasses, purses, wallets, and even an occasional set of false teeth plummeting to the bottom of the track, so be sure to find a safe place for your possessions before the ride starts. It's also turbulent enough to upset the stomachs of those so unwise as to ride it immediately after eating—but not so harrowing that knees shake for more than a minute or two after "touchdown." (Those who chicken out at the last minute have access to an exit.)

Note: Guests who are under 44 inches are not permitted to ride, and you must be in good health and free from heart conditions, motion sickness, back or neck problems, or other physical limitations to ride. Expectant mothers should skip the trip. Children under 7 must be accompanied by an adult.

TOMORROWLAND INDY SPEEDWAY:

Little cars that burn up the tracks at this attraction provide most of the background noise in Tomorrowland. Kids especially enjoy the herky-jerky driving experience.

The vehicles have rack-and-pinion steering and disc brakes, but unlike most cars, they run along a track. Yet, even expert drivers have trouble keeping them going in a straight line. (Don't panic when you notice the lack of a brake pedal—when you take your foot off the gas, the car comes to a quick, if not screeching, halt.) The one-lap tour of Tomorrowland takes about five minutes.

Note: You must be at least 52 inches tall to drive the cars by yourself. There is no height requirement to ride shotgun. Babies younger than 12 months may not ride.

WALT DISNEY'S CAROUSEL OF PROGRESS: First seen at New York's 1964–65 World's Fair and moved here in 1975, this 20-minute experience showcases the evolution of the American family and how life changed—and ostensibly progressed—with the advent of electricity. The hook here is that as a scene ends, the audience moves to the next one—not unlike a being on a carousel (hence the name of the attraction). This is a great place to escape the crowds and heat, not to mention take a much needed load off weary feet.

Shopping

No one travels all the way to the Magic Kingdom just to go shopping. But as many a first-time visitor has learned with some surprise, shopping is one of the most enjoyable pastimes here.

The Magic Kingdom's boutiques and stores stock much more than just Disneyana. Along with the more predictable items in Main Street shops, it's possible to find cookbooks and stoneware dishes, pirate hats and toy frontier rifles, 14-karat gold charms and filigreed costume jewelry. In Adventureland, shops boast many items imported from the exotic regions the area represents. Throughout the park, stores generally have merchandise that complements the themes of the various lands.

In some shops, you can watch people at work—a candy maker pouring peanut brittle in the Main Street Confectionery, a glassblower crafting wares in Main Street's Crystal Arts, and the like. And every store offers a selection of items, from the inexpensive to the not-so-inexpensive.

Finally, some advice. We recommend shopping in the early afternoon, rather than at the end of the day, when the shops are more crowded. However, keep in mind that Main Street shops do stay open a half hour after park closing, in case you need any last-minute gifts on the way out of the park. Also note that purchases may be stored for the day in lockers located near the park's entrance or, in the case of very large items, sent to package pickup. WDW resort guests may arrange for purchases to be sent to their hotel rooms free of charge. Purchases may be shipped on request. Note that this service has been suspended in the past and may not be offered during your visit.

Main Street

THE CHAPEAU: This Town Square shop is the place to buy Mouse ears and have them monogrammed, and to shop for straw hats, baseball caps, and assorted other headgear.

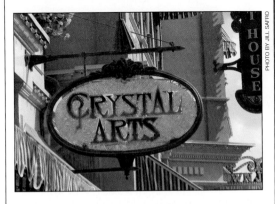

PHOTO BY JILL SAFRO

CRYSTAL ARTS: Cut-glass bowls, vases, glasses, and plates glitter in the mirror-backed cases of this crystal-chandeliered emporium. An engraver or a glassblower is always at work by the bright light that floods through the big windows. Presented by the Arribas Brothers.

MAGIC KINGDOM

Where to Eat in the Magic Kingdom

A complete listing of all eateries—full-service restaurants, fast-food emporiums, and snack shops—can be found in the *Good Meals, Great Times* chapter. See the Magic Kingdom section, beginning on page 226.

DISNEY & CO.: The wallpaper at this shop is Victorian and the woodwork elaborate; old-fashioned ceiling fans twirl slowly overhead. This store stocks a selection of games and plush toys and clothing for young adults.

DISNEY CLOTHIERS: This shop features an array of clothing, including sweatshirts and sleepwear, all of which incorporate Disney characters in some way. Bags, jewelry, watches, and other accessories round out the selection.

EMPORIUM: Framed by a two-story-high portico, the Magic Kingdom's largest gift shop (which has expanded, taking over the space formerly occupied by the Center Street flower garden and the Harmony Barber Shop) stocks stuffed animals and toys, sundries, film, T-shirts, and more.

The cash registers always seem to be busy, especially toward the end of the afternoon and before park closing. Nearby lockers make for convenient storage of purchases.

Don't forget to peer into the windows, which usually feature elaborate displays ranging from seasonal themes to character tableaux from the latest Disney movie.

FIREHOUSE GIFT STATION: Authentic firefighting paraphernalia provides the backdrop for a variety of firefighter and pet-related

Let It Rain

The show doesn't stop just because of a storm. Instead, shops throughout the Magic Kingdom sell plastic Mickey ponchos to outfit guests who have left their own rain gear back home, at their hotel, or in the car.

products, such as Mickey Mouse firefighter souvenirs, and reproductions of historical firefighting objects.

HARMONY BARBER SHOP: Situated next door to the Main Street Car Barn, the quaint, old-fashioned setting for this working shop (complete with occasional appearances by a harmonizing quartet) merits a peek even if you have no need for a trim. It's open from 9 A.M. to 4:30 P.M. daily. This is a popular spot for a child's first haircut.

MAIN STREET ATHLETIC CLUB: Sports-related gifts and apparel are the hallmarks of this shop. The merchandise features images of Disney characters pursuing their favorite sports. The shop also stocks golf shirts with a small Mickey embroidered on the pocket.

MAIN STREET CONFECTIONERY: Tasty chocolates are sold in this old-fashioned pink-and-white paradise. A delight at any time of day, but especially when the cooks in the shop's glass-walled kitchen are pouring peanut brittle onto a table to cool. Then the candy sends up clouds of aroma that you could swear were being fanned out onto the street. The peanut brittle is for sale in small bags, along with jelly beans, marshmallow crispy treats, and dozens of other confections that will satisfy any sweet tooth.

MAIN STREET PACKAGE PICKUP: This is the place to go if you have any Magic Kingdom purchases "sent to the front of the park." Allow at least three hours for the package to get here. It's near the Train Station.

MAIN STREET MARKET HOUSE: An old-fashioned spot, with cookies, candy, and housewares. Past wares have included specialty tins, napkin rings, and espresso cups.

NEWSSTAND: No newspapers are sold in the Magic Kingdom—even at its newsstand, which is near the park entrance. (It's to the left, just inside the turnstiles.) The stand sells character merchandise and souvenirs.

THE SHADOW BOX: Watching Rubio Artist Co. silhouette cutters snip black paper into the likenesses of children is one of Main Street's more fascinating diversions.

TOWN SQUARE EXPOSITION HALL: A combination camera center and museum, Exposition Hall features exhibits celebrating the history of photography. This is the spot for film, batteries, collectible pins, photo albums, disposable cameras, and picture frames. It's also possible to have your photo snapped and superimposed onto a Disney background—be it in front of Cinderella Castle, beside Disney villains, or in the Hundred Acre Wood. These photos can be made into posters, plaques, or mouse pads.

UPTOWN JEWELERS: Designed to resemble a turn-of-the-century collectibles shop, this spiffy store specializes in jewelry and other gift items, including an extensive selection of pins. One counter stocks souvenir charms in 14-karat gold and sterling silver, among them Tinker Bell, Cinderella Castle, and the Walt Disney World logo (a globe with mouse ears). There's also a selection of Disney character figurines. Clocks and watches in all shapes and sizes are available here, including Mickey Mouse watches in a variety of configurations.

WHEELCHAIR AND ECV RENTAL: Inside the turnstiles on the right as you enter the Magic Kingdom, this rental concession offers a limited number of wheelchairs and electric convenience vehicles. They are available on a first-come, first-served basis. (Hold onto your receipt—it'll get you a replacement wheelchair or ECV should yours mysteriously disappear during the day.) Keep in mind that wheelchairs and ECVs rented here cannot be taken outside the park itself.

Adventureland

AGRABAH BAZAAR: Clothing with a safari theme is featured at this shop. In addition, look for souvenirs of the *Aladdin*, *Jungle Book*, and *Winnie the Pooh* ilk—many with a safari theme.

ISLAND SUPPLY: This small tropical surf shop features a surprisingly large selection of surfing attire and accessories.

PLAZA DEL SOL CARIBE BAZAAR: Ahoy there, mateys! A swashbuckler's delight, the joint adjoining the Pirates of the Caribbean sells stuff celebrating both the attraction and the feature films of the same name. It also stocks nautical gifts and other pirate booty, including Jolly Roger flags, rings, dolls, sailing-ship models, ships in a bottle, and eye patches. If that's not enough treasure for you, check out the candy and snacks, straw hats (including colorful oversize sombreros), piñatas, pottery, straw bags, clothing, and artificial flowers. This is one of our favorite shops.

ZANZIBAR TRADING COMPANY: Across from Adventureland's famed "Egg Roll Wagon," this corner shop stocks jungle collectibles including hand-crafted wood items imported from Kenya: giraffes, letter openers, and rain sticks. Also found here are straw and woven items, baskets, and drums.

Frontierland

BIG AL'S: Named for the most popular (and least talented) member of the Country Bears, this riverfront shop is known for its selection of headwear, including Davy Crockett caps.

BRIAR PATCH: Toys and cuddly character items, plus Magic Kingdom logo merchandise are featured wares at this shop, located near the Splash Mountain exit. There's also a pair of rocking chairs for those who need to take a load off.

FRONTIER TRADING POST: This is the place to shop for collector pins and the associated accoutrements. Since it's got the largest selection of pins in the park, they might want to rename this the Pin Trading Post.

PRAIRIE OUTPOST & SUPPLY: Stop by this turn-of-the-century general store for candy, coffee, and cookies. Decorative items such as candles are also for sale.

Liberty Square

HERITAGE HOUSE: Early American reproductions predominate the stock of this store next to The Hall of Presidents. Parchment copies of famous American documents are popular with youngsters. Collectors might be tempted to snap up Americana items from books to clothing. Tucked into a corner is a family name history and coat of arms area. Campaign buttons, flags, T-shirts, and Statue of Liberty items are also available.

LIBERTY SQUARE PORTRAIT GALLERY: In the midst of Liberty Square, guests may have their portraits drawn in this open-air studio.

MADAME LEOTA'S CART: This shop gives guests on their way to The Haunted Mansion a taste of things to come, with monster masks and ghoulish goodies. There are items featuring scenes and characters from the classic attraction, too. It's also the place to pick up an invisible pooch. FYI: Madame Leota is the spirit featured in the crystal ball inside the Haunted Mansion.

YANKEE TRADER: This quaint little shop near The Haunted Mansion is filled with housewares, snow globes, picture frames, and blankets. Weary soles, er, souls enjoy the rocking chairs on the porch.

YE OLDE CHRISTMAS SHOPPE: A wide variety of festive and decorative Christmas items, including tree-top dolls, automated

display characters, angel figurines, and souvenir ornaments—Disney-themed and traditional—is available year-round.

Fantasyland

THE KING'S GALLERY: This shop inside Cinderella Castle features a line of crystal and medieval creations such as swords and shields. In addition, it stocks items related to Cinderella herself (including glass slippers), as well as her castle. This is also the place to pick up limited-edition art items.

POOH'S THOTFUL SHOP: Located at the exit of The Many Adventures of Winnie the Pooh, this shop has wares featuring the folks from the Hundred Acre Wood.

SIR MICKEY'S: Expect to find all sorts of Disney souvenirs in this shop with a theme based on *The Brave Little Tailor*—the cartoon in which Mickey defeats a giant to win the hand of Princess Minnie. (It was one of the most elaborate and expensive Mickey Mouse cartoons ever made.)

TINKER BELL'S TREASURES: Can't get enough Disney princess merchandise? Stop here for toys, costumes, dolls, and kids' clothing, plus personalized beaded jewelry.

Mickey's Toontown Fair

COUNTY BOUNTY: Disney character memorabilia, featuring all the favorites, can be found in this colorful spot under the big tent. Look for costumes, children's apparel, autograph books, key chains, candy, and more. Don't miss the doll-making exhibit or the winning entries from previous fairs, including the famous "most-upside-down cake," baked by Daisy Duck.

Tomorrowland

MERCHANT OF VENUS: The place for anything and everything Stitch, from plush toys to games to clothing.

MICKEY'S STAR TRADERS: This is one of the better places to go in the Magic Kingdom for Disney-themed items: plush toys, towels, hats, shirts, dishes, candy, etc. Film, sunglasses, and sun-care products are also available. The Tomorrowland Transit Authority passes through here, too.

Entertainment

In this most magical corner of the World, a tempting slate of live performances ranks among the more serendipitous discoveries. The Magic Kingdom's entertainment mix includes dazzling high-tech shows and old-fashioned numbers alike. To keep apprised of the offerings on any given day, stop at City Hall upon arrival at the park to pick up a current guidemap and Times Guide.

While specifics are subject to change, the following listing is a good indication of the Magic Kingdom's repertoire. As always, we advise calling 407-824-4321 to confirm schedules.

CASEY'S CORNER PIANO: A pianist tickles the ivories of a snow-white upright daily at Casey's Corner restaurant on Main Street.

DAPPER DANS: You just might encounter a barbershop quartet while strolling down Main Street. Conspicuously clad in straw hats and striped vests, the ever-so-jovial Dapper Dans tap-dance and let one-liners fly during their short four-part-harmony performances.

FIREWORKS: "Wishes," a dynamite, pyrotechnic extravaganza, is presented most nights when the Magic Kingdom stays open after dark. Narrated by Jiminy Cricket, this is one of the biggest, boldest, and truly eye-popping fireworks shows ever presented in the park. Showtime varies—check a park Times Guide for specifics. Wishes is ideally viewed from Main Street, U.S.A., but can be seen from many vantage points. It is presented rain or shine.

FLAG RETREAT: At about 5:10 P.M. each day (check a current Times Guide), patriotic music fills the air as a color guard marches to Town Square, in Main Street, U.S.A., and takes down the American flag that flies from the flagpole. On special occasions, a band plays live music. WDW veterans should know that the doves that used to take part in the ceremony are enjoying a hard-earned retirement.

DISNEY DREAMS COME TRUE PARADE: This parade, created especially for the Magic Kingdom park, invites guests to celebrate Disney magic and make a dream come true. The interactive parade, which has festive floats, as well as every Disney character imaginable, begins in Frontierland and winds its way up Main Street, U.S.A.

STORYTIME WITH BELLE: In Fairytale Garden near Cinderella Castle, Belle invites young friends to help act out the story of "Beauty and the Beast."

SWORD IN THE STONE CEREMONY: Several times each day, a child is appointed temporary ruler of the realm by pulling the magical sword, Excalibur, from the stone in front of Cinderella's Golden Carrousel. Merlin the Magician presides over the ceremony.

Holiday Happenings

It's a rare holiday that passes quietly in the Magic Kingdom. During certain holidays, such as Christmas, New Year's Eve, and the Fourth of July, this Kingdom usually breaks curfew, staying open extra late and stepping up its nighttime entertainment. On these occasions, special performances of the SpectroMagic parade and the fireworks are often in store. Of course, entertainment plans are subject to change, so it's important to call 407-824-4321 for current schedules.

EASTER: Easter is a delightful, if a bit crowded, time to visit the Magic Kingdom. Mr. and Mrs. Easter Bunny have been known to appear in the park to help guests celebrate the occasion.

FOURTH OF JULY: The busiest day of the summer—and with good reason: there's a double-size fireworks extravaganza whose explosions light up the skies not only above Cinderella Castle, but also over Seven Seas Lagoon. It's a thrilling display.

HALLOWEEN: This most spooky of holidays is celebrated on select nights from mid-September through October (though not necessarily on Halloween itself) with a special-ticket event: Mickey's Not-So-Scary Halloween Party. The park closes a bit early on nights when the party takes place. (Guests bearing tickets to the party can stay in the park.) Expect characters in costume, creepy music and fog effects, and trick-or-treating throughout the park. It's a hoot! Mickey's Boo-to-You Halloween Parade takes place, as does a special edition of the fireworks show. Visit *www.disneyworld.com* or call 407-824-4321 to order tickets to the party.

CHRISTMAS: A towering Christmas tree goes up on Main Street and the Magic Kingdom is decked out as only Disney can do it. On select nights in November and December, the Magic Kingdom hosts a special-admission celebration known as Mickey's Very Merry Christmas Party.

The festivities, complete with complimentary hot chocolate and cookies and snow flurries on Main Street, include a running (or two) of Mickey's Very Merry Christmas Parade and holiday shows, plus a special Wishes fireworks show. There are special performances during the day—even the Country Bears get into the act. Disney characters are on hand, too.

The Christmas party is a very popular (and enjoyable) event. Purchase tickets way ahead of time. And don't forget to wear red and green!

NEW YEAR'S EVE: It has always been true that on December 31 the throngs here are body to body. Expect a dazzling, super-size fireworks display and oodles of happy holiday decorations. There's plenty of nip in the air as the evening goes on, so dress accordingly.

Where to Find the Characters

Mickey's pals make appearances throughout the day. Alice and her Wonderland friends show up in Fantasyland, as does Ariel. Belle reads stories to guests in Fairy Tale Garden, near the Castle. The Diamond Horseshoe Saloon is also an excellent spot to see characters. Character meals at Crystal Palace, Cinderella's Royal Table, and Liberty Tree Tavern offer guests a chance to meet their favorites. But the best place is at Toontown Fair, where guests can meet Mickey and his buddies, as well as Disney princesses. Characters may greet guests in Town Square at park opening time. Check a Times Guide for updated information.

SpectroMagic Lights Up the Park

SpectroMagic, the dazzling parade which first premiered during Disney World's 20th anniversary celebration, has gotten rave reviews, and taken its place among Disney's must-sees. (Its beloved predecessor, the Main Street Electrical Parade, can currently be seen at Disney's California Adventure, in Anaheim, California.)

Fiber-optic cable and threads are the conduits for shimmering lights that create everything from the "hair" on King Triton's beard on one float to daisy petals on another. Some 600,000 miniature bulbs light up in wild, changing patterns, moving in perfect concert with sound effects and a dramatic musical score.

SpectroMagic follows the Magic Kingdom's traditional parade route (heading from Main Street, U.S.A., to Frontierland and vice versa). There are excellent viewing locations throughout the route, with many along the curbs of Main Street. It gets very crowded there, so you must plan to claim your foot of curb about 45 minutes to an hour and a half ahead of time (particularly for the earlier running).

The parade lights up the Magic Kingdom during all peak seasons and select evenings throughout the year.

Timing Tip: When the parade runs twice a night, the earlier presentation is always significantly more crowded than the later one. So, if your family hasn't collectively run out of steam, stick around for the late show. You'll be glad you did.

Note: Some performances may be canceled due to inclement weather.

Hot Tips

- Start the day by picking up a Fastpass assignment for your favorite attraction.

- If the weather's steamy, dress toddlers in waterproof diapers. Then they'll be free to frolic in the fountains in Fantasyland and Mickey's Toontown Fair.

- If there are two performances of the evening parade, the later one tends to draw smaller crowds.

- If you're driving to the park, start out very early. Most people arrive between 9:30 A.M. and 11:30 A.M., and the roads and parking lots are jammed. Plan to be at the gates to the Magic Kingdom before they open, and then be at the end of Main Street when the rest of the park opens.

- Wear very comfortable shoes: You'll be spending a lot of time on your feet. (Note that no bare feet are permitted in the park.)

- Dying to meet Mickey Mouse? Head for the Judge's Tent in Mickey's Toontown Fair. (You have to go through his house to get there.) He greets visitors all day, every day.

- You can usually get in line for an attraction right up until the minute the park closes.

- Avoid the mealtime rush hours by eating early or late: before 11:30 A.M. or after 2 P.M., and before 5 P.M. or after 8 P.M.

- At busy times, take in these less-packed attractions: Walt Disney World Railroad, Liberty Square Riverboat, Hall of Presidents, and Tomorrowland Transit Authority.

- Check the Tip Board for information on the wait times for popular attractions.

- Break up your day. Consider heading back to your hotel (if it's not too far) for some swimming. Be sure to hold on to your admission pass, stroller and/or wheelchair receipt(s), and your parking stub, so that you can re-enter the Magic Kingdom.

- If your party decides to split up, set a meeting place and time. Avoid meeting in front of Cinderella Castle, since this area can become quite congested.

- If an attraction has two lines, the one on the left usually will be shorter.

- For a full-service meal, be sure to make reservations in advance by calling 407-WDW-DINE (939-3463).

- There are picnic facilities at the Transportation and Ticket Center (TTC).

- Park guests have the right to chicken out at any time while waiting in line. In other words, should you or a member of your party have second thoughts about soaring on Space Mountain, visiting with the grinning ghosts of the Haunted Mansion, or another attraction, simply inform an attendant and you'll be discreetly whisked out a special exit.

- If you've rented a stroller, consider returning it just before the night's fireworks presentation. That way, after the show, you'll be able to make a beeline for your bed rather than stand in a line to return your stroller.

- Merchandise found in shops at Walt Disney World is also available through mail order. Call 407-363-6200 for info.

- Travel light. The fewer bags you have, the faster you'll pass through security.

- Allow extra time to get through the turnstiles on the way into the park—security and the "ticket tag" system can make for big delays—especially during peak times and on "Extra Magic Hours" days.

Epcot

HAPPY 25th Birthday

EPCOT

Imagine a place whose entertainment inventory includes both a rich sampling of world cultures and a fun, enlightening journey to the technological frontier. You now have an inkling of the eye-opening and mind-broadening potential of Epcot—a place that's evolved most imaginatively in each of the twenty-five years it's been open.

Walt Disney suggested the idea back in 1966: "Epcot will be an experimental prototype community of tomorrow that will take its cue from the new ideas and technologies that are emerging from the creative center of American industry." It would never be completed, he said, but would "always be introducing and testing and demonstrating new materials and systems." On October 1, 1982, Walt Disney's dream became a reality. Test Track puts guests on the thrilling inside track of the fast and perilous world of automobile testing. Soarin' delivers the breath-taking sensation of flight. And classics like the Universe of Energy and Imagination! continue to ignite the creative forces within us all.

The park consists of two areas of exploration: Future World and World Showcase. The former examines ideas in science and technology in ways that make them seem not only comprehensible but downright irresistible. The latter celebrates the diversity of the world's peoples, portraying a stunning array of nations, with extraordinary devotion to detail.

Think of Epcot as Disney's playground for the curious and the thoughtful. The experiences it delivers—all of them wonders of the real world— continue to amaze, educate, inspire, and (of course) entertain.

WORLD SHOWCASE

FUTURE WORLD

WORLD SHOWCASE LAGOON

MOROCCO

FRANCE

INTERNATIONAL GATEWAY

JAPAN

THE AMERICAN ADVENTURE

UNITED KINGDOM

ITALY

CANADA

IMAGINATION!

GERMANY

THE LAND

CHINA

THE SEAS

NORWAY

SHOWCASE PLAZA

MEXICO

INNOVENTIONS WEST

TEST TRACK

INNOVENTIONS EAST

MISSION: SPACE

SPACESHIP EARTH

WONDERS OF LIFE

To Buses

UNIVERSE OF ENERGY

Entrance Plaza

N

Getting Oriented

Double the Magic Kingdom park and you have an idea of the size of Epcot. As for layout, the park is shaped something like a giant hourglass. The pavilions of Future World fill the northern bulb, while the international potpourri called World Showcase occupies the southern bulb. Future World is anchored on the north by the imposing silver "geosphere," dubbed Spaceship Earth.

As you pass through Epcot's main Entrance Plaza, Spaceship Earth looms straight ahead. Pathways curve around the 180-foot-tall geosphere, winding up at Innoventions Plaza. Here, in addition to a show fountain, you'll see signs for Innoventions, whose two buildings cradle the east and west sides of the plaza. Beyond this central area, there are two roughly symmetrical north-south avenues; these are dotted with the six pavilions that form the outer perimeter of Future World. Mission: SPACE, Test Track, Wonders of Life, and Universe of Energy flank Spaceship Earth on the east, while Imagination!, The Land, and The Seas with Nemo & Friends lie to the west.

In World Showcase, the international pavilions are arranged around the edge of sparkling World Showcase Lagoon, with The American Adventure directly south of Spaceship Earth on the lake's southernmost shore. A walkway from Future World leads to the World Showcase Promenade, a 1.2-mile thoroughfare that wraps around the lagoon, winding past each World Showcase pavilion in the process.

HOW TO GET THERE

Take Exit 67 off I-4. Continue along to the Epcot Auto Plaza; if you park in a distant lot, take a tram from the parking lot to the park's main entrance.

By WDW Transportation: From the Grand Floridian, Contemporary, and Polynesian: hotel monorail to the Transportation and Ticket Center (TTC), then switch to the TTC-Epcot monorail. From the Magic Kingdom: express monorail to the TTC, then switch to the TTC-Epcot monorail. From Downtown Disney: bus to any resort, then transfer to an Epcot bus or boat. From the Disney-MGM Studios, Animal Kingdom, all other Walt Disney World resorts, and the resorts on Hotel Plaza Boulevard: buses.

Note: A second Epcot park entrance, called

International Gateway, provides entry directly to World Showcase. It may be reached via walkways and the *FriendShip* water launches from the Swan, Dolphin, Yacht and Beach Club, and BoardWalk resorts. The boat deposits guests between the France and United Kingdom pavilions. It is possible to purchase theme park admission here, at Epcot's "back door."

PARKING

All-day parking at Epcot is $9 for day visitors (free to Disney resort guests with a resort ID, as well as annual passholders). Attendants will direct you to park in one of several lots named for steps in the creative process, such as Discover and Imagine. Trams circulate regularly, providing transportation between the distant lots and the main entrance. Be sure to note the section and aisle in which you park. Parking tickets allow for re-entry to the area (and the other theme parks) throughout the day.

HOURS

Future World is usually open from about 9 A.M. to 7 P.M. World Showcase hours are about 11 A.M. to 9 P.M. During certain holiday periods and the summer months, hours are extended. It's best to arrive at least a half hour before the posted opening time, particularly during these busy seasons. On select days, the park opens one hour early or stays open three hours late for Disney resort guests only. Call 407-824-4321 for current schedules, or visit *www.disneyworld.com.*

GETTING AROUND

Water taxis, called *FriendShip* launches, ferry guests across the World Showcase Lagoon. Docks are located near Mexico, Canada, Germany, and Morocco. (The only other way to traverse the vast area is on foot.)

Admission Prices

ONE-DAY BASE TICKET
(Restricted to use only in Epcot. Prices do not include sales tax and are subject to change.)
Adult $63
Child* $52
*3 through 9 years of age; children under 3 free

Park Primer

EPCOT

BABY FACILITIES

There are changing tables and facilities for nursing mothers at the Baby Care Center in the Odyssey Center, between Test Track and Mexico. Disposable diapers are kept behind the counter at many Epcot shops; just ask.

CAMERA NEEDS

The Camera Center in Entrance Plaza and World Traveler at International Gateway stock memory cards, film, batteries, and disposable cameras. Stop at the Camera Center or at ImageWorks in Imagination! to transfer images from media cards to a CD. It's possible to print digital photos at the ImageWorks shop.

DISABILITY INFORMATION

Nearly all attractions, shops, and restaurants are accessible to guests using wheelchairs. Parking for guests with disabilities is available. Additional services are available for guests with visual and hearing disabilities. The *Guidebook for Guests with Disabilities* is available at Guest Relations. It provides a detailed overview of all services. For more information, turn to the *Getting Ready to Go* chapter of this book.

FIRST AID

Minor medical problems can be handled at the First Aid Center, in the Odyssey Center, between Test Track and Mexico. Keep in mind that many guests could avoid a trip to First Aid simply by staying well hydrated. If you have an emergency, notify an employee.

INFORMATION

Guest Relations, which is located next to Spaceship Earth, is equipped with guidemaps, Times Guides, and a helpful staff.

LOCKERS

Lockers are found immediately west of Spaceship Earth. Cost is $5, plus a $2 refundable deposit for unlimited use all day.

LOST & FOUND

Lost and Found is located at Guest Relations in Innoventions East. To inquire about lost items after your visit, call 407-824-4245. If you find an item, present it to a park employee.

LOST CHILDREN

Report lost children at Guest Relations or the Baby Care Center, and alert an employee.

MONEY MATTERS

There are ATMs at the main entrance, on the path between Future World and World Showcase, and at The American Adventure. Some foreign currency may be exchanged at Guest Relations. Credit cards (American Express, JCB, Discover, Diner's Club, Visa, MasterCard, Disney gift cards, and The Disney Visa Card), traveler's checks, Disney Dollars, Disney gift cards, and WDW resort IDs are accepted for admission and merchandise, as well as meals at most restaurants.

PACKAGE PICKUP

Epcot shops can arrange for most purchases to be transported (for free) to the Gift Stop in Entrance Plaza or International Gateway in World Showcase for later pickup.

SAME-DAY RE-ENTRY

Be sure to retain your ticket if you plan to return later the same day. A hand stamp is no longer required.

SECURITY CHECK

Guests entering Disney theme parks will be subject to a security check. Backpacks, parcels, purses, etc., will be searched by security personnel before guests are permitted to enter.

STROLLERS & WHEELCHAIRS

Strollers, wheelchairs, and Electric Convenience Vehicles (ECVs) may be rented from venues at both park entrances. Wheelchairs are also available at the Gift Stop. Cost is $10 for strollers and wheelchairs. A "Length-of-Stay" rental yields a $2-per-day discount. It's $35 a day for an ECV, plus a $5 refundable deposit. Quantities are limited. ECVs tend to sell out early. Keep your rental receipt; it can be used that same day to get a replacement at Epcot or another theme park.

TIP BOARD

Check this digital board in Innoventions Plaza throughout the day to learn current waiting times for the most popular attractions.

Future World

A mere listing of the basic themes covered by the pavilions at Future World—agriculture, communications, car safety, the ocean, energy, health, imagination, and space—tends to sound a tad academic. But when these serious topics are presented with a special flair, they become part of an experience that ranks among Disney's most entertaining.

Some of these subjects are explored in the course of lively and unusual "adventures," involving a whole arsenal of motion pictures, special effects, and Audio-Animatronics figures so lifelike that it is hard to remain unmoved. The basic elements are also appealing in their own right, from the palm-dotted Entrance Plaza to the dramatic fountain just past Spaceship Earth, the many-faceted "geosphere" that has become the universal symbol of Epcot.

The park is so vast that it's hard to know what to do first. Many guests simply stop at Spaceship Earth on their way into Future World. As a result, they end up spending more time waiting in line than they need to. A wise alternative is to save Spaceship Earth for later in the day (when the lines inevitably thin out), and head for Soarin', the "less intense, non-spinning" Mission: SPACE, The Seas with Nemo & Friends, and Test Track (if motion sickness isn't an issue for you) as soon as the park opens (the lines tend to stay long throughout the day). Take in as many Future World attractions as time allows, making sure to see the Image Works playground in the Imagination! pavilion, and save World Showcase for the evening hours. This strategy works well for families. (Refer to page 32 for a detailed version of this plan of attack.)

Another alternative—one that requires quite a bit of extra walking, but can help skirt a long line or two—is to explore Future World until World Showcase opens at 11 A.M. Then, in the afternoon, when many guests have shifted over to World Showcase, return to the Future World area. Innoventions is not only an interesting spot to pass the busy hours after lunch, but also a cool refuge when high temperatures prevail outdoors. And although queues can be found during peak seasons at Soarin', Mission: SPACE, Test Track, Imagination!, The Seas with Nemo & Friends, and The Land throughout most of the late morning and afternoon,

the period from late afternoon until park closing is usually less hectic. But don't forget to make it back to World Showcase in time to see the nighttime spectacular, IllumiNations: Reflections of Earth.

Spaceship Earth

As it looms impressively just above the Earth, this great faceted silver structure looks a little bit like a spaceship ready to blast off. It appears large from a distance, and it seems even more immense when viewed from directly underneath. It's no surprise that some visitors simply stop beneath it and gawk.

The show inside, which explores the continuing search by human beings for evermore efficient means of communication, remains one of Epcot's compelling—if not a thrill a minute—attractions. It's a slow-moving, narrated journey through time.

A common misconception about Spaceship Earth is that it is a geodesic dome. Not so. It is a geosphere. A geodesic dome is only half a sphere, while Spaceship Earth is almost

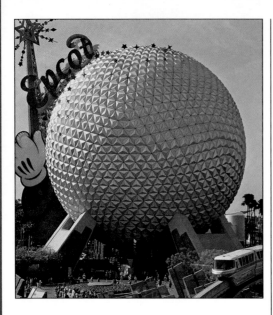

completely round. Affectionately known to many simply as "the Ball," Spaceship Earth is indeed a sight to behold.

Noted science-fiction writer Ray Bradbury, together with consultants from the Smithsonian Institution, the Los Angeles area's prestigious Huntington Library, the University of Southern California, and (among others) the University of Chicago, collaborated with Disney in developing this memorable 14-minute journey. It begins in an inky-black time tunnel, complete with a musty smell that suggests the dust of ages, and continues through history from the days of Cro-Magnon man (30,000 or 40,000 years ago) to the future.

The attraction features interesting special effects, such as the flickering candles in the scene where a monk has nodded off and the smell of smoke coming from the fall of Rome. Every scene is executed in exquisite detail. The symbols on the wall of that Egyptian temple really are hieroglyphics, and the content of the letter being dictated by the pharaoh was excerpted from a missive actually received by an agent of a ruler of the period.

All of these sights are enough to keep heads turning as the "time machines" wend their way upward. The most dazzling scene is saved for the ride's finale, when the audience is

Hot Tip!

The line for Spaceship Earth is usually quite long during the early morning hours and relatively short in the late afternoon and evening.

placed in the heart of a communications revolution amid interactive global networks that tie all the peoples of the world together.

GATEWAY GIFTS AND CAMERA CENTER: These two shops are located near the entrance to Spaceship Earth. The former sells Epcot souvenirs—shirts, mugs, toys, etc.—as well as sunscreen, tissues, and the like. Film and various other Kodak products, including disposable cameras, are sold at the Camera Center.

Innoventions

Where else but Disney World would the information superhighway intersect with The Road to Tomorrow? It does at Innoventions, a forward-thinking showplace that encourages guests to experience futuristic technologies today. It's an opportunity to test products that may soon change the way we live and work. Equally important, Innoventions offers an unintimidating environment where you don't need to know how to program a VCR to be able to try out supercomputers or send video e-mail messages.

Hot Tip!

Keep an eye (or ear) out for a talking trash can inside the Electric Umbrella restaurant and a talking drinking fountain near the Imagination! pavilion.

An introduction hosted by Tom Morrow 2.0, a mini-robot and "a friend to technology," provides an overview of the new Innoventions experience, as well as some navigational tips. Once Tom's had his say, it's time to follow The Road to Tomorrow, a long, winding thoroughfare that snakes throughout Innoventions, and along which the exhibits are found.

The displays change often, making one of Walt Disney's original dreams for Epcot a reality. Employees will answer questions from curious—or skeptical—visitors.

Innoventions covers two buildings, referred to as Innoventions East and West. The outside area between the pavilions is filled with color, light, spinning mobiles, and sidewalks glistening with fiber-optic lighting effects.

Above all, count on spending time exploring the exhibit areas (at least an hour or two). There's so much to see and do that curiosity will often get the better of any schedule here.

Hot Tip!

Innoventions Plaza is home to Pin Central. This area, between Innoventions East and West, is the pin-trading headquarters for Epcot. (Of course, there are many other pin-trading locations throughout Walt Disney World.)

MOUSE GEAR: This enormous shop used to be called the Centorium. Though the name has changed, the selection remains top-notch. Mouse Gear stocks Disney character memorabilia, key chains, T-shirts, hats, books, candy, mugs, photo albums, jewelry, towels, footwear, Figment (the purple dragon from Epcot's Imagination! pavilion) toys, and much more—making this the best source for character merchandise in Epcot. There are also items related to the park itself, along with Disney-themed apparel and children's clothing. It is one of the best shops at Disney, and it stays open at least a half hour longer than the park does. It's a nice place to browse as the crowds exit the park after IllumiNations.

THE ART OF DISNEY EPCOT GALLERY: This is Epcot's spot for a unique assortment of Disney collectibles. The store showcases a wide variety of Disney animation art, including production cels, hand-painted limited-edition cels, character figurines, fine-art serigraphs, and lithographs.

The Seas with Nemo & Friends

Welcome to the largest facility ever dedicated to humanity's relationship with the ocean. It was designed by Disney Imagineers, in cooperation with distinguished oceanographic experts and scientists.

Though it enjoys the distinction of being one of Future World's original pavilions, what used to be known as The Living Seas is as fresh as ever—thanks to a little clownfish called Nemo and some of his fishy friends.

Once inside, guests can find the animated critters' real-life counterparts, including clownfish, blue tangs, sharks, and puffer fish.

The pavilion also features a ride, an interactive encounter with an animated turtle, and an engaging post-show area. Little ones enjoy frolicking in Bruce's SharkWorld—a hands-on

Under the Sea

Three behind-the-scenes tours offer guests a closer look at life in The Seas with Nemo & Friends under-water environs. DiveQuest gives certified scuba divers the opportunity to explore one of the world's largest aquariums. Epcot Seas Aqua Tour lets guests snorkel The Seas. Dolphins in Depth offers guests the chance to learn about dolphin behavior as they closely observe researchers and trainers interacting with dolphins. Reservations for either tour can be made by calling 407-WDW-TOUR (939-8687). For more information on both of these programs, turn to page 212 of the *Everything Else in the World* chapter.

play area that celebrates the ocean's toothiest residents. From there, take a look at a simulated Caribbean coral reef environment. Finally, the crowning jewel of the pavilion: Turtle Talk with Crush.

 TURTLE TALK WITH CRUSH: If ever there was an attraction that left guests smiling and asking "How do they do that?!"—this is it. The concept is simple enough—a 10-minute, animated show featuring the surfer-dude sea turtle from *Finding Nemo*. The amazing part? The cartoon critter interacts with the audience. In doing so, he imparts turtle-y wisdom, answers questions, and cracks more than a few jokes. You have to see it to believe it. To do that, you'll have to wait in line—it's extremely popular with guests of all ages. It's like, totally awesome, dude.

PHOTO BY JILL SAFRO

THE SEAS WITH NEMO & FRIENDS

ATTRACTION: Brand-spanking new, this undersea adventure is fun for all ages. In it, guests climb aboard a "clam-mobile" and enter a colorful coral reef. It seems Nemo has wandered off again and his teacher, Mr. Ray, needs help finding him. So keep your eyes peeled! There's a bit of suspense involved, but rest assured, it all ends happily.

CARIBBEAN CORAL REEF: The man-made reef exists in an enormous tank that holds about six million gallons of water and more than 60 species of sea life. Among the 2,000 or so inhabitants are turtles, angelfish, sharks, dolphins, and diamond rays. It's worth it to stop by as the park opens—that's usually when breakfast is served to the fish!

Guests sometimes get to see scuba divers testing and demonstrating the newest diving gear and underwater monitoring equipment as they carry on training experiments with dolphins. This pavilion is an especially big hit with young guests.

The Land

Occupying six acres, this enormous skylighted pavilion examines the nature of one of everybody's favorite topics—food. It also gives guests a chance to soar above the clouds in a celebration of flight. A film, *The Circle of Life*, uses characters from *The Lion King* to deliver an entertaining yet inspirational message about humanity and the environment. A boat ride explores farming in the past and future.

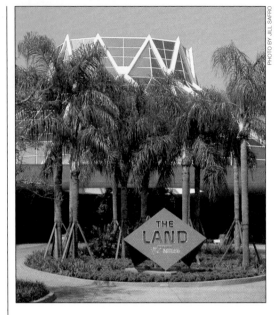

Narration gives visitors the chance to learn about the experimental agricultural techniques practiced in the pavilion.

Timing Tip: Soarin' is a wildly popular attraction. So much so that Fastpass assignments may be all gone before noon. It's best to visit first thing in the morning and get a Fastpass while the gettin's good!

LIVING WITH THE LAND: FP The 13½-minute boat ride through the rain forest and greenhouses in this pavilion opens with a dramatic storm scene. Guests sail through tropical rain forests, prairie grain fields, and a family farm. As the boat passes through each realistic setting, the guide offers commentary on humanity's ongoing struggle to cultivate and live in harmony with the land. Note the details that make each setting so convincing, such as sand blowing over the desert and light flickering from the TV in the farmhouse window.

In the next segment, guests enter a plant research laboratory and solarium. Here, our planet's major food crops are being grown in research projects, along with rare new crops that may someday help meet Earth's ever-growing dietary needs.

The guide on each boat provides information on the crops being grown. Also of interest are the experiments being conducted to explore the practice of farming fish, and a desert farm area, where plants get nutrients through a drip irrigation system that delivers just the right amount of water—important in a dry climate.

As unreal as they appear, all the plants on view in the experimental greenhouses are living. In contrast, those in the biomes (the ecological communities viewed from the boat ride) were made in Disney studios out of lightweight plastic that simulates the cellulose found in real trees. The trunks and branches were molded from live specimens; the sycamore in the farmhouse's front yard, for example, duplicates one that stands outside a Burbank, California, car wash. Thousands of polyethylene leaves were snapped on.

BIRNBAUM'S
★BEST★ SOARIN': FP Up, up, and away! On this high-flying new Epcot attraction (it's been thrilling visitors at Disney's California Adventure park for years), you'll be suspended in a hang glider 45 feet in the air, above a giant IMAX projection dome, and treated to an aerial tour of some of the most awe-inspiring landscapes the state of California has to offer.

With the wind in your hair and your legs dangling in the breeze, the multi-passenger hang glider feels so convincingly real that you may even be tempted to pull up your feet for fear of tripping over a treetop as you dip down toward the ground. During the rather peaceful journey, flyers glide toward the Upper Yosemite Falls of Yosemite Valley, past an active naval aircraft carrier in San Diego Bay, by San Francisco's Golden Gate Bridge, and then down over the vast deserts in Death Valley and the lush wine country of Napa Valley. In all, the airborne trip takes about four minutes and employs synchronized wind currents, scent machines, and a moving musical score set to a film that wraps 180 degrees around you, making this a thoroughly enveloping experience.

Note: You must be 40 inches tall and free

Hot Tip!
Got a rumbly in your tumbly? Head for Sunshine Seasons in The Land pavilion. There's a variety of counter-service choices—apt to please even the pickiest of eaters.

of back problems, heart conditions, motion sickness, and other physical limitations to ride. It's calmer than traditional "thrill" rides, but the sensation of flight is quite realistic. If you're afraid of heights, sit this one out.

CIRCLE OF LIFE: This 20-minute film uses animation and live action to illustrate some of the dangers to our environment, as well as potential solutions. Presented as a fable featuring *The Lion King* favorites Simba, Timon, and Pumbaa, the film takes an optimistic approach to a serious subject. It is shown in the Harvest Theater, just inside the entrance to The Land.

Club Cool

Future World's Club Cool (formerly known as Ice Station Cool) is a great place to beat the heat. Located near Innoventions, it is Coca-Cola's International Tasting Station. Here, you can sample eight different soft drinks from around the world, some tastier than others.

After you've quenched your thirst, courtesy of the Coca-Cola Company, you may have a desire to do some shopping. Not coincidentally, there's plenty of Coke merchandise to choose from (at this point, you will have to open your wallet if you'd like a souvenir).

At press time, Club Cool was open for business during Future World's regular operating hours.

Soon after the film begins, Simba's startled by the exuberant shout of "Timber!" and is drenched by the splash of a fallen tree in the water. The culprits are none other than his friends Timon and Pumbaa, who are clearing the savanna for the development of the Hakuna Matata Lakeside Village. Simba seizes the opportunity to tell them a tale about creatures who sometimes forget that everything is connected in the Circle of Life: humans.

Simba demonstrates to Timon and Pumbaa the consequences of progress, as his lessons are driven home by visual evidence of humans' mistreatment of the air, water, and land. (Timon: "And everybody was *okay* with this?") The effect is a mix of entertainment and a message about responsibility.

Imagination!

The oddly shaped pyramids that house the Imagination! pavilion are striking to behold. They certainly set the stage for the engaging experiences inside, some of which are among the most whimsical at Epcot. The undisputed crown jewel here is a dazzling 3-D movie called Honey, I Shrunk the Audience. Guests are also invited behind the scenes of the Imagination Institute in an attraction known as Journey Into Imagination with Figment.

Another pavilion highlight is the pair of quirky fountains outside—the Jellyfish Fountains, which spurt streams of water that spread out at the top, looking for an instant like their namesake sea creature, and the Leap Frog Fountains, which send out smooth streams of water that arc from one garden plot to another in the most astonishing fashion. Kids just can't get enough of them.

Timing Tip: During peak seasons, the queue outside seems to be longest from about 10 A.M. to noon and remains fairly lengthy throughout most of the day. Count on spending up to an hour at this pavilion.

JOURNEY INTO IMAGINATION WITH FIGMENT: He's back! Figment, the tiny purple dragon with the orange wings and yellow eyes, is on hand to guide guests on an imaginative quest. The goal? To figure out, once and for all, the best way to capture your imagination.

The journey takes place at Imagination Institute, where guests are invited to tour the institute's various labs such as the Sight Lab, the Sound Lab, and the Smell Lab. All in all, it's a tame experience, save for the occasional blast of air or flashing lights.

Nostalgia buffs, take note: The classic song "One Little Spark," which made its debut with the original incarnation of this attraction, underscores the show once more.

PHOTO BY JILL SAFRO

IMAGEWORKS: "WHAT IF" LABS: It's a rare ImageWorks visitor who doesn't experience at least some of the emotion felt by the little kid who cried when her parents tried to tear her away. That's not surprising, because the area is filled with activities that give every visitor the chance to have some fun while stretching the imagination.

Although this interactive wonderland recently underwent extensive refurbishment, it has retained some old favorites. A true highlight for youngsters (though guests of all ages appreciate it) is an area called Stepping Tones. It's hopscotch with a musical twist. Another popular attraction invites guests to wave their arms conductor style and, by doing so, trigger a cacophony of sounds, some more melodious than others.

A recent addition to this imaginative playground encourages guests to morph pictures of themselves into flowers, puppies, and even cartoon characters. Once you've been transformed into a daisy or a superhero, you can send the image to friends (or even yourself) via the Internet. Plan to spend up to an hour exploring these entertaining labs.

IMAGEWORKS SHOP: This spot at the exit to the ImageWorks: "What If" Labs offers merchandise themed to the Imagination! pavilion (including the ever-popular Figment). It also provides a service whereby your image can be captured by computer and reproduced onto items such as ornaments and crystal cubes. You can have your mug slapped onto a poster, or a variety of other accessories. Film, disposable cameras, and other photographic essentials are available, too.

BIRNBAUM'S BEST★ **HONEY, I SHRUNK THE AUDIENCE:** **FP** Welcome to the Imagination Institute, workplace of Professor Wayne Szalinski, the featured character in the three "Honey" movies: *Honey, I Shrunk the Kids*; *Honey, I Blew Up the Kid*; and *Honey, We Shrunk Ourselves*. Rick Moranis, Marcia Strassman, and the kids reprise their familiar film roles at this 18-minute attraction.

In the pre-show area, guests see a movie about imagination. Then they are welcomed to the Imagination Institute and given an overview of what they will see inside the theater.

> ## Hot Tip!
> Honey, I Shrunk the Audience is known to frighten small children and more than the occasional grown-up (especially those who may be spooked by snakes or mice).

Professor Szalinski is to be presented with the Inventor of the Year Award, and will demonstrate several of his inventions. On the way into the theater, guests are provided with "protective goggles" (3-D glasses) to shield their eyes from the flying debris that can come loose during new-product demonstrations.

Once the audience is seated, Szalinski is nowhere to be found. Then he suddenly zooms off the screen in his new HoverPod, out of control and miniaturized by his shrinking machine. Szalinski's son Nick steps in to demonstrate the "Dimensional Duplicator," a machine that can make copies of anything. As Nick switches on the machine, his brother drops a pet mouse into the duplicating chamber and hits the number 999. Suddenly hundreds of mice pour out of the screen in an effect that leaves guests squirming.

Nick gets rid of the mice with Professor Szalinski's No-Mess Holographic Pet System, which projects a 3-D cat out into the audience to scare away the mice. The cat morphs into a lynx and a lion before overheating and exploding. Just then, Szalinski returns, blows himself up to normal size, and demonstrates his new, more powerful, shrinking machine.

Of course, the machine spins out of control and accidentally shrinks the audience and Nick. While the audience is miniaturized, the theater shakes with every on-screen footstep. When apparent giants crouch down to ogle guests in the theater, it's a rare person who doesn't feel diminished to ant proportions.

Hot Tip!

Early mornings and late evenings are the least congested times to visit Epcot's Imagination! pavilion.

The effects are believable, particularly when Adam picks up the theater and shows it to his mom. Motion effects in the theater add to the realism, as does the pet snake that gets loose. The audience is eventually brought back to normal size, of course, although not without incident. The attraction has one last surprise in store, which we won't divulge.

Note: The effects in this attraction give some guests the heebie-jeebies, especially those afraid of snakes or mice. If you suspect that you or any of your kids will have an adverse reaction, consider skipping the movie and heading to ImageWorks while the rest of your party watches the movie.

Timing Tip: This attraction tends to be less crowded very early or later in the day.

Test Track FP

BIRNBAUM'S ★BEST★ Fasten your safety belt! This industrial-looking pavilion puts guests through the frenetic motions of automobile testing. As vehicles progress along the track, they whiz down straightaways, hug hairpin turns, and face near-collisions—and not always in ideal road conditions. En route, riders learn how tests are performed in real facilities (called proving grounds) and discover why certain procedures are crucial to car safety.

Before developing the attraction, Disney Imagineers toured GM proving grounds around the country. The result: From the steely facade to the rows of authentic testing equipment inside, Test Track bears more than a passing resemblance to the real thing.

The experience begins with a pre-show walking tour of the plant that reveals the incredible amount of component testing performed before automakers commit to production. Guests witness automotive testing vignettes, with everything from human interface (our courageous, crash-prone counterparts) to tires, brakes, air bags, and even seats being put through their paces.

The computer-controlled, six-seater vehicles are equipped with video and audio, but no steering wheels or brake pedals. The roads bear the familiar lines and signage of the real world, adding to the attraction's realism.

The five-minute ride begins with an uphill acceleration test. Then the suspension gets a workout, as vehicles descend over a bumpy surface that puts the wheels at odds with one another. During environmental testing, riders feel the heat and get the shivers as vehicles pass first through a radiant heat chamber, then a cold chamber. Roadside robots pitch in by spraying the fenders and door panels with water to test for corrosion.

The ride takes a dramatic turn during the road-handling segment. Vehicles course along a winding road, complete with mountain scenery, and into a darkened tunnel. Passengers hear a horn blast, see the high beams of a tractor trailer, and swerve to avoid the truck. As they emerge, there is a crash; guests round a corner to witness a barrier crash test. Their own vehicles then accelerate toward the barrier.

A long straightaway feeds into a series of banked turns and another straight shot that sends vehicles rocketing around the pavilion at top speed (up to 65 miles per hour).

Note: Kids under 7 must be accompanied by an adult; guests under 40 inches cannot ride; passengers must be free of back problems, heart conditions, motion sickness, and other physical limitations. Pregnant women are advised to sit this one out.

Hot Tip!

If you don't mind splitting up your party, head for the "single rider" lines at Test Track and Mission: SPACE. They move faster than the standby line.

Mission: SPACE FP

Think you've got "the right stuff"? Well, this is your chance to prove it. Epcot's out-of-this-world attraction has a bold mission—to give you a chance to feel the excitement and extreme intensity of space travel without ever leaving the planet.

There are actually two ways to travel to Mars at this attraction: the original, "intense," way and the newer, "less intense," experience. The original Mission: SPACE attraction provides a galaxy of thrills for many brave and sturdy theme park guests. The adventure begins with a white-knuckle blast-off of a spacecraft (which has rather snug seating for four) on an important mission to Mars. The sustained G-force during the launch is intended to be most realistic. Once en route, expect a rather strange, spectacular sensation. It's not quite weightlessness, but according to astronauts who've felt the real thing, it's pretty darn close. (So much so that it also tends to duplicate the not-so-spectacular sensation of space sickness. In fact, Mission: SPACE has the dubious distinction of being the first attraction in theme park history to be equipped with motion-sickness bags.)

Throughout the journey, you're expected to work with your fellow crew members (assuming the roles of navigator, captain, engineer, and pilot) to accomplish the mission. We recommend ignoring this call to duty and keeping your eyes glued to the screen. This will allow you to sit back and enjoy the ride and decidedly downsize the dizziness factor.

The original attraction can wreak havoc on the equilibrium. To cut the chances of losing

Hot Tip!

Epcot is bigger than it seems, so allow yourself plenty of time to get from place to place. (It takes about a half hour to walk from Spaceship Earth to The American Adventure in World Showcase.) Keep this in mind if you have made reservations at a restaurant or hope to secure a nice fireworks viewing location on the World Showcase promenade.

your lunch, keep your eyes open at all times and fixed on the screen in front of you. You may be tempted to tilt your head or shut your eyes. Don't. (We promise you will arrive on Mars whether you fulfull your astronaut duty or not.)

All guests must be at least 44 inches tall and free of back and heart problems, motion sickness, and other physical limitations. Pregnant women should skip the trip, as should anyone with claustrophobic tendencies. In fact, if you have any health issues whatsoever, sit this out. And don't eat before riding!

Bottom line? Most guests who don't get queasy on the highly intense version tend to rave about Mission: SPACE. For us, well, we're proud to admit we choose the alternative, gentler version of this ride. It's intended for those who have health issues or simply would rather not take the risk. The experience is a bit different on "Mission: SPACE-lite," but at least it gives everyone a chance to ride without turning green. The effects may be toned down, but they are quite extraordinary. We thoroughly enjoy the "less intense," non-spinning mission to Mars.

EPCOT

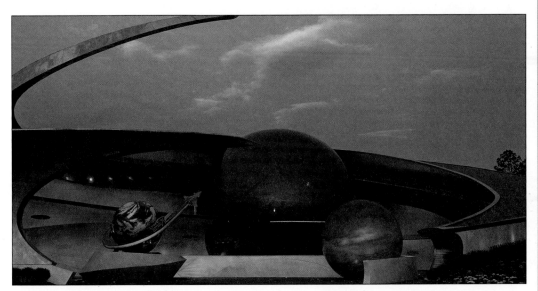

Wonders of Life

The 72-foot-tall steel DNA molecule at the entrance to this pavilion beckons guests to humorous and informative experiences related to health. While it is only open during busy periods (usually summer and holiday times), it is quite popular. Housed in a geodesic dome and two attached buildings, this pavilion allows guests to enjoy both a serious and an amusing look at health, fitness, and modern lifestyles. Wonders of Life also boasts Body Wars, Epcot's dramatic simulator ride—a fast and furious (and bloody) journey through the human body.

Once inside the building, guests find themselves at the Fitness Fairgrounds. In the middle is a theater that shows a 14-minute film called *The Making of Me*. It's a story starring Martin Short as a man who wonders how he came into existence. To find out, he travels back in time to the birth of his parents, their first few years together, and their decision to have a child—him. Footage from an actual delivery is part of the film; it is sensitively presented and provides an accessible and touch-

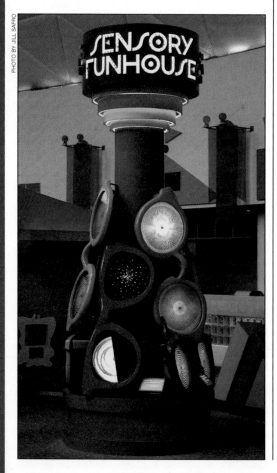

ing view of childbirth. Parents should be aware that the film is a teeny bit graphic and may not be suitable for some children. It also leaves a few key questions unanswered, thereby allowing parents to satiate their kids' appetite for knowledge on a case-by-case basis.

There are plenty of hands-on activities in areas surrounding the theaters. The Sensory Funhouse offers hands-on activities for the young and young at heart. It's the Disney version of a children's museum, where education and entertainment go hand in hand.

At the Lifestyle Revue, guests punch in such information as age, weight, height, exercise habits, whether they smoke, and perceived stress levels at an interactive computer terminal. The computer then processes the information and offers some advice on how to lead a healthier and less stressful existence.

Frontiers of Medicine, located toward the back of the Fitness Fairgrounds, features the only completely serious segment of Wonders of Life. Here, guests can see scientific and educational exhibits of leading developments in medicine and health sciences. The exhibits change regularly.

CRANIUM COMMAND: This area of the Wonders of Life pavilion welcomes guests into the mind of a 12-year-old kid. The pre-show sets the mood as a brief animated film explains what you are about to see. General Knowledge is recruiting pilots for an assortment of new brains. There are jokes aplenty, many of which go right over the heads of young kids. Buzzy, our star pilot, fumbles through basic training and gets assigned to one of the most volatile brains of them all, that of an adolescent boy.

Inside a 200-seat theater, the enormously exaggerated head of our 12-year-old subject is piloted by Buzzy, a delightfully goofy Audio-Animatronics figure. The two large eyes are actually rear-projection video screens, and it is through them that the audience gets an idea of how a young boy thinks and reacts. The other animated participant, General Knowledge, helps Buzzy learn which portion of the mind is required for a particular situation.

The right and left sides of the brain, the stomach, the heart, and the adrenal gland are all represented by perfectly cast celebrities. One such actor is George Wendt (Norm from *Cheers*), operating the stomach. Other characters include Bobcat Goldthwait as the adrenal

gland, Dana Carvey and Kevin Nealon (Hans and Franz of *Saturday Night Live* fame) as the heart, Charles Grodin as the left brain, and Jon Lovitz as the right brain.

Cranium Command is a whimsical and entertaining (not to mention educational) show—one of Epcot's best. This 19-minute presentation is fast-paced and packed with so many details that you'll notice new things even after seeing it many times.

BIRNBAUM'S ★BEST★ BODY WARS: The same state-of-the-art technology that sends guests on a rollicking ride through outer space at the Star Tours attraction at the Disney-MGM Studios also exists at Wonders of Life in the form of this five-minute thrill ride. After boarding the vehicles, which are actually the same type of flight simulators employed by military and commercial airlines in pilot training, guests are whisked away on a rough and exciting ride through the human body. Movie buffs will think immediately of the films *Fantastic Voyage* and *Inner Space*.

The queue area features exhibits from a fictional company specializing in the latest technology in the miniaturization of human beings. Park guests pass through two special-effects portals and are ready to do a routine medical probe of the human body—from the inside.

During the course of this bumpy trip, a scientist is dispatched to remove a splinter that has made its way beneath the patient's skin. Guests go along for the ride but end up on a rescue mission when the scientist is attacked by a white blood cell. Of course, there are some problems along the way, making this trip seem out of control.

Note: This is a somewhat rougher ride than Star Tours, its simulator-ride counterpart at the Disney-MGM Studios. Signs posted outside Body Wars warn that passengers must be free of back problems, neck problems, heart conditions, motion sickness, and other such physical limitations. Pregnant women should not ride Body Wars. Children must be at least 40 inches tall to ride. Finally, if the sight of blood makes you woozy, this attraction is probably not for you.

Universe of Energy

BIRNBAUM'S ★BEST★ In the mood for a chuckle? Set a course for this attraction. You'll get a few giggles and learn something to boot.

Although it's easy to spot this pavilion's mirrored pyramid, the facade does not provide any clue at all to the 45 minutes of surprises in store. One of the most technologically complex experiences at Epcot, a show called Ellen's Energy Adventure consists of several movies and a ride-through segment. None of these is exactly what guests might expect. This is especially true after the pavilion's 1996 major renovation, which repackaged the attraction, placing its legendary Audio-Animatronics dinosaurs and lofty environmental message in a humorous and much more personal context.

The show begins with a film (featuring a few familiar faces). In it, a character named Ellen is watching *Jeopardy!* One of the contestants is Ellen's annoying college roommate, Judy.

Ellen plays along but keeps striking out, particularly in the ENERGY category. As she watches, her neighbor Bill Nye, the Science

Hot Tip!

As home to a 45-minute attraction, the Universe of Energy is a great place to take a load off your feet and give your body a chance to cool off. And it's pretty darn funny, too!

PHOTO BY JILL SAFRO

Guy, pops in and is aghast at Ellen's ignorance. Shortly thereafter, Ellen dozes off.

Ellen dreams she is a contestant on the show, competing against her former friend Judy and Albert Einstein. This time, all of the questions are about energy. As Einstein ponders and Ellen fumbles, Judy is racking up points. Ellen, who has a negative score ("this nightmare game is a lot harder than the home version"), decides to freeze her dream and ask Bill Nye, the Science Guy, for some help.

The second segment leads guests into a theater, where Bill vows to educate Ellen about the importance of energy. He persuades her to travel back in time to see where some of our energy sources came from. Suddenly (but very slowly), the whole seating area rotates, then breaks up into six sections that inch forward. The vehicles embark with Ellen upon an odyssey through the primeval world. Enormous prehistoric trees crowd the forest. Apatosauruses wallow in the lagoon out front. A lofty allosaurus battles with an armored

stegosaurus, and an elasmosaurus bursts out of a tide pool with frightening suddenness—all under the watchful gaze of winged pteranodons. (This zone may spook toddlers.)

Next, guests move out of the forest and view a montage of pictures capturing the history of civilization, from cave dwellers to the present. (Keep your eyes peeled for the wacky caveman who discovers fire—chances are, you'll recognize him, too.) The issue of alternative-energy sources is raised, and the message is that there is no save-all source, but rather there are many possibilities with promise.

The attraction winds up with Ellen returning to the game show of her dreams. This time, she's beating her friend Judy, who is not at all happy about how much Ellen has learned during the commercial break. To win, she must name the one energy source that will never be depleted. (We won't reveal the answer, but we're not too proud to brag about getting it right.)

Almost as intriguing as the attraction is the technology behind it. The vehicles weigh about 30,000 pounds when fully loaded with passengers, yet are guided along the floor by a wire that is only *one-eighth inch thick*.

Did You Know?

There are two acres of solar panels on the rooftop of Future World's Universe of Energy pavilion. Together, they generate 15 percent of the energy it takes to power the attraction housed inside. (It's enough energy to run six average homes.)

World Showcase

Noble sentiments about humanity and the fellowship of nations, which have motivated so many world's fairs in the past, also inhabit World Showcase. But make no mistake about it: This area of Epcot is unlike any previous international exposition.

The group of pavilions that encircles World Showcase Lagoon (a body of water that is about the size of 85 football fields, with a perimeter of about 1.2 miles) demonstrates Disney conceptions about participating countries in remarkably realistic, consistently entertaining styles. You won't find the real Germany here—rather, the country's essence, much as a traveler returning from a visit might remember what he or she saw.

Shops, restaurants, and attractions are housed in a group of structures that is an artful pastiche of all the elements that give that nation's countryside and towns their distinctive flavor. Although occasional liberties have been taken when scale and proportion required them, careful research governed the design of every nook and cranny.

Equally impressive is the cuisine. With no fewer than eleven upscale eateries to choose from, it's no wonder some guests here do

nothing but nosh. (That is especially true during Epcot's popular Food and Wine Festival, a time when dozens more nations contribute to an already fortified international menu. See page 10 for additional information.)

In the shops, many of the wares represent the country in whose pavilion they are sold. Craftspeople are occasionally on hand to demonstrate their arts. Thanks to special cultural-exchange programs and recruiting efforts, many World Showcase staffers hail from the countries the pavilions represent.

A diverse lineup of entertainment ensures that all visitors experience more than a little culture, foreign or otherwise. The entertainment is as authentic as the Disney casting directors can make it, with native performers commonly featured and new festivities always in the works.

Hot Tip!

World Showcase pavilions may open at 11 A.M. or later. However, guests may use the International Gateway entrance as much as a half hour prior to Future World's official opening time.

Pavilions are described in the order in which they would be encountered while moving counterclockwise around the World Showcase Lagoon after crossing the bridge from Future World.

Canada

Celebrating the many beauties of the U.S.A.'s neighbor to the north, the area devoted to the Western Hemisphere's largest nation is complete with its own mountain, waterfall, rushing stream, rocky canyon, mine, and splendid garden massed with colorful flowers. There's even a totem pole, a trading post, and an elaborate, mansard-roofed hotel similar to ones built by Canadian railroad companies as they pushed west around the turn of the 20th century. All this is imaginatively arranged somewhat like a split-level house, with the section representing French Canada on top, and another devoted to the mountains alongside it and below. From a distance, the Hôtel du Canada, the main building here, looks like little more than a bump on the landscape—as does Epcot's single Canadian Rocky Mountain. But up close they both seem to tower as high as the real thing.

The gardens were inspired by the Butchart Gardens, in Victoria, British Columbia, a famous park created on the site of a limestone quarry. The hotel is modeled after Ottawa's Victorian-style Château Laurier. Entertainment may be provided by a troupe of Celtic rock musicians, called "Off-Kilter." They perform on a stage facing the promenade.

O CANADA!: This 18-minute motion picture, presented in Circle-Vision 360 inside Canada's mountain, portrays the Canadian confederation in all its coast-to-coast splendor—the prairies and plains, sparkling shorelines and

rivers, and the untouched snowfields and rocky mountainsides surround you. The Royal Canadian Mounted Police also put in an appearance. All the maritime provinces are pictured, with their covered bridges and sailing ships, as is Montreal, with its old-world cafes and churches; the scene in the Notre Dame Basilica, with its organ booming and choirboys in attendance, is particularly stirring.

The great outdoors gets equal play. In one scene, snow geese take off all around the screen, and the beating of their wings is positively thunderous. Eagles, possums, mallards, bobcats, wolves, bears, deer, bison, and herds of reindeer can also be seen.

Filmed, too, were steers being roped at a rodeo and the chuck wagon race that takes place every year at that great provincial fair known as the Calgary Stampede. Skiers in the vast and empty Bugaboos, dogsledders, and ice-skaters are featured in the winter scenes; in a hockey game, the sound system almost perfectly conveys the scratch of skates on ice and the sharp whack of sticks slamming against the puck. And throughout, the motion picture provides a you-are-there feeling that makes all of this spectacular scenery still more memorable. Note that there are no seats in this theater.

NORTHWEST MERCANTILE: The first shop to the left upon entering the pavilion's plaza features merchandise by Roots, a Canadian apparel label. The Roots line features athletic attire, shoes, and fragrances. The shop also stocks plush toys, maple syrup, and other Canada-themed collectibles. Skeins of rope, tin scoops, lanterns, and antique ice skates hanging from the long beams overhead set the mood, together with the structure itself.

LA BOUTIQUE DES PROVINCES: This small shop inside Hôtel du Canada, which features a variety of items with an *Anne of Green Gables* theme, also proffers Linda Edgington decoupage, pewter, and other items crafted by Canadian artists.

United Kingdom

In the space of only a few hundred feet, visitors to this pavilion stroll from an elegant London square to the edge of a canal in the rural countryside—via a bustling urban English street framed by buildings that constitute a veritable rhapsody of historic architectural styles. But one scene leads to the next so smoothly that nothing ever seems amiss. Here again, note the attention to detail: the half-timbered High Street structure that leans a bit, the hand-painted "smoke" stains that make the chimneys look as if they had been there for centuries. When a thatched roof is required, it's right where it should be—though the roof may be made of plastic broom bristles because fire regulations prohibit the real thing. Off to the side is a pair of scarlet phone booths identical to those that used to be found around the U.K. And there are eight architectural styles characteristic of the streetscapes, from English Tudor to Georgian and English Victorian.

There is no major attraction in this pavilion; instead, it features half a dozen shops and a pub that serves a selection of beers and ales that would be the toast of any "local" in London itself. There's lots of entertainment, including a group of comedians called the World Showcase Players, who, when not engaged in general clowning on the World Showcase Promenade, coax audience members into participating in their farcical playlets. In the pub, a pianist has been known to play late into the evening. A mop-topped quartet known as the British Invasion occasionally plays Beatles tunes in the garden courtyard. They're a true crowd-pleaser. (Entertainment is subject to change.)

THE CROWN & CREST: This shop looks like a backdrop for a child's fantasy of the days of King Arthur, with its high rafters decked out with bright banners, vast fireplace (and crossed swords above), and wrought-iron chandelier. "Pub mugs," glasses that serve yards of beer, limited-edition chess sets, and passport stamp sets are the stock-in-trade at this emporium adjoining the Sportsman Shoppe. Name histories and family crests are also available.

SPORTSMAN SHOPPE: Head here for clothing and accessories centered on uniquely British locales and events. You can expect to

Hot Tip!

A great place to watch IllumiNations is from the Rose & Crown Pub in the United Kingdom pavilion. Try to snag a lagoonside table—whether within the pub's boundaries or in the self-serve sitting area nearby—about 30 minutes before the show is set to begin. (Note that on nights when the wind is blowing directly toward the Rose & Crown, it might be better to grab a bite and watch the show from Mexico's La Cantina, on the other side of the lagoon.)

find Wimbledon tennis garb, golf items from Scotland's Royal and Ancient Golf Club at Saint Andrews, plus Rugby shirts. Don't miss the tartan map on the wall opposite The Crown & Crest; it identifies plaids from Glen Burn and Gordon to Langtree and St. Lawrence. Outside, the shop resembles a stone manor built during the last half of the 16th century.

THE TEA CADDY: Fitted out with heavy wooden beams and a broad fireplace to resemble the Stratford-upon-Avon cottage of William Shakespeare's wife, Anne Hathaway, this shop stocks English teas, both loose and in bags, in a wide variety of flavors. Other items include teapots, china, biscuits, and assorted candies.

PHOTO BY JILL SAFRO

THE TOY SOLDIER: This shop presents a nice selection of British toys, as well as a rather extensive selection of merchandise featuring the gang from the Hundred Acre Wood: Winnie the Pooh, Piglet, Eeyore, and Tigger, too.

THE QUEEN'S TABLE: This shop (opposite the Sportsman Shoppe) may be one of the loveliest in Epcot. This is particularly true of the store's elegant Adams Room, embellished with elaborate moldings, hung with a crystal chandelier, and painted in cream and robin's-egg blue. The setting is a lovely background for the perfumes, soaps, and other fragrant items that are available.

Don't neglect to inspect small, serene Britannia Square outside the shop farthest from the promenade. But for its small size and the Florida climate, it feels like London itself.

THE MAGIC OF WALES: This small emporium offers pottery, jewelry, souvenirs, and hand-crafted gifts.

International Gateway

International Gateway, informally known as Epcot's back door, is located between the United Kingdom and France pavilions. Here you'll find:

FRIENDSHIP LANDING: Disney's water taxis, known as *FriendShip* boats, ferry guests to the Yacht and Beach Club, BoardWalk, and the Swan and Dolphin Resorts, and finally to the Disney-MGM Studios (which is the last stop before the boat returns to the resorts and back to Epcot). The dock is located outside the International Gateway turnstiles.

GATEWAY GIFTS: Candy, convenience items, souvenirs, and a package pickup depot are located at this spot near the France entrance.

Where to Eat in Epcot

A complete listing of all eateries—full-service restaurants, fast-food emporiums, and snack shops—can be found in the *Good Meals, Great Times* chapter. See the Epcot section, beginning on page 231.

WORLD TRAVELER: Disney fashions, home items, character merchandise, and Epcot souvenirs are among the items for sale here.

STROLLER AND WHEELCHAIR RENTAL: Strollers and wheelchairs are available for rent at this location. Remember to keep your rental receipt; it can be used on the same day in the Magic Kingdom, the Disney-MGM Studios, Animal Kingdom, or again in Epcot, should you leave and return later on. It is also possible to get a replacement stroller here.

France

The buildings here have mansard roofs and casement windows so Gallic in appearance that you may expect to see some sad Bohemian poet looking down from above. A canal-like offshoot of the lagoon seems like the Seine itself; the footbridge that spans it recalls the old Pont des Arts. There's a kiosk nearby like those that punctuate the streets of Paris and a bakery whose heavenly rich aromas announce its presence long before it's visible.

Shops sell perfumes and other items. Their roofs are of real copper or slate, and the cabinetry is finely crafted. Galérie des Halles—the iron-and-glass-ceilinged market that Paris once counted as one of its most beloved institutions—lives again. But perhaps most special of all are the people. Hosts and hostesses who hail from Paris and the French provinces answer questions in French-accented English. Keep an eye out for Server Amusant, the comedic waiter who does one heck of a balancing act.

Some interesting background notes: The dusty rose-colored, lace-trimmed costumes that the hostesses wear were inspired by the dresses in *Le Bar aux Folies-Bergère* by the Impressionist painter Edouard Manet, and the main entrance to the pavilion recalls the architecture of Paris, most of which was built during the *Belle Epoque* ("beautiful age"), the last decades of the 19th century.

Don't miss the garden on the opposite side of this arcade. It is one of the most peaceful spots in World Showcase.

BIRNBAUM'S BEST **IMPRESSIONS DE FRANCE:** Shown in the Palais du Cinéma, a little theater that's not unlike the one at Fontainebleau, this enchanting 18-minute film takes viewers on a trip through France.

The film shows off a beautiful tree-dotted estate, fields and vineyards at harvest time, a flower market and a pastry shop, a glacier, and a harbor full of squawking gulls. Viewers visit the Eiffel Tower; Versailles and its gilt Hall of Mirrors (just outside Paris); Mont Saint Michel; the French Alps; and Cannes, the star-studded resort city on the Mediterranean coast. All this is even more appealing thanks to a superb sound track, consisting almost entirely of the music of French-classical composers.

The exceptionally wide screen adds yet another dimension. This is not a Circle-Vision 360 film like the movies shown at China and Canada. The France film used only five cameras, and it is shown on five large projection surfaces—200 degrees around. It's a beautiful film, one of the park's best. We recommend stopping for a French pastry break after the show.

PLUME ET PALETTE: This is one of the loveliest shops in World Showcase. The Art Nouveau style is reflected in the curves that embellish the wrought-iron balustrade edging the mezzanine and the moldings that decorate cherry-wood cabinets and shelves. Among the wares are French fragrances and soaps.

LA SIGNATURE: Another beautiful spot, this boutique features a selection of Guerlain cosmetics and fragrances.

L'ESPRIT DE PROVENCE: This little shop stocks a selection of dinnerware and kitchen accessories from the Provence region of Southern France.

LES VINS DE FRANCE: Selections in this lovely wine shop range from the inexpensive to the pricey, from *vin ordinaire* going for

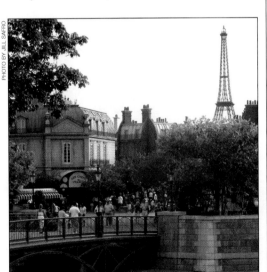

several dollars to upward of $99 for a rare vintage. Wine tastings are held here to sample the offerings (note that a charge is levied for each taste). Those who don't want to carry their purchases may have them dispatched to a package pickup location (either at the Park's Future World entrance or at the International Gateway entrance in World Showcase) for retrieval later in the day (be sure to allow at least two hours for packages to make it to their destination).

SOUVENIRS DE FRANCE: Everything from Eiffel Tower statues to CDs with music by French composers is the stock-in-trade at this location near the exit of the cinema. Gifts are themed to the artwork of renowned French artists, such as Monet and Renoir. Mugs, tote bags, umbrellas, and picture frames are among the offerings available. The area is based on Paris's now-demolished Les Halles, the city's old fruit and vegetable market.

Morocco

Nine tons of tile were handmade, hand cut, and shipped to Epcot to create this World Showcase pavilion. To capture the unique quality of this North African country's architecture, Moroccan artisans came to Epcot to practice the mosaic art that has been a part of their homeland for thousands of years. Koutoubia Minaret, a detailed replica of the famous prayer tower in Marrakesh, stands guard at the entrance. A courtyard with a

Hot Tip!

Don't try to fit all of the World Showcase movies into one day, especially if you are traveling with kids.

fountain at the center leads to the Medina (Old City). Between the traditional alleyways and the more modern sections are the pointed arches and swirling patterns of the Bab Boujouloud gate, a replica of the one that stands in the city of Fez. An ancient working waterwheel irrigates the gardens, and the motifs repeated throughout the buildings include carved plaster and wood, tile, and brass. Mo'rockin takes over the courtyard, with musicians playing Western music with an Arabic twist. (Entertainment may change.)

MOROCCAN NATIONAL TOURIST OFFICE: An information center offering literature useful in planning a visit to Morocco, this is also the place to inquire about experiencing a "Morocco Tour." The guided tour of the pavilion includes an in-depth description of the culture, history, and architecture of Morocco. Tours are held daily at 1 P.M., 3 P.M., and 5 P.M. They are free to all Epcot park guests and last from about 20 to 45 minutes.

TANGIER TRADERS: This is the place to shop if you're in the market for a fez, woven belts, leather sandals and purses, and other traditional Moroccan clothing and accessories.

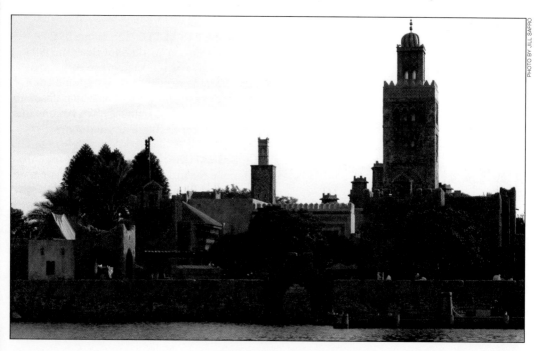

PHOTO BY JILL SAFRO

MARKETPLACE IN THE MEDINA: Handwoven baskets, sheepskin wallets and bags, assorted straw hats, drums, sandals, postcards, scarves, and small carpets are among the available wares.

THE BRASS BAZAAR: Interspersed among the decorative brass plates in this store are ceramic pitchers, planters, pots, ornate bottles of rosewater, serving sets, soapstone carvings, wooden collectibles, books, framed prints, and other Moroccan wares.

SOUK AL MAGREB: This small waterside enclave located on the World Showcase promenade spills over with crafted brass work. Moroccan baskets and leather goods also abound. In addition to henna tattoos (provided by a resident tattoo artist), one can also pick up toy camels, hats, and shirts.

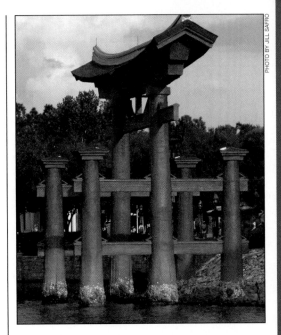

PHOTO BY JILL SAFRO

Japan

Serenity rules in Japan. Except, of course, when the pavilion resounds with traditional music performed by a drum-playing duo or group.

The landscaping, designed in accordance with traditional symbolic and aesthetic values, contributes to the pavilion's peaceful mood. Rocks, which in Japan represent the enduring nature of the Earth, were brought from North Carolina and Georgia (since boulders are scarce in the Sunshine State). Water, symbolizing the sea (which the Japanese consider a life source), is abundant; the Japan pavilion garden has a stream and pools inhabited by *koi* (fish). Evergreen trees, which in Japan are symbols of eternal life, are here in force.

> ## Did You Know?
> The five stories of the Japanese pagoda symbolize earth, water, fire, wind, and sky.

Disney horticulturists created this very Japanese landscape using few plants native to that country because the climate there is so different from that of Florida. Among the few trees here native to Japan are the *sago*, near the courtyard entrance to the Yakitori House; the two Japanese maple trees, identifiable by their small leaves, not far away (near the first stairway from the promenade on the left side of the courtyard as you face it); and the prickly monkey-puzzle trees, near the walkway to the promenade, on

The American Adventure side of the pagoda. Needle-sharp thorns make the latter the only species of tree that monkeys cannot climb.

The pagoda was modeled after an eighth-century structure located in the Horyuji Temple, in Nara, Japan. The striking *torii* gate on the shore of World Showcase Lagoon derives from the design of the one at the Itsukushima shrine in Hiroshima Bay.

BIJUTSU-KAN GALLERY: Housing a changing cultural display, this small museum has offered, among other exhibitions, "Netsuke— Historic Carvings of Old Japan," a showcase of traditional Japanese art forms, and, more recently, the Kitahara Collection of Tin Toys, featuring toys produced from 1880–1970.

MITSUKOSHI MERCHANDISE STORE: There are kimonos, T-shirts bearing Japanese characters, traditional headdresses, and a selection of bowls and vases meant for flower arranging for sale at this spacious store set up by Mitsukoshi—a four-century-old retail firm.

The shop features a large selection of kimonos, as well as chopsticks, bonsai, jewelry, china, paper fans, and origami products. There is also a bounty of snacks, candies, and tea. The pleasant atmosphere and wide variety of merchandise make this establishment a most rewarding experience for both the casual browser and the serious shopper.

The building's design was inspired by the Gosho Imperial Palace, which was constructed in Kyoto in A.D. 794.

The American Adventure

BIRNBAUM'S BEST When it came to creating The American Adventure, the centerpiece of World Showcase, Disney Imagineers were given relatively free rein. So the 110,000 bricks of the imposing Colonial-style structure that houses a spectacular show, fast-food restaurant, and souvenir shop are the real thing—patiently crafted *by hand* from soft Georgia clay.

The show inside stands out because of its wonderfully evocative settings, its detailed sets, and the 35 superb Audio-Animatronics players, some of the most lifelike ever created by the Disney organization. A stellar a cappella vocal group called Voices of Liberty periodically serenades guests in the building's foyer. By all means, catch a performance.

THE AMERICAN ADVENTURE SHOW: One of the outstanding Epcot attractions, this 26-minute presentation celebrates the American spirit from our nation's earliest years right up to the present. Beginning with the arrival of the Pilgrims at Plymouth Rock and their hard first winter on the western shore of the Atlantic, the Audio-Animatronics narrators—an amazingly lifelike Ben Franklin and a convincing, cigar-puffing Mark Twain—recall key people and events in American history: the Boston Tea Party, George Washington and the grueling winter at Valley Forge, the influential abolitionist Frederick Douglass, the celebrated 19th-century Nez Percé chief Joseph, and many more. The Philadelphia Centennial Exposition is remembered, along with women's rights campaigner Susan B. Anthony, telephone inventor Alexander Graham Bell, and the steel giant and philanthropist Andrew Carnegie. Naturalist John Muir converses onstage with Teddy Roosevelt. Charles Lindbergh, Rosie the Riveter, Jackie Robinson, Marilyn Monroe, and Walt Disney are represented. So are John Wayne, Lucille Ball, Margaret Mead, John F. Kennedy, Martin Luther King, Jr., and Billie Jean King.

The idea is to recall episodes in history, both

Hot Tip!

While all of the seats in the American Adventure theater provide good views, the sound quality is best in the middle and toward the front.

negative and positive, that contributed to the growth of the spirit of America, either by engendering "a new burst of creativity" (in the designers' words) "or a better understanding of ourselves as partners in the American experience." It hasn't been updated in a while, but it is still rather compelling.

For information about how each of the many featured historical figures spoke during his or her lifetime, researchers contacted historians and cultural institutions—the Philadelphia Historical Commission, the State Historical Society of Missouri, the Department of the Navy's Ships Historical Branch, and others. When recordings were not available, educated guesses were made: Alexander Graham Bell's voice was created on the basis of contemporary comments about his voice's clarity, expressiveness, and crisp articulation, combined with the fact that his father taught elocution.

A highlight of the show is the majestic music played throughout by the Philadelphia Symphony Orchestra.

Seats toward the front of the house give the best view of the Audio-Animatronics figures. If you

have some extra time before the show, be sure to read the inspirational quotes on the walls—Jane Addams, Charles Lindbergh, Herman Melville, and Ayn Rand are among the Americans who are quoted.

AMERICAN HERITAGE GALLERY: Located inside the American Adventure pavilion, the addition of this art gallery brought Epcot's grand total to six. Its inaugural exhibition, called "Echoes of Africa," explores the connection between historical African art and its influence and significance as interpreted by contemporary African-American artists.

HERITAGE MANOR GIFTS: Visit this shop to find Americana in all of its red-white-and-blue glory. Gifts include patriotic clothing, flags, and books about American history.

AMERICA GARDENS THEATRE: An ever-changing slate of entertainment is presented throughout the year in this lakeside amphitheater in front of The American Adventure pavilion. Showtimes are also posted on the promenade and in the Times Guide.

Be sure to note the pruning of the western sycamores overhead: The old-fashioned pollarding method used, which involves trimming the treetops flat and allowing the lower branches to interlock, produces a thick canopy. The flower beds are planted appropriately with red, white, and blue blossoms.

Italy

The arches and cutout motifs that adorn the World Showcase reproduction of the Doge's Palace in Venice are just the more obvious examples of the attention to detail lavished on the individual structures in this relatively small pavilion. The angel perched atop the scaled-down campanile was sculpted on the model of the original, right down to the curls on the back of its head. It was then covered with real gold leaf, despite the fact that it was destined to be set almost 100 feet in the air.

The other statues in the complex, including the sea god Neptune presiding over the fountain in the rear of the piazza, are similarly exact. And the pavilion even has an island like Venice's own, its seawall appropriately stained with age, plus moorings that look like barber poles, with several distinctively Venetian gondolas tied to them. St. Mark the Evangelist is also remembered, together with the lion that is the saint's companion and Venice's guardian; these can be seen atop the two massive columns that flank the small arched footbridge that connects the island to the mainland. The only deviation from Venetian reality is the alteration of the site of the Doge's Palace in reference to the real St. Mark's Square.

The quaint pavilion is equally interesting from a horticultural point of view. The island boasts kumquat trees, citrus plants typical of the Mediterranean, and a couple of olive trees that can be seen on both sidewalls of the Enoteca Castello and La Bottega Italiana. Originally located in a Sacramento, California, grove, the olive trees arrived in Florida via flatbed truck a bit slimmer than when they started out. (Arizona border inspectors decreed that the trees be trimmed to the ten-foot width required by state law; therefore, the ancient olives were shorn en route. The hardy trees survived, leaving only their scars to remind visitors of the ordeal; the darker bark is what remains of the original, while the lighter areas are new growth.) The tall, narrow trees that stand like dark columns are Italian cypresses, which are extremely common in their native country.

ENOTECA CASTELLO: This shop on the edge of the piazza features a selection of red and white Italian wines. Items such as chocolate, espresso, cookbooks, and decorative bottle toppers are also on hand.

IL BEL CRISTALLO: There is an abundance of fine leather goods, including purses, wallets, and bags inside this shop (just off the promenade on the Germany side of the piazza). Other featured wares include scarves, ties, fragrances, and jewelry.

LA BOTTEGA ITALIANA: This shop sells an eclectic blend of decorative ceramics and glassware, plus an assortment of masks.

Germany

There are no villages in Germany quite like this one. Inspired by various towns in the Rhine region, Bavaria, and the German north, it boasts structures reminiscent of those found in urban enclaves as diverse as Frankfurt, Freiburg, and Rothenburg. There are stair-stepped rooflines and towers, balconies and arcaded walkways, and so much overall charm that the scene seems to come straight out of a fairy tale. The beer hall to the rear is almost as lively as the one at Munich's famed Oktoberfest, especially late in the evening. The shops, which offer a range of merchandise from wine and sweets to ceramics and cuckoo clocks, toys, and books—and even art—are so tempting that it's hard to leave the area empty-handed.

The elements that constitute the Germany pavilion are described here as they would be encountered walking from west to east (counterclockwise) around the cobblestone-paved central plaza, which is known as the St. Georgsplatz, after the statue at its center. St. George, the patron saint of soldiers, is depicted with a dragon that legend says he slew during a pilgrimage to the Middle East.

Try to time your World Showcase peregrinations to take you to Germany on the hour, when the handsome, specially designed glockenspiel at the plaza's rear can be heard chiming in a melody composed specifically for the pavilion.

DAS KAUFHAUS: This two-story structure, whose exterior is patterned after a merchants' hall known as the Kaufhaus (located in the German town of Freiburg in Breisgau), stocks hand-painted eggs (some painted on the premises), glassware, and housewares. Film and sundries are also available.

VOLKSKUNST: Small and exceptionally appealing, this establishment is filled with a burgher's bounty of German timepieces, plus a smattering of other items made by hand in the rural corners of the nation. As for cuckoo clocks, some are small and unobtrusive, while others are so immense that they'd look appropriate only in some cathedral-ceilinged hunting lodge. This is also the place to pick up a traditional German beer stein.

DER TEDDYBAR: Located adjacent to Volkskunst, this toy shop would be a delight if only for the lively mechanized displays: Some of the stuffed lambs and the dolls wearing folk dresses (called *dirndls*) have been animated so that tails wag and skirts swirl in time to German folk tunes. The shop is also home to one of Walt Disney World's best selections of toys, including an assortment of expensive stuffed keepsakes from Steiff. Last but not least, the dolls are simply wonderful— you can even have one created to your personal specifications.

KUNSTARBEIT IN KRISTALL: This shop to the left of the Biergarten features Austrian and crystal jewelry, tall beer mugs, wineglasses in traditional German tints of green and amber, and crystal decanters. Guests may have glassware etched on the spot.

SUSSIGKEITEN: It's a mistake to visit this tiny confectionery shop on an empty stomach: Chocolate cookies, butter cookies, and almond biscuits mix with caramels, nuts, and pretzels on the shelves, and there are boxes upon boxes of *lebkuchen*, the spicy chewy cookies traditionally baked in Germany at Christmas, not to mention Gummy Bears (which the packages announce as *Gummibaeren*). Be sure to note the attractive display of old Bahlsen sweets by the door.

WEINKELLER: The Germany pavilion's wine shop, situated between the cookie shop and the crystal shop toward the rear of St. Georgsplatz, offers about 50 varieties of German wine. Wine tastings are held here daily. The selection includes not only those vintages meant for everyday consumption, but also fine estate wines. These are white (with a few exceptions), because white wine constitutes the bulk of Germany's vinicultural output. (Only 20 percent of all German bottlings are red.) The setting itself is quite attractive—low-ceilinged and cozy, and full of cabinets embellished with carvings of vines and bunches of grapes.

DIE WEIHNACHTS ECKE: This is a shop that can set a visitor's mind to thoughts of Christmas—even on the hottest dog days of summer. Ornaments, decorations, and gifts manufactured by various German companies line the shelves of this store. Among them are wood carvings made in the German town of Oberammergau, nutcrackers, and a whole collection of "smokers" (carved wooden dolls with a receptacle for incense and a hollow pipe for the smoke to escape).

GLAS UND PORZELLAN: Featuring glass and porcelain items made by the German firm of Goebel, this is an attractive establishment with rope-turned columns, curved moldings, delicate scrollwork, and tiny carved rosettes. But no matter how attractive the background, the stars of the show are the M. I. Hummel figurines that Goebel makes. Cherubic, rosy-cheeked children, shown carrying baskets, trays, umbrellas, and other items—depicted as in the drawings of a young German nun named Berta Hummel—are favorites of collectors around the world. There is always an elaborate showpiece at the center of the shop, and a Goebel artist is here to demonstrate the process by which Hummel creations are painted and finished.

China

Dominated by the Disney equivalent of Beijing's Temple of Heaven and announced by a pair of banners that offer good wishes to passersby (the Chinese characters translate to: "May good fortune follow you on your path through life" and "May virtue be your neighbor"), this pavilion conveys a level of serenity that offers an appealing contrast to the hearty merriment of the bordering Germany and the gaiety of nearby

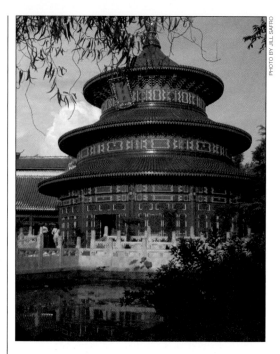

Mexico. Part of this quiet environment is the by-product of the soothing, traditional Chinese music. Live flute, zither, or dulcimer music is performed inside the Temple of Heaven, while agile acrobats do tricks in the courtyard. The gardens also make a major contribution. They are full of rosebushes native to China, and there is a century-old mulberry tree (to the left of the main walkway into the pavilion), with a pomegranate tree and a wiggly-looking Florida native known as a water oak nearby.

The number of stones in the floor of the pavilion's main structure is not random; the center stone is surrounded by nine stones because nine is considered a lucky number in China. Around the edge of the outer room rise 12 columns—because 12 is the number of months in the year and the number of years in a full cycle of the Chinese calendar. Be sure to stand on the round stone in the center: every whisper is amplified.

Village Traders

Located between the Germany and China pavilions, this open-air shop sports a selection of gift items from Africa, India, and Australia. Browse through such souvenirs as wind chimes, handbags, hats, and, of course, T-shirts.

A spacious emporium is devoted to Chinese wares, and two restaurants add to the overall atmosphere. However, all this is secondary to the motion picture shown inside the Temple of Heaven—a Circle-Vision 360 film that is one of the most diverting World Showcase attractions. Keep in mind that this is a standing-room-only experience.

REFLECTIONS OF CHINA: This new presentation shows the beauties of a land that few Epcot visitors have seen firsthand—and does it so vividly that it's possible to see the film twice and still not fully absorb all the wonderful sights.

The film replaces "Wonders of China," the Circle-Vision 360 movie that played at Epcot's China pavilion since 1982. Just as with the original, filmmakers used nine cameras to capture cultural and scenic images that will wrap completely around viewers. The tour includes stops in Hong Kong, Macau, Beijing, and Shanghai.

This updated film includes footage of many landmarks, such as the 2,400-year-old Great Wall and Tian'anmen Square, as well as some newer cultural developments. Overall, it showcases the majesty of this ancient country and highlights some of the more dramatic changes that have taken place over the past 20 years. Note that the theater has no seats.

HOUSE OF WHISPERING WILLOWS: When exiting, pass by the House of Whispering Willows, an exhibit of ancient Chinese art and artifacts. Changed about every six months, it invariably includes fine pieces from well-known collections.

YONG FENG SHANGDIAN: This vast Chinese emporium, located off the narrow, charming Street of Good Fortune, offers a huge assortment of merchandise—silk robes, prints, paper umbrellas, embroidered items, and more. Trinkets, moderately priced items, and expensive antiques are available. The calligraphy on the curtains wishes passersby good fortune, long life, prosperity, and happiness.

Norway

Set between Mexico and China is Norway, a pavilion added to the World Showcase mix in 1988. Built in conjunction with many Norwegian companies, the pavilion celebrates the rich history, folklore, and culture of one of the Western world's oldest countries.

The cobblestone town square is an architectural showcase of the styles of such Norwegian towns as Bergen, Alesund, and Oslo. There's also a Norwegian castle fashioned after Akershus, a 14th-century fortress still standing in Oslo's harbor; the castle here houses the Akershus restaurant. Few can resist walking into the bakery for a taste of its treats. In a show of modernity, a statue of Norway's living legend, marathoner Grete Waitz, stands behind the bakery. Shops stock handicrafts and folk items: hand-knit woolens, wood carvings, and glass and metal artwork.

For a free guided tour of the pavilion in addition to a crash course in Norwegian culture and architecture, stop by the Norway Tourism desk.

MAELSTROM: FP Visitors tour Norway by boat—16-passenger, dragon-headed longboats inspired by those Eric the Red and other Vikings used a thousand years ago. The five-minute voyage begins in a tenth-century Viking village, where a ship is being readied to head out to sea. Seafarers then find themselves in a mythical Norwegian forest, populated by trolls who cause the boats to plummet backward, through a maelstrom, to the grandeur of the Geiranger fjord, where the vessel nearly spills over a waterfall. After a plunge through a rocky passage, the boats wind up in the

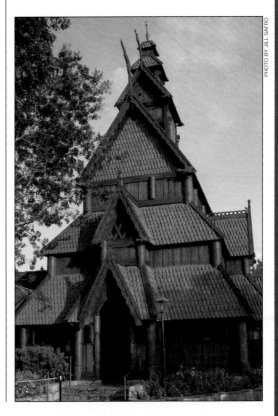
PHOTO BY JILL SAFRO

stormy North Sea. As the boats pass the legs of an oil rig, the storm calms and a coastal village appears on the horizon.

Survivors disembark and enter a movie theater, where the journey continues on-screen for five more minutes. If you wish to skip the flick, walk straight through the theater to exit.

STAVE CHURCH GALLERY: Inside the wooden stave church, there is a small exhibit that explores Vikings and Norwegian culture. It's interesting (and sad) to note that only 30 stave churches remain in Norway today.

THE PUFFIN'S ROOST: Norwegian gifts, sweaters, activewear, fragrances, jewelry, Christmas items, pewter, candy, toys, and trolls are the wares for sale at this shop.

Mexico

The tangle of tropical vegetation surrounding the great pyramid that encloses this pavilion and the Mexican restaurant at the lagoon's edge on the promenade provide only the barest suggestion of the charming area inside.

Dominated by a re-creation of a quaint plaza at dusk, the pyramid's interior is rimmed by balconied, tile-roofed, colonial-style structures. Crowding a pretty fountain area is a quartet of stands selling Mexican handicrafts, and to the left is a shop stocked with other handsome wares. The Mariachi Cobre band keeps things lively. To the rear, the San Angel Inn, a corporate cousin of the famous Mexico City restaurant, serves authentic Mexican fare. Behind it, the pavilion's main show chronicles Mexican culture from earliest times right up to the present.

Take a look at the cultural exhibit inside the

PHOTO BY JILL SAFRO

pyramid entrance on the way in. Note that the building itself was inspired by Meso-American structures dating from the third century A.D.

EL RIO DEL TIEMPO: THE RIVER OF TIME: Over the course of this simple six-minute boat trip, sprinkled with vignettes of pre-Columbian, Spanish colonial, and modern Mexican life, visitors greet a Mayan high priest, watch performers dance, and are assailed by vendors at a market. A band dressed to look like skeletons entertains at one juncture (in a reference to the Day of the Dead, a holiday celebrated in Mexico with candies and sweets shaped like skulls and skeletons). The cheery montage of film, props, and Audio-Animatronics figures is reminiscent of It's a Small World, though on a much smaller scale.

PLAZA DE LOS AMIGOS: Even if you're not in a buying mood, make a point of stopping by to take a look at this bustling marketplace. Brightly colored paper flowers, sombreros, malachite, baskets, mariachi music (available on CD), and pottery make this *mercado* (market) at the plaza's center as bright and almost as lively as one in Mexico itself. The brilliantly hued papier-mâché piñatas that figure strongly in the scenery here are quite popular. Authentic pre-Colombian figures are on display. Also available for purchase are spices, salsa, liquors (emphasis on tequila), cocktail accessories, candy, film, and Mexican musical instruments.

EL RANCHITO DEL NORTE: Located on the lagoon side of World Showcase Promenade, this spot features gifts and souvenirs from Mexico.

LA FAMILIA FASHIONS: Traditional and modern Mexican accessories for everyone in the family; the handcrafted silver jewelry is a major draw.

Showcase Plaza

PORT OF ENTRY: A children's shop carrying infants' and kids' clothing, girls' character dresses, plush dolls, and toys.

DISNEY TRADERS: Merchandise combining the charms of classic Disney characters and World Showcase themes is the primary stock-in-trade. Sunglasses, film, and sundries are also available.

Entertainment

Epcot presents an intriguing array of live performances each day, making it very important to consult a park Times Guide when you arrive. For updates, call 407-824-4321.

AMERICA GARDENS THEATRE: The venue alongside the lagoon at The American Adventure pavilion hosts an ever-changing program of live entertainment. Check a Times Guide for current offerings.

ILLUMINATIONS—REFLECTIONS OF EARTH: This nighttime spectacular presents the entire history of our planet in 13 minutes—from its creation to the present and a look toward the future. A dazzling mix of lasers, fireworks, fountains, and music, this show is a highlight of any Epcot visit.

The extravaganza, visible from anywhere on the World Showcase Promenade, takes place nightly at closing time. There are excellent viewing locations all around the World Showcase lagoon. Note that additional viewing areas have been added to the stretch between the Germany and China pavilions.

KIDCOT FUN STOPS: There is an activity area in each of the countries of World Showcase and at Future World's Test Track, The Seas with Nemo & Friends, and The Land. These spots allow young guests to play games and make crafts that are native to different cultures. Note that these areas are best enjoyed by small children.

WORLD SHOWCASE PERFORMERS: It's all but impossible to complete a circuit of World Showcase without catching a few performances en route. Keep an eye on the schedule to take in live entertainment at each pavilion, often performed by natives of the country represented. Among the possibilities: worldly comedians, a Mexican mariachi band, Moroccan belly dancers, Chinese acrobats, Canadian rock band, African storytellers, and more.

Holiday Happenings

During certain holidays, such as the Fourth of July, Christmas, and New Year's Eve, Epcot usually stays open extra late and presents added entertainment for the occasion. Call 407-824-4321 for details.

CHRISTMAS: Epcot celebrates this holiday with a nightly tree-lighting ceremony, a lighted archway that hugs the path to Showcase Plaza, and a candlelight choral processional.

The Candlelight Processional, a stirring presentation of traditional holiday songs, features a reading of the Christmas story by a celebrity narrator. This is a very popular event (and one of our favorites!). Disney characters are on hand for a nightly tree-lighting, too.

Hot Tips

- On your way into the park, pick up a free guidemap and a Times Guide. Consult the entertainment schedule first thing.

- Lines throughout Epcot are longest at mid-day and shortest in the early evening.

- During peak seasons, preferred reservation times at Epcot's table-service restaurants book quickly—make reservations as far in advance as possible. However, some tables may be available on a first-come, first-served basis (with a bit of a wait). Arrive a few minutes ahead of your reservation time.

- Most World Showcase restaurants seat guests until park closing. To make advance plans, call 407-WDW-DINE (939-3463).

- Check the Tip Board in Innoventions Plaza for wait times at the most popular attractions and adjust your plans accordingly. And use Fastpass whenever possible.

- Interactive fountain areas at Epcot provide guests of all ages with an opportunity to cool off. Be sure to pack swimsuits (or waterproof diapers) for little ones who will undoubtedly spend time splashing in the water.

- If you plan to play at Image Works, the interactive play area inside Imagination!, take along the e-mail address of a friend. It may come in handy.

- Allow plenty of time to explore the hands-on exhibits at Innoventions East and West, and Image Works in the Imagination! pavilion.

- When it comes to park-hopping, Epcot is an ideal park to hop to. It's usually open late.

- *FriendShip* water taxis are unlikely to transport you across World Showcase Lagoon any faster than a brisk walk, but they are a peaceful, foot-friendly way to make the half-mile-plus journey.

Where to Find the Characters

Classic Disney characters, such as Mickey Mouse, Chip, and Dale, host all meals served at the Garden Grill restaurant in The Land pavilion in Future World. Disney princesses invite you to join them for a meal at Norway's Akershus Royal Banquet Hall. Characters also appear at the Epcot Character Connection in Innoventions West in Future World. Figment greets guests at Journey Into Imagination, inside the Imagination pavilion. Check a park Times Guide for schedules and greeting locations.

Disney-MGM Studios

The Disney-MGM Studios park has been described as "the Hollywood that never was and always will be." A bit hokey, perhaps—but also true. Enter the gates and the mosaic of flashy neon, chromed Art Deco, and streamlined architecture, and star-gazing street characters immediately plunge you into the Hollywood of the 1940s. A nostalgic view of the moviemaking capital has been combined with revealing backstage tours, a variety of TV- and movie-themed attractions, and a delightful selection of eateries to create this Walt Disney World enclave. Throw in a character-laden motorcade parade, and the result is an entertainment wallop worthy of a rave review.

The Studios' water tower, known to punsters (for obvious reasons) as the "Earffel Tower," is reminiscent of the structures looming over Hollywood studios of the Golden Age. Here, however, it gets that special Disney touch— it's capped by a Mouseketeer-style hat. In true Hollywood style, this established star is somewhat upstaged by a relative newcomer: a towering Sorcerer Mickey hat, stationed at the far end of Hollywood Boulevard.

Since opening, the park continues to expand and evolve. Its eclectic lineup of classic attractions is joined by thrilling newcomers: an enhanced (and scarier) Tower of Terror, the rollicking Rock 'n' Roller Coaster, a dynamic vehicle stunt show, and an explosive struggle between good and evil in Fantasmic! Each adds a whole new dimension to the Hollywood term *action*.

A Beauty and the Beast — Live on Stage!

B Fantasmic!

C The Twilight Zone Tower of Terror

D Rock 'n' Roller Coaster

E The Magic of Disney Animation

F Playhouse Disney — Live on Stage!

G Walt Disney: One Man's Dream

H Voyage of The Little Mermaid

I Disney-MGM Studios Backlot Tour

J American Film Institute Showcase

K Honey, I Shrunk the Kids Movie Set Adventure

L Muppet★Vision 3-D

M Star Tours

N Indiana Jones Epic Stunt Spectacular

O Sounds Dangerous starring Drew Carey

P The Great Movie Ride

Q Lights, Motors, Action! Extreme Stunt Show

·········· Parade Route

Getting Oriented

While the Disney-MGM Studios is much smaller than Epcot, the park has a sprawling layout with no distinctive shape or main thoroughfare. As such, the Studios can be a bit of a challenge to navigate. Be sure to study a guidemap as you enter.

The park entrance is at Hollywood Boulevard. This shop-lined avenue leads straight to Hollywood Plaza, address of the Studios' Chinese Theater, a replica of Mann's Theatre that doubles as the site of The Great Movie Ride (it's hidden behind the giant Sorcerer Mickey hat). Walking along Hollywood Boulevard, toward the plaza, you'll come to Hollywood Junction. Here, a wide, palm-fringed thoroughfare known as Sunset Boulevard branches off to the right.

Stroll down Sunset Boulevard and you'll come across The Hollywood Hills amphitheater, home of Fantasmic! and Rock 'n' Roller Coaster. At the street's far end is The Hollywood Tower Hotel, home of The Twilight Zone™ Tower of Terror. The strip is also graced with shops, the Sunset Ranch Market, and the Theater of the Stars amphitheater, where Beauty and the Beast—Live on Stage is performed daily.

Stand in Hollywood Plaza, facing the Chinese Theater and you'll notice an archway just off to your right. This leads to Animation Courtyard. Mickey Avenue, the street veering off to the left of Animation Courtyard, leads to the Disney-MGM Studios Backlot Tour. If you turn left off Hollywood Boulevard and go past Echo Lake, you're on course for such attractions as Sounds Dangerous starring Drew Carey, Indiana Jones Epic Stunt Spectacular, and Star Tours. Just beyond Star

Tours there is another entertainment zone, near the Streets of America (in the backlot area). The biggies to see here: Muppet*Vision 3-D, Lights, Motors, Action!, and the Honey, I Shrunk the Kids Movie Set Adventure.

HOW TO GET THERE

Take Exit 64B off I-4. Continue about half a mile to reach the parking area. Take a tram to the park entrance.

By WDW Transportation: From the Swan, Dolphin, Yacht and Beach Club, and BoardWalk: boat or walkway. From Fort Wilderness: bus from the Settlement stop. From the Magic Kingdom: ferry or monorail to the TTC, then bus to the Studios. From Epcot, Animal Kingdom, all other Walt Disney World resorts and the resorts on Hotel Plaza Boulevard: bus. From Downtown Disney: bus to any WDW resort and transfer to a Studios bus or boat.

PARKING

All-day parking at the Studios is $9 for day visitors (free to WDW resort guests and annual passholders). Trams circulate regularly, providing transportation from the parking area to the park entrance. Be sure to note the section and the aisle in which you park. The parking ticket you receive allows for re-entry to the parking area throughout the day.

HOURS

The Disney-MGM Studios is usually open from 9 A.M. until about one hour after sunset. During certain holiday periods and summer months, hours are extended. It's best to arrive about 20 minutes before the posted opening time—guests are often let in early. Depending on the season, some stage shows do not open until late in the morning.

Admission Prices

ONE-DAY BASE TICKET
(Restricted to use only in the Disney-MGM Studios. Prices do not include sales tax and are subject to change.)
Adult $63
Child* $52
*3 through 9 years of age; children under 3 free

Park Primer

BABY FACILITIES

Changing tables and facilities for nursing mothers can be found at the Baby Care Center at Guest Relations near the park entrance.

CAMERA NEEDS

The Darkroom on Hollywood Boulevard stocks memory cards, batteries, and disposable cameras. Film is sold in several Studios shops, but is no longer processed on-site.

DISABILITY INFORMATION

Most Walt Disney World attractions, restaurants, shops, and shows are accessible to guests using wheelchairs. Additional services are available for guests with visual or hearing disabilities. For a detailed overview of the services offered, including transportation, parking, attraction access, and more, pick up a copy of the *Guidebook for Guests with Disabilities* at Guest Relations. For more information, refer to the *Getting Ready to Go* chapter.

FIRST AID

Minor medical problems can be handled at the First Aid Center, located next to Guest Relations at the park entrance.

INFORMATION

Guest Relations, located just inside the park entrance, has free guidemaps and Times Guides and an ever-resourceful staff. To make same-day dining arrangements for certain Studios eateries, head over to the booth at the junction of Hollywood and Sunset boulevards.

LOCKERS

Lockers, found by Oscar's Super Service, near the entrance, cost $5 per day (plus a $2 refundable deposit) for unlimited use. They may be rented from the Crossroads of the World kiosk, directly across from Oscar's classic pickup truck. Your receipt entitles you to a locker at any other theme park on the same day (not including the deposit).

LOST & FOUND

Located near the park entrance, past the turnstiles on the right. To report lost items after your visit, call 407-824-4245.

LOST CHILDREN

Report lost children at Guest Relations, or alert a Disney employee to the problem.

MONEY MATTERS

There is an ATM just outside the park entrance, and one inside Toy Story Pizza Planet Arcade. In addition to cash, credit cards (American Express, Visa, Discover, JCB, Diner's Club, the Disney Visa Card, and MasterCard), traveler's checks, Disney gift cards, and Walt Disney World resort IDs are accepted for admission, merchandise, and meals at all restaurants. Some snack carts and souvenir stands accept cash only.

PACKAGE PICKUP

Shops can arrange for purchases to be transported to package pickup at the Lost and Found (by the park entrance), where they can be picked up later. The service is free.

SAME DAY RE-ENTRY

Be sure to retain your ticket if you plan to return later the same day. A hand-stamp is no longer required for re-entry.

SECURITY CHECK

Guests entering Disney theme parks will be subject to a security check. Bags will be searched by Disney security personnel before guests are permitted to enter the park.

STROLLERS & WHEELCHAIRS

Strollers, wheelchairs, and Electric Convenience Vehicles (ECVs) may be rented from Oscar's Super Service, inside the park entrance on the right. Cost for strollers and wheelchairs is $10. A double stroller costs $18. A "Length of Stay" rental ticket saves wheelchair- and stroller-renters $2 a day. Cost for ECVs is $35, plus a $5 refundable deposit. Keep the receipt —it can be used on the same day for a replacement at any theme park. Quantities are limited.

TIP BOARDS

Check the Tip Boards at the junction of Hollywood and Sunset boulevards and on the Streets of America to learn the waiting times for the most popular attractions in the park. Attendants can answer questions, too.

The Main Attractions

The Disney-MGM Studios has a brand of attractions altogether unique. Some offer guests behind-the-scenes looks at the creative and technical processes that generate television, movies, and animation. Others go so far as to allow guests to gain a bit of showbiz experience along with the insight. Still others present popular characters and stories in new forms—from stage shows to thrill rides.

Many shows and attractions are presented at scheduled times, or keep shorter hours than the park itself—consult a Times Guide or the park's Tip Board for starting times.

The Twilight Zone™ Tower of Terror FP

BIRNBAUM'S ★BEST★ The Hollywood Tower Hotel is the creepy home of a spectacular thrill ride. On the facade of the 199-foot-tall building hangs a sparking electric sign. As the legend goes, lightning struck the building on Halloween night in 1939. An entire guest wing disappeared, along with an elevator carrying five people.

The line for the ride runs through the lobby, where dusty furniture, cobwebs, and old newspapers add to the eerie atmosphere. As guests enter the library, they see a TV brought to life by a bolt of lightning. Rod Serling invites them to enter The Twilight Zone.

Guests are led toward the boiler room to enter the ride elevator. (This is your chance to change your mind about riding. Simply ask the attendant to direct you toward the "chicken exit.") Once you take a seat in the elevator, the doors close and the room begins its ascent. At the first stop, the doors open and guests have a view down a corridor. Among the many effects is a ghostly visit by the hotel guests who vanished. The doors close again and you continue your trip skyward.

At the next stop, you enter another dimension, a combination of sights and sounds reminiscent of *The Twilight Zone* TV series. In fact, Disney Imagineers watched each of the 156 original *Twilight Zone* episodes at least twice for inspiration. This part of the ride is a disorienting experience, in part because the elevator moves horizontally.

What happens next depends upon the whim of Disney Imagineers, who have programmed the ride so that the drop sequence is chillingly random. At the top (about 157 feet up), passengers can look out at the Studios below. Once the doors shut, you plummet 13 stories. The drop lasts about two seconds, but it seems a whole lot longer.

Just when you think it's over, the elevator launches skyward, barely stopping before it plunges again. And again. As you exit, Rod Serling claims this is the kind of thing "they don't tell you about in any guidebook." It's been our privilege to prove him wrong.

From the time you are seated, the trip takes about five minutes. Note that you must be at least 40 inches tall to ride. It is not recommended for pregnant women, those with a heart condition, or people with back and neck problems. Though thrilling (and scary), the drops are surprisingly smooth. Still, if you'd rather not experience the sensation of being a human yo-yo, sit this one out.

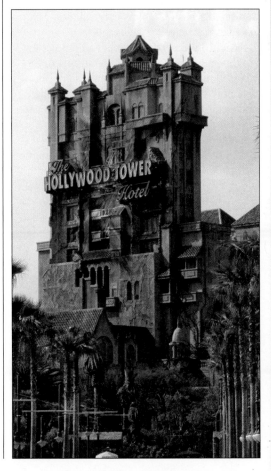

FP = Fastpass attraction (see page 25)

Rock 'n' Roller Coaster Starring Aerosmith FP

 The fastest roller coaster in Walt Disney World history is guaranteed to rock your world. Rock 'n' Roller Coaster is ideally suited for those who consider the Tower of Terror a little on the tame side.

The indoor attraction reaches a speed of nearly 60 miles per hour—in 2.8 seconds flat. Other twists include two loops and a corkscrew—marking the first time Disney has turned guests upside down on American soil.

Hot Tip!

You'll need to stop at a locker (near the park entrance) before riding Rock 'n' Roller Coaster—there's no place to store loose articles in the ride vehicles.

The ride's premise is this: The rock band Aerosmith has invited you to a backstage party. The only thing standing between you and the big bash is a classically chaotic Los Angeles freeway.

To get to the party on time, you'll have to zip through the nighttime L.A. streets in a stretch limo. The ride vehicles (designed to resemble limousines) are equipped with a high-tech sound system (five speakers per seat make for a mega-decibel ride), and the remainder of the journey features rockin' synchronized sound—adding a very dramatic

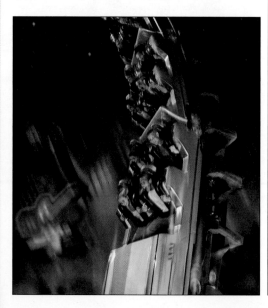

dimension to the roller coaster experience most daredevils have come to expect.

You must be free of back, neck, and heart problems to experience this topsy-turvy tour. Expectant mothers should sit this one out. Guests must be at least 48 inches tall to ride.

Beauty and the Beast —Live on Stage

Here's the show that inspired the Broadway musical. Several times each day, Belle, Gaston, Mrs. Potts, and the rest of the cast of the Disney film *Beauty and the Beast* come to life at the 1,500-seat Theater of the Stars, near the Tower of Terror, on Sunset Boulevard.

PHOTO BY JILL SAFRO

The 30-minute show is as entertaining as they come. The staging's just right and the music's simply addictive as it traces the classic tale—from Belle's dissatisfaction with her life in a small French town to the climactic battle between the staff of the Beast's castle and Gaston and the townspeople. Lumière and friends perform the song "Be Our Guest" with a delightful display of dancing flatware. Check a park Times Guide for performance schedule.

The Magic of Disney Animation

This attraction gives guests an insider look at the creative process behind Disney's many animated blockbusters.

The majority of the action takes place in a theater. Here, you'll be greeted by a jovial, knowledgeable host and treated to a whimsical explanation of how Disney animators bring characters to life. This segment of the tour is cohosted by Mushu, the wisecracking little dragon from the film *Mulan*. After breezing past desks once used by animators, you'll be invited to take part in a group animation lesson. The capacity for this part of the tour is smaller than the rest, so you may have to wait a bit to get in. If you don't want to stick around, there is an exit.

There's a little treat at the end of the tour: Copies of some of the Academy Awards won by the Disney animation team are on display, along with drawings from famous films. Note that the working animation facility has been shuttered, so there are no actual animators to spy on anymore.

Before moving on, spend some time browsing at the Animation Gallery, where Disney animation cels, exclusive limited-edition reproductions, books, figurines, and many other collectibles are for sale.

Voyage of The Little Mermaid FP

One of the Disney-MGM Studios' most popular attractions, this is a 17-minute live musical production, adapted from the Disney animated classic. The show is presented in a theater with an underwater feel. In it, many of the film's beloved animated characters, such as Flounder and Sebastian, are brought to life by puppeteers. The show opens with a lively rendition of "Under the Sea," then animated clips from the movie are shown as people join the puppets onstage.

Ariel is the star and performs songs from the film. Prince Eric makes an appearance, and an enormous Ursula glides across the stage to steal Ariel's voice. Of course, as in the movie, the happy ending prevails. The story line is a little bit disjointed, hopping from scene to scene, and some of the signature songs are missing. However, most viewers are familiar with the film, so this choppiness doesn't detract much from the show.

There are many special effects, including cascading water, lasers, and a lightning storm

that may be a bit frightening for very young children. Note that many of the effects are best enjoyed from the middle to the rear of the theater. Keep in mind that, although this is a Fastpass attraction, performances are still presented at scheduled times throughout the day. Current showtimes are always listed on the Times Guide (available at many locations throughout the park).

Playhouse Disney– Live on Stage!

Put on your dancing shoes! Bear, Tutter, Pip, Pop, and the rest of the gang will be disappointed if you don't join in the fun as they perform playful ditties from their Disney Channel show. Most popular with preschoolers, this stage show gets off to a bit of a slow start: Bear is sound asleep. Once audience members rouse him from his nap (no easy task), he bursts into song, welcoming one and all to his big, blue house. Later, Bear invites his new friends to investigate the day's mail, pay tribute to his beloved home, search for Shadow, and, of course, do the Bear Cha-Cha.

The performance space, which resembles a working TV studio, holds large crowds (of mostly tiny people) at a time. There are no seats, but there's plenty of room to sprawl out on the carpeted floor. This show is presented at Playhouse Disney in the Animation Courtyard area of the theme park. Expect to see characters from *JoJo's Circus, Stanley, Book of Pooh*, and other Disney Channel favorites. Times Guides list performance times.

Disney-MGM Studios Backlot Tour

Guests go backstage to see and experience some little-known aspects of TV and movie production on a tour of sets and prop stations. The 30-minute tour runs throughout the day.

The first stop is a large, outdoor special-effects area. This zone features a water tank, and teaches guests how special-effects–laden waterborne scenes can be created on a set.

Guests then board the trams and travel to the backlot. Trips begin with a look at the vast wardrobe department. More than 100 designers create costumes for Disney's movie, TV, and other entertainment projects—and with 2.5 million garments for its workers, Disney World has the planet's largest working wardrobe. Famous costumes are on display.

The tram then passes through the camera, props, and lighting departments. A look into the scene shop reveals carpenters at work on sets that will later be finished on the soundstages.

Where in Central Florida can you find an active oil field in the middle of a dry, rocky, barren desert canyon prone to flash floods? In

Catastrophe Canyon! As the guide will tell you, crews are filming a movie in which a backstage tram gets stuck in the canyon during a flash flood. But supposedly it's safe to go in because they're not filming today.

In a series of special effects, a rainstorm begins. Then there's an explosion, complete with flames that are so hot even riders on the right side of the tram feel them, followed by a flash flood that is so convincing, it forces everyone to lean the other way. The road underneath the tram shifts and dips, lending even more reality to the adventure.

From Catastrophe Canyon, the tram rides by the Streets of America, where reproduced building facades line urban streets. Though the brickwork looks authentic, these backless facades are constructed mostly of fiberglass and Styrofoam. The skyscrapers, including the Empire State Building and the Chrysler Building, are actually painted flats. Forced perspective (the same technique that makes Cinderella Castle appear taller than it is) makes the four-story Empire State Building appear as if it were the actual 104-story structure. After the tour, if crews are not filming, guests may explore the Streets of America area on foot. (It is possible to visit the area without experiencing

the backlot tour.) The tram may also pass through the Lights, Motors, Action! Extreme Stunt show theater.

Lights, Motors, Action! Extreme Stunt Show FP

When it comes to action, this attraction takes the phrase "cut to the chase" quite seriously. Here, tires squeal and flames burst as cars hurtle over trucks and jet skis rocket from a canal. The overall guest experience is twofold. On the one hand, it is a thrilling display of seemingly death-defying feats, and on the

---

Hot Tip!

Guests on the left side of the tram may get wet at Catastrophe Canyon, while those on the right stay dry. Choose accordingly.

other, it's an inside, backstage peek at how the movie-magic happens.

Taking place in a huge theater beyond the Streets of America (on a site once occupied by Residential Street), the show is presented several times a day. Check a Times Guide for showtimes and arrive early (or get a Fastpass). This lavish show was originally presented at Disneyland Paris, where it is known as Moteurs . . . Action! Parts may be too loud or intense for some small children (i.e., a stunt-person is set on fire).

PHOTO BY JILL SAFRO

American Film Institute Showcase

Though it is the final stop on the Backlot Tour, it is possible to visit this treasure chest of Hollywood memorabilia without taking the tour itself. Costumes, props, and set pieces used in recent, as well as classic, movies and television programs are on display in this ever-changing exhibit.

Although showcased items will be different when you visit (most recently, there was a preponderance of paraphernalia paying tribute to Hollywood villains), displays have included Barbara Stanwyck's costume from *Sorry, Wrong Number*, the police car from *Dick Tracy*, an Academy Award won by the film *My Fair Lady*, concept artwork from *Toy Story*, and live-action sets and stop-motion puppets from *James and the Giant Peach*.

The Great Movie Ride

Housed in a full-scale reproduction of historic Mann's Chinese Theatre, this 19-minute attraction captivates guests' imaginations from the get-go. The queue area winds through a lobby and into the heart of filmmaking, where movie scenes are shown on a large screen.

Hot Tip!
Don't miss the special tribute to the man who started it all: Walt Disney himself. The exhibit, entitled "Walt Disney: One Man's Dream" is housed in a theater on Mickey Avenue.

The guided tour begins in an area reminiscent of the hills of Hollywood (which, as the famous, now abbreviated, sign indicates, was once known as Hollywoodland) in its heyday. As a ride vehicle whisks guests under a vibrant marquee, they are transported to the celluloid world of yesteryear. About 60 dancing mannequins atop a cake greet guests in a replay of the "By a Waterfall" scene from the Busby Berkeley musical *Footlight Parade*.

Gene Kelly's memorable performance from *Singin' in the Rain* is the next scene, in which rain seems to drench the soundstage but does not dampen the spirits of the Audio-Animatronics representation of Mr. Kelly. (Gene Kelly personally inspected his likeness.) Then Mary Poppins and Bert the chimney sweep entertain (Julie Andrews and Dick Van Dyke, respectively), as Mary floats from above via her magical umbrella and Bert sings "Chim Chim Cher-ee" from a rooftop.

From the world of musical entertainment, guests segue to adventure. James Cagney recreates his role from *Public Enemy* as the ride

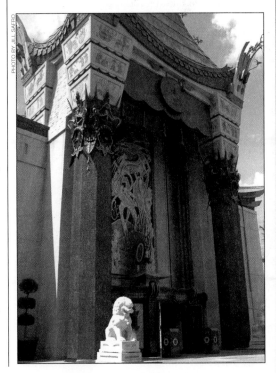

PHOTO BY JILL SAFRO

proceeds along Gangster Alley. A mob shootout begins and puts guests in the midst of an ambush. An alternate route leads to a western town, where John Wayne can be seen on horseback eyeing some would-be bank robbers. When the thieves blow up the safe and flames pour from the building, heat can be felt from the trams.

As the ride vehicle glides into the spaceship from *Alien*, Officer Ripley guards the corridor while a slimy monster threatens riders from overhead. (Note that this and other scenes may upset young children.)

The legendary farewell from *Casablanca* is also depicted, complete with a lifelike Rick and Ilsa. (Ingrid Bergman's daughter Isabella Rossellini has brought her kids here to "see Grandma.") Guests are moved from the airfield to the swirling winds of Munchkinland, where a house has just fallen on the Wicked Witch of the East. Her sister, as portrayed by Margaret Hamilton, appears in a burst of smoke. This Audio-Animatronics figure is impressively realistic (and scary). But happy endings prevail, and guests follow Dorothy and company along the Yellow Brick Road to the Emerald City of Oz. As the ride draws to a close, guests view a montage of memorable moments from classic films.

Timing Tip: If the queue extends outside the building, you're in for a long wait. It takes about 25 minutes to reach the ride vehicles once you've entered the theater.

Sounds Dangerous Starring Drew Carey

As you streak around a hairpin curve, precariously positioned in the driver's seat of a speeding car, you may want to check the security of your safety belt. Don't bother. There are no seat belts. Why? As its name indicates, this attraction only *sounds* dangerous. The majority of the action takes place in your head, thanks to a personal headset and some remarkably convincing stereo sound effects.

This 3-D audio adventure occurs inside a television soundstage. Audience members (that's you) are on hand to watch a new show being filmed. The program, *Undercover Live*, follows a detective (played by Drew Carey) as he attempts to solve cases in the real world. Drew sports a tiny camera on his tie, so the audience can see and hear all the action.

Initially, all goes according to plan. Drew infiltrates a warehouse owned by the United Snowglobe Company. He suspects they are smuggling something, though he can't put his finger on exactly what the contraband is. (Nor does he catch on after brushing past a box labeled SMUGGLED DIAMONDS, KEEP CLEAR.)

As Drew breaks into a suspect's office, he pulls the camera out of his tie tack, to give the audience a closer look at his lock-picking prowess. The unexpected appearance of a security guard sends a wave of panic over our hero, and he quickly hides the camera . . . in his mouth. Snap, crackle, blackout—the camera's video feed shorts out. Fortunately, the audio is unaffected, so it's on with the show!

From here on in, it's all about 3-D sound. (Drew Carey actually wore tiny microphones on his ears to achieve this effect.) Drew's mad pursuit to catch the bad guys takes audience members everywhere from a room full of buzzing honeybees to a barbershop for a quick trim and blow-dry. The case is finally resolved at the circus, but not before a close encounter with a prancing pachyderm.

The show, which runs continuously, lasts about 12 minutes. Generally fun for everyone, it does have its dark and spooky (remember the bees?) moments. It may be a bit unsettling for kids under the age of 7.

Indiana Jones Epic Stunt Spectacular FP

Earthquakes, fiery explosions, and assorted other dramatic events give guests some insight into the science of movie stunts and special effects at this 2,000-seat amphitheater. Stunt people re-create scenes from Indiana Jones films to demonstrate the skill required to keep audiences on the edge of their seats. Show director Glenn Randall, who served as stunt coordinator of such films as *Raiders of the Lost Ark*, *Poltergeist*, *E.T.*, and *Jewel of the Nile*, calls the show "big visual excitement."

But the 30-minute show isn't all flying leaps. Guests also see how the elaborate stunts are pulled off—safely—while the crew and an assistant director explain what goes on both in front of and behind the camera.

In one segment, a scene from *Raiders of the Lost Ark* is staged. A 12-foot-tall rolling ball chases a Harrison Ford look-alike out of the temple. The steam and flames are so intense that the audience can feel the heat. The crew then dismantles the set, revealing the remarkable lightness of movie props, as assistants roll the ball uphill for the next show.

In a scene at a busy "Cairo" street market, "extras" chosen from the audience play the famous scene in which Indiana Jones pulls a gun while others are fighting with swords. The explosive action continues and leads to a desert finale in which the hero and his sweetheart make a death-defying escape.

There are moments during this show when audience members might wonder if something has actually gone wrong. But by revealing tricks of the trade, the directors and stars show that what appears to be dangerous is actually a safe, controlled bit of movie magic.

Star Tours FP

BIRNBAUM'S BEST This attraction, which was inspired by George Lucas's series of *Star Wars* movies, offers guests a chance to board StarSpeeders that are the same type of flight simulators regularly employed by the military and commercial airlines to train pilots. By synchronizing a stunning film with the virtually limitless motion of the simulator, the ride allows guests to truly feel what they see.

Visitors enter an area where the famed *Star Wars* characters R2-D2 and C-3PO are working for a galactic travel agency. They spend their time in a bustling hangar area servicing the Star Tours fleet of spacecraft. Riders board the craft for what is intended to be a leisurely trip to the Moon of Endor, but the five-minute ride quickly develops into a harrowing flight into the depths of space, including encounters with giant ice crystals and laser-blasting fighters. The flight is out of control from the start, as the rookie pilot comically proves that Murphy's Law applies to the entire universe.

This is a very turbulent trip through the galaxy. Passengers must be free of back problems, heart conditions, motion sickness (do not ride on a full stomach!), and other physical limitations. Pregnant women are not permitted to board. Guests must be at least 40 inches tall, and children under 7 must be accompanied by an adult; kids under 3 are not allowed to ride.

Muppet*Vision 3-D

One of the most entertaining attractions at the Studios, this 3-D movie is quite remarkable. As with so many other Disney theme park attractions, much of the appeal is in the details. A funny 12-minute pre-show gives clues about what's to come. Once inside the theater, many will notice that it looks just like the one from Jim Henson's classic TV series *The Muppet Show*. Even the two curmudgeonly fellows, Statler and Waldorf, are sitting in the balcony, bantering with each other and offering their typically critical commentary on the show.

The production comes directly from Muppet Labs, presided over by Dr. Bunsen Honeydew—and his long-suffering assistant, Beaker—and introduces a new character, Waldo, the "Spirit of 3-D." Among the highlights is Miss Piggy's solo, which Bean Bunny turns into quite a fiasco. Sam Eagle's grand finale leads to trouble as a veritable war breaks out, culminating with a cannon blast to the screen from the rear balcony, courtesy of everyone's favorite Swedish Chef.

The 3-D effects, spectacular as they may be, are only part of the show: There are appearances by live Muppet characters, fireworks, and lots of funny details built into the walls of the huge theater. Including the pre-show, expect to spend about 29 minutes with Kermit and company. Shows run continuously throughout the day.

Hot Tip!

Even if you plan to skip Fantasmic!, it's good to know when it's being presented. Plan to hit the exit about 15 minutes after the 26-minute show is scheduled to begin. That way you'll beat the potential post-show bottleneck at the turnstiles.

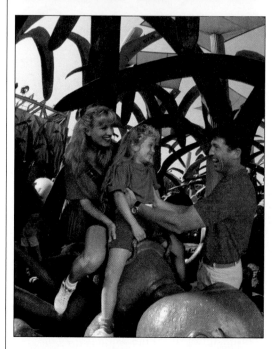

Honey, I Shrunk the Kids Movie Set Adventure

The set for the backyard scenes of the classic Disney movie has been re-created as an oversize, soft-surface playground. Enter it and experience the world from an ant's perspective.

Blades of grass soar 30 feet high, paper clips are as tall as trees, and Lego toys are practically big enough to live in. There are caves to explore (under the giant mushrooms) and many climbing opportunities (tremendous tree stumps and sprawling spiderwebs are among the better ones). Kids love to crawl into the discarded film canister and slide out along an oversize piece of film.

A leaky hose also provides entertainment as it squirts in a slightly different location each time. The props make everyone look and feel as though they were, indeed, shrunk by *Honey, I Shrunk the Kids'* Professor Wayne Szalinski. It holds the greatest appeal for younger guests.

Shopping

Hollywood Boulevard

CELEBRITY 5 & 10: Modeled after a 1940s Woolworth's, this large shop carries housewares such as lamps, candles, aprons, bath items, and Mickey ice cube trays, plus items that can be personalized.

COVER STORY: A small area located just through The Darkroom, this is the place to pick up your picture if you've had it taken by any of the park photographers.

CROSSROADS OF THE WORLD: In the middle of the entrance plaza, Mickey Mouse keeps watch from atop this Hollywood Boulevard landmark. The kiosk deals mostly in pins, but has some souvenirs and guidemaps. This is also the place to stop if you'd like to rent a locker.

THE DARKROOM: The Art Deco facade of this shop allows guests to peer through an aperture-like window. Cameras (including the disposable kind), film, and camera accessories are sold.

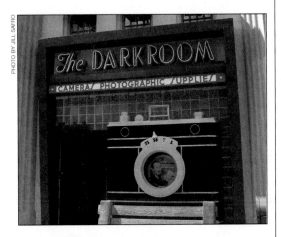

PHOTO BY JILL SAFRO

KEYSTONE CLOTHIERS: Women's and men's fashions and accessories are the specialties of the house.

L.A. CINEMA STORAGE: A great source for kids' stuff, with a nice variety of clothing and toys for infants, toddlers, and small children. Many items, such as watches, toys, and candy, feature classic Disney characters, including Mickey, Minnie, Donald, Goofy, and the like. There is also a "Create Your Own Mr. Potato Head" station.

MICKEY'S OF HOLLYWOOD: The place to find character T-shirts, sweatshirts, hats, plush toys, watches, socks, wallets, bags, books, and sunglasses, plus items emblazoned with the Walt Disney Studios logo.

MOVIELAND MEMORABILIA: This kiosk, located just to the left of the Studios' main entrance, stocks stuffed toys, hats, sunglasses, film, key chains, and other souvenirs.

SID CAHUENGA'S ONE-OF-A-KIND: Autographed photos of past and present matinee idols and sports stars, old movie magazines and posters, and assorted Hollywood memorabilia, such as lunch boxes, mugs, magnets, and books have been among the many celebrity-oriented collectibles with which Sid's been willing to part—for a price.

Sunset Boulevard

LEGENDS OF HOLLYWOOD: A tribute to Disney's animated legend, Winnie the Pooh. Expect to find an abundance of shirts, hats, and other colorful merchandise featuring everyone's favorite chubby little cubby—plus his pals from the Hundred Acre Wood.

MOUSE ABOUT TOWN: The best source for sports apparel featuring the famed mouse subtly embroidered onto sportswear, sweatshirts, and jackets. The Mouse also purveys golf-related apparel and accessories. Expect to find hats, ties, shirts, jackets, and more.

ONCE UPON A TIME: The exterior of this shop replicates the Carthay Circle Theatre, in Hollywood, where *Snow White and the Seven Dwarfs* premiered in 1937. The shop specializes in holiday items, with an emphasis on Christmas. For a fee, a Disney artist will customize a character sketch for you.

ROCK AROUND THE SHOP: Survive the Rock 'n' Roller Coaster and earn the right to shop here (okay, you can sneak into the shop from the outside, too). Expect to find music-related items such as drumsticks and CDs.

SUNSET CLUB COUTURE: A sophisticated selection of jewelry and mostly Mickey watches includes limited-edition pieces and pocket watches. A Disney artist can customize character watches on the spot.

SUNSET RANCH: This open-air shop carries Disney character hats, totes, and apparel, plus sunscreen, film, and sundries.

SWEET SPELLS: This shop, which is within the Beverly Sunset building, has a super selection of candy, cookies, and other ooey, gooey snack items. The caramel apples are to die for.

TOWER GIFTS: Inside the Hollywood Tower hotel, near the ride exit (but accessible from the outside), this spot offers Hollywood Tower Hotel merchandise.

VILLAINS IN VOGUE: All villains, all the time. Look for souvenirs and clothing featuring your favorite Disney bad guys (and girls). The shop is within the Beverly Sunset building, adjacent to Sweet Spells.

Beyond the Boulevards

AMERICAN FILM INSTITUTE SHOWCASE: Looking for items featuring the likes of Marilyn Monroe, Abbott and Costello, or Lucille Ball? Head here. There is also a supply of Three Stooges stuff. Nyuk, nyuk, nyuk.

ANIMATION GALLERY: Don't overlook this shop in the Animation Building, where limited-edition figurines, Disney animation cels, books, statues, and other collectibles ensure great browsing, even if buying isn't on your mind.

THE DISNEY STUDIO STORE: Expect to find T-shirts, hats, and accessories inspired by Disney films at this Animation Courtyard shop. Items featuring the park's logo are available, too.

GOLDEN AGE SOUVENIRS: Located beside Sounds Dangerous starring Drew Carey, this tiny shop stocks items such as hats, sunglasses, film, and souvenirs.

IN CHARACTER: In front of the Voyage of The Little Mermaid, this costume shop has everything a child needs to dress like a Disney prince or princess.

INDIANA JONES ADVENTURE OUTPOST: Next to the Indiana Jones attraction, you'll discover adventure clothing, as well as memorabilia emblazoned with the Indy insignia.

STAGE 1 COMPANY STORE: Situated near the exit of Muppet*Vision 3-D, guests can find toys, shirts, and other merchandise with the likenesses of Kermit the Frog, Miss Piggy, Fozzie Bear, and other Muppet characters.

TATOOINE TRADERS: This shop near the exit of the Star Tours attraction offers intergalactic souvenirs tied to the ever-growing family of *Star Wars* films, as well as the ever-popular Star Tours attraction.

THE WRITER'S STOP: This cozy nook next to the Sci-Fi Dine-In Theater has fresh-brewed coffee, souvenirs, CDs, and a small selection of reading material—plus cookies!

Where to Eat at the Studios

A complete listing of eateries at the Studios—full-service restaurants, fast-food emporiums, and snack shops—can be found in the *Good Meals, Great Times* chapter. See the Disney-MGM Studios section, beginning on page 238.

Entertainment

As you might expect from a park fashioned in the image of Hollywood's heyday, the Disney-MGM Studios knows how to put on a show. Basically, in these parts, it's always showtime. Pick up a free guidemap and Times Guide (at Guest Relations or any shop in the park), not only to check attraction starting times but also to find out what other entertainment is on tap.

While specifics may change, the following list is a good indication of the Studio's stage presence. As always, we advise calling 407-824-4321 for entertainment schedules.

DISNEY STARS AND MOTOR CARS PARADE: The Disney-MGM Studios celebrates Hollywood's golden era with a cavalcade of stars. This processional, presented as a colorful motorcade, features souped-up cars occupied by super stars. Classic Disney and Pixar characters are joined by friends from Disney Channel shows, not to mention members of the Muppets, Power Rangers, and *Star Wars* crews.

STREETMOSPHERE CHARACTERS: This troupe of performers infuses Hollywood Boulevard with old-time, Tinseltown ambience. Would-be starlets searching for their big break, fans seeking guests' autographs, and gossip columnists chasing leads entertain daily.

Holiday Happenings

The park usually stays open extra late to mark holidays such as New Year's Eve, the Fourth of July, and Christmas. During these times, lots of special entertainment is often in store. Call 407-824-4321 for up-to-the-minute schedules.

CHRISTMAS: The Osborne Family Spectacle of Lights is the Studios' brilliant, twinkling homage to the season. The recently revised (and somewhat downsized) display featuring millions of lights (provided by Little Rock businessman Jennings Osborne and his family) is a perennial favorite. It's presented in the area known as the Streets of America. For updates, visit *www.disneyworld.com*.

Trip the Light Fantasmic!

BIRNBAUM'S BEST Fantasmic!, a lavish musical production, plays nightly at The Hollywood Hills Amphitheater on Sunset Boulevard. A dramatic mix of fireworks, fountains, lasers, and Disney characters, it invites guests to take a peek into the dream world of Mickey Mouse.

Though similar to its Disneyland counterpart, half of this 26-minute production is original. The action follows Mickey through a series of dreams. In the first dream, he appears on a mountain, shoots fireworks from his fingertips, and conducts an orchestra of colorful fountains. (Guests seated up front get spritzed.) Soon Mickey is plagued by nightmares as Disney villains take over his dreams. (This part has been known to scare small children.) In the end, the Mouse and his pals prevail (of course!).

Seating begins about 90 minutes before show-time—though some guests line up even earlier. Check a Times Guide for the schedule.

We recommend sitting toward the back—the view is good and it's easier to get out after the show. There is standing room, too.

After the finale, plan to sit for a bit. It can take 20 minutes for the crowd to exit the theater.

Timing Tip: On nights when Fantasmic! is presented twice, see the last show. Afterward, as the masses exit the park, take some time to browse the shops that keep their doors open after hours.

Hot Tips

- Some attractions keep shorter hours than the park itself. Check a Times Guide when you arrive. It lists current hours and schedules.

- Check the Studios Tip Board often to get an idea of showtimes and crowds.

- See Rock 'n' Roller Coaster, Tower of Terror, Voyage of The Little Mermaid, and Star Tours early in the day, before crowds build up.

- Snag a spot along Hollywood Boulevard about 20 to 30 minutes before the Stars and Motor Cars parade.

- Tower of Terror is a popular attraction with long lines. Use Fastpass whenever possible. And never ride immediately after a meal.

- The line for The Great Movie Ride is generally the longest early in the morning and immediately following the afternoon parade.

- For a full-service meal, make restaurant reservations when you arrive, at either Hollywood Junction or these eateries: 50's Prime Time Cafe, Hollywood Brown Derby, Sci-Fi Dine-In Theater, or Hollywood & Vine. For reservations, call 407-WDW-DINE (939-3463) up to four months ahead of your preferred dining date.

- The shops on Hollywood Boulevard are open a half hour past park closing.

- Park hoppers take note: There is a water taxi link between the Disney-MGM Studios and Epcot. The boat docks to the left as you exit the Studios. You may also reach Epcot, as well as all other parks, by bus. Ambitious athletes may choose to walk. (It'll take you at least 15 to 30 minutes to make the trip on foot.)

- The Hollywood Brown Derby, Mama Melrose's Ristorante Italiano, and Hollywood and Vine offer a dinner-and-show combination: a meal followed by Fantasmic!, complete with reserved V.I.P. seating. It's a great way to avoid the time-consuming hassle of waiting for the show. Reservations can be made up to 180 days in advance by calling 407-WDW-DINE (939-3463).

- Many attractions and shows stop admitting guests prior to the park's closing time (and some don't open until a few hours after the park does). Check a Times Guide for schedules. Attractions that you may enter up until the very last minute include Rock 'n' Roller Coaster, The Twilight Zone™ Tower of Terror, The Great Movie Ride, Muppet*Vision 3-D, and Star Tours.

- If you choose to skip Fantasmic!, plan to exit the park before the show ends. This way, you'll avoid the inevitable bottleneck at the exit. If you're watching the show, consider making your exit before the big finale.

Where to Find the Characters

You'll find Disney characters such as Buzz Lightyear and Woody from *Toy Story* by Al's Toy Barn. They may be joined by Jessie, Bullseye, or some other *Toy Story* friends. Tigger greets guests outside his trailer on Mickey Avenue. Mickey mingles with parkgoers inside a building off Mickey Ave. *Monsters, Inc.* characters greet guests on Commissary Lane, while JoJo and Goliath may be spotted on Mickey Avenue. The Power Rangers sometimes patrol the Streets of America. Check a park Times Guide for specifics, or inquire at Guest Relations.

Disney's Animal Kingdom

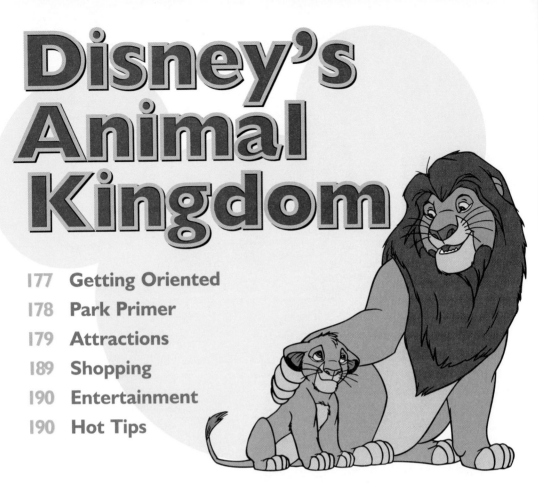

With a mix of lush landscapes, thrilling attractions, and close encounters with exotic animals, this is clearly a theme park raised to a different level of excitement. Here, guests do more than just watch the action—they live it. They become paleontologists, explorers, and students of nature. And if, by doing so, they leave with nothing more than a great big smile, Disney will have accomplished one of its major goals. But many guests come away with a little bit more: a renewed sense of respect for our planet and for the life-forms we share it with (not to mention a few boffo souvenirs).

The attractions at Disney's Animal Kingdom are meant to engage, entertain, and inspire. They immerse guests in a tropical landscape and introduce them to wondrous creatures from the past and present—as well as a few that exist only in our collective imagination.

The park, which is accredited by the American Zoo and Aquarium Association, is home to more than 1,700 animals representing 250 different species. Most of the creatures are of the animate variety, as opposed to the Audio-Animatronics kind. Despite that, you won't see many beasts behind bars here. Instead, you'll go on safari and see a menagerie of wild critters living in spacious habitats, with remarkably few separations visible to the naked eye.

The following pages will help you get the most out of your visit to Disney's Animal Kingdom. It is, after all, a jungle out there.

ASIA

I Flights of Wonder at Caravan Stage

J Maharajah Jungle Trek

K Kali River Rapids

L Expedition Everest

DINOLAND U.S.A.

M Dinosaur

N The Boneyard playground

O Finding Nemo — The Musical

P Chester & Hester's Dino-Rama!

AFRICA

A Kilimanjaro Safaris

B Pangani Forest Exploration Trail

C Wildlife Express to Rafiki's Planet Watch

D Rafiki's Planet Watch

DISCOVERY ISLAND

E The Tree of Life

F Discovery Island Trails

G It's Tough to be a Bug!

CAMP MINNIE-MICKEY

H Festival of the Lion King

Getting Oriented

Though Disney's Animal Kingdom encompasses about five times the area of its Magic counterpart, one need not be in training for the Olympics to tackle it. (Most of the land is reserved for non-homo-sapien critters.) By all estimates, pedestrians rack up about the same mileage in one day here as they do in a day at Epcot.

The park's layout is relatively simple: a series of sections, or "lands," connected to a central hub. In this case, the hub is Discovery Island (formerly known as Safari Village), an island surrounded by a river, and home to the Tree of Life, the park's icon. A set of bridges connects Discovery Island with other lands: the Oasis, DinoLand U.S.A., Asia, Africa, and Camp Minnie-Mickey.

As you pass through Animal Kingdom's entrance plaza, you approach the Oasis. Feel free to meander at a leisurely pace, absorbing the soothing ambience of a thick, elaborate jungle, or you can proceed more quickly and plan to revisit this relaxing region later on. Each of several pathways deposits you at the foot of a bridge leading to Discovery Island. As you emerge from the Oasis, you'll see the awe-inspiring Tree of Life, a 14-story Disney-made tree, looming ahead. The tree, which stands near the middle of the island, is surrounded by Discovery Island Trails. Off to the southwest is the character-laden land known as Camp Minnie-Mickey.

To the southeast lies DinoLand U.S.A., home of countless prehistoric animals, a fossil dig, a high-spirited stage show called Finding Nemo—the Musical, and an attraction that's sure to induce a mammoth adrenaline surge: Dinosaur. Behind Discovery Island and to the northwest is Africa, where guests may go on an African safari, explore a nature trail, and take the Wildlife Express train to Rafiki's Planet Watch, the park's research and education center.

Asia is northeast of Discovery Island. Here, guests come face-to-face with the yeti, aka abominable snowman on the Expedition Everest thrill ride, encounter real tigers on the exotic Maharajah Jungle Trek, and take a daring journey through the rain forest on a raft at the splashy Kali River Rapids.

HOW TO GET THERE

Take Exit 65 off I-4. Then follow the signs to Disney's Animal Kingdom. Trams run between the parking lot and the main entrance.

By WDW Transportation: From all Walt Disney World resorts: buses. From Downtown Disney: bus to any resort or the TTC, then transfer to an Animal Kingdom bus. From the Magic Kingdom: ferry or monorail to the TTC, then bus to Animal Kingdom. From Epcot, the Disney-MGM Studios, and the resorts on Hotel Plaza Boulevard: buses.

PARKING

All-day parking at Animal Kingdom is $9 for day visitors (free to Walt Disney World resort guests with presentation of resort ID). Trams circulate regularly, providing transportation from the parking area to the park entrance. Be sure to note the section and aisle in which you park. Also, be aware that the parking ticket allows for re-entry to the parking area throughout the day.

HOURS

Although hours are subject to change, the gates are generally open daily from about 9 A.M. until about an hour after dusk. During certain holiday periods and the summer months, hours may change. It's best to arrive up to a half hour before the official opening time. For current schedules, call 407-824-4321 or visit *www.disneyworld.com.*

Admission Prices

ONE-DAY BASE TICKET
(Restricted to use only in Disney's Animal Kingdom. Prices do not include sales tax and are subject to change.)
Adult $63
Child* $52
*3 through 9 years of age; children under 3 free

Park Primer

BABY FACILITIES

Changing tables and facilities for nursing mothers can be found at the Baby Care Center on Discovery Island, near Creature Comforts. It's also possible to purchase certain necessities, such as formula and diapers, at this facility.

CAMERA NEEDS

Camera supplies and disposable cameras can be purchased at Garden Gate Gifts, Disney Outfitters, Duka La Filimu, Mombasa Marketplace, and Chester and Hester's Dinosaur Treasures. Images may be transferred to CDs at Garden Gate Gifts. Note that film processing is no longer available.

DISABILITY INFORMATION

Nearly all of the Animal Kingdom attractions, shops, and restaurants are accessible to guests using wheelchairs. Additional services are available for guests with visual or hearing disabilities. The *Guidebook for Guests with Disabilities* provides a detailed overview of the services available, including transportation, parking, and attraction access. (For additional information, refer to the *Getting Ready to Go* chapter.)

FIRST AID

Minor medical problems can be handled at the First Aid Center, located on Discovery Island on the northwest side of the Tree of Life, near Creature Comforts.

INFORMATION

Guest Relations, located just inside the park entrance, is equipped with guidemaps, Times Guides, and a helpful staff. Free guidemaps are also available in many shops.

LOCKERS

Lockers are found just inside the main entrance area, near Guest Relations. Cost is $5 (plus a $2 refundable deposit) for unlimited use all day.

LOST & FOUND

The department is located at Guest Relations, just inside the park entrance. To report lost items after your visit, call 407-824-4245.

LOST CHILDREN

Report lost children at the park's Baby Services, near Creature Comforts on Discovery Island, or alert the closest Disney employee to the matter.

MONEY MATTERS

There is an ATM at the entrance to the park. Currency exchange can be handled at Guest Relations. Disney Dollars, in $1, $5, and $10 denominations, are also available at Guest Relations. In addition to cash, credit cards (American Express, Diner's Club, Discover Card, JCB, Visa, MasterCard, and the Disney Visa), Disney gift cards, traveler's checks, and Disney resort IDs are accepted for admission and merchandise, and for meals at most restaurants. Some snack carts accept cash only.

PACKAGE PICKUP

Shops can arrange for purchases to be sent to Garden Gate Gifts for later pickup (packages should be ready for pickup about three hours after purchase). The service is free.

SAME-DAY RE-ENTRY

Be sure to retain your ticket if you plan to return later the same day. It is no longer necessary to have your hand stamped.

SECURITY CHECK

Guests entering Disney theme parks may be subject to a security check. Expect backpacks, parcels, purses, etc., to be searched.

STROLLERS & WHEELCHAIRS

Strollers, wheelchairs, and Electric Convenience Vehicles (ECVs) may be rented at Garden Gate Gifts. The cost is $10 for strollers and wheelchairs (double strollers cost $18 plus a day). "Length-of-Stay" rentals yield a $2-per-day discount; $35 for ECVs, plus a $5 refundable deposit. Quantities are limited (and they run out early in the day). Keep your receipt; it may be used the same day to get a replacement here or at the other theme parks.

TIP BOARD

There is a Tip Board on Discovery Island. Check it to learn the current wait times for popular park attractions.

The Oasis

Traditionally, one has to travel across a long, sunbaked stretch of desert in order to experience the soothing atmosphere of a tropical oasis. With that in mind, think of the Animal Kingdom parking lot as a concrete version of the Sahara. Once you've trekked across it, your journey takes you through the park's front gate and entrance plaza. What's that up ahead? Could it be a towering African tree? Here in Central Florida? It must be a mirage.

But, no. Within seconds you arrive at the Oasis, a thriving tropical garden filled with waterfalls, running streams, and lush vegetation. The transition is by no means a subtle one. Guests are immediately enveloped in a world of nature. The peaceful setting is most idyllic.

Though not a full-fledged "land" per se, this small jungle simply oozes atmosphere. It is thick and elaborate and comes complete with critters. (Some are more difficult to spot than others. When searching for the naturally camouflaged creatures, remember to look up occasionally.) As park visitors walk along the pathways, they may catch glimpses of different kinds of animals, from deer and iguanas to anteaters and birds. As in the rest of the

Animal Kingdom, there is the illusion that guests are walking among the wildlife.

The Oasis is at once an exciting and calming experience. It sets the stage for what's to come. Guests have several options once they've entered the Oasis. They can continue on a northerly path, making tracks toward the Tree of Life and across a bridge to Discovery Island. They can proceed at a more snail-friendly pace, keeping a tally of the various life forms that slither by. Or they can simply take time to stop and smell the flowers.

> **"I have learned from the animal world. And what everyone will learn who studies it is a renewed sense of kinship with the Earth and all of its inhabitants."**
> **— Walt Disney**

Timing Tip: Making a trip through the Oasis is the only way to get in (and out of) Animal Kingdom. Some paths can become congested during the hours closest to opening and closing times. To beat the crowds, use a path to the left when you enter and exit the park.

Discovery Island

Once you've passed through the Oasis, you will come to a bridge spanning a peaceful river. The bridge leads to Discovery Island, an area at the center of Animal Kingdom and the hub from which all other realms of the park may be reached.

Discovery Island is defined by the brilliant colors, tropical surroundings, and equatorial architecture of Africa and the South Pacific. The facades of the buildings are all carved and painted based on the art of nations from around the world. Don't fail to notice all the bright, whimsical folk-art images representing various members of the animal kingdom.

This island is the shopping and dining center of Animal Kingdom. Many of the park's fast-food restaurants can be found here, including Pizzafari and Flame Tree Barbecue.

Hot Tip!

Take a moment to study a guidemap as you enter Animal Kingdom. It will give you a sense of the layout. The park Times Guide provides information about show-times for Festival of the Lion King, Finding Nemo—the Musical, and other attractions.

By far the most striking element on Discovery Island is the Tree of Life. It is on the map, but chances are you'll have no trouble finding it. Rising from the middle of the island and as tall as a 14-story building, the Tree of Life is hard to miss.

The Tree of Life

The Tree of Life is the dramatic 145-foot icon of Disney's Animal Kingdom. The imposing tree, with its swaying limbs and gnarled trunk, looks an awful lot like the real thing—from a distance. Up close, it's apparent that this is a most unusual bit of greenery. Covered with more than 325 animal images, it is a swirling tapestry of carved figures, pain-stakingly assembled by a team of artisans. The tree, though inorganic, stands as a symbol of the connected nature of life on Earth. We think Joyce Kilmer would have approved.

DISCOVERY ISLAND TRAILS: Walkways that snake around the Tree of Life allow guests to get a close-up view of the trunk and even play a game of "spot the animals." (The spiraling animal images go all the way to the top of the tree. You'll need binoculars if you hope to see them all.) Scattered about the tree's base is a variety of animal habitats. Animals can be seen in a very open, somewhat traditional park-like setting, with lush grass, trees, and other vegetation. Among the creatures you may recognize are macaws, flamingos, and deer. Others to which you may be introduced for the very first time as you meander through the exhibits include capybaras (huge rodents with an affinity for swimming) and ring-tailed lemurs (not quite monkeys' uncles, more like cousins). The trails are accessible from several points around the tree.

Hot Tip!

Children under age 5 may have enjoyed the film *A Bug's Life*, but few of them fancy It's Tough to be a Bug! As a matter of fact, it terrifies many of them.

BIRNBAUM'S ★BEST★ **IT'S TOUGH TO BE A BUG!:** FP Inside the trunk of the Tree of Life is a 430-seat auditorium featuring an eight-minute, animated 3-D movie augmented by some surprising "4-D" effects. The stars of the show are the world's most abundant inhabitants—insects. They creep, crawl, and demonstrate why, someday, they just might inherit the Earth. It's a bug's-eye view of the trials and tribulations of their multi-legged world.

As guests enter "The Tree of Life Repertory Theater," the orchestra can be heard warming

up amid the sounds of chirping crickets. When Flik, the emcee (and star of *A Bug's Life*), makes his first appearance, he dubs audience members honorary bugs and instructs them to don their bug eyes (3-D glasses). Then the mild-mannered ant introduces some of his not-so-mild-mannered cronies, including a Chilean tarantula, dung beetles, and "the silent but deadly member of the bug world"— the stink bug. What follows is a manic, often humorous, revue.

Note: The combination of intense special effects and frequent darkness tends to frighten toddlers and young children. In addition, anyone leery of spiders, roaches, and their ilk is advised to skip the performance, or risk being seriously bugged.

DISNEY'S ANIMAL KINGDOM

Africa

The largest section of Animal Kingdom, Africa is bigger than the Magic Kingdom all by itself. This 110-acre, truer-than-life replica of an African savanna is packed with pachyderms, giraffes, hippos, and other wild beasts. All guests enter Africa through Harambe, a village based on a modern East African coastal town. It is the dining and shopping center of Animal Kingdom's Africa.

The instant you walk across the bridge to Harambe, you are transported to Africa. Everything here is authentic, from the architecture to the landscaping to the merchandise in the marketplace. The result was achieved after Disney Imagineers made countless trips to the continent. After seven years of observing, filming, and photographing the real thing, they re-created it here in North America.

The animals that live here, however, are not re-creations. They are quite real, most varied, and extremely abundant. In fact, this chunk of land puts the *animal* in Disney's Animal Kingdom.

Kilimanjaro Safaris FP

BIRNBAUM'S ★BEST★ The Kilimanjaro Safaris has something for everyone: beautiful landscapes, majestic, free-roaming animals, and a thrilling adventure. It is everything you may expect from a trip to Africa, and a whole lot more.

The 18-minute safari begins with a brief introduction from a guide who does double duty as your driver.

Once you climb aboard the ride vehicle, look at the plates above the seat in front of you. They will help you identify the animals you see. And have those cameras ready.

As the vehicle travels along dirt roads, you'll spot free-roaming wild animals: zebras, gazelles, hippos, elephants, warthogs, rhinos, lions, and more. Some animals wander near your vehicle, and others cross its path. (Relax. Only the harmless critters will approach. Others, such as lions and cheetahs, only *appear* to invade your safe, personal space.)

Hot Tip!

There's no need to stampede toward the the Kilimanjaro Safaris ride first thing in the morning—the animals are out and active throughout the day. That said, if you do ride early, consider coming back later in the day. The beauty of this attraction is that you tend to see something new each time.

The majesty of the Serengeti may lull you into a state of serenity, but it's merely the calm before the storm. You'll soon be jostled and jolted as the vehicle crosses pothole-filled terrain and rickety bridges—one of which puts you close to a horde of sunbathing crocodiles.

The safari experience takes a dramatic turn when a band of renegade ivory poachers is discovered hunting for elephants. Your guide chases the outlaws and takes you along for the ride. If you're prone to motion sickness, back trouble, or have other physical limitations, you may want to sit this one out. The ride is a rather bumpy one.

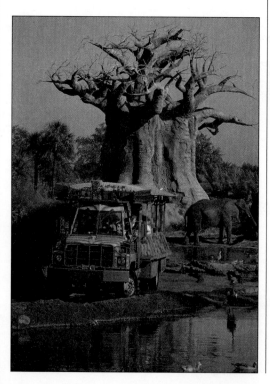

Pangani Forest Exploration Trail

This self-guided walking trail winds past communities of gorillas and other rare African animals. Access it at the end of the Kilimanjaro Safaris or by the entrance in Harambe.

The first major stop on the trail, the name of which translates to "place of enchantment" in Swahili, is the Research Station. The station contains exhibits, including naked mole rats. Just outside are a free-flight aviary and an aquarium teeming with fish. Not far away is the hippo exhibit, which provides close-up views of hippopotamuses both in and out of water.

Farther along the trail there is a scenic overlook point, where you can get an unobstructed view of the African savanna. This is also known as the "Timon" exhibit, featuring a family of perky meerkats. Afterward, you may catch an up-close glimpse (through a glass wall) of a cavorting gorilla or two.

As you come to the end of the suspension bridge, you'll find yourself in a beautiful green valley. Congratulations! You've finally reached the gorilla area—an experience well worth the wait. (Note that you may have to wait a little bit longer for that first gorilla sighting. Our evolutionary cousins have been known to play hide-and-seek in the lush vegetation.)

Rafiki's Planet Watch

This attraction could undergo changes for 2007. The description that follows reflects its press-time incarnation.

On the east side of the village of Harambe is the Harambe Train Station. That's where you board the Wildlife Express and experience a behind-the-scenes look at a Disney park while en route to Rafiki's Planet Watch.

As part of the 5½-minute trip, you'll glide past the buildings where elephants, rhinos, and giraffes sleep at night. A guide narrates throughout the trip. All guests disembark at the Rafiki's Planet Watch station. (You must reboard the train to return to Harambe.)

While Animal Kingdom's stories often carry a conservation theme, this part really brings the message home. This area is the park's conservation headquarters. It's also a veterinary lab, as well as the research and education hub.

"Much of the world's wildlife is in imminent danger," says Judson Green, former chairman of Walt Disney Attractions. "Disney is working to save endangered animals, but we also hope to motivate our guests to support wildlife programs that are in urgent need of support." After spending some time at Rafiki's Planet Watch, visitors just might have the motivation they need. Exhibits are geared to spark curiosity and awe about wildlife and conservation efforts around the world. Here are a few highlights:

Affection Section: An animal encounter area with critters to see and touch. Most of the animals are exotic breeds of familiar petting-zoo types: goats, sheep, pigs, etc. However, this is still an enjoyable experience for young guests. So is the elephant fountain just outside the gate. It's an entertaining way to rinse little hands after frolicking with the fauna.

Animal Cams: Guest-operated video cameras that observe animals throughout Animal Kingdom as they go about their daily business.

Animal Health & Care: A tour of veterinary labs and research facilities.

Eco Heroes: A set of touch-sensitive video kiosks that allow guests to interact with famous biologists and conservationists.

EcoWeb: A computer link to conservation organizations around the world.

Rafiki's Planet Watch Video: An interactive video, hosted by Rafiki, that gives guests information about endangered animals.

Song of the Rainforest: A thoroughly entertaining "3-D" audio show that surrounds guests with sounds of the rain forest.

Rafiki's Planet Watch is about a five-minute walk from the train depot. In addition to its educational appeal, this is also one of the best places to cool off at Animal Kingdom.

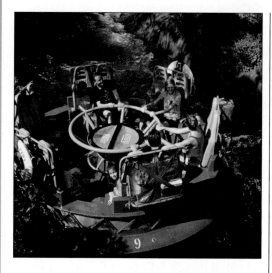

On the far side of a Himalayan-style bridge, beyond an ancient temple, lies the tranquil village of Anandapur (Sanskrit for "place of delight"). The buildings' design was inspired by structures in Thailand, Indonesia, and other Asian countries known for their rich architectural history.

A product of Disney Imagineering, the village epitomizes the complex, enduring relationship between the animals and ecosystems of the Asian continent. The tiny village borders an elaborate re-creation of a Southeast Asian rain forest. As such, Disney's Asia is an ideal location for trekking through the lush jungle, shooting the rapids on a raging river, and gazing upon the multi-hued inhabitants of this treasured terrain.

Kali River Rapids FP

 Before guests board rafts at Kali (pronounced *KAH-lee*) River Rapids, a wise voice admonishes that "the river is like life itself, full of mysterious twists and turns." What the voice *doesn't* say is that this particular river is also full of splashing water and a blazing inferno. This may be business as usual for some daring souls, but for most of us, these elements make for one dramatic, drenching adventure.

All guests begin the journey in the offices of Kali River Rapids Expeditions, a river rafting company. A slide show offers information on the sometimes unscrupulous business of logging—how it has ravaged the rain forest and

> ## Hot Tip!
> Everyone and everything gets wet on Kali River Rapids. Any items that simply must stay dry should be stored in a locker or with a non-riding member of your party.

deprived animals of their habitats. However, thanks to ecotourism (among other things), there is hope. Peaceful voyages give people a new appreciation and sense of responsibility for this endangered land.

A 12-seater raft whisks "ecotourists" up a watery ramp and through an arching tunnel of bamboo. It proceeds onward, through a hazy mist and past remnants of an ancient shrine. As the raft moves along curves of the river, guests enjoy views of undisturbed rain forest.

The tranquility is shattered by a startling sight. A huge chunk of forest has been gutted by loggers. On both sides of the river, the forest has vanished. As guests absorb the image, they are besieged by more disturbing sights and sounds. Straight ahead, the river is choked with a tangled arch of burning logs— and the raft is headed straight for it. Suddenly, the rain forest isn't the only thing endangered.

Kali River Rapids is an especially soggy experience. It is the rare guest who leaves the ride without a thorough soaking. Should you wish to repel as much precipitation as possible, pack a plastic poncho.

Note: This is a bumpy adventure. In order to experience it, you must be at least 38 inches tall. It is not recommended for pregnant women, those with a heart condition, people with back or neck problems, or anyone who wishes to stay dry.

Maharajah Jungle Trek

 Welcome to the jungle! The Maharajah Jungle Trek is a self-guided walking tour of a tropical paradise, complete with roaming tigers, gushing waterfalls, and dense greenery. Throughout the expedition, trekkers encounter a deluge of flora and fauna typically found in the rain forests of Southeast Asia. Tapirs, Komodo dragons, and a conglomeration of colorful birds call this corner of Animal Kingdom home. Majestic Asian tigers can be spotted stalking ancient ruins, strategically separated from would-be prey. Deer and antelope graze and frolic nearby, blissfully oblivious of their fearsome neighbors' proximity.

Approximately midway through the thicket stands a rustic, tin-roofed assembly hall. Step inside to witness the breathtaking sight of giant fruit bats showing off their six-foot wingspans. As you look through the windows, thinking that the crystal-clear glass was cleaned by a super-diligent window washer, think again. There is no glass in some of the windows—and, therefore, *nothing* separating you

from the giant creatures fluttering about on the other side. What keeps the big bats from getting up close and personal with guests? They're a lot less interested in humans than humans are in them. (Can't say that we blame them.) Note that some viewing areas are adorned with wire or glass—for guests who are more comfortable with a bat buffer.

Flights of Wonder

A 1,000-seat, open-air theater, the Caravan Stage features performances by actors wearing nothing but feathers and the occasional crown. Members of more than 20 different bird species have starring roles in Flights of Wonder, a high-flying celebration of the winged wonders of the world. Hawks, owls, falcons, and even chickens have been known to awe spectators as they swoop, soar, and strut their stuff in each 20-minute performance. Some demonstrate how they hunt. Others display their grape-grabbing or money-grubbing talents. Check a park Times Guide for the schedule. This show has morphed quite a bit from its original incarnation. It's a hoot!

Expedition Everest FP

BIRNBAUM'S ★BEST★ Walt Disney World's mountain range is a bit more intense these days, as the world's tallest mountain—Everest—has risen from the peaceful village of Serka Zong in Animal Kingdom's Asia. Like its sister peaks, Space, Splash, and Big Thunder, this E-ticket precipice promises to deliver "coaster thrills, spills, and, chills." Does it deliver on that promise? Boy, does it ever!

Hot Tip!
Fastpass assignments for Expedition Everest tend to be gone soon after the park opens. Get yours as early as possible.

The attraction features an old tea train chugging and churning as it climbs up and around snowcapped peaks. Suddenly, the track comes to an end in a gnarled mess of twisted metal. Lurching forward and backward, the train hurtles through caverns and icy canyons before depositing guests in the presence of the legendary Yeti (aka the Abominable Snowman)—who's not too happy that you've scaled the mountain he so fiercely protects.

Feeling up to the challenge of a dramatic, high-speed train ride? If you are free of heart, back, and neck problems, are not pregnant, have no fear of heights (or abominable snowpeople), and are at least 44 inches tall, go for it. As always, never eat right before experiencing a ride as topsy-turvy as this one.

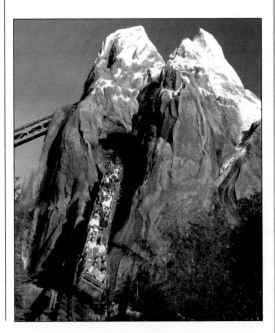

DISNEY'S ANIMAL KINGDOM

DinoLand U.S.A.

If the look and feel of DinoLand U.S.A. seems familiar, there's a reason: It was designed to capture the flavor of roadside America. It is a mixture of culture and kitsch—the likes of which you might stumble upon during a cross-country road trip. Here, you'll come face-to-face with fossil fanatics, jump into gigantic footprints, and browse through a typically tacky roadside souvenir stand, where you can pick up some dinosaur mementos for the folks back home.

This corner of Animal Kingdom comes complete with its own dramatic entrance: a 50-foot skeleton of a brachiosaurus. As guests stroll beneath the bones, they find themselves smack in the middle of a paleontological dig. Here, guests of all ages (especially little ones) have the chance to play paleontologist as they dig through a fossil-packed pocket of dino discovery.

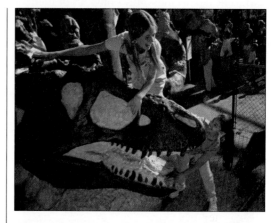

> ## Did You Know?
> Many of the benches in Disney's Animal Kingdom are made of recycled plastic milk jugs. It takes 1,350 jugs to make a single bench!

The dinosaurs that dwell here, though often quite animated, are all of the inanimate variety. But do keep your eyes peeled for the prehistoric life-forms that actually *live* in this land. That is, for real creatures that exist in the here and now, but whose ancestors kept company with the likes of the carnotaurus and its cousins from the Cretaceous Era.

The Boneyard

The Boneyard gives guests—especially the very young ones—an opportunity to dig for fossils in a discovery-oriented playground. They will excavate the ancient bones of a mammoth in this re-creation of a paleontological dig (think huge sandbox). They will also unearth clues that may help them solve the mystery of how and when the creature met its untimely demise.

For serious "boneheads" who just aren't satisfied with simple digging, there are plenty of other bone-related activities here. You can bang out a primitive tune on a bony xylophone (it's located near the car; to make a

sound, simply press on a rib), zip down prehistoric slides, and work your way through a fossil-filled maze. While exploring, watch your step: If you accidentally wander into a giant dinosaur footprint, you'll be greeted with an ominous roar.

While in DinoLand, be sure to check out the OldenGate Bridge. It's a gateway structure made from a dinosaur skeleton. The bridge links one end of The Boneyard with the other. This is a good place to take young kids while other members of your party ride Dinosaur.

Chester & Hester's Dino-Rama!

A colorful land-within-a-land, Chester and Hester's is an area ideally suited for young thrill seekers. Located just beyond The Boneyard playground, this wild-and-woolly, carnival-like zone features old-fashioned midway games and two rides: Primeval Whirl and TriceraTop Spin.

PRIMEVAL WHIRL: FP A small roller coaster (with spinning cars) that seems to have been plucked from a traveling fair, this ride has a familiar feel to it. By all means, give it a whirl—it's a truly wild ride. You must be at least 48 inches tall to spin.

TRICERATOP SPIN: The ride is apt to please fans of the Magic Kingdom's Dumbo, the Flying Elephant, and the Magic Carpets of Aladdin. Guests ride in one of the 16 flying dinos, each of which resembles an oversize tin toy. It's tame when compared to its Dinosaur attraction neighbor, but worth checking out—especially for young dinosaur groupies.

Dinosaur FP

BIRNBAUM'S ★BEST★ This dizzying adventure begins with guests being strapped into vehicles and catapulted back in time to complete a dangerous, albeit noble, mission: to rescue the last iguanodon—a 16-foot plant-eating dinosaur that you may remember from the Disney film *Dinosaur*—and bring him back to the present. The iguanodon, which lived more than 65 million years ago (during the Cretaceous Period), just might hold the answer to the mysterious disappearance of his dino brethren.

Throughout the frenetic quest to locate the elusive iguanodon, you cling to an out-of-control vehicle while dodging blazing meteors and a mix of friendly and ferocious dinosaurs.

Soon you encounter the carnotaurus—a fearsome, carnivorous dinosaur. The carnotaurus, which has horns like a bull and a face like a toad, is a remarkably unsightly specimen.

All of the dinosaurs are especially fierce-looking and move as though they were alive. Even their nostrils move as they "breathe."

This 3½-minute attraction offers more than a thrill a minute. You rocket through time, are practically pelted by meteors, and narrowly escape becoming a dino dinner as the carnotaurus suddenly turns the tables and chases after *you*.

Guests reach the attraction through the Dino Institute, a museum-like building deep in the heart of DinoLand. Here, you'll be treated to a pre-show by Bill Nye, the Science Guy, (audio only) and see a dinosaur skeleton and an assortment of fossils and other artifacts.

This is an extremely rough (and dark) attraction. You must be at least 40 inches tall to experience it. It is not recommended for pregnant women, those with a heart condition, or people with back or neck problems. Small kids will certainly be frightened.

Finding Nemo— The Musical

Dinoland is just about as far off Broadway as one could be. Yet this show's got the ingredients of a Broadway smash: beloved characters (i.e., Marlin, the overprotective clownfish dad; Nemo, his curious son; and Dory, the endearing royal blue tang with the short-term memory loss); original songs by a Tony-winning composer (Robert Lopez); dancers; acrobats; and the theatrical puppetry of Michael Curry (who designed the richly detailed character puppets seen in the Broadway version of Disney's *The Lion King*). You can catch this 30-minute dazzler at the newly enclosed and air-conditioned Theater in the Wild. Check a park Times Guide for showtimes—and get there early.

Camp Minnie-Mickey

What would a theme park be without a gregarious cast of handshaking characters? You will find the patented Disney character experience in all of its animated glory in Camp Minnie-Mickey. Set deep in a dense forest, this land is really a summer camp frequented by Mickey Mouse and all of his pals.

To find the characters, guests follow one of four short trails. Each one leads to an open-air hut, occupied by the likes of Mickey Mouse, Minnie Mouse, Donald Duck, Daisy Duck, or Goofy. Different Disney characters make appearances at these meet-and-greet pavilions throughout the day. Be sure to have the autograph books and cameras ready.

Camp Minnie-Mickey is also the home of two shows—one starring the cast of *The Lion King* and the other, Pocahontas herself. Check a Times Guide for schedules.

Festival of the Lion King

BIRNBAUM'S ★BEST★ In addition to rustling up grubs in Camp Minnie-Mickey, the talented cast of *The Lion King* performs a 30-minute stage show in the Lion King Theater (which is now completely enclosed and thoroughly air-conditioned).

Presented in the round, this lavish revue is as bright and boisterous as they come. The dramatic opening features a parade of performers in colorful animal costumes. What follows is an intriguing, energetic interpretation of the film, including songs, dances, and acrobatics. With the exception of Timon, who plays himself, lead characters are portrayed by humans draped in bold African costumes.

Songs include Scar's nasty version of "Be Prepared," as well as "Can You Feel the Love Tonight?," "The Circle of Life," and a rousing rendition of "The Lion Sleeps Tonight."

Timing Tip: Although this enclosed theater accommodates nearly 1,400 guests at a time, we recommend arriving at least 30 minutes before the performance time. Take our word for it: It's worth the wait.

Pocahontas and Her Forest Friends

The forest is in trouble, and Pocahontas is worried. "It is being cut down limb by limb," she tells Grandmother Willow. "They are leaving nothing in their path."

And so the stage is set for this 12-minute presentation in Grandmother Willow's Grove. the grim premise soon gives way to a more positive outlook, as Pocahontas is reminded that there is one creature of the forest who has the power to protect it. But which one?

Pocahontas begins a quest to find the mystery creature. Along the way, she learns that many forest dwellers have special talents. Among them are skunks, rabbits, raccoons. and even a snake—all of them real. At the end of this sweet and simple musical fable, Pocahontas learns a very important lesson about preserving the forest—as do members of the audience.

Note: The theater space is small, so arrive early to get a seat. Also, because live animals star in the production, no food is permitted.

Get Involved

When it comes to conservation efforts, the folks at the Walt Disney Company want you to do as they say—and as they do: The Disney Wildlife Conservation Fund helps non-profit groups protect and study endangered and threatened animals and their habitats. Among those groups are the ASPCA, Dian Fossey Gorilla Fund, Jane Goodall Institute, and the Wildlife Conservation Society. And guests who "Add a Dollar" help, too.

Of course, as a trip to Animal Kingdom makes clear, there are many ways to help our planet's wild inhabitants. Stop by Rafiki's Planet Watch during your visit. There, you can get information about conservation efforts in your neck of the woods. Don't leave your enthusiasm behind when you leave the park!

Shopping

Entrance Area

GARDEN GATE GIFTS: Located near the entrance to the Oasis, this is the place to rent strollers and wheelchairs. Film and disposable cameras are for sale. This is also the park's package-pickup location.

OUTPOST: This small shop, located just outside the park's entrance, features a variety of character merchandise and Animal Kingdom souvenirs.

Discovery Island

BEASTLY BAZAAR: Safari hats with Mickey, Pooh, or Pluto ears; Disney's Animal Kingdom logo watches; character figurines; and plush toys clad in safari garb are among the wares offered in this shop, designed as a celebration of aquatic animals. There's a selection of kitchen, bath, and home-decor items. Note that items offered may change.

CREATURE COMFORTS: This shop offers items for kids—toys, clothes, costumes, hats, and more.

DISNEY OUTFITTERS: Nature-themed gifts and apparel are the stock-in-trade here. There's an abundance of clothing (for the whole family). Make a point of checking out the authentic carved animal totem poles in the center room—they are most impressive.

ISLAND MERCANTILE: This sprawling shop is themed as a shipping company that celebrates working animals—camels, elephants, beavers, and others. Here, you'll find character merchandise, clothing, candy, and Disney paraphernalia. Note that this shop stays open about a half hour after Animal Kingdom closes for the day.

Did You Know?

Many of the costumes worn by Animal Kingdom cast members are made of wood—actually, a natural fabric called lyocell, made from wood pulp. The pulp is harvested from trees grown specifically for this fabric.

Africa

DUKA LA FILIMU: Situated near the entrance to Kilimanjaro Safaris, this is an ideal place to load up on film for your trip.

MOMBASA MARKETPLACE AND ZIWANI TRADERS: An African marketplace and trading company, these connected shops feature animal toys, safari clothing, T-shirts, books, and Africa-themed gifts such as pottery, masks, and musical instruments.

OUT OF THE WILD: Located just outside the exit of Rafiki's Planet Watch, this open-air shop stocks a variety of souvenirs, including shirts, hats, notebooks, and toys.

DinoLand U.S.A.

CHESTER & HESTER'S DINOSAUR TREASURES: Themed as an American road-side souvenir stand, this shop pays homage to all reptiles and prehistoric animals. Its focus is reflected in an assortment of wacky items strewn about the shop.

Entertainment

AFRICAN ENTERTAINMENT: Contemporary sounds of Africa often fill the air as bands serenade guests passing through the village of Harambe. Storytellers have been known to perform animal tales from time to time.

ANIMAL ENCOUNTERS: Enjoy up-close encounters with some of the smaller members of the animal kingdom as they wander the park with their human keepers.

MICKEY'S JAMMIN' JUNGLE PARADE: Animal Kingdom celebrates the wonders of the natural world in this peppy parade. It features familiar Disney characters—including Mickey Mouse, Minnie Mouse, Goofy, Donald Duck, and Rafiki—cruising in jazzy jalopies. Stilt-walkers and puppets put in appearances, too. Check a Times Guide for the parade schedule.

Hot Tips

- Arrive at the park 20 minutes before park opening time. Animal Kingdom often kicks off the day with "The Adventure Begins"—a character-laden musical celebration. It's a very Disney way to start the day.

- Island Mercantile on Discovery Island stays open a half hour after the park closes.

- Most of Animal Kingdom's attractions take place outdoors. Don't become overheated! Make a point of slipping into an air-conditioned shop or restaurant from time to time to cool off.

- Narrow, winding paths; grooved pavement; and hilly terrain make this the most challenging Disney theme park in which to navigate a wheelchair.

- Check the Animal Kingdom Tip Board often to get an idea of showtimes and crowds.

- The line for Kilimanjaro Safaris tends to dwindle a bit by midday. See it then (the experience is enjoyable at any time of day).

- Get a Fastpass for Expedition Everest first thing in the morning—they are often gone before lunch time.

- Rainforest Cafe generally keeps longer hours than the park does.

- When the weather gets steamy, keep a refillable water bottle with you at all times.

- If you plan to park hop, Animal Kingdom is a good park at which to begin the day.

Where to Eat in Animal Kingdom

A complete listing of eateries at Disney's Animal Kingdom—table-service restaurants, fast-food spots, and snack stands—can be found in the *Good Meals, Great Times* chapter. See the Animal Kingdom section, beginning on page 241.

Everything Else in the World

While the total turf of the World encompasses about 47 square miles, the theme parks cover less than 1,000 acres. Much of the remaining Walt Disney World terrain is crammed with irresistible activities of a variety and quality seldom found anywhere else.

There's superb golf and tennis, beaches for sunbathing, lakes for motor-boating, fishing, and sailing, canoes to rent and winding streams to paddle along, bicycles for hire, campfire sites, horseback riding, race-car driving, nature trails, and picnic grounds. The recreation options continue with Typhoon Lagoon, a lushly landscaped, state-of-the-art water park complete with surfing lagoon; and Blizzard Beach, a thrilling watery wonderland that translates the hallmarks of a ski resort to the realm of swimming.

A quartet of lavish spas provides guests with ample opportunity to pamper themselves silly. Intriguing "backstage" programs invite the curious to slip behind the scenes and learn about the workings of Walt Disney World. Add to all that Downtown Disney, a dining, shopping, and amusement district encompassing Pleasure Island, an after-dark entertainment complex; the Marketplace, a colorful assortment of shops and restaurants; and the West Side, a cluster of themed eateries, unique shops, and interactive entertainment experiences. It seems this really is a World without end.

Downtown Disney

Sprinkled across 120 waterfront acres are the shops, nightclubs, restaurants, and entertainment sites that collectively make up Downtown Disney. Like the downtown area of any thriving metropolis, Disney's Downtown consists of several distinct neighborhoods. In this case, they are known as the Marketplace, Pleasure Island, and the West Side. Unlike a typical downtown, however, the Disney depiction dispenses with the downside. You won't see litter on the streets, unsightly storefronts, or weary workers rushing home at five o'clock. You *will* see a series of spirited spots designed solely for your dining, shopping, and partying pleasure.

Judging by the throngs that descend upon this place, Downtown Disney is *the* place to be after dark. That said, it can get a tad congested—especially on the roads leading here. However you're traveling, allow plenty of extra time to get to and from this fun zone. Note that all sections are connected by walking paths. For information, visit *www.disneyworld.com* or call 407-939-2648.

Downtown Disney Essentials

GUEST RELATIONS: Between Team Mickey Athletic Club and Ghirardelli Soda Fountain & Chocolate Shop in the Marketplace, and across from Wetzel's Pretzels on the West Side, these information centers are also the place to go for help making reservations, Lost and Found, stroller and wheelchair rental, theme park tickets, and more. There is an ATM near Team Mickey Athletic Club in the Marketplace, by Wetzel's Pretzels on the West Side, and near Pleasure Island's Rock 'n' Roll Beach Club.

HOW TO GET THERE: Downtown Disney is accessible from exits 67 and 68 off I-4.

By WDW Transportation: From Old Key West, Port Orleans French Quarter and Riverside, and Saratoga Springs: boats or buses. From all other WDW resorts: bus. There is no direct transportation from Disney theme parks to Downtown Disney. The Marketplace is within walking distance of several resorts on Hotel Plaza Blvd. For more information, turn to *Transportation & Accommodations*.

By Taxi: Yellow cabs service the Downtown Disney area. The cost to most WDW resorts is usually $8 to $20.

Note: Stick with authorized taxis such as Checker Cabs and avoid independent cabs. Their fees aren't regulated and are often outrageous.

West Side

Pleasure Island

PLEASU

Marketplace

Located on the shores of Lake Buena Vista, the Marketplace is a relaxing setting for shopping, dining, and much more. The waterside enclave is sprinkled with gardens featuring whimsical topiaries. Kids are fond of the Downtown Disney Marketplace Carousel (tucked between Pooh Corner and Earl of Sandwich). And adults may enjoy a drink at Cap'n Jack's Margarita Bar.

While many guests opt to eat in a restaurant, others grab a bite from the Earl of Sandwich and sit at waterfront tables. (Refer to *Good Meals, Great Times* for restaurant information.) Afterward, some gravitate toward the marina for boating or fishing. (Turn to the *Sports* chapter for details.) There is no admission charge to visit the Marketplace.

Shopping

The descriptions below suggest the types of wares each store offers. Most shops in the Downtown Disney Marketplace are usually open daily from 9:30 A.M. to 11 P.M.

ARRIBAS BROS.: This shop sells handcrafted items from Spanish artisans and designers. Large cut-glass bowls and vases are available, along with mugs, sculptures, and other wares, all of which can be engraved.

THE ART OF DISNEY: Disney animation cels, porcelain figures, ceramics, posters, and other collectibles are available at this engaging gallery.

BASIN: Products designed to clean you up and calm you down are the stock-in-trade at this soothing Marketplace establishment. Candles, soaps, and bath crystals are just some of the wares on hand. A sampling area allows shoppers to try before they buy. The bath bombs are the best!

DISNEY'S DAYS OF CHRISTMAS: Here is the best place to deck the halls Disney style— it's the largest Christmas shop on Disney property. In addition to many character items, the shop boasts a large assortment of hand-crafted ornaments. Other items to look for: Christmas cards, candles, Santa hats with Mouse ears, and books. Many items can be personalized.

DISNEY'S PIN TRADERS: This shop boasts a tremendous assortment of collector pins and various pin-collecting accessories. In fact, this is Walt Disney World's most elaborate pin-trading center.

DISNEY TAILS: A pet-pampering palace, this shop proffers fresh-baked animal treats, toys, leashes, collars, and pet gear that can be personalized. Resist the urge to bring Fido for the shopping spree—only service animals are allowed in.

DISNEY'S WONDERFUL WORLD OF MEMORIES: Housed in the spot that was once 2 R's Reading and Riting, this shop is now scrapbook central. In addition to pre-packaged kits and other scrapbooking supplies (including stickers and stationery), several stations allow guests to create their own scrapbook pages and postcards.

Marketplace

GOOFY'S CANDY COMPANY: One-stop shopping to satisfy all your sugary cravings, this shop has a sumptuous selection of chocolates, a dipping kitchen, and much more.

LEGO IMAGINATION CENTER: World of Disney's next-door neighbor, this shop is a showcase for larger-than-life Lego models, including dinosaurs and scary aliens. It also invites guests to flaunt their creativity in an outdoor interactive play area. The store stocks Lego products and educational toys. By the way, that sea serpent in Buena Vista Village Lake is also made of Legos.

MICKEY'S MART: Mickey's all about bargains, in this "everything is $10 or less" establishment.

MICKEY'S PANTRY: Stop here for mugs, glasses, cooking utensils, plus teas and coffees.

ONCE UPON A TOY: A sprawling toy box of a store, this site features interactive areas, colorful displays, and an outdoor play space. All the big brand names are represented, as are a few of the smaller ones.

TEAM MICKEY ATHLETIC CLUB: A cavernous store with a locker-room motif, this shop is the perfect setting for sports clothing, active wear, and sports equipment. You'll find items with Disney characters in sporting poses emblazoned on them.

WORLD OF DISNEY: A gigantic space stuffed with a huge selection of Disney merchandise, this is the place for one-stop shopping. Twelve themed rooms provide the backdrop for the array of goods. Characters are available on everything from watches to luggage.

Cinderella's Fairy Godmother recently set up shop in the refurbished Princess Room. Her Bibbidi Bobbidi Boutique, which is run by "Fairy Godmothers in training," caters to princess-wannabes ages 3 and up. Here kids can get their faces painted with glitter makeup, do their nails, and even design tiaras. An Audio-Animatronics princess sings songs, too. The boutique is open from 9:30 A.M. to 6 P.M. daily, seven days a week. Reservations are strongly encouraged; call 407-WDW-STYLE (939-7895).

There's a haven for pirate fans here, too. The Adventure Room invites young swashbucklers to sail the high seas, hoist the Jolly Roger, and fill treasure chests with buccaneer booty. They can make pirate hats and chat with Rusty Blade (an Audio-Animatronics pirate) and his pet parrot, Pollyanna.

Where to Eat at Downtown Disney

A complete listing of restaurants, bars, and snack spots can be found in the *Good Meals, Great Times* chapter. See the Downtown Disney restaurant listing, beginning on page 243. Most restaurants here are open from about 11:30 A.M. to midnight. Planet Hollywood serves until 1 A.M. West Side spots may serve as late as 2 A.M.

Pleasure Island

A six-acre nighttime entertainment complex, Pleasure Island delivers a wealth of options that nicely top off a day in the parks. In addition to clubs, there are several restaurants and shops here in the central area of Downtown Disney.

Most clubs open at 8 P.M. and don't close until 2 A.M. Admission is no longer required at the gate, but is required to enter most individual venues. Admission to Pleasure Island venues is an option with the "Water Park Fun & More" add-on to the Magic Your Way Base Ticket. It's also included with a Premium Annual Pass. A Pleasure Island annual pass, which grants access to all venues, costs $59.59 ($48.95 to renew). Guests under age 18 must be accompanied by a parent or guardian.

> ## Hot Tip!
> Drivers take note: In order to prove that you are 21 years old, you must present an official photo ID. So if your mug is not emblazoned on your license, be sure to bring it *and* a photo ID. Otherwise, you will not be allowed to imbibe—even though your driver's license is, indeed, the real McCoy.

Cocktails and soft drinks are available at all of the clubs. The drinking age in Florida is 21. Guests who are 18, 19, and 20 will be admitted to the clubs (except Mannequins and BET SoundStage Club Thursday through Sunday) but will not be served alcohol. A valid U.S., foreign, or international driver's license with a photo, an active U.S. military identification card, or a passport must be presented as proof of age.

Clubs

ADVENTURERS CLUB: "Explore the unknown, discover the impossible" states the credo posted at the entrance. The place is modeled after the paneled libraries and elegant salons of similar clubs of the 19th century and is packed with memorabilia. Most of the items on display were collected at garage sales, antique shows, and shops from around the world by Disney Imagineers.

> ## When it's Time to Change...
> ...you've got to rearrange. Or at least shake things up a bit. Though nothing was official at press time, we see possible changes in Pleasure Island's not-too-distant future. No, we're not psychic, but we can't help but notice that all the shops have mysteriously disappeared. Exactly what's in store for P.I. may be a mystery, but we're hoping that the end result will be an island we'd want to be stranded on.

The two-story club is littered with "stuff," so stroll around and snoop all you like. If you have a seat at the bar, ask the bartender to work some magic; your stool may slowly sink toward the floor. In the library, a haunted organ sets the scene for outrageous storytellers. The show is a little silly, but fun.

MANNEQUINS: This is the place to head to dance the night away. Lights, contemporary dance music, and an overall exuberant atmosphere dominate the scene. The name of the club comes from the many mannequins serving as props.

The main dance floor is actually a big turntable, and the music is provided by a deejay. The lighting is a major attraction, with 60 robotically controlled lighting instruments and a matrix of lights behind the stage.

Note that guests must be at least 21 years old

(with valid proof of age) to enter Mannequins Thursday through Sunday. As the most intense of Pleasure Island's nightclubs, this spot draws quite a few young adults, of both the guest and local resident varieties.

At press time there was a possibility that Mannequins would get a major overhaul—but we're assured the spinning dance floor will definitely be sticking around.

BET SOUNDSTAGE CLUB:

Dancing and other audience-engaging activities combine to make BET SoundStage Club a unique entertainment experience. The club welcomed its first visitors in 1998. (It's operated by BET Holdings, Inc., which owns Black Entertainment Television.)

In keeping with the BET musical tradition, the club features the best in rhythm and blues and hip-hop. Early in the evening, a veejay cues up videos by contemporary urban artists and encourages everyone to take to the dance floor. A selection of appetizers may be available.

Call 407-WDW-2648 for show information. BET SoundStage is restricted to guests 21 and older Thursday through Sunday.

COMEDY WAREHOUSE:

A comedy troupe performs five times each evening. There are five comedians and one musician. It's a show that features improvisational comedy based on audience suggestions. Every seat offers a good view, even if the stools are a little tough on bad backs. Popcorn is the snack of choice. The comedy isn't quite cutting edge, but it's all in good fun.

8TRAX:

Got a penchant for the Partridge Family? Does Abba have a special place in your heart? If so, make tracks for 8TRAX. Music from the early seventies and the disco era fills this dance spot. To keep things in a nostalgic mode, the staff even dresses in polyester. The club also features eighties music for the seventies-challenged.

This description was accurate at press time, but this club may undergo changes in 2007.

MOTION:

This high-energy dance club has a cobalt blue interior and features Top 40 tunes, courtesy of an in-house deejay. The dance floor is quite spacious. It's often quite chilly in here. Plan accordingly.

This description was accurate at press time, but Motion may be re-Imagineered in 2007.

RAGLAN ROAD:

Straight from the Emerald Isle, this establishment captures the charm of an authentic Irish pub—not surprising, as all of the furnishings were designed and built in Ireland. Culinary temptations are courtesy of Kevin Dundon, one of Ireland's best-known chefs. The entertainment here is as free-flowing as the stout—expect a mix of traditional and contemporary music, storytelling, and dance. Raglan Road, which is owned and operated by Great Irish Pubs Florida, is in the space previously occupied by the Pleasure Island Jazz Company. Pleasure Island Club admission is not required for entrance. *Slainte!* (That's Gaelic for "Cheers!")

ROCK 'N' ROLL BEACH CLUB:

A combination of dancing and surfer-style decor awaits guests here. The dance floor is on the lowest level of the building, and there are billiard tables and games on the other two floors. Live bands perform hits from the 1960s to the present. The atmosphere is a little frenetic but nonetheless exciting. Light snacks are available. There are now two stairways for entering and exiting the venue.

Shopping at Crossroads

Originally conceived by the WDW folks, the Crossroads of Lake Buena Vista shopping center, near the resorts on Hotel Plaza Boulevard, is a convenient dining and shopping area. The center is anchored by a Gooding's supermarket, which is open 24 hours a day.

West Side

When Disney's shopping and entertainment district underwent its latest growth spurt, it did so in true American style: It went west. The West Side boasts a wide variety of restaurants, shops, movies, and clubs. Although it does not have an admission fee, some venues may charge a cover.

AMC THEATRES: The most popular multi-screen movie theater complex in the state of Florida is also one of the largest. The 24 screens show an impressive selection of current movie releases. The seats are roomy and comfortable, and the sound system is first-rate. (It was developed by George Lucas, the creative force behind the series of *Star Wars* blockbusters.) For current schedules, call 407-298-4488.

BONGOS CUBAN CAFE: Situated across from the AMC Theatres on the edge of Buena Vista Village Lake, Bongos echoes the style of clubs in Miami's South Beach. Created in part by Gloria Estefan, it features the flavors and rhythms of Cuba and other Latin American countries. The bold design is dramatic, yet whimsical. Guests dine and, if the mood strikes, even dance amid the colorful, tropical decor (and one remarkably oversized pineapple, which houses a multi-level cocktail lounge).

The food here moves to a Latin beat as well, with a slate of traditional and nouvelle Cuban dishes. There is entertainment on Friday and Saturday nights.

CIRQUE DU SOLEIL: The building that towers over all the others at Downtown Disney West Side is actually a tent—a circus tent. It's the home of a most extraordinary entertainment experience: Cirque du Soleil. This original show, titled La Nouba, is a Walt Disney World exclusive.

Known for its high energy and artistic performances, Cirque du Soleil shows feature a mix of acrobatics and modern dance combined with colorful costumes and dramatic original music. A cast of more than 70 international performers showcase their physical talents twice a day, five days a week.

Tickets for the show may be purchased up to six months in advance. Call 407-939-7600 or visit *www.disneyworld.com* for information or to order tickets. If you have not already purchased tickets to La Nouba, consider stopping by the Cirque du Soleil box office at Downtown Disney West Side—some seats may be available at the last minute. Note that the show is quite popular.

DISNEYQUEST: This imaginative entertainment complex features high-tech activities that engage kids and grown-ups alike. Sometimes described as a self-contained, interactive theme park, the five floors under the DisneyQuest roof are divided into four "zones": Explore, Score, Create, and Replay.

Each zone features rides and games from the simple (classic video games like Asteroids, in Replay) to some of the more technologically advanced (e.g., Create's CyberSpace Mountain, in which guests not only design gravity-defying roller coasters but get to ride their creations in a simulator).

Other stops on the tour include Buzz Lightyear's AstroBlaster (bumper cars that let you shoot balls at other drivers), Mighty Ducks Pinball Slam (which turns players into human joysticks), Sid's Create-a-Toy (a computer terminal that allows guests to assemble their own twisted toys), the family-oriented Virtual Jungle Cruise (a turbulent river-raft ride into a primeval world), and Pirates of the Caribbean: Battle for Buccaneer Gold (a swashbuckling shipboard adventure).

Expect to be engaged for two to three hours (or until sensory overload sets in). DisneyQuest is open daily from late morning till late evening. Admission covers most games. It's included with a Premium Annual Pass and the "Water Park Fun & More" add-on for a Magic Your Way base ticket. (If admission isn't included with your pass, pay at the entrance.)

HOUSE OF BLUES: A combination restaurant–music hall with standing room for 2,000, House of Blues was inspired by one of America's most celebrated musical traditions. There is a lively dose of jazz and country, plus a little bit of R & B and some rock 'n' roll thrown into the music mix. The old-fashioned Southern cooking lures diners here—especially on Sunday mornings, when the chefs prepare an all-you-can-eat buffet feast, complemented by live gospel music. Tickets can be purchased through Ticket Master (407-839-3900; *www.ticketmaster.com*) or the House of Blues box office (407-934-2583).

The House of Blues restaurant features a mélange of Delta-inspired cuisine, including jambalaya, *étouffée*, and bread pudding.

WOLFGANG PUCK CAFE: There are three dining areas in this two-story restaurant—an express counter, a cafe, and a more formal dining room on the second floor—plus a sushi bar. All feature the celebrated chef's signature pizzas, rotisserie chicken, and other specialties.

Shopping

CANDY CAULDRON: Stop here for some homemade Southern-style sweets in an open candy kitchen.

HOYPOLOI: The glass, ceramics, sculpture, jewelry, and other eclectic, decorative items on display here make this shop seem more like an art gallery. It's worth a peek.

MAGIC MASTERS: You won't believe your eyes when you enter this mysterious little shop. There's no merchandise on display. There is simply a list of magical items, from crystal balls to linking handcuffs to a "wizard and book" (whatever that means). The cashier does double duty as the in-house magician. It's one of the more entertaining shops at WDW.

MAGNETRON: Your fridge will never be the same once you've paid a visit to this specialty magnet shop with its eclectic assortment of 50,000 magnets.

MICKEY'S GROOVE: Look for novelty headwear, toys, and pins with a Mouse motif.

PLANET HOLLYWOOD ON LOCATION: This shop specializes in Planet Hollywood–brand merchandise.

POP GALLERY: A West Side newcomer, this gallery features artist-signed limited sculptures and paintings, and high-end gift items. There's a champagne bar, too. Hence the "pop."

SOSA FAMILY CIGARS: In addition to offering premium cigars, this shop showcases the art of hand-rolling. Feel free to puff away here—the shop's a smoking zone.

STARABILIAS: The spotlight here is on memorabilia—music, television, movie—allowing you to bring a piece of Hollywood to the folks back home.

SUNGLASS ICON: Looking to change your eyeglass image? Slip on shades that have been sported by the stars—or at least replicas of their shades.

VIRGIN MEGASTORE: This store has a huge selection of music, from classical to contemporary. Listening stations allow guests to sample some of the musical fare. DVDs and books are also available.

BoardWalk

A stroll at Disney's BoardWalk is a journey back in time. Inspired by the Middle Atlantic seaside attractions of the early 1900s, BoardWalk recaptures the carefree atmosphere of that bygone era. The resort is surrounded by restaurants, clubs, and amusements similar to those enjoyed by beachgoers of yesteryear. It's bordered by a wood-planked walkway, which hugs the shore of Crescent Lake. By day, BoardWalk is a peaceful place to soak up sun, enjoy lunch, or simply walk the boards. After dark, the place turns into a twinkling center of nighttime activity—some of it elegant, some of it downright raucous.

Wyland Galleries, which features the world's foremost marine environmental art, is one of the more calming diversions. WildWood Landing challenges onlookers to test their luck and skill at a collection of classic carnival games. And strolling performers enchant passersby of all ages with magic shows, balloon tricks, or other antics.

BoardWalk is open to everyone. Although there is no admission price, individual venues may charge a cover. There is a $8 charge for valet parking (even for guests who are staying at a Disney resort). Self-parking is free. For more restaurant information, refer to *Good Meals, Great Times.*

Clubs

ATLANTIC DANCE: This is a lovely atmosphere in which to dance the night away. A deejay cranks up tunes, tempting guests to twist and shout on the spacious dance floor. Live bands, some big, some small, play on select occasions.

In addition to traditional cocktails, the club serves specialty drinks. Sample one in the "big room" or on the waterfront balcony.

Guests must be 21 or older, with a legal photo ID, to enter. There was no cover charge at press time, but that could change. Hours are generally 9 P.M. until 2 A.M., Tuesday through Saturday.

This club is known for reinventing itself: Specifics may be different during your visit.

ESPN CLUB: This club aims to please sports enthusiasts of all kinds, from the casual armchair quarterback to the most rabid fanatic. It includes a broadcasting facility, arcade, and table-service restaurant and bar.

More than 100 televisions broadcast live sports events, so guests always know the score. (Need to make a pit stop at a crucial moment of the game? Don't sweat it . . . there are even TVs in the bathrooms.)

The ESPN Club has three sections. As you enter, you're on the 50-yard line at The Sidelines. You can catch a game on a television monitor above the "penalty box" bar or sit at a nearby table. Beer, wine, and soft drinks are available, as is the usual pub fare.

Sports Central, the main dining area, has a big screen, showing—what else?—the big game. The kitchen is open until 11 P.M. for meals, 12:30 A.M. for appetizers.

The Yard Arcade, a gameroom with an "urban playground" motif, lets you play the latest sports-themed video games while listening to the big game of the moment.

JELLYROLLS: You might want to warm up your vocal cords before crossing the threshold. They don't call it a sing-along bar for nothing: Guests are expected to sing, clap, and join in the fun at this warehouse home of dueling pianos. You'll hear everything from Gershwin to *Grease*. The piano players take requests, so plan ahead. Write the request—a cocktail napkin will do—and slip it onto the piano. (Although it's not required, we recommend slipping a tip along, too. It will increase the odds of your hearing the request *and* help the musicians pay their rent.)

Jellyrolls is open from 7 P.M. until 2 A.M. nightly. There is usually an $8–$10 cover charge to enter. (Note that the cover charge may vary.) To get in, you must be at least 21 years old and willing to prove it.

Water Parks
Typhoon Lagoon

This watery playground was inspired by an imagined legend: A typhoon hit a tiny resort village many years ago, and the storm—plus an ensuing earthquake and volcanic eruption—left the village in ruins. The locals, however, were resourceful and rebuilt their town as this "wateropolis."

The centerpiece of Typhoon Lagoon is a huge watershed mountain known as Mount Mayday. Perched atop its peak is the *Miss Tilly*, a marooned shrimp boat originally from Safen Sound, Florida. *Miss Tilly*'s smokestack erupts every half hour, shooting a 50-foot flume of water into the air.

The surf lagoon is huge: Thrilling slides snake through caves, tamer ones offer twisting journeys, and tiny slides entertain small kids. And the new Crush 'n' Gusher is a thrilling addition. Note that children under 10 must be accompanied by an adult.

SURF POOL: The main swimming area contains nearly three million gallons of water, making it one of the world's largest wave pools. The Caribbean-blue lagoon is surrounded by a white-sand beach, and its main attraction is the waves that come crashing to the shore every 90 seconds. The less adventurous can loll about in two relatively calm tide pools, Whitecap Cove and Blustery Bay.

CASTAWAY CREEK: This 2,100-foot circular river that winds through the park offers a lazy, relaxing orientation to Typhoon Lagoon. Tubes may be borrowed for free and are the most enjoyable way to make the trip along the three-foot-deep waterway. The ride takes guests through a rain forest, where they are cooled by mists and spray; through caves and grottoes that provide welcome shade on hot summer days; and through an area where "broken" pipes from a water tower unleash showers on helpless passersby. There are exits along the way, where guests can hop out for a while and do something else. It takes 20 to 35 minutes to ride around the park without taking a break.

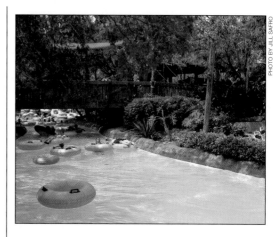

PHOTO BY JILL SAFRO

CRUSH 'N' GUSHER: This "water coaster" thrill ride is one of a kind. In it, daredevils are whisked along a series of flumes and tossed and turned as they weave through an abandoned tropical fruit factory. There are three spillways to choose from: Banana Blaster, Coconut Crusher, and Pineapple Plunger.

GANGPLANK FALLS, KEELHAUL FALLS, AND MAYDAY FALLS: These white-water rides offer guests a variety of slippery trips, two of them in inner tubes. All of the slides course through caves and waterfalls, and past rockwork, making the scenery an attraction in itself. Gangplank Falls gives families a chance to ride together in a three- to five-passenger craft.

HUMUNGA KOWABUNGA: These three speed slides, reported to have been carved into the landscape by the historic earthquake, will send guests zooming through caverns at speeds of 30 miles per hour. The 214-foot slides each offer a 51-foot drop, and the view from the top is a little scary. But it's over before you know it, and once-wary guests hurry back for another try. Guests are also warned that they should be free of back trouble, heart conditions, and other physical limitations to take the trip. Guests must be at least 4 feet tall to ride any of the Humunga Kowabunga speed slides. Pregnant women are not permitted to ride.

STORM SLIDES: The Jib Jammer, Rudder Buster, and Stern Burner body slides send guests off at about 20 miles per hour down winding fiberglass slides, in and out of rock formations and caves and through waterfalls. It's a somewhat tamer ride than Humunga Kowabunga, but still offers a speedy descent. The slides run about 300 feet, and each offers a different view and experience.

SHARK REEF: Guests borrow snorkel equipment for a swim through a coral reef, where they come face-to-face with sharks and fish. The reef is built around a sunken tanker. The sharks, by the way, leopard and bonnethead, are passive members of the species. Everyone must shower before entering. Guests must be older than age 5 to experience Shark Reef. Kids under 10 must be accompanied by an adult.

KETCHAKIDDEE CREEK: Open only to those 4 feet tall or under, this area has small rides for pint-size visitors. Children must be accompanied by an adult. There are slides, fountains, waterfalls, squirting whales and seals, a mini-rapids ride, an interactive tugboat, and a grotto with a veil of water that kids love to run through.

SURFING: Surf clinics are offered on select mornings before the park opens. For information, call 407-WDW-SURF (939-7873).

Essentials

WHEN TO GO: Typhoon Lagoon gets very crowded early in the day. Hours vary seasonally, but the park is generally open from 10 A.M. to 5 P.M., with extended hours in the summer months. All of the pools are heated in the winter. Note that this park is usually closed for refurbishment during certain winter months. The park may also close due to bad weather. Call 407-824-4321 for updates.

EXTRA MAGIC HOURS: Typhoon Lagoon may open one hour early for guests staying in a Walt Disney World-owned-and-operated hotel (plus the Hilton on Hotel Plaza Blvd.) provided that they can prove it and have a valid ticket. The park stays open three hours later for these guests one night a week during the 2-week Easter period and 12 summer weeks.

HOW TO GET THERE: Bus service begins from all resorts approximately one hour before Typhoon Lagoon opens for the day.

The buses stop at the water park and then at the Downtown Disney Marketplace before 10 A.M. After 10 A.M., resort buses stop at the Marketplace and then Typhoon Lagoon. Buses stop running to the water park about one hour after it closes. Parking is free.

LOCKER ROOMS: Restrooms with showers and lockers are located close to the entrance. Other restrooms are available farther into the park. Small lockers cost $5 plus a $5 deposit to rent for the day, while large lockers cost $7 plus a $5 deposit. Towels rent for $1; life jackets and tubes are available free of charge.

WHERE TO EAT: Both Typhoon Lagoon restaurants offer similar fare and outdoor seating. Leaning Palms, which was known as Placid Palms before the typhoon hit, was renamed to fit its somewhat unorthodox architecture. Burgers, pizza, salads, ice cream, and assorted snacks are sold here. Typhoon Tilly's Snack Shack serves chicken tenders, wraps, barbecued pork sandwiches, and ice cream. Let's Go Slurpin' offers frozen drink specialties and spirits. Guests may bring their own food or enjoy fare from the restaurants in designated picnic areas. Alcoholic beverages and glass containers may not be brought into the park. Coolers are allowed.

FIRST AID: A first-aid station capable of handling minor medical problems is located just to the left of Leaning Palms.

BEACH SHOP: Singapore Sal's, located near the park's main entrance, is set in a ramshackle building left a bit battered by the typhoon. Swimsuits, sunglasses, hats, towels, sunscreen, souvenirs, water shoes, and Typhoon Lagoon logo products are available.

Admission Prices

Prices do not include sales tax and are subject to change. **Note:** Admission is an option with a Magic Your Way ticket that includes a Water Park Fun & More add-on and is included with a Premium Annual Pass.

	Adults	Children*
One-Day Ticket	$35.00	$29.00
Annual Pass	$99.95	$80.50

*3 through 9 years of age; children under 3 free

Blizzard Beach

A wintry, watery wonderland, Blizzard Beach is said to be the result of a freak storm that dropped a mountain of snow onto Walt Disney World, prompting the quick construction of Florida's first ski resort. When temperatures soared and the snow began to melt, designers prepared to close the resort. But when they spotted an alligator sliding down the slopes, they realized that they had created an exhilarating water adventure park. The slalom and bobsled runs became downhill waterslides. The ski jump is one of the world's tallest (120 feet) and fastest (60 miles per hour) free-fall speed slides.

The centerpiece of Blizzard Beach is the snowcapped Mount Gushmore and its Summit Plummet. Most of the more thrilling runs are found on the slopes of this mountain, which tops out at 90 feet. At the summit, swimmers have a choice of speed slides, flumes, a white-water raft ride, and an inner-tube run. Guests may reach the top of Mount Gushmore via chairlift. The lift has a gondola for guests with disabilities. There are stairs, too.

This is the most action-packed Disney water park yet, with enough activities for the entire family to fill at least a day. Note that kids under 10 must be accompanied by an adult.

MELT-AWAY BAY: This one-acre pool at the base of Mt. Gushmore is equipped with its own wave machine. No tsunamis here, however—just a pleasant, bobbing wave.

CROSS COUNTRY CREEK: This meandering 3,000-foot waterway circles the entire park. A slow current keeps visitors moving merrily along.

Hot Tip!

Early birds get the lounge chairs around these parts. If you want to snag a chair at any of Disney's water parks, arrive as close to park opening as possible.

Inner tubes, which are free, are the most pleasant way to travel. The ride includes a trip through a bone-chilling ice cave, where guests are splashed with the "melting ice" from overhead.

SUMMIT PLUMMET: The thrilling ride begins 120 feet in the air on a platform 30 feet above the top of Mount Gushmore. Brave souls travel about 60 miles per hour down a 350-foot slide. Near the top, guests pass through a ski chalet. To those watching from below, riders seem to disappear into an explosion of mist. You must be at least 4 feet tall to take the plunge.

SLUSH GUSHER: This relatively tame, double-humped waterslide offers a brisk journey through a snow-banked mountain gully. Topping out at 90 feet, Slush Gusher is the tallest slide of its kind. You'll find it on Mount Gushmore, next to Summit Plummet. Guests must be at least 4 feet tall to ride.

TEAMBOAT SPRINGS: The longest family white-water raft ride in the world takes six-passenger rafts down a twisting, 1,400-foot series of rushing waterfalls.

TOBOGGAN RACERS: An eight-lane water-slide sends guests racing over a number of dips. They lie on their stomachs on a mat and travel headfirst down the 250-foot route.

SNOW STORMERS: A trio of flumes descends from the top of the mountain. Guests race down on a switchback course that includes ski-type slalom gates.

RUNOFF RAPIDS: On this inner-tube run, guests careen down three twisting, turning flumes in a single or double tube.

DOWNHILL DOUBLE DIPPER: Guests travel down these two parallel 230-foot-long racing

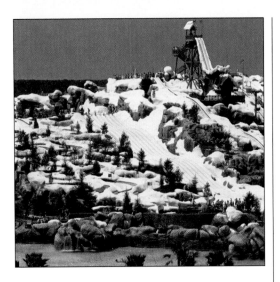

slides at speeds of up to 25 miles per hour. The partially enclosed water runs feature ski-racing graphics, flags, and time clocks. You must be 48 inches tall to ride.

SKI PATROL TRAINING CAMP: An area designed specifically for preteens, Frozen Pipe Springs looks like an old pipe and drops sliders into eight feet of water. The Thin Ice Training Course tests agility as kids try to walk along broken "icebergs" without falling into the water. Snow Falls's "wide" slides allow a parent and child to ride together. At the Ski Patrol Shelter, guests grab on to a T-bar for an airborne trip. At any point in the ride they can drop into the water below. Ski patrol participants also experience Cool Runners, where riders can count on hurtling and whirling over lots of moguls on twin inner-tube slides. No bunny slopes for these brave daredevils.

TIKE'S PEAK: A kid-size variation of Blizzard Beach, this attraction features miniature versions of Mount Gushmore's slides and a snow-castle fountain play area. Adults must be accompanied by a child to enter this zone.

Essentials

WHEN TO GO: As a guest favorite, Blizzard Beach tends to get very crowded early in the day. Hours vary seasonally, but the park is generally open from 10 A.M. to 5 P.M., with extended hours in summer. All pools are heated in winter. Blizzard Beach is often closed for refurbishment during certain winter months. It may also close due to inclement weather. For schedules, call 407-WDW-PLAY (939-7529).

EXTRA MAGIC HOUR: Blizzard Beach may open one hour early for guests staying in a Walt Disney World-owned-and-operated hotel (plus the Hilton on Hotel Plaza Boulevard) provided that they can prove it and have a valid ticket.

HOW TO GET THERE: Blizzard Beach is served by the buses that go to and from Animal Kingdom. There is service to and from Epcot and the Disney-MGM Studios, as well. Parking is free.

LOCKER ROOMS: There are restrooms with showers near the main entrance. Other restrooms and dressing rooms are located around the park. Small lockers cost $5 plus a $5 deposit for the day, while large lockers cost $7 plus a $5 deposit. Towels rent for $1, and life jackets and tubes may be used for free.

WHERE TO EAT: Burgers, hot dogs, fruit salads, and drinks are available at Lottawatta Lodge, in the main village area. Two snack stands with limited offerings are located in more remote areas: Avalunch and The Warming Hut. Polar Pub offers drink specialties and spirits. There are picnic areas for those who prefer to pack their own food. Alcoholic beverages and glass containers may not be brought into the park. Coolers are allowed.

FIRST AID: Minor medical problems are handled at this station near the main entrance.

BEACH SHOP: The Beach Haus stocks bathing suits, T-shirts, shorts, sunglasses, hats, sunscreen, beach towels, and more.

Admission Prices

Prices do not include sales tax and are likely to change. **Note:** Admission is an option with a Magic Your Way ticket that includes a Water Park Fun & More add-on and is included with a Premium Annual Pass.

	Adults	Children*
One-Day Ticket	$35.00	$29.00
Annual Pass	$99.95	$80.50
Combo Ticket	$42.50	$34.50

(Includes one-day admission to Blizzard Beach and Disney's Winter Summerland miniature-golf course.)

*3 through 9 years of age; children under 3 free

Daredevil Disney

EVERYTHING ELSE IN THE WORLD

You've catapulted through the galaxy on Space Mountain, survived the role of crash dummy on Test Track, and become something of a human yo-yo on the Twilight Zone Tower of Terror. Now what? Believe it or not, there are plenty of thrills awaiting you outside the theme park turnstiles. Some of them, such as the wedgie-inducing slides at the water parks, are well known. Others may be lower key, but they're definitely high octane. Here's a rundown of our favorite theme-park-alternative thrill rides.

PARASAILING: Even if you've never had the urge to be a human kite, consider giving this a whirl. After a simple lift-off from the back of a boat, you and your parachute gradually climb skyward. Before you know it, you're eye level with the roof of the Contemporary resort hotel. A few peaceful minutes later, the hotel and the nearby Magic Kingdom appear to have shrunk considerably. It's not unlike the illusion of flying over London in Peter Pan's Flight. Only this flight's no illusion: You're really 450 or so feet above it all. And don't worry about the landing. It's as smooth as the trip itself. The attendants simply reel you in for a soft touchdown on the back of the boat.

For information on prices and reservations, turn to page 219.

STOCK CAR RACING: Few people can say they've ridden shotgun in a race car, let alone driven one. And this is the real deal. Whether you do it as a driver or a passenger, the Richard Petty Driving Experience is guaranteed to deliver the adrenaline surge of a lifetime. The track is off the beaten path, so

some Disney guests fail to notice it. Those who do tend to come back for more.

For the ride-along experience, you'll don a helmet and climb through the window into the passenger seat. Buckle up and . . . you're off! The big challenges here: (1) not obsessing over the speedometer (it may reach 145 mph) and (2) keeping your head straight (the force from the extreme velocity tends to push noggins to the right).

The expert driver will take you inches from the wall and zip in and out of traffic. (Yes, there are other cars on the track at the same time.) If you're in the driver's seat, you'll have an expert driver to follow. Tailgate at your own risk.

For details on pricing (it's not cheap) and reservations, turn to page 224.

SURFING: When the sun comes up, so does the surf at Disney's Typhoon Lagoon. On select days, guests can take part in a surf clinic taught by competitive surfers. Instructors control the height of the waves—and they give Mother Nature a run for her money.

If you've never hung ten before, know this: It ain't easy. But once you've managed to get up on a board, it's a blast.

For more information, call 407-939-7873.

WATERSKIING: Florida weather being what it is (hot!), waterskiing (as well as wakeboarding and tubing) never really goes out of season. It's a refreshing way to see the sights of Bay Lake—and a serious workout to boot. Sammy Duvall instructors are on hand to assist. For more information, see page 220.

MOTORBOATING: If you've been to Walt Disney World before, you've no doubt seen folks tooling about in zippy, little motorboats. But have you ever actually given one a try? It's an experience we highly recommend.

For starters, the watercraft known as Sea Raycer boats are indeed speedy. And it's an experience everyone can enjoy (though guests need to be at least 12 years old and at least 5 feet tall to drive). Magic Kingdom resorts require that at least one person per boat have a valid driver's license. Expect to pay about $24 for a half hour. Be sure to wear a watch—as you're apt to lose track of time. For more information, turn to page 219.

Fort Wilderness

In a part of the state where campgrounds tend to look like dried pastures—barren and very hot—the Fort Wilderness Resort and Campground, located almost due east of the Contemporary resort, is an anomaly—a forested, 700-acre wonder of tall slash pines, white-flowering bay trees, and ancient cypresses hung with Spanish moss. Seminole Indians once hunted and fished here.

There are more than a thousand campsites arranged in several campground loops; among them, Wilderness Cabins are available for rent, completely furnished and fitted with all the comforts of home. For information about lodging options, refer to our *Transportation & Accommodations* chapter.

Scattered throughout the campground loops are sporting facilities, including two tennis courts and many small playgrounds, basketball, tetherball, and volleyball courts. Fort Wilderness has riding stables (with rather mellow horses), two swimming pools, a marina full of boats, a canoe livery, a beach, bikes and golf carts for rent, and a nature trail. Some facilities are available to campground guests only; some are open to all guests, no matter where they happen to be staying.

There's a pony farm (which offers rides to young guests) and a barn that's home to the horses that pull the Magic Kingdom's Main Street trolleys. The barn houses a small museum that celebrates horses and the cherished role they've played in Disney history.

Two stores—the Settlement Trading Post and the Meadow Trading Post—stock campers' necessities, a limited supply of groceries, and souvenirs. And then there's Pioneer Hall, the home of the Hoop-Dee-Doo Musical Revue dinner show (described in the *Good Meals, Great Times* chapter). This rustic structure (made of white pine shipped from Montana) also houses a popular (and reasonably priced) buffet restaurant and a small lounge area. Mickey's Backyard Barbecue is offered here during busy times of the year.

BEACHES AND SWIMMING: The beach on the shore of Bay Lake is a good spot for sunning or snoozing in a hammock. There are also two pools for campers' use. Note that the beaches and pools are open to Fort Wilderness guests only. Swimming is not allowed at the beach.

BIKE RENTALS: Bikes may be rented at the Bike Barn for trips along the bike paths and roadways of Fort Wilderness—or just for getting around. Bikes cost about $8 per half hour or $21 per day.

BLACKSMITH SHOP: The pleasant fellow who shoes the draft horses that pull trolleys in the Magic Kingdom is on hand most mornings to answer questions and talk about his job; occasionally, guests may watch him at work, fitting the big animals with the special polyurethane-covered, steel-cored horseshoes that are used to protect the horses' hooves. This shop is located at the Tri-Circle-D Ranch.

BOATING: Fort Wilderness is ribboned with tranquil canals that make for delightful canoe trips of one to three hours—or longer if you take fishing gear and elect to wet your line. Canoe rentals are available at the Bike Barn for about $7 per half hour or $11 per hour. Pedal boats (about $7 per half hour or $11 per hour) may also be rented here for use in the canals. For a trip around Bay Lake, zippy little Sea Racer boats, Boston Whaler Montauks, and pontoon boats are available for rent at the marina, at the north end of the campground. (Refer to the *Sports* chapter for details.)

CAMPFIRE PROGRAM: Held nightly (weather permitting) near the Meadow Trading Post at the center of the campground, this evening program features Disney movies, a sing-along, and cartoons. Chip and Dale often put in an appearance. It's open to WDW resort guests only (no charge).

CARRIAGE RIDES: Guests may enjoy a relaxing and intimate carriage ride through

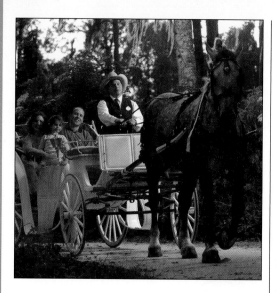

the picturesque grounds of Fort Wilderness. The rate for each 25-minute ride is $35.

Small carriages can hold up to two adults and a small child. Larger carriages fit 4 adults or 2 adults and up to 3 small kids. Reservations are a must. Rides are offered nightly. Call 407-WDW-PLAY for information or to make a reservation. Walk-up reservations are sometimes possible. (Ask the driver about buying tickets. If they're available, expect to pay with cash or a Disney Resort ID card. Credit cards are not accepted.) Rides may be canceled due to inclement weather. Cancelations must be made at least 24 hours ahead to avoid paying full price.

Note that guests are picked up in front of Crockett's Tavern at Pioneer Hall. Feel free to bring your own liquid refreshments.

ELECTRIC CART RENTALS: Available at the Bike Barn (about $46 for 24 hours) for sightseeing or transportation. Renters must be 18 years old and have a valid driver's license. Reservations are necessary; call 407-824-2742 for reservations and additional information.

ELECTRICAL WATER PAGEANT: Originally presented for the dedication of the Polynesian Luau in 1971, this cavalcade of lights is presented nightly on the waters of Bay Lake and the Seven Seas Lagoon. The simple pageant consists of two strings of seven barges, each carrying a 25-foot-tall screen of lights featuring King Neptune and creatures of the sea. And it's all set to music. The show can be seen from the beach at Fort Wilderness, as well as from the Contemporary, Polynesian, and Grand Floridian resorts. (We've caught it

while waiting for the monorail at the Magic Kingdom, too.) Ask for the schedule at your resort's lobby concierge desk.

FISHING EXCURSIONS ON BAY LAKE: Walt Disney World's restrictive fishing policy means plenty of angling action—largemouth bass weighing two to eight pounds, mainly—for those who sign up for fishing excursions.

The fee ranges from about $200 to $230 for up to five people for a two-hour excursion (one additional hour is about $90) and includes gear, a guide, and soft drinks; no license is required. The price varies based on time of day, with the early morning trips commanding the highest rate.

Note that all fishing is strictly catch-and-release. Call 407-WDW-BASS (939-2277) for exact times and to make reservations.

FISHING IN THE CANALS: In addition to largemouth bass, catfish and panfish can be caught here as well. Those without their own gear will find cane poles and lures for sale at the trading posts; equipment is also available for rent at the Bike Barn. Cane poles are about $4 per half hour. Rods and reels are about $6 per hour or $10 per day. Bait costs about $4. No license is required. Fort Wilderness resort guests may toss their lines in right from the shore. All Walt Disney World fishing is strictly catch-and-release.

LAWN MOWER TREE: The tree that mysteriously grew around a lawn mower is a Fort Wilderness point of interest worth seeking out. It's just off the path leading to the marina, across the way from the Meadow Trading Post.

PONY FARM: This enclave just behind Pioneer Hall is home to some friendly ponies. Pony rides, offered seasonally, are available between 10 A.M. and 5 P.M. for $4. (The pony-ride weight limit is 80 pounds.) The farm is a good place to visit before the Hoop-Dee-Doo Musical Revue.

TENNIS: Two tennis courts are available; play is on a first-come, first-served basis.

TRAIL RIDES: Guided horseback trips depart four times daily from the Trail Blaze Corral and take riders on a leisurely, meandering ride through the Florida wilderness, where it is not uncommon to see birds, deer, and even an occasional alligator. Galloping is not part of the experience, so you don't need riding know-how to sign up. Cost is about $42 per person. No children under 9 are permitted to ride. There is a weight limit of 250 pounds. Reservations are necessary; call 407-WDW-PLAY (939-7529) up to 90 days in advance.

TRI-CIRCLE-D RANCH: This corner of Fort Wilderness is the place that the world champion Percherons and the draft horses that pull trolleys down Main Street in the Magic Kingdom call home. You may watch them chomping on their food and occasionally see young colts and fillies as well. The Tri-Circle-D insignia above the barn door—two small circles atop a large one with the letter *D* inside—is the WDW brand. The barn is also the site of a museum that pays tribute to horses and their role in Disney history.

PLAYGROUNDS, VOLLEYBALL, TETHER-BALL, AND BASKETBALL COURTS: These are scattered throughout the camping loops. There is no charge to use the courts.

WAGON RIDES: The wagon departs from Pioneer Hall at 7 P.M. and 9:30 P.M. and carries guests on a trip through wooded areas near Bay Lake. Each ride lasts about 45 minutes and concludes at Pioneer Hall.

Purchase tickets from the wagon ride host: $8 for adults, $5 for children 3 through 9. Kids under 12 must be accompanied by an adult.

On nights when the Magic Kingdom offers a fireworks presentation, Fort Wilderness offers "fireworks wagon rides." These excursions are

in addition to those regularly scheduled. Expect fireworks wagon rides to depart at 8:30 P.M. for a 9 P.M. fireworks show. The fireworks are viewed from a distance, but the experience is made special by plugging into the show's audio sound track.

Group wagon rides are available by calling 407-824-2734 (24 hours in advance). The price is $300 per hour.

WILDERNESS SWAMP TRAIL: A three-quarter-mile trail, this smooth footpath into the woods skirts the marshes along the shore of Bay Lake, then plunges into a forest thick with tall, straight-standing cypress trees. It is near Marshmallow Marsh, at the northern end of the campground.

Essentials

HOW TO GET THERE: From outside the World, take Magic Kingdom Exit 64B off I-4 onto US 192, go through the Magic Kingdom Auto Plaza, and bearing to your right, follow the Fort Wilderness signs. This is the most expeditious way to go, even for WDW resort guests.

By WDW Transportation: Buses or boats. Buses can get you just about anywhere, but allow yourself plenty of time—the system, while efficient, is time-consuming.

Boats are also available from Magic Kingdom marinas (about a 30-minute ride) and from the Contemporary and Wilderness Lodge resorts (about a 25-minute ride). For details about WDW Transportation, see the *Transportation & Accommodations* chapter.

WHERE TO EAT: For a description of the Trail's End restaurant at Fort Wilderness, refer to the *Good Meals, Great Times* chapter.

The Settlement Trading Post, located not far from the beach at the north end of the campground, and the Meadow Trading Post, located near the center of Fort Wilderness, also offer a limited supply of food staples. For serious grocery shopping, head to Goodings at Crossroads or another nearby supermarket. Ask for directions at the Lobby Concierge.

> ## Hot Tip!
> River Country, Walt Disney World's (and the real world's) original water park, was closed indefinitely when this book went to press. It is not expected to be open in 2007.

WDW Spas

For many guests, a day at the theme parks is an exciting test of physical endurance—complete with sprinting (say, from Dumbo to Space Mountain before that Fastpass time expires), weight lifting (toting tired toddlers), and long-distance hiking (covering more than a mile to reach the American Adventure pavilion from Epcot's front gate—and back again!). Fortunately, there are many ways to rest and rejuvenate weary bones, throbbing feet, and noise-addled noggins. Chief among them is a visit to a soothing spa (ahhhh). There are four such spots on Disney property, open to WDW resort guests and day visitors alike.

GRAND FLORIDIAN SPA: A short walk from the Grand Floridian Resort, this casual retreat is located right next to the tennis courts. Though far from plush, the facility's saunas, steam rooms, whirlpools, and even the locker rooms promote pampering. Specialties of the house include aromatherapy baths, a deluxe facial, complete with hand and foot massage, and a cooling lavender body wrap, guaranteed to take the sting out of any sunburn. Other services include aromatherapy and massage (including shiatsu, Swedish, sports, and one specially designed for expectant mothers). Manicures, pedicures, and other hand and foot treatments are also available.

Health club hours are generally from 6 A.M. to 9 P.M., but may vary. Treatment hours are usually 8 A.M. to 8 P.M. daily. Prices start at about $115 for a 50-minute massage and about $125 for a facial. Full- and half-day packages are available. For more information, call 407-824-2332 or visit *www.disneyworld.com*. Reservations are accepted up to one year in advance.

Spa Tips

• Reserve treatments far in advance and be sure to confirm all appointments.

• If you'll feel more comfortable with either a male or a female spa therapist, make the request when you make your reservation. The spas strive to accommodate such requests whenever possible.

• Plan to arrive a few minutes early. That'll give you time to change and relax.

• If you're scheduled for a body treatment, leave all clothes in a locker. Robes (and slippers) are provided.

• Don't forget to remove all jewelry before a treatment. (You can leave it in the safe in your resort room.)

• Bathing suits are optional for the separate men's and women's saunas and whirlpools.

• It's always a good idea to take a quick shower before a treatment—especially if you've been at the beach or running around theme parks beforehand.

• Drink plenty of water after your spa experience. It'll counter any dehydrating effects.

MANDARA SPA AT THE DOLPHIN: As exotic as it is peaceful, this new retreat pampered its first visitors in the latter half of 2005. Guests have been stepping up to swap their stress for smiles ever since.

Mandara, which has locations throughout the world, specializes in treatments that are meant to reflect the "beauty, spirit, and traditions of ancient times, along with the soul and ritual of Asian culture." The spa menu showcases Balinese massage, a variation of Swedish massage, that was developed in Bali. It incorporates stretching, "vigorous yet relaxing" movements, and elements of shiatsu. Of course that's just one of many services offered here—all of which emphasize physical wellness and spiritual well-being. Other treatments include the Mandara Four Hand massage, Elemis Aroma Stone Therapy, and Elemis Deep Tissue Muscle massage. The Elemis Visible Brilliance Facial ($150) is perfect for sensitive skin, providing a deep pore cleansing

Hot Tip!

The spas at the Grand Floridian and at Saratoga Springs offer My First Facial, My First Manicure, and My First Pedicure for guests ages 4 to 12.

while smoothing wrinkles. And the exotic Frangipani Body Nourish Wrap ($220 for 75 minutes) includes 50 minutes of massage and incorporates a special oil from the rare and fragrant Balinese Frangipani flower.

In addition to Balinese-inspired architecture, two interior gardens provide retreats before guests begin the spa ritual. The goal here is to provide a place for guests to rejuvenate their minds as well as those aching "I can't believe I covered four theme parks in two days!" muscles. For more information, call 800-227-1500 or visit *www.swandolphin.com.*

THE SPA AT DISNEY'S SARATOGA SPRINGS: Terra-cotta-colored tiles and teal towels accent this spa's ten treatment rooms. Signature services include the Warm Seafoam Mud Wrap and Seaweed Hydro-Massage. Also on tap: aromatherapy, reflexology, sports and Swedish massage, and hydrotherapy, plus a variety of body wraps and scrubs. Manicures, pedicures, and facials are also options. The locker rooms are equipped with a steam room, sauna, and whirlpool.

Located on the shore of Buena Vista Village Lake, the spa is in the Fitness Center at the Saratoga Springs resort. Hours are generally from 8 A.M. to 8 P.M., but vary seasonally. A 50-minute massage costs about $115, with facials going for about $125 (plus gratuity). Full- and half-day packages are available. For information, call 407-827-4455. Reservations are taken up to six months ahead.

THE SPA AT BUENA VISTA PALACE: A plush, peaceful place, this spa is as well equipped as they come. One-way glass provides natural, picture-window views from (but not into) the 14 treatment rooms. High-tech chairs with whirlpool foot baths and back-massage capability make getting a pedicure a real event. And a cool-mud Theme Park Leg Relief Wrap can put the spring back in the step of even the most labored lower limbs. Landscaped, outdoor whirlpools, plus locker room saunas and steam rooms, are there to aid the relaxation process.

Among the many treatments from which to choose are aromatherapy and massage, including shiatsu, Swedish, deep-tissue, and reflexology. A variety of special facials (including one for sun-stressed skin), baths (herbal, mud, mineral, and seaweed), scrubs, and wraps are available. An adjacent salon offers the usual lineup of services.

The Spa at the Buena Vista Palace hotel is situated opposite the Downtown Disney Marketplace, on Buena Vista Drive. Hours are usually 8 A.M. to 8 P.M., but vary seasonally. A 25-minute massage costs about $75, and facials are about $120 (plus a 20 percent gratuity). Full- and half-day packages are available, as are custom packages. For information, call 800-996-3426 or 407-827-3200. Reservations are accepted up to one month in advance.

Internet Access at WDW

We'll resist the urge to chastise you for insisting on checking your e-mail while on vacation (since we're similarly obsessed) and instead happily report that all Walt Disney World resorts offer in-room high-speed Internet access. Of course you'll need to supply the laptop and connection cable—and pay $9.95 for each 24-hour period that you choose to use the service.

For those guests who prefer not to be tethered to the wall while exploring the Net, do know that Wi-Fi (wireless fidelity) is a reality at several locations. You can use the service for $4.99 per hour or for $9.95 for 24 hours at a time. As it is not provided by the Walt Disney Company, it will not be billed to your room, like most purchases made on Disney property. Instead, you'll pay via the Internet itself, using a credit card. Of course, your computer must be Wi-Fi ready. At press time, the following resorts had areas that offered wireless Internet service: BoardWalk, Contemporary, Coronado Springs, Grand Floridian, Yacht and Beach Club, and the Swan. Note that in-room high-speed Internet service (with a connection cable) is also available at the Swan and Dolphin.

Finally, if you'd like to access the Internet but prefer not to lug your own computer, simply ask your Lobby Concierge to direct you to the nearest resort business center. There you can check your e-mail, peruse the news, manage your fantasy sports teams, and more. Fees vary—be sure to inquire before you start surfing.

Just for Kids

Walt Disney World may appeal to the kid in all of us, but some activities are intended for the actual young—not just the young at heart. With the exception of the Princess Tea Party, the following programs are intended for guests who can't remember life before the Internet. (The programs take place at the Grand Floridian, but are available to all youngsters who visit Walt Disney World.) The programs are all quite popular—and accommodate a limited number of guests—call as early as possible to make your reservation: 407-WDW-DINE (939-3463).

ALBATROSS TREASURE CRUISE: Thar be treasure in Crescent Lake! Kids are invited to follow clues and join in the hunt. The 2-hour quest takes young adventurers to several stops and includes a reading of the "The Legend of the Albatross." Lunch (PB&J sandwiches, cookies, and a juice box) is served at the final port of call. The ship weighs anchor at the Yacht Club marina Wednesday and Saturday at 9:30 A.M. Cost per child is about $30. It's open to potty-trained guests ages 4–10. Participants should wear socks and sneakers.

GRAND ADVENTURES IN COOKING: Aspiring chefs can jump-start their careers in this sweet program at the Grand Floridian resort. Over the course of an hour or so, kids may decorate their own chef hat and apron, as well as contribute to a culinary creation—which they can share with happy guests lounging in the resort lobby. It's open to potty-trained kids between the ages of 4 and 10. Reservations are required and may be made up to 180 days ahead. The cost is about $30 a kid.

MY DISNEY GIRL'S PERFECTLY PRINCESS TEA PARTY: Young regals (and their grown-up guardians) are encouraged to dress like their favorite princess for this festive tea party, offered daily from 10:30 A.M. to noon (except Tuesdays and Saturdays) in the Garden View Lounge at Walt Disney World's Grand Floridian resort. The tea party is hosted by Miss Rose Petal, a magical rose from Aurora's garden that has come to life to lead story-telling, sing-alongs, and a princess parade. Guests may take a break from sipping tea and eating cake to visit with Princess Aurora, aka Sleeping Beauty. Have those cameras and autograph books ready.

All guests between the ages of 3 and 11 receive a "My Disney Girl" doll, dressed as Princess Aurora, plus accessories. The cost for one adult and child (ages 3–11) is $225, including tax and gratuity. Each additional child is $150, while an extra adult pays $75. Reservations are required and may be made up to 180 days ahead.

WONDERLAND TEA PARTY: Fans of Alice and her Wonderland friends will have a blast at this party presented at 1900 Park Fare at Disney's Grand Floridian resort. During the hour-long event, kids make and eat cupcakes and enjoy a light lunch. They'll also be treated to a story and have tea with the characters. The cost is about $30 per child, ages 4–10 (potty-trained). The tea party is offered Monday through Friday at 1:30 P.M. Reservations are required and are available 180 days in advance.

PIRATE ADVENTURE: Ahoy there, mateys! In this adventure, young pirates don red bandannas and hit the high seas in search of treasure. The ship shoves off at the Grand Floridian marina each Monday, Wednesday, Thursday, and Saturday at 9:30 A.M. From there, it visits exotic ports of call (other resort marinas), where guests collect valuable treasures and enjoy lunch. It's available to potty-trained kids ages 4–10. Cost per child is about $30. Reservations are required and are available up to 180 days ahead. Note that participants should wear socks and sneakers.

Specialty Cruises

At Walt Disney World, every evening ends with a bang—which comes in the form of elaborate pyrotechnic displays. Two such presentations, the Magic Kingdom's Wishes fireworks and Epcot's IllumiNations: Reflections of Earth, are seen by thousands of park-goers on a nightly basis. However, these dazzling displays are also enjoyed by a privileged few, far removed from the hubbub of the theme park crowds, yet close enough to marvel at the subtleties of each brilliant burst. These are the guests who chose to book a boat for a specialty cruise. This vintage vantage point is available to everyone, provided that the rates don't break the budget and that reservations are made in advance. Of course, there is the other extreme: a peaceful, moonlit cruise on the quiet waterways of the World. This option is also available to guests who book a specialty cruise.

Reservations are accepted up to 24 hours ahead; advance reservations, accepted up to 90 days ahead, are strongly recommended. While specifics may change, the following is a good indication of what was available at press time.

> ## Hot Tip!
> If you plan to enjoy a scenic fireworks cruise, pack a sweater. It can get chilly out there on the open seas—even during summer.

THE GRAND 1: This striking 45-foot Sea Ray yacht escorts up to 14 guests at a time. A private tour of the Seven Seas Lagoon and Bay Lake culminates with a front-row seat for the Magic Kingdom's fireworks, when possible. (The vessel drops anchor in the vicinity of the park entrance, aligning itself as closely with Cinderella Castle as possible.)

The *Grand 1* departs from the Grand Floridian, but stops at the Polynesian, Contemporary, Wilderness Lodge, or Fort Wilderness Lodge on request. It costs about $400 per hour to rent, with the per-boatload fee covering up to 14 guests, plus a driver and a deckhand. Call 407-824-2682 to reserve it.

PONTOON BOATS: More practical than luxurious, Disney's fleet of pontoon boats still deliver a crowd-pleasing cruise experience.

The boats, which accommodate up to 10, take guests on tours of the Seven Seas Lagoon and Bay Lake, near the Magic Kingdom, as well as Crescent Lake, near Epcot's World Showcase. Those in the Magic Kingdom area are treated to VIP viewing of that park's fireworks show, Wishes, while Epcot-area cruisers take in IllumiNations: Reflections of Earth, when available. Larger pontoon boats carry the Wishes soundtrack—a special treat!

Pontoon cruises last about one hour. Magic Kingdom fireworks excursions depart from the Grand Floridian, Polynesian, Contemporary, Wilderness Lodge, and Fort Wilderness marinas. IllumiNations cruises leave from Yacht Club marinas. The cost (which includes a driver) starts at about $200 to $250 per boatload. Call 407-WDW-PLAY (939-7529) for reservations.

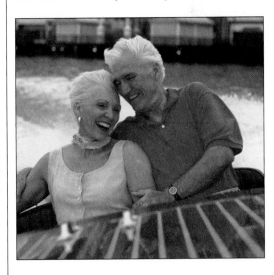

THE BREATHLESS: This elegant, open-air motorboat is a sleek 24-foot reproduction of a 1930s mahogany runabout. Named after the Dick Tracy character, the vessel is equipped with bench seats and fits up to seven guests.

Moored at the Yacht and Beach Club marina, the *Breathless* escorts private parties around Crescent Lake and adjoining waterways by day and night. All cruises depart from a dock at the Yacht and Beach Club, but requests for pickups at the BoardWalk resort marina will be honored.

The one-hour IllumiNations cruise costs about $200. Prices are per boatload (for up to seven passengers) and include a driver. Call 407-WDW-PLAY (939-7529) for reservations.

Behind-the-Scenes Tours

Disney Adult Discoveries programs offer the chance to experience Walt Disney World from the inside out. Most of the guided behind-the-scenes tours are only open to visitors 16 and older (though there are a few exceptions). Guests are required to carry a photo ID when attending backstage programs. Tours and prices (which include tax) are subject to change; for information or to make reservations, call 407-WDW-TOUR (939-8687). **Note:** Tours marked with an asterisk (*) may be included with the Magic Your Way Premium Package, though restrictions may apply.

AROUND THE WORLD AT EPCOT (daily at 8:30 and 9:30 A.M.): An hour-long tour around the World Showcase Lagoon with a twist. Instead of using your feet, you'll take in the sights and sounds from a Segway Human Transporter (a personal transportation device). The minimum age is 16, while the maximum weight is 250 pounds. Minors must get the signature of a parent or guardian. Cost is $80, plus park admission. Tours start at the Guest Relations lobby inside the main entrance. Guests should arrive 15 minutes early.

BACKSTAGE MAGIC (Monday through Friday): This is one of WDW's best programs. Highlighting the 7-hour exploration of the Magic Kingdom, Disney-MGM Studios, and Epcot may be an underground tour of the Magic Kingdom's Utilidors—Disney's tunnel system. Lunch is included, as are a few surprises. Cost is $199. Park admission is not required or included.

BACKSTAGE SAFARI* (Monday, Wednesday, Thursday, Friday): This 3-hour tour takes guests through backstage animal facilities, such as the veterinary hospital and elephant barn at Disney's Animal Kingdom. The cost is $65, plus theme park admission.

DISNEY'S FAMILY MAGIC TOUR* (daily): Families may participate in this 2-hour, scavenger hunt through the Magic Kingdom. The cost is $27 per guest (above age 3). Park admission is not included, but is required.

DIVEQUEST (daily): The highlight of the 2½-hour program is a 40-minute underwater adventure—complete with sharks, turtles, rays, and other fish—in The Seas with Nemo & Friends aquarium. Participants must present proof of current scuba certification. Cost is $140. Guests ages 10 and 14 must dive with a parent or guardian. Gear is provided. Park admission is not required or included.

DOLPHINS IN DEPTH (weekdays at 9:45 A.M.): This 3-hour program teaches guests about dolphin behavior as they interact with the animals and observe researchers and trainers working with them. Cost is $150 and includes a souvenir T-shirt. Park admission is not required or included. Wet suits are provided; wear your own swimsuit.

EPCOT SEAS AQUA TOUR (daily at 12:30 P.M.): A new 2½-hour program that lets guests learn about and interact with ocean life in The Seas with Nemo & Friends pavilion. First, guests watch a video about sea creatures, then they join them in their habitat using a Supplied-Air Snorkel system. Cost is $100 (all profits go to the Disney Wildlife Conservation fund). Gear is included, as are refreshments, a T-shirt, and a group photo of the experience. Guests must wear a bathing suit. Park admission is not required or included.

GARDENS OF THE WORLD* (Tuesday, Thursday): Hosted by a horticulturist, this 3-hour program guides guests through a study of plants, flowers, and trees at Epcot's World Showcase. Cost is $59, plus park admission.

HIDDEN TREASURES OF WORLD SHOWCASE* (Tuesday, Thursday): This 3½-hour tour takes guests to the international pavilions at Epcot. The focus is on international art, architecture, and traditions. Cost is $59, plus park admission.

KEYS TO THE KINGDOM* (daily): A 4½-hour tour that offers an on-site orientation to the history and workings of Walt Disney World's original theme park, the Magic Kingdom. Guests visit an attraction (waiting in the regular attraction line) and take a peek at the Utilidors (the legendary tunnels underneath the park). Cost is $60, plus theme park admission.

THE MAGIC BEHIND OUR STEAM TRAINS* (Monday, Tuesday, Thursday, Saturday):
A 3-hour tour that gives guests an inside look at the Walt Disney World Railroad. In addition to an exploration of Walt Disney's passion for steam trains, guests visit the backstage "roundhouse" where the steam trains are stored, and join the opening crew as they prepare for the daily railroad operation in the Magic Kingdom.

Guests must be at least 10 to take the tour. Cost is $40 per person. Theme park admission is required, but not included.

MICKEY'S MAGICAL MILESTONES*:
(Monday, Wednesday, Friday at 9 A.M.): A 2-hour celebration of the world's most successful mouse includes visits to Magic Kingdom attractions and locations that retrace his storied career. Tours cost $25 per person (plus park admission) and start at the Guided Tour Garden next to City Hall on Main Street, U.S.A. Guests should arrive 15 minutes early and wear their most comfortable walking shoes (expect to cover quite a bit of territory). The tour is recommended for guests ages 10 and up.

THE UNDISCOVERED FUTURE WORLD*
(Monday, Wednesday, Friday at 9 A.M.): Walt Disney dreamed about making the world a better place. In this 4-hour tour, guests are taken back to the creation of Epcot and learn about Walt's lofty ambitions and his legacy.

Guests walk to all Future World pavilions and learn how each area celebrates humanity's accomplishments and challenges. The goal is to share the vision behind the park.

Cost is $49 per person. Guests must be at least 16 years old to attend this walking program. Theme park admission is required, but not included.

WILD BY DESIGN* (Thursday, Friday at 8:30 A.M.):
A 3-hour experience that invites guests to learn how art, architecture, historical artifacts, and storytelling were combined to create Disney's Animal Kingdom. The tour takes place in the park, not behind the scenes. As guests explore various lands, a guide offers insight into the complexities of caring for wild

animals and their habitats.

A light continental breakfast is served at the halfway point of the tour. Cost is $58 per person. Theme park admission is required, but not included. Guests must be at least 14 years old to attend the program. Given prior notice, this outdoor walking tour can accommodate guests with special needs.

YULETIDE FANTASY (seasonal):
A festive 3½-hour experience, this program showcases the way Disney weaves stories and folklore into decorations found in the theme parks and resorts. It offers a unique perspective on how colors, textures, architecture, and illusions help WDW deck the halls for the holidays.

Cost is $69 per person. Theme park admission is not included or required. Guests must be at least 16 years old to participate. All guests must present a photo ID.

It's a Celebration

What happens when a little bit of Disney magic spills over to the real world? A town called Celebration, Florida. Founded in 1996 by a subsidiary of the Walt Disney Company, the town is surrounded by 4,700 acres of protected greenland.

The homes, with their front porches and picket fences, hark back to a much simpler time in American history. Built along a scenic lakeside promenade, downtown Celebration is a pleasant place to relax outdoors.

With the addition of the Celebration Hotel, which opened in fall 1999, guests can do more than just visit this quaint little town—they can move in! (If only temporarily.)

The 115-room, four-diamond hotel is situated lakeside in downtown Celebration. Guest accommodations include an environmental sound and music system, phone with data-port, hair dryer, iron with board, and a safe. There is ample meeting space in addition to a pool, whirlpool, fitness center, lobby bar, and breakfast buffet.

Note that Plantation Room is the only eatery here—but guests need only cross the street to find other spots in which to dine.

Architect Graham Gund based the design of the hotel on a 1920s Florida wood-frame look. With its big roofs, low eaves and dormers, and wraparound porches, the hotel reinforces the small-town theme of Celebration.

Guests can shop, stroll, skate, or simply enjoy a picnic by the lake. There are several village parks, miles of nature trails, and the Celebration Golf Club's 18-hole public golf course (rates range from $49 to $129). Near the par-72 course is a 3-hole youth course where Tiger Woods wannabes can practice their golf swings.

The community's retail and business district invites visitors to enjoy a variety of dining, shopping, and entertainment spots, including a bookstore, antiques shop, ice cream parlor, diner, and movie theater.

Located southeast of the intersection of U.S. 192 and I-4 near Kissimmee, Celebration is about a ten-minute drive from Walt Disney World. For information, call 407-566-2200, or write: Celebration Information; 610 Sycamore Street, Suite 310; Celebration, FL 34747. Or visit *www.celebrationfl.com* to see what's happening during your visit.

Sports

Many first-time visitors don't realize that Disney World provides a plethora of sporting opportunities. Within WDW's 27,000-plus acres there are more tennis courts than at most tennis resorts, and more holes of championship-caliber golf than at most golf centers, plus so many other diversions—from fishing and biking to boating, swimming, parasailing, and horseback riding—that the quantity and variety are matched by few other vacation destinations.

So while the family golfers are pursuing a perfect swing on one of five first-rate, 18-hole courses, tennis buffs can be wearing themselves out on the courts, sailors can be sailing, water-skiers can be skimming back and forth across powerboat wakes, and anglers can be casting away in hopes of hooking a big bass. Those who prefer to spectate rather than participate can visit a virtual sports mecca at Disney's Wide World of Sports complex, an enormous state-of-the-art facility that hosts a staggering array of sporting events, both amateur and professional. And those who prefer the sedate can treat themselves to a soothing spa treatment.

Instruction, as well as guides, drivers, and assorted supervisors, makes every sport as much fun for beginners as for hard-core aficionados. Moreover, the ready accessibility of WDW sporting activities—via an excellent system of public transportation (see *Transportation & Accommodations*)—means that no family member need curtail playtime to chauffeur others around.

Note: *All prices are subject to change.*

A Matter of Courses

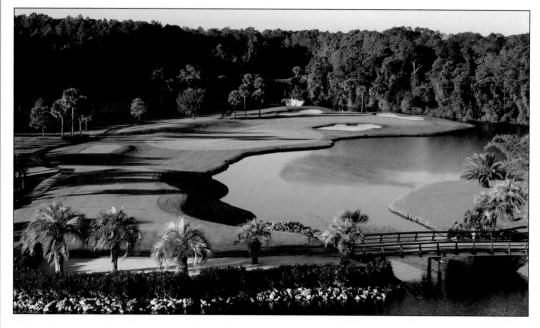

Most people don't immediately think of Walt Disney World when they contemplate a golf vacation. Yet there are six superb courses here: the Magnolia, the Palm, and the nine-hole Oak Trail are situated across from the Polynesian resort and extend nearly to the borders of the Magic Kingdom. A short drive away is the Lake Buena Vista course, whose fairways are framed by Saratoga Springs Resort and Spa and Old Key West resort. Osprey Ridge and Eagle Pines play from the Eagle Pines and Osprey Ridge Golf Club.

While the original Joe Lee–designed courses (the Palm, Magnolia, and Lake Buena Vista) won't set anyone's knees to knocking in terror from the regular tees, all three are demanding enough to have merited the status of a stop on the PGA Tour tournament trail.

Tom Fazio designed Osprey Ridge to offer a reasonable challenge for beginners as well as more advanced players. Eagle Pines, designed by Pete Dye, is a low-profile layout built level with, or lower than, the surrounding land.

Depending on the tee from which a golfer plays, Disney courses will prove challenging and/or fun, and all are constructed to be especially forgiving for the mid-handicap player.

PALM & MAGNOLIA: The wide-open, tree-dotted Magnolia measures 5,232 yards from the front tees, 6,642 from the middle, and a staggering 7,516 from the back. The Palm is tighter, with more wooded fairways and nine water hazards; it measures 5,311 yards from the front, 6,461 from the middle, and 7,010 from the back. Both courses have received a four-star ("outstanding") rating from *Golf Digest* magazine. The Magnolia and Palm share two driving ranges and putting greens.

Oak Trail: This nine-hole, 2,913-yard layout, a walking course tucked into a corner within the Magnolia, was designed for beginners and junior golfers, but it has some tough holes, including two par 5s.

OSPREY RIDGE & EAGLE PINES: These two par-72 courses play from the Eagle Pines and Osprey Ridge Golf Club. The Tom Fazio–designed Osprey Ridge measures 5,402 yards from the front tees, 6,680 from the middle, and 7,101 from the back. It takes guests into remote areas as it winds through wooded landscape near Fort Wilderness. Dramatic contouring puts some tees 20 to 25 feet above the basic grade. In contrast, the Pete Dye–designed Eagle Pines is a low-profile layout. It plays 4,838 yards from the front tees, 6,309 from the middle, and 6,772 from the pro tees. Many fairways are bordered by scrub and pine needles; water comes into play as well. Osprey Ridge and Eagle Pines share a driving range and a putting green.

LAKE BUENA VISTA COURSE: This Joe Lee design measures 5,194 yards from the front tees, 6,264 from the middle, and 6,749 from the rearmost markers. Among the shortest of the 18-hole, par-72 courses, it has a fair amount of water, and its tree-lined fairways are Disney's narrowest. The course is well suited for beginners but challenges experienced players. A driving range and putting green are available.

Essentials

WHEN TO GO: January through April is peak golfing season. To beat the crowds, play on a Monday or Tuesday, tee off in the late afternoon, and take advantage of low summer rates. From May through late September, guests pay about $64 at Osprey Ridge and Eagle Pines, and about $64 at Lake Buena Vista, Palm, and Magnolia after 10 A.M. After 3 P.M., the price drops significantly at Osprey Ridge, Eagle Pines, Palm, and Magnolia. Annual golf memberships (available to Florida residents only, for about $53) net discounts during this period, too.

RESERVATIONS: Call 407-WDW-GOLF (939-4653) or visit *www.disneyworldgolf.com* to confirm rates and to secure tee-off times. From January through April, morning and early afternoon tee times should be reserved well in advance; starting times after 3 P.M. are often available at the last minute. Those buying a Magic Your Way Premium or Platinum package may reserve tee times up to 120 days prior to their check-in date. Guests with confirmed reservations at a WDW resort or at a resort on Hotel Plaza Boulevard may reserve 90 days ahead and save up to $10 per round. Others may book tee times 60 days ahead. Reservations must be made with a major credit card. Cancellations must be made at least 48 hours ahead to avoid paying in full.

FEES: At the 18-hole courses, greens fees (including a required cart) vary with the course and season. Rates range from about $60 to $169 for guests at WDW resorts and the resorts on Hotel Plaza Boulevard, and from about $50 to $190 for day visitors. Twilight rates, available throughout the year, begin in midafternoon and run about $53 to $80. Cost

for adults to play Oak Trail is $38 for 9 holes; juniors (17 and under) pay $20 for 9 holes. Afternoon rates, known as "twilight rates," may yield steep discounts. Prices include tax and are likely to rise in 2007.

INSTRUCTION: At the Walt Disney World Golf Studio at the Palm and Magnolia, private 45-minute lessons cost $75 for adults, $50 for juniors (up to age 17). Lessons are customized to all levels of experience. Video analysis may be used. More experienced golfers may consider booking back-to-back lessons for a 90-minute playing session. Reservations are necessary and may be made up to 120 days in advance; call 407-WDW-GOLF (939-4653).

DRESS: Proper golf attire is required. Shirts must have collars and any shorts must be Bermuda length.

EQUIPMENT RENTAL: Equipment can be rented at all courses; club rentals range from about $48 to $59 for men and $48 for women, depending on the season. Photo ID and major credit card (for the $500 refundable deposit) are required for club rentals. Range balls (about $6 per basket) are among the items available.

Tournaments

The Golf Classic at the Walt Disney World resort is one of the biggest spectator events on Disney's sports calendar. It features 144 of the PGA Tour's top players and usually takes place in October. Guests who plan to golf during their WDW vacation are advised not to visit during tournament week. (You may, however, play with the pros if you are willing to pay for it.)

For additional information about the PGA Tour's Classic and other special Walt Disney World golf events, call 407-WDW-GOLF (939-4653). Private tournaments may be arranged by calling 407-938-3870. Dates are subject to change.

Tennis, Everyone

No one comes to Walt Disney World strictly for a tennis vacation; it just doesn't exude the country-club ambience of a tennis resort, where everyone is totally immersed in the game. But the facilities and instruction programs here are extensive enough that such holidays are possible. Certainly, playing a couple of sets of tennis on one of the World's resort courts is a good way to unwind after a morning in a park.

The Grand Floridian Resort and Spa is "center court" for WDW tennis. It boasts a pair of soft-surface clay courts. Professional programs and clinics are available, as are private or group lessons, seasonal camps, and organized convention-style tournaments for groups of at least 10 players. Experienced players may take part in the "Play the Professional" program. All WDW tennis activities are overseen by M.D. Tennis, Inc.

All other Walt Disney World tennis is played on hard courts. Fort Wilderness, Yacht and Beach Club, Saratoga Springs, and BoardWalk have two; Old Key West has three; and the Swan and Dolphin share a four-court facility. With the exception of the Grand Floridian courts (which are available to guests of that resort only), tennis courts may be used by guests staying at any Disney-owned-and-operated resort. The courts at Fort Wilderness may be used by day guests. There is a fee to play at the Grand Floridian. All other courts are free. For information or to make reservations, call 407-WDW-PLAY (939-7529).

Essentials

WHEN TO GO: Courts are often open from 8 A.M. to 7 P.M. daily (hours are seasonal; call ahead for exact times); courts at the Swan and Dolphin are open 24 hours; lighted courts are available at each of them. In February, March, April, June, and July the courts may endure heavy use, but there is often a lull between noon and 3 P.M., and again from dinnertime

until closing time. January, October, and November are prime months for tennis.

Equipment rental is limited at Walt Disney World. Guests should bring their own tennis racquets and balls.

All courts are available on a first-come, first-served basis. During very busy periods, the length of time a single group of players can occupy a court is restricted to two hours on any morning, afternoon, and evening.

DRESS: Tennis whites are appropriate, but not required, for play on Disney's courts. Tennis shoes are a must.

B.Y.O.R.

Though it may be possible to rent or borrow a tennis racquet at one of Disney's resort courts, we recommend bringing your own equipment. While you're at it, pack a can or two of tennis balls as well. (Even if you can buy these on property, they're likely to be cheaper if purchased in the real world.)

Waters of the World

Boating

Walt Disney World is the home of the country's largest fleet of pleasure boats. Cruising on Bay Lake and the Seven Seas Lagoon can be excellent sport, and a variety of boats are available for rent at WDW resort marinas. Bay Lake excursions originate from the Contemporary, on the lake's western shore; Wilderness Lodge, on the south shore; and Fort Wilderness, which occupies the lake's southeastern shore. The Polynesian and Grand Floridian resorts send boaters out from their marinas on the southern shore of Seven Seas Lagoon. The Caribbean Beach resort leases watercraft for use on its own 45-acre Barefoot Bay. The Yacht and Beach Club, BoardWalk, Swan, and Dolphin share a boating haven in 25-acre Crescent Lake. And marinas at Port Orleans, Old Key West, and the Downtown Disney Marketplace set guests up to cruise the waterways adjoining the 35-acre Lake Buena Vista. Guests at Coronado Springs may rent watercraft for use on the 15-acre Lago Dorado.

To rent, day visitors and resort guests alike must show a resort ID, a driver's license, or a valid passport. Rental of certain craft may carry other requirements (described below). Note that no privately owned boats are permitted on any Walt Disney World waters. Also, all prices and times are subject to change.

BOSTON WHALER MONTAUK BOATS: These 17-foot, motorized boats are a good choice for relaxing cruises. They accommodate up to six adults, and may be rented for about $32 per half hour at the Downtown Disney Marketplace, Polynesian, Contemporary, Grand Floridian, Wilderness Lodge, Coronado Springs, Yacht and Beach Club, Old Key West, Port Orleans, Caribbean Beach, and Fort Wilderness marinas.

CANOEING: A long paddle down the smooth, wooded Fort Wilderness canals is such a tranquil way to pass a misty morning that it's hard to remember that the bustle of the Magic Kingdom is just a short launch ride away. Canoes are available for rent at the Bike Barn at Fort Wilderness (about $7 per half hour, $11 per hour). Most excursions last one to three hours; those with fishing gear often last longer. Canoes may also be rented at the Caribbean Beach and Port Orleans Riverside marinas. (Note that fishing from canoes is not allowed.) Ocean Kayaks (open-top kayaks) may be rented at La Marina at Coronado Springs and at the marina at Port Orleans Riverside (about $7 per half hour, $11 per hour).

MOTORBOATS: Particularly when the weather is warm, there are always dozens of small boats zipping back and forth across Bay Lake, Seven Seas Lagoon, Lake Buena Vista, Crescent Lake, and Barefoot Bay. These are called Sea Raycer boats, and they're just as much fun as they look. The boats, which are remarkably fast, are so small that a rider feels every bit of speed, and they whiz around quickly enough so that a lot of watery terrain can be covered in a half-hour-rental period (for about $23).

Sea Raycer boats can be rented at the Grand Floridian, Polynesian, Wilderness Lodge, Contemporary, Yacht and Beach Club, Fort Wilderness, Caribbean Beach, Coronado Springs, Port Orleans Riverside, Old Key West, and Downtown Disney Marketplace marinas. When the weather is warm, lines form at about 11 A.M. and stay fairly constant until about 4 P.M. Guests must be at least 12 years old and 5 feet tall to rent Sea Raycer boats. Children under the minimum age and height may ride as passengers but they are not allowed to drive the boat. At Magic Kingdom resort marinas, at least one person in a boat must have a valid driver's license.

PARASAILING: Excursions are offered at the Contemporary resort marina. Each seven- to ten-minute flight costs about $90 for one person, $140 for two to ride tandem. Reservations are necessary and may be made up to 90 days ahead; call 407-939-0754.

PEDAL BOATS: These craft rent for about $7 per half hour or $11 per hour at the Caribbean Beach, Port Orleans, Coronado Springs, Old Key West, and Swan and Dolphin marinas. Watercraft are available to all guests at all locations. Hydro Bikes (boats resembling bicycles affixed to pontoons) may be rented at the Swan and Dolphin when it isn't too windy; single-bike units cost about $8 per half hour at each location; doubles, about $16 per half hour at the Swan and Dolphin.

PONTOON BOATS: Motorized, canopied platforms on pontoons are perfect for families, inexperienced sailors, and visitors more interested in serenity than in thrills. Available at most resort marinas, the 21-foot craft hold up to ten adults and cost about $42 per half hour. Guests must be at least 18 years old to rent a pontoon boat.

SAILBOATS: The running room and usually reliable winds of Bay Lake and Seven Seas Lagoon make for good sailing, and the Grand Floridian, Polynesian, and Wilderness Lodge marinas rent a variety of craft so that guests might get a little wind in their sails on the 600-acre expanse. Various types of sailboats are available; models accommodate two to six people and rent for about $25 to $33 per hour. Experience is required for rental of catamarans, available at the Grand Floridian.

WATERSKIING, WAKEBOARDING, AND TUBING: Ski boats with Sammy Duvall instructors and equipment ($140 an hour, for

one to five guests) are available at the Contemporary resort marina. Watercraft may be reserved here, too. Reservations must be made at least 24 hours in advance and may be made up to 90 days ahead; call 407-939-0754.

Fishing

The 70,000 bass with which Bay Lake was stocked in the mid-1960s have grown and multiplied as a result of WDW's restrictive fishing policy. (It's strictly catch-and-release.) No angling is permitted on Bay Lake or the Seven Seas Lagoon, except on the guided fishing expeditions. Largemouth bass weighing two to eight pounds are the most common catch.

Fishing excursions are presented by BASS, the world's largest fishing organization. Guests who participate in a WDW excursion receive a one-year BASS membership, which includes 11 issues of *Bassmaster Magazine*, a membership pack with a membership card, decal, member handbook, eligibility to compete in national events, discounts, and other benefits.

Excursions depart from the marinas daily (call 407-939-2277 for exact times and prices); five people can be accommodated on a trip. The trip lasts two hours and includes guide, gear, and refreshments (coffee and soft drinks). Guides will pick up guests at the Contemporary, Polynesian, Grand Floridian, Fort Wilderness, and Wilderness Lodge marinas.

Other trips depart from Downtown Disney Marketplace marina at 7 A.M., 10 A.M., and 1:30 P.M. for fishing on Lake Buena Vista and adjoining waterways. Guides will also pick up guests at Old Key West, Saratoga Springs, and Port Orleans Riverside and French Quarter. Two-hour excursions accommodate up to five anglers and include guide, gear, and refreshments. Kids under 16 must be accompanied by an adult.

Anglers might also consider two-hour tours that depart from the Yacht and Beach Club at 7 A.M., 10 A.M., and 1:30 P.M. All trips accommodate up to five people. Two-hour trips depart the BoardWalk dock at 7 A.M., 10 A.M., and 1:30 P.M. daily. A guide, gear, and refreshments are included.

Coronado Springs and Caribbean Beach resorts offer 2-hour excursions on Nitro bass boats that accommodate one or two guests. They depart from the resort marinas at 7 A.M., 10 A.M., and 1:30 P.M. daily. The $200 to $230 price includes equipment and a guide.

Special fishing excursions for kids ages 6 through 12 depart Monday through Friday from BoardWalk resort, and on weekends from the Magic Kingdom resorts—the Contemporary, Grand Floridian, Polynesian, Fort Wilderness, and Wilderness Lodge. Refreshments are provided, as is bait.

Reservations for all fishing excursions must be made at least 24 hours in advance and may be made up to 90 days ahead; call 407-WDW-BASS (939-2277).

Fishing on your own—again, strictly catch-and-release—is permitted in the canals at Fort Wilderness and the stocked fishing hole at Port Orleans Riverside. Fort Wilderness guests may toss in lines from any campground canal shore. Licenses are not required. Rods and reels, and cane poles are available for rent at the Fort Wilderness Bike Barn. Bait (in the form of worms) may be purchased. Poles may also be rented at Port Orleans Riverside and Coronado Springs.

Swimming

Between Bay Lake and Seven Seas Lagoon, Walt Disney World resort guests have five miles of powdery white-sand beach at their disposal. Although the beaches are strictly for sunbathing and sandcastle construction, swimmers may splash in one of the many pools that come in every shape and size imaginable. Typhoon Lagoon and Blizzard Beach (see *Everything Else in the World*) only add to the fun.

BEACHES: When Walt Disney World was under construction during the mid-1960s, Bay Lake had an 8-foot layer of muck on its bottom. The lake was drained and cleaned, and below the muck, engineers unearthed the pure, white sand that now edges Walt Disney World resort shorefronts, most notably at the Contemporary, Grand Floridian, Caribbean Beach, and Fort Wilderness. These four sections of beach, plus the ones at the Polynesian, Wilderness Lodge, Yacht and Beach Club, Coronado Springs, and Swan and Dolphin, make up WDW's sandy areas. They aren't walk-forever strands, but they are long enough that most people don't bother to go to the end. Note that all Disney resort beaches are open only to those guests staying at the respective hotels. Swimming is not permitted.

POOLS: Walt Disney World resorts have at least one pool apiece. With the exception of the sister resorts (Yacht and Beach Club; Port Orleans French Quarter and Riverside;

All-Star Movies, All-Star Music, and All-Star Sports; and Swan and Dolphin), which share some of their recreational facilities, WDW hotel pools are open only to guests staying at those resorts. This policy was initiated to prevent overcrowding. Note that the pools are heated in winter.

Featuring one pool apiece are the Animal Kingdom Lodge and Port Orleans French Quarter. The Grand Floridian, Contemporary, Polynesian, Fort Wilderness, Wilderness Lodge, and the All-Stars have two pools each. BoardWalk and Pop Century feature three pools, Coronado Springs and Old Key West have four swimming holes each, Port Orleans Riverside has six, and Caribbean Beach has seven. The Yacht and Beach Club resorts have between them three unguarded pools plus a small water park, called Stormalong Bay, that features slides, jets, and a sand-bottomed wading area. Saratoga Springs resort has three pools. The Swan and Dolphin share a lovely, themed grotto pool with a slide, one huge rectangular pool, and a third smaller pool. For descriptions of the themed pools at Walt Disney World resorts, consult the *Transportation & Accommodations* chapter.

There are no diving boards; swimmers in search of a big splash should head for Blizzard Beach or Typhoon Lagoon. Lifeguards are on duty during most daylight hours at the resort's main pools. In addition, each of the resorts on Hotel Plaza Boulevard has its own pool.

Disney's Wide World of Sports Complex

Variety is the name of the game at Disney's Wide World of Sports complex. The multi-million-dollar complex invites athletes and spectators alike to dive into more than 30 types of sporting experiences. It's a grand slam for die-hard sports fans.

The 220-acre facility hosts amateur and professional events in everything from archery to wrestling. The home of many Amateur Athletic Union (AAU) championship events is also the spring training site for Major League Baseball's Atlanta Braves. The 2003 Super Bowl champion Tampa Bay Buccaneers have held training camp here, too.

Designed as a modern vision of old-time Floridian building styles, the architecture harks back to the days when sports facilities were extensions of their neighborhoods; to that end there is even a town commons.

The complex includes a baseball stadium; a field house that accommodates basketball, wrestling, and volleyball; a track-and-field complex; tennis courts; and multipurpose fields fit for football, soccer, and more. Given the possibilities, sports-loving spectators have a world of choices on their hands.

A general-admission ticket costs about $11 for adults and $8 for kids ages 3 through 9. Tickets may be purchased at the front gate and allow guests to watch all "nonpremium"

events. Note that guests are only admitted on days when events are scheduled. (Though guests may also patronize All Star Cafe.)

Tickets to premium events, such as Atlanta Braves spring training games (beginning in late February or early March), may be purchased through TicketMaster (407-839-3900; or *www.ticketmaster.com*) and include general admission to the complex.

Premium tickets may also be purchased at the Wide World of Sports complex box office on the day of an event, depending on availability. Prices vary, depending on the event. Note that, in addition to traditional seats, the baseball stadium has lots of lawn seating.

Essentials

HOW TO GET THERE: WDW resort guests can take a bus to the Disney-MGM Studios and transfer to a bus to the Sports Complex. Allow at least an hour for the bus commute (more if you're attending a premium event). Transportation specifics are subject to change. If you are driving, take exit 65 off I-4 to Victory Way. The complex is between U.S. 192 and Osceola Parkway. Parking is free.

WHERE TO EAT: The big-ticket eatery here is All Star Cafe. TVs and a deejay keep you posted with current scores from around the sports world.

There are more than 30 concessions for those seeking a somewhat lighter bite. They offer hot dogs, popcorn, soft drinks, and beer (not to mention peanuts and Cracker Jack), as well as a few more substantial, yet just as portable, snacks.

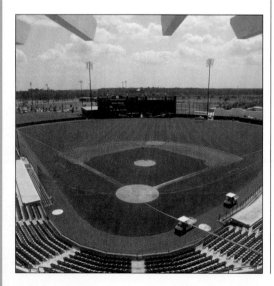

Touch Base

Get the scoop on all the action at Disney's Wide World of Sports by calling 407-WDW-GAME (939-4263) or visiting the website: *www.disneyworldsports.com*.

More Sporting Fun

BIKING: Pedaling along the rustic pathways and lightly trafficked roads at Fort Wilderness can be a pleasant way to spend a couple of hours. Both areas are spread out, so bicycles are a practical way to get around. Bikes are available for rent at Old Key West, Wilderness Lodge, Port Orleans, Caribbean Beach, BoardWalk, Yacht and Beach Club, Saratoga Springs, and Coronado Springs. The cost is about $8 an hour or $22 per day. Bikes with training wheels or baby seats are available. Helmets are mandatory and may be borrowed for free.

JOGGING: Except from late fall to early spring, the weather is usually much too steamy in Central Florida for jogging. If you run very early in the morning in warm seasons, the heat is somewhat less daunting. The 1.4-mile promenade around the lake at the Caribbean Beach resort is ideal for jogging, as is the three-quarter-mile promenade that surrounds Crescent Lake, a waterway that's bordered by the Swan and Dolphin, Yacht and Beach Club, and BoardWalk resorts, and the nearly mile-long path circling Coronado Springs' Lago Dorado. Fort Wilderness and the Wilderness Lodge share a three-quarter-mile path with exercise stations. Old Key West also has scenic routes. Courses are all about one mile in length.

MINIATURE GOLF: The Fantasia Gardens Miniature Golf complex, located near the Swan, Dolphin, and BoardWalk resorts, offers players two 18-hole courses themed to the Disney film *Fantasia*. The Fantasia Fairways course offers a difficult layout sure to tantalize serious golfers. It features traditional golf obstacles, such as sand traps, water hazards, doglegs, and roughs. Don't be fooled by the small size of the course—the challenges are big. (At press time, the record for the par-61 course was 50.)

Fantasia Gardens, on the other hand, is all in fun, with clever things (a dancing hippo, xylophone stairs, brooms dumping buckets of water) at every hole. The degree of difficulty varies from hole to hole, but overall, this is an easy course to conquer. There are several challenges out there, however. Hole 15, for example, is one of the trickier ones. Here golfers aim through four minigeysers that randomly squirt water into the air.

Disney's Winter Summerland miniature golf course is a mere stone's throw from the Blizzard Beach water park. Designed as a vacation retreat for Santa and his elves, the two 18-hole courses boast a delightfully festive atmosphere, complete with Christmas carol sound tracks. The sandy-surface course is just a bit more of a challenge than its snowy-surface counterpart.

A round on any course costs about $10 for adults, $8 for kids ages 3 through 9. The second round is half price. Typical playing time is about an hour. Hours are generally 10 A.M. to 11 P.M., but vary seasonally. For additional information, call 407-WDW-PLAY (939-7529).

SPAS AND HEALTH CLUBS: While some of the fitness centers within WDW hotels are reserved for guests staying at the resort that houses them, several have open-door policies and are accessible to all WDW resort guests. Health clubs include the Contemporary Health Club, Sturdy Branches at Wilderness Lodge, Zahanati at Animal Kingdom Lodge, La Vida at Coronado Springs, The Spa at Saratoga Springs, Muscles & Bustles at

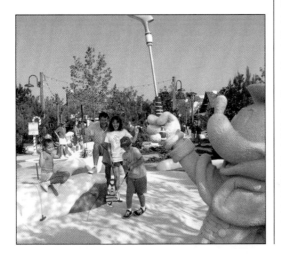

BoardWalk, the Health Club at the Grand Floridian, Resort Fitness Center at Old Key West, Ship Shape at the Yacht and Beach Club, and the fitness center at the Swan. Registered guests may use their respective resort's facility for free. Guests not registered in a resort with a health club can still use the facilities for a $12 fee. The Contemporary Health Cub has strength and cardio equipment, cardiovascular machines, and massage. Others have more extensive equipment. Ship Shape has a whirlpool and steam room. Muscles & Bustles has a steam room, and massage services. La Vida has a tanning bed and massage.

The spas are located at the Grand Floridian Spa & Health Club, the Saratoga Springs Resort & Spa, the Dolphin resort, and the Buena Vista Palace. The Spa at Saratoga Springs has a modern facility with the best lineup of exercise machines on Disney property. There are special spa packages available at each of these resorts.

STOCK CAR RACING: The Richard Petty Driving Experience (RPDE) takes motorsports fans out of the grandstands and into a scene that most can only dream about: behind the wheel of a stock car. The RPDE, located at the Walt Disney World Speedway, near the Magic Kingdom guest parking lot, is a training ground for racer wannabes. It offers two different levels of actual driving experience: "Rookie Experience" and "Experience of a Lifetime."

For the less "driven" daredevils, there is the "Riding Experience," which sends guests zooming around the track at blazing speeds while still maintaining their passenger status. No reservations are required for the Riding Experience. Rides begin at 9 A.M. daily. The cost is about $100, plus tax.

The Rookie Experience includes instruction and eight high-speed (up to 145 miles per hour) laps around the one-mile oval track, as well as a warm-up and a cool-down lap. The three-hour program costs about $380, plus tax. Reservations are required.

The King's Experience is a total of 18 laps behind the wheel. Cost is about $750, plus tax. Reservations required.

The Experience of a Lifetime is a 30-lap program completed over three sessions. Participants work on building speed and establishing a comfortable driving line. The cost is about $1,300, plus tax. Reservations are a must.

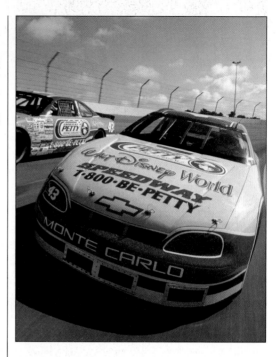

The RPDE operates daily year-round, with the exception of dates on which actual races are held at the WDW Speedway. Shuttle transportation is provided from the Transportation and Ticket Center (TTC). Call 800-237-3889 for information or to make reservations. To drive, guests must have a valid license and the ability to drive a stick shift. Prices are subject to change.

TRAIL RIDES: Guided horseback rides into pine woods and scrubby palmetto country set off from the front of Fort Wilderness four times daily. This trip is not meant for seasoned gallopers—you can't wander off on your own. The horses have been culled for gentleness, so trips are especially suitable for novices. Cost is about $42 per person for a 45-minute tour. Kids under 9 are not allowed to ride, and there's a weight limit of 250 pounds. (Younger kids can saddle up on ponies at the Fort Wilderness Pony Farm.) Reservations are necessary, and can be made up to 30 days ahead by calling 407-WDW-PLAY (939-7529).

VOLLEYBALL & BASKETBALL: Except for the volleyball court at Typhoon Lagoon, courts are reserved for WDW resort guests. The Grand Floridian, Yacht and Beach Club, Fort Wilderness, Swan and Dolphin, Coronado Springs, and Old Key West have volleyball courts. Contemporary, Fort Wilderness, and Old Key West have basketball hoops.

SPORTS

Good Meals, Great Times

Although fast food is in great supply, it is hardly the entire Walt Disney World dining story. Epcot adds international flavors to the WDW menu. Tempting options at the other theme parks, BoardWalk, and Downtown Disney—not to mention new dining frontiers in the ever-growing brood of WDW resorts—make deciding where to eat a mouthwatering dilemma. Disney's ongoing effort to expand its culinary horizons has certainly been successful, producing prominent palate-pleasers such as California Grill and Artist Point, plus family favorites like Chef Mickey's and Cinderella's Royal Table.

Because there's such a large number and variety of eateries around the World, this chapter presents dining information in two formats. First, we've included an area-by-area rundown—a comprehensive section whose descriptions of food purveyors, including sample menu options, will prove most helpful when you get hungry in a particular part of the World. Second, we've compiled a collection of what we consider to be the best restaurants in a particular category. To select these standouts, we looked at the menu, theme, and overall enjoyability of each restaurant. And, of course, we sampled the food.

Finally, in the chapter's last section, we offer a guide to the varied lounges of the World, along with a briefing on Disney's reservations system and dinner show options—and assurance that great times are destined to follow.

The lion's share of eateries here in Walt Disney World's first theme park are fast-food spots. These establishments' colorful facades and costumed servers are natural extensions of the fantasy surrounding the park's seven distinct "lands." The healthy variety of food available on the fly is a testament to Magic Kingdom visitors' typical preference for a quick bite with no need for firm plans. For those who prefer an all-out meal, the park's handful of table-service restaurants offer fine mealtime escapes.

First Things First

The letters at the end of each entry refer to the meals served there: breakfast (B), lunch (L), dinner (D), or snacks (S).
• When you see a not-so-hidden Mickey (🐭) at the end of an entry, it means that eatery was a Disney Dining Plan* participant at press time (see page 19 for details).
• Eateries in this chapter have been designated inexpensive (under $15), moderate ($15 to $29), expensive ($30 to $50), and very expensive ($51 and up). Prices are based on an adult-sized meal consisting of a beverage, entrée, and either one appetizer, side order, or dessert (not including tax and tip). These classifications are reflected by dollar symbols at the end of each entry (all symbols are defined by the key at the bottom of each page). Note that breakfast and lunch generally cost less.
• All Walt Disney World restaurants and fast-food spots (except some with outside seating or at the Swan and Dolphin resorts) are nonsmoking only. Some restaurants at BoardWalk and Downtown Disney have set aside special sections for smokers.
• Reservations for most table-service restaurants (and all dinner shows) should be made in advance by calling 407-WDW-DINE (939-3463).
    We recommend calling 407-WDW-DINE to confirm all WDW restaurant information.
*Disney Dining Plan locations are subject to change without notice.

Adventureland
Fast Food & Snacks

ALOHA ISLE: This snack stand located near the Swiss Family Treehouse sells refreshing pineapple spears and juice, along with other tropical offerings, including pineapple floats and the especially popular frozen Dole Whip pineapple soft serve. It's a Magic Kingdom classic. **S** S

EL PIRATA Y EL PERICO: The Spanish name of this snack stand, located across from the Pirates of the Caribbean attraction, translates to "The Pirate and the Parrot." The offerings here include several traditional Mexican items, such as tacos, taco salads, and nachos, as well beef empanadas (pastry filled with beef and vegetables). Note that this spot operates on a seasonal basis. **L S** S-$$ 🐭

PHOTO BY JILL SAFRO

SUNSHINE TREE TERRACE: Offerings at this snack spot located near The Enchanted Tiki Room—Under New Management are some of the most refreshing in the Magic Kingdom: orange, raspberry, and lemon slushes, and a citrus swirl—ice cream swirled with juicy slush. Cappuccino, espresso, and soft drinks are also available. **S** S

Fantasyland
Table Service

CINDERELLA'S ROYAL TABLE: Newsflash: Cinderella is now in the house for breakfast *and* lunch! Known as the Once Upon A Time breakfast and A Fairy Tale lunch, both meals include visits by the ever-popular Cinderella and her princess friends. Come supper time, guests are entertained by Fairy Godmother during the Dreams Come True dinner.

Hostesses at this festive establishment wear Renaissance-inspired garb and address guests as "my lady" or "my lord." The hall itself is high-ceilinged and as majestic as the old mead hall it is designed to represent. Its second-story setting offers a pleasantly peaceful view of Fantasyland. Decor tends to royal blues and purples, with tapestry-backed chairs. (Cinderella's royal throne is in the lobby of the restaurant. Feel free to try it out—it makes for a nice photo op.)

At lunch and dinner guests of the princess dine on menu items such as herb-crusted pork, prime rib, and seared salmon. The all-inclusive cost for breakfast is about $32 for adults and $22 for kids ages 3 through 9; lunch is about $34 for adults, $23 for kids 3 through 9; dinner is about $40 for adults, $25 for kids ages 3 through 9. The price includes a photo imaging package. Reservations are necessary. *A 180-day advance booking is required for all meals*, along with payment *in full*. Cancellations must be made at least 24 hours in advance to receive a refund. This is an extremely difficult table to reserve—don't get little ones' hopes up until you actually book it. **B L D** $$$ ❤

Fast Food & Snacks

ENCHANTED GROVE: A small stand that's the perfect spot to cool off with a lemonade, lemonade slush, or strawberry slush/soft-serve vanilla ice cream swirl. **S** $

MRS. POTTS' CUPBOARD: Ice cream gets top billing at this window. There are soft-serve cones; hot fudge, strawberry shortcake, and brownie sundaes; and shakes and floats. **S** $

PINOCCHIO VILLAGE HAUS: Located near It's a Small World (some tables offer a peek at the attraction via sizable picture windows), this is another one of those Magic Kingdom restaurants that seem a lot smaller from the outside than they really are, thanks to a labyrinthine arrangement of a half dozen rooms decorated with antique cuckoo clocks, oak peasant chairs, and murals depicting characters from Pinocchio's story—Figaro the Cat, Cleo the Goldfish, Monstro the Whale, and Geppetto, the puppet's creator. The menu offers pizza, Italian sandwiches, soups, and salads. **L D S** $–$$ ❤

SCUTTLE'S LANDING: Soft drinks and frozen carbonated beverages are the big draw at this snack spot located near the Dumbo the Flying Elephant attraction. **S** $

Frontierland
Fast Food & Snacks

PECOS BILL CAFE: Sooner or later, almost every guest passing from Fantasyland into Frontierland—ambling along the banks of the river on their way to Splash Mountain—walks by Pecos Bill Cafe. Cheeseburgers, sandwiches, salads, and hot dogs are the staples. If you'd rather not get fries, let them know when you place your order. The excellent fixin's bar (which includes fresh lettuce and tomato, sautéed mushrooms and onions, pickles, and cheese sauce) and ample seating make this spot one of the most popular fast food restaurants in the Magic Kingdom—it's one of our favorites, too. **L D S** $–$$ ❤

Liberty Square
Table Service

LIBERTY TREE TAVERN: At this pillared and porticoed eatery opposite the riverboat landing, the floors are wide oak planks, the wallpaper looks as if it might have come from Williamsburg, the curtains hang from cloth loops, and the venetian blinds are made of wood. The rooms are chock-full of mementos that might have been found in the homes of Thomas Jefferson, George Washington, and Ben Franklin, and the window glass was made using 18th-century casting methods. Such charming environs make the food served therein seem almost secondary.

> ## Hot Tip!
> Hungry for more information about WDW dining? If so, we highly (and immodestly) recommend *Birnbaum's Guide to Walt Disney World Dining 2007*.

❤ Disney Dining Plan participant at press time

The à la carte lunch includes fish, pot roast, turkey, creamy New England clam chowder, sandwiches, and soups.

Dinner, an all-you-can-eat feast served family-style, is hosted by Disney characters. Menu items have included salad, roast turkey, flank steak, pork chop, Stouffer's macaroni and cheese, mashed potatoes, garden vegetables, and stuffing (the restaurant is pretty much Stouffer's central). The character dinner costs about $28 for adults and $13 for children ages 3 through 9. Note that desserts and some beverages cost extra. Reservations are suggested. **L D** $$-$$$ ♥

Fast Food & Snacks

COLUMBIA HARBOUR HOUSE: A fast-food fish house with a touch of elegance. Fried fish, fried chicken strips, vegetarian chili or clam chowder, and assorted sandwiches (including a vegetarian option) and salads grace the menu. (If you order salad, request the dressing on the side or risk it being saturated.) The food is usually quite good, and there are enough antiques and other knick-knacks decking the halls to raise this establishment, located near the Liberty Square entrance to Fantasyland, well above the ordinary. Model ships, copper measures, harpoons, nautical instruments, little lace tieback curtains, and low-beamed ceilings give the restaurant a cozy air. The upstairs dining rooms are particularly charming. **L D S** $-$$ ♥

SLEEPY HOLLOW: Ice-cream-cookie sandwiches, funnel cakes, caramel corn, and other desserts—all made fresh before your eyes—are the sweets for sale at this savory snack stand located in The Hall of Presidents' neighborhood, near the Liberty Square bridge. It's pleasant to eat and relax on the secluded brick patio outside. It has a lovely view of Cinderella Castle. **S** S

Main Street
Table Service

CRYSTAL PALACE: What's the big draw here? Winnie the Pooh and his pals are here three meals a day. One of the Magic Kingdom's cherished landmarks, this spot takes its architectural cues from a similar structure that once stood in New York, and from San Francisco's Conservatory of Flowers, which still graces that city's Golden Gate Park. The place is quite spacious, with tables scattered amid a Victorian-style indoor garden, complete with fresh flowers and hanging greenery. Tables in the front look out on flower beds, while those at the east end have views of a courtyard. The restaurant is located on a pathway at the end of Main Street, U.S.A.

Four topiaries—Winnie the Pooh, Tigger, Eeyore, and Piglet—greet guests at the entrance, a sign of the character presence here. None other than Winnie the Pooh himself and his pals from the Hundred Acre wood circulate throughout meals.

Offerings vary according to season and available produce. The all-you-can-eat buffet

PHOTO BY JILL SAFRO

Healthier Options

Health-conscious folks need not abandon all restraint for want of suitable sustenance. Most restaurants offer low-fat, low-cholesterol, low-salt, low-carb, and vegetarian entrées. Even fast-food stands now feature healthier fare such as fresh salads, grilled chicken sandwiches, fresh fruit, turkey burgers, and nonfat frozen yogurt. If you have any special requests or allergies, make them known when you book your restaurant reservation. It's a good idea to confirm any special requests before you leave home and to remind your server once you arrive.

B breakfast **L** lunch **D** dinner **S** snacks $ *under $15* $$ *$15-$29* $$$ *$30-$50* $$$$ *$51 and up*

features a full variety of traditional breakfast items every morning; a salad bar, deli bar, pasta dishes, chicken, and fish for lunch; and spit-roasted beef, chicken, pastas, fish, carved meats, and inventive sides for dinner. The evening salad bar, with its grilled vegetables, peel-and-eat shrimp, cold pasta salads, and variety of greens and grains, is first-rate. Kids love the ice-cream-sundae bar offered at lunch and dinner. Cost for breakfast is about $19 for adults and $11 for children ages 3 through 9; lunch is about $21 for adults and $12 for children; dinner is about $28 for adults and $13 for children. Reservations are suggested. **B L D** SS-SSS

PLAZA RESTAURANT: This airy, many-windowed establishment, around the corner from the Plaza Ice Cream Parlor, is done up in mirrors with sinuous Art Nouveau frames. The menu offers chef's salads, burgers, and hot and cold sandwiches—plus ice cream, milk shakes, malts, floats, and the biggest sundaes in the Magic Kingdom. Reservations are suggested. **L D S** SS

TONY'S TOWN SQUARE: The decor was inspired by Walt Disney's classic feature *Lady and the Tramp* (which can be viewed in the restaurant's waiting area). The terrazzo-style patio offers a fine view of Town Square (though tables there are in very limited supply). The lunch menu offers Italian specialties, including paninis (sandwiches). Pizzas with selected toppings are good bets. Other staples include Caesar salad, sandwiches, and pasta.

At dinner, select from chicken Florentine, steak, grilled pork chop, and spaghetti, along with daily specials. For dessert, tempting Italian sweets complement a cup of espresso or cappuccino. Reservations are suggested. **L D** SSS

Fast Food & Snacks

CASEY'S CORNER: The small round tables at this old-fashioned red-and-white stop on the west side of Main Street (adjacent to Crystal Palace) spill out onto the sidewalk. Except when the weather is hot, this baseball-themed spot is great for ballpark favorites—hot dogs in jumbo sizes, fries, brownies, soft drinks, and coffee. During daytime hours a pianist plinks away on the restaurant's white upright. There's also a back room with bleacher seating. (Seats face a screen showing cartoons with a sporting theme.) **L D S** S

MAIN STREET BAKERY: If the sight of this old-fashioned storefront doesn't lure you in, the aroma most certainly will. The Main Street Bakery is a pleasant place for a light breakfast, lunch, midmorning coffee break (they have espresso and cappuccino drinks in addition to straight Nescafe), or midafternoon rest stop. Assorted pastries, cakes, and pies are the main temptations. Also offered are premade sandwiches, fresh cookies: chocolate chunk, oatmeal raisin, sugar, and Nestlé's Original Toll House recipe. Ice-cream-cookie sandwiches are "built to order." **B L S** S

PLAZA ICE CREAM PARLOR: Ice cream lovers from all over the country converge on this corner of the park, which boasts the Magic Kingdom's largest variety of hand-scooped ice cream flavors. **S** **S**

Tomorrowland
Fast Food & Snacks

AUNTIE GRAVITY'S GALACTIC GOODIES: This small spot located across from the Tomorrowland Indy Speedway (between Merchant of Venus and Mickey's Star Traders) offers refreshing smoothies, soft-serve ice cream, sundaes, floats, fruit cups, juice, and soft drinks. **S** **S**

COSMIC RAY'S STARLIGHT CAFE: The largest fast-food location in the Magic Kingdom is located directly across from the Tomorrowland Indy Speedway. Three menus are offered at separate sections along the lengthy counter. *Bay 1* serves rotisserie chicken, chicken strips, and barbecue ribs; *Bay 2* has cheeseburgers, vegetarian burgers, and hot dogs; and *Bay 3* offers soups, Caesar salads, wraps, and barbecue sandwiches. Kosher selections are available. An Audio-Animatronics lounge lizard known as Sunny Eclipse entertains diners with cheesy songs and (bad) jokes in the dining area. **L D S** **S–$$**

LUNCHING PAD AT ROCKETTOWER PLAZA: Located at the base of the Astro Orbiter in the center of Tomorrowland's sprawling concrete plaza, this small dining spot offers sizable smoked turkey legs, character cookies, frozen soda slushies, and soft drinks. **S** **S**

TOMORROWLAND TERRACE NOODLE STATION: Just east of the Plaza restaurant on Main Street, U.S.A., this sleek spot on the edge of Tomorrowland serves Asian salads, stir-fry and noodle bowls, egg rolls, and pot stickers. There are some particularly pleasant tables situated toward the water that look past the graceful willow trees nearby, an impressive topiary sea serpent, not to mention Cinderella Castle. **L D S** **S**

PHOTO BY JILL SAFRO

B breakfast **L** lunch **D** dinner **S** snacks $ *under $15* $$ *$15-$29* $$$ *$30-$50* $$$$ *$51 and up*

In Epcot

The various areas that make up Epcot offer a spectrum of eating options that extends from the usual burgers and fries to mouthwatering international specialties. Future World counts a please-all food court among its fast-food spots, plus two table-service restaurants whose menus and atmospheres innovatively reflect the themes of the pavilions they inhabit. World Showcase, on the other hand, is characterized by international flavors. Here, the cuisine of each country is served in settings that strive to transport visitors, if just for the duration of their meal. While the abundance of appealing table-service restaurants makes World Showcase a very popular dining destination, the promenade is also ringed with fast-food spots, most of which feature international fare. Reservations are an important part of the Epcot dining equation. (To make arrangements, call 407-WDW-DINE.) Character meals are options for breakfast, lunch, and dinner in Future World (for specifics on dining with Disney characters, see page 252).

Future World
Table Service

CORAL REEF (The Seas with Nemo & Friends): Decorated in cool greens and blues to complement its surroundings, this restaurant offers diners a panoramic view of the coral reef through large windows. The windows are eight feet high and more than eight inches thick. The dining room has several tiers, so all guests get a decent view. The menu features fresh fish and shellfish—including catfish, mahimahi, shrimp, and salmon—prepared in a number of delectable ways. Landlubber selections, such as as New York Strip and pan-seared chicken breast, are also available. The menu may vary seasonally. Reservations are suggested. **L D** $$$ 🐭

GARDEN GRILL (The Land): Sleek wood-trimmed booths illuminated with brass lamps help to make this a festive eatery. The restaurant itself revolves (very slowly), moving past a mural of giant sunflowers and above scenes of the thunderstorm, sandstorm, prairie, and rain forest featured in the Living with the Land boat ride. The scenes were designed with diners in mind, and provide them with a peek into a farmhouse window that's out of viewing range of the waterborne passengers.

Chip and Dale (and friends) host two character meals each day. Lunch and dinner menus feature rotisserie meats, grilled flank steak, and fried catfish. There is a separate menu for children. Cost is about $21 for adults lunch, $28 for dinner. Kids pay about $12 for lunch and $13 for dinner. Beverages and dessert are included. Meals are served family style (communal platters for the table). Reservations are suggested. **L D** $$-$$$ 🐭

Fast Food & Snacks

ELECTRIC UMBRELLA (Innoventions Plaza): This large fast-food establishment is decorated in shades of blue, mauve, and magenta. The fare may not be imaginative, but the restaurant is a good bet when the weather is temperate enough to allow dining at the tables on the terrace outside—or when bound for World Showcase with finicky eaters in tow. Offerings include burgers, chicken strips, tossed salads, sandwiches, hot dogs, and soft drinks. Beer is served, too. **B L D S** $-$$ 🐭

FOUNTAIN VIEW ESPRESSO AND BAKERY (Innoventions Plaza): Fresh-baked goods and desserts—such as croissants, cheesecake, cookies, and more—can be found at this sleek spot across from the Fountain of Nations. Espresso, cappuccino, and smoothies are among the assorted beverages available here. **B S** $-$$ 🐭

SUNSHINE SEASONS (The Land): One of the most interesting of the Future World dining options, this handful of diverse stands is on the lower level of the Land pavilion. There is ample seating at tables beneath colorful hot-air balloons. Note that it can be extremely busy at mealtimes, and the dining area gets downright chaotic. Because of the wide variety of foods available here, this is one of the best places in Epcot for a family that can't agree on what to eat—there's bound to be something for everyone.

Sandwich Board is home of the roasted vegetable Cuban sandwich, Black Forest ham and salami grinders, and more. The **Soup and Salad Shop**'s creative salads include roasted beet and goat cheese and seared tuna with sesame rice wine dressing. Three different soups are made fresh daily. **The Grill Shop** features rotisserie chicken and ancho-rubbed rotisserie beef chimichurri. The latter is served on flatbread with tabbouleh and greens. Moroccan rotisserie chicken and grilled salmon are also offered. **Wok Shop** serves Mongolian beef with jasmine rice, and noodle bowls such as chicken chili garlic. The **Bakery** offers fresh-made desserts. In addition to the house specialty—Soarin' Creme Brulée—expect to find brownies, ice cream, and other sweet treats. There is also a "grab and go" area that stocks items such as sushi, fruit and cheese plates, salads, and snacks. `B L D S` `$-$$` 🐭

World Showcase
Table Service

AKERSHUS ROYAL BANQUET HALL (Norway): The Norwegian castle of Akershus dominates Oslo's harbor, and is the most impressive of all Norway's medieval fortresses. It is actually half fortress and half palace, and many of its grand halls continue to be used for elaborate state banquets. At Epcot's castlelike Akershus, guests are treated to authentic royal

Norwegian cuisine. They also get to dine with royalty—as Disney princesses interact with guests during all three meals every day of the week.

An all-inclusive price entitles lunch and dinner guests to enjoy dishes that don't often leave Scandinavia. Included in the family style sampling of the Norwegian *koldbord* is smoked salmon and seafood, Norwegian cheese, and chilled salads. Norwegian-inspired entrées include fresh seafood, beef, and poultry selections. A child's menu is available. Dessert and soft drinks are included.

If you can't snag a reservation at Cinderella Castle, Akershus's Princess Storybook meals are an excellent alternative. While guests enjoy the all-you-can-eat fare (bacon, eggs, breads, and other traditional American breakfast selections are brought to your table), Disney princesses wander about and mingle with guests. Belle, Jasmine, Snow White, Sleeping Beauty, and even Mary Poppins have made appearances. Note that the character appearance schedule varies. Reservations are suggested. A deposit of $10 per person is required for all meals. Breakfast costs about $23 for adults (age 10 and up) and $13 for kids (ages 3–9); lunch is about $25 (adults) and $14 (kids); dinner costs about $29 (adults) and $14 (kids). `B L D` `$$-$$$` 🐭

BIERGARTEN (Germany): Located at the rear of the St. Georgsplatz in the Germany pavilion, this huge, tiered restaurant is every bit as jolly as Alfredo's restaurant in the Italy pavilion. This is partly because of the long tables that encourage a certain togetherness among guests—and partly because beer is served in oversize steins. But equal credit for the *gemütlich* atmosphere must go to the restaurant's lively entertainment.

There are scheduled appearances by traditional Bavarian musicians—each clad in lederhosen or dirndl—who play accordions, cowbells, a musical saw, and a harplike stringed instrument known as the "wooden laughter." The entertaining shows take place at scheduled times in the dining room. The schedule is usually posted at the door. Diners are usually invited to join the fun on the dance floor. The food is hearty and presented as an all-you-can-eat buffet, featuring all sorts of sausages (bratwurst, *Debrizinger*, *Bauernwurst*), frankfurters, rotisserie chicken, homemade spaetzle, assorted cold dishes, potato salad, cucumber salad, and many more

German specialties. Because entertainment is intermittent, there's plenty of time to enjoy the pleasant setting. Reservations highly recommended, particularly during peak seasons (book as early as possible). **L D** **$$-$$$** ✿

BISTRO DE PARIS (France): One flight above Les Chefs de France, this restaurant evokes the charm of early 20th-century Paris. A traditional bistro menu (created by the same trio of French chefs responsible for the fare at Chefs de France) features such robust "preludes" as the grilled quail and *fois gras* sampler.

The brief entrée menu includes honey-roasted rack of lamb, roasted venison, and Maine lobster. The heartiness of the fare makes it an especially good dining choice in cool weather. Reservations are suggested. *Note that this restaurant accepts reservations up to 30 days ahead.* **D** **$$$$**

LE CELLIER STEAKHOUSE (Canada): Tucked away on the lowest level of the pavilion near Victoria Gardens, this low-ceilinged, lantern-lighted, stone-walled establishment looks a little like the ancient wine cellars for which it is named. It offers a menu of Canadian foods, with hearty sandwiches and steak salads available for lunch. Canadian Alberta Beef is added to the offerings at dinner. The cheese soup is scrumptious..

Maple-glazed salmon, rosemary garlic seared chicken, and unique pasta dishes round out the entrée selections. For dessert, try the classic *crème brûlée* or chocolate cake. Canada's own Moosehead and Labatt beers and Inniskillin wine are served. The tempting menu makes Le Cellier Steakhouse a prime destination. Reservations are suggested. **L D** **$$-$$$** ✿

LES CHEFS DE FRANCE (France): This charming restaurant has a bright, airy feel, with yellow and cream-colored walls drenched in natural light. It boasts a large glass-enclosed "outside" dining area with a conservatory motif.

Behind the restaurant's well-appointed scenes, a team of internationally acclaimed chefs—Paul Bocuse, Roger Vergé, and Gaston Lenôtre—have prepared a tempting nouvelle menu. Bocuse operates a restaurant outside Lyons, France, and Roger Vergé runs one just north of the French Riviera. Together with Gaston Lenôtre (widely recognized as France's premier preparer of pastries and other dessert delicacies), they form a most unusual, and absolutely formidable, gastronomic trio. Their menu features fresh ingredients readily available from Florida purveyors. In addition, the restaurant imports as many key ingredients from France as possible.

As you might expect, the fare here is delightfully French, but the foundation of the menu is nouvelle cuisine, which involves lighter sauces using less cream and butter than in classic French cooking. Menu items include beef tenderloin, duck, and lamb. Soups and appetizers, such as onion soup and escargot, are all-day staples. Apple tart, chocolate crêpes, peach melba, and chocolate mousse cake are dessert specialties of note.

Be aware that this can be one of the most expensive of all World Showcase restaurants. Reservations are suggested (book as early as possible). **L D** $$$–$$$$

L'ORIGINALE ALFREDO DI ROMA

RISTORANTE (Italy): This restaurant's trompe l'oeil paintings make diners believe they're seeing real scenes, rather than mere murals, and lend character to the decor of this popular establishment. As in the famous Roman restaurant of the same name (where fettuccine Alfredo was invented in 1914), the house specialty is, fittingly enough, fettuccine Alfredo—wide, flat noodles tossed in a sauce made of butter and imported Parmesan cheese. But many other sizes and shapes of pasta are also available. There is also a number of less familiar Italian preparations involving chicken, seafood, sausage, and veal.

At lunchtime, it's also possible to order pizza. For dessert, choose from specialties such as cannoli, tiramisu, ricotta cheesecake, or homemade gelato. Even if you don't eat here, it's fun to stop and just peer through the glass kitchen windows to watch the cooks cranking out the rigatoni, ziti, linguine, lasagne, fettuccine, and spaghetti (which, the menu reminds guests, were brought from Europe to America by Thomas Jefferson in 1786). Reservations are suggested. **L D** $$$

MARRAKESH (Morocco): The most savory part of the Morocco pavilion features traditional and modern Moroccan cuisine. Waiters are dressed in traditional Moroccan costumes. Menu specialties include roast lamb, chicken brochette, beef shish kebob, and couscous (steamed semolina served with your choice of lamb, chicken, or vegetables). Sampler platters are also available. The tilework was done by Moroccan craftsmen. Belly dancers and musicians entertain diners at lunch and dinner. Reservations are suggested. **L D** $$$

MITSUKOSHI (Japan): A complex of dining and drinking spots, all run by the Japanese firm for which it is named, occupies the second level of the large structure on the west side of the Japan pavilion. There are two options:

Tempura Kiku occupies a small corner of the Mitsukoshi building that's devoted to the batter-dipped, deep-fried chicken, beef, sea-

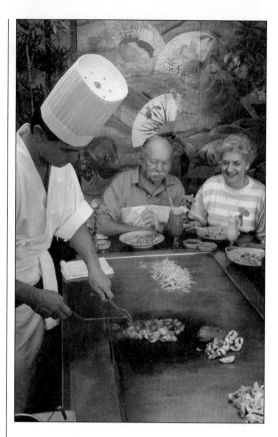

food, and fresh vegetables that are collectively known as tempura. The individual tidbits are crisp and delicious. Sushi and sashimi round out the offerings. Seating is first come, first served. **L D** $$$

Teppanyaki Dining Room is composed of five rooms not unlike those popularized by the Benihana chain all around America. Guests sit counter style around large grills while white-hatted chefs chop vegetables, meat, and fish at lightning speed and then stir-fry it all just as quickly. Whether the chopping and cooking accompany a mildly comic routine depends on the chef, but in any case, the establishment is quite convivial. The seating arrangements make it natural to strike up a conversation with fellow diners; in fact, it's almost impossible to keep to yourself. Reservations are suggested. **L D** $$$

NINE DRAGONS (China): This stop on Epcot's varied international restaurant tour transports guests back to the time of Imperial China when in the palatial dining room. Meals are presented family style, and allow guests to sample provincial cuisines such as *Sichuan* beef in spicy broth, Xinjiang-style lamb chop, and honey sesame chicken from the Kiangche region of China. Guests who prefer dim sum can select from appetizers such as shrimp and pork spring rolls and salad (served in a vase). A selection of imported Chinese teas, beers, and wines is available. The dessert menu features red-bean ice cream, caramel ginger ice cream, and no-sugar-added chocolate mousse. Reservations are suggested. **L D** **$$$** 🍸

ROSE & CROWN PUB AND DINING ROOM

(United Kingdom): The fare here tends toward pub grub—that is, fish-and-chips and traditional meat pies. For lunch, however, it's also possible to order Bangers and Mash (sausages with mashed potatoes), vegetable curry, prime rib, or the Ploughman's Lunch (sliced turkey and ham, English cheeses, and fresh bread). For an appetizer, we recommend the sautéed mushrooms in cream sauce on puff pastry. For dessert there's warm apple crumble topped with ice cream and a sticky toffee pudding, sherry-flavored sponge cake, and chocolate cake with Guinness mousse. Bass ale from England, and Harp lager and Guinness stout, from Ireland, are on tap.

(They're served cold, in the American fashion, not at room temperature, as some British guests may prefer.)

The decor is pretty, mainly polished woods, etched glass, and brass accents. In fine weather it's pleasant to lunch under a canopy on the terrace outside and watch the *FriendShip* water taxis cruising across World Showcase Lagoon. On the little island just to the east, the wind ruffles the leaves of the Lombardy poplars, a species of tree that is found along roadsides all over Europe.

As for the pub's architecture, it incorporates three distinct styles. The wall facing the World Showcase Promenade is reminiscent of urban establishments popular in Britain since the 1890s, while that on the south side evokes

London's 17th-century Cheshire Cheese pub, with its brick-walled flagstone terrace, slate roof, and half-timbered exterior. The canal facade, with its stone wall and clay-tile roof, reminds visitors of the charming pubs so common in the English countryside.

The pub section of the Rose & Crown serves such snacks as Stilton cheese and fresh fruit platters, and fish-and-chips—along with all the brews noted above and traditional British mixed drinks, such as shandies (Bass ale and ginger ale), lager with lime juice, black velvets (Guinness stout and champagne), and black and tans (Bass ale and Guinness stout). The pub is quite popular, so it's often necessary to queue up at the door. Note that the pub section also spills out onto the World Showcase promenade—where the first-come, first-served waterside tables make for a nice spot to sip a drink and, possibly, enjoy some fish-and-chips from a nearby window. Reservations are not available in the pub areas, but suggested for the adjacent dining room. **L D S** **$$$** 🍸

SAN ANGEL INN (Mexico): The food at this establishment located to the rear of the plaza inside the Mexico pyramid (a corporate cousin of the famous Mexico City restaurant of the same name) may come as a surprise to most visitors. Although the tacos and tortillas and other specialties that usually fall under the broad umbrella of Mexican food are available, the menu also offers a wide variety of more subtly flavored fish, poultry, and meat dishes.

To start, there's *queso fundido* for two (melted cheese and Mexican pork sausage with corn or flour tortillas). As entrées, the menu offers grilled tenderloin of beef served with a chicken enchilada, guacamole, and refried beans; *plato Mexicano* (beef taco, quesadilla, and refried beans for lunch; at dinner substitute beef tenderloin or tampiquena for the quesadilla); *ensalada mexicana* (greens with grilled chicken, tomatoes, avocado, turnip, cheese, and cactus strips tossed in a tortilla shell); plus much more that is good and tasty. Mexican desserts are largely unfamiliar to many diners, with the possible exception of the custard known as flan, but are well worth trying. Dos Equis beer and margaritas make good accompaniments. Reservations are suggested. **LD** **$$$** 🐭

Fast Food & Snacks

BOULANGERIE PATISSERIE (France): This bakery and pastry shop in the France pavilion is not hard to find: Just follow the wonderful aroma, then watch the crowds line up to consume the flaky croissants, éclairs, fruit tarts, and chocolate mousse. The treats are served under the management of the stellar trio of chefs who operate the popular Les Chefs de France restaurant not far away: Paul Bocuse, Roger Vergé, and Gaston Lenôtre. Hint for those who hate to wait: This has become a favorite snacking spot among Epcot veterans; your best bet is to stop here as soon as World Showcase opens or half an hour before park closing. **S** **S-$$** 🐭

CANTINA DE SAN ANGEL (Mexico): Located along the World Showcase Promenade, just outside the entrance to Mexico's pyramid, this no-nonsense quick-service stand serves beef-filled soft tortillas; *tacos al carbón*, flour tortillas filled with grilled chicken breast strips, onions, and

PHOTO BY JILL SAFRO

peppers, served with refried beans and salsa; and *churros*, a sort of fried dough rolled in cinnamon and sugar. The Cantina is a good choice for a simple snack, and even more so for its outdoor lagoonside seating. Beer and margaritas are available. **LDS** **$-$$** 🐭

COOL POST (between Germany and China): This is a perfect spot for a refreshing cold drink. Frozen yogurt and ice cream are also served. **S** **$** 🐭

KRINGLA BAKERI OG KAFE (Norway): Tucked between the Norway pavilion's wooden church and a cluster of shops, this popular eating spot serves *kringles*, sweet candied pretzels reserved for special occasions in Norway; heart-shaped waffles topped with powdered sugar and jam; almond-pastry sticks; and *smørbrøds*, open-face sandwiches of smoked salmon, roast beef, or turkey. We're intrigued by the scrambled eggs wrapped in smoked salmon. There is a shaded outdoor eating area. **LDS** **$-$$** 🐭

LIBERTY INN (The American Adventure): To many visitors from other countries, American food means burgers, hot dogs, chicken, and fries, and these are the staples at the Liberty Inn, located to the left of The American Adventure show on the far side of the World Showcase lagoon. Salads, sandwiches, and apple cobblers round out the selections. The place is good for kids and unadventurous eaters. **LDS** **$-$$** 🐭

LOTUS BLOSSOM CAFE (China): Adjacent to Yong Feng Shangdian shopping gallery in the China pavilion, this fast-food counter offers orange chicken rice bowls, salads with peanut dressing, egg rolls, and soup. Peach-flavored iced tea, oolong tea, and bubble teas are available. There is a covered outdoor seating area nearby. **LD** **$-$$** 🐭

REFRESHMENT PORT (Canada): Another good spot for a quick thirst quencher or a McDonald's-style snack. Located on the World Showcase promenade, stop here for fries, chicken McNuggets, and McFlurries. **S** **$** 🐭

SOMMERFEST (Germany): Bratwurst sandwiches, soft pretzels, Black Forest cake, apple strudel, Lowenbrau beer, and wine are offered at this covered spot, located toward the rear of the pavilion; seating is nearby. **LDS** **$-$$** 🐭

TANGIERINE CAFE (Morocco): Named for the Moroccan city of Tangier, this casual spot serves lentil salad, hummus, and tabbouleh, as well as rotisserie chicken, beef, and lamb presented as sandwiches (served on Moroccan bread) and combination platters. Coffees and pastries are available. **L D S** **$–$$** 🍴

YAKITORI HOUSE (Japan): Located in the gardens to the left of the plaza, the restaurant occupies a scaled-down version of the 16th-century Katsura Imperial Summer Palace, in Kyoto; sliding screens, lanterns, and kimono-clad servers add to the authentic atmosphere.

Among the fare here is *sukiyaki beef*, a stewlike concoction flavored with soy sauce, spices, and the Japanese rice wine known as sake, served over rice. That staple, along with teriyaki chicken (it's basted with soy sauce and sesame oil as it broils), sushi, and Japanese sweets and beverages, typifies the offerings here. The menu has included green tea and red bean ice cream. The nearby garden serves as a peaceful respite for those who wish to take a break from the hustle and bustle of a busy Epcot day. **L D S** **$–$$** 🍴

YORKSHIRE COUNTY FISH SHOP (United Kingdom): Located next to the Rose & Crown Pub, this walk-up window serves Harry Ramsden's famous (and delicious) fish-and-chips, plus beverages. **L D S** **$–$$** 🍴

Epcot Mealtime Tips

- The international restaurants of World Showcase offer some of the best dining on the property. Since many of them are very popular, it's a good idea to arrange advance reservations for any table-service restaurants by calling 407-WDW-DINE (939-3463) long before arriving. However, it's important to note that some tables may be available for same-day seating. To make arrangements, head to Guest Relations first thing in the morning or to the kiosk located by the Tip Board in Innoventions Plaza. Meals may also be booked at the individual restaurants.

- Don't dismiss the idea of an early seating if you can get it: a 5 P.M. dinner may not only be welcome, but it may also provide the opportunity to spend the most pleasant and uncrowded evening hours enjoying the Epcot attractions.

- Lunch provides guests with another chance to enjoy the most popular Epcot restaurants. It also has an additional appeal: With reservations for 1 P.M., it's possible to spend some of the busiest hours in the park consuming a pleasant meal while less fortunate visitors are waiting in some of the longest lines of the day.

- If you aren't able to secure reservations for a meal, don't despair. There are many satisfying alternatives to a table-service restaurant. Japan has Tempura Kiku, a full-service spot with batter-dipped, deep-fried meats and vegetables, and Yakitori House, good for skewered bits of barbecued chicken and sushi. Sample simple Mexican specialties at Cantina de San Angel (whose lagoonside tables provide a view of the sun setting behind Epcot). Also try the sandwiches at Kringla Bakeri og Kafe, in Norway, or the fish-and-chips in the United Kingdom.

- Cravings for conventional fast foods will be satisfied at the Electric Umbrella, in Innoventions, and at the Liberty Inn, in The American Adventure. The Sunshine Seasons, in The Land pavilion, offers a bit of everything. (However, it can get extremely congested at mealtime rush hours.)

- The most unadventurous eaters can still find something pleasing—even in the more exotic restaurants of World Showcase. If you're undecided, ask at Guest Relations to see a booklet describing the menus. Keep in mind that most restaurants have menus for kids.

In the Disney-MGM Studios

The eateries at the Disney-MGM Studios are a breed apart. Some feature decor that returns guests to a bygone era; others recapture memorable moments from the big or small screen. All reprise a beloved part of Hollywood's star-studded heritage. The Studios has five full-service restaurants, whose atmospheres and menus are so distinct they satisfy altogether different moods and whims. Reservations are available for these dining rooms; call 407-WDW-DINE (939-3463). A solid—and fairly diverse—ensemble of fast-food places hits the spot for eaters on the move.

Table Service

50'S PRIME TIME CAFE: The setting is straight out of your favorite classic sitcoms of the 1950s. Each of the plastic-laminate kitchen tables is set under a pull-down lamp, evoking a suburban kitchenette. Televisions around the room broadcast black-and-white clips from favorite fifties comedies (all related to food). Guests are waited on by "Mom" (and other family members) with considerable enthusiasm—they make recommendations and encourage everyone to keep their elbows off the table and clean their plates (*or no dessert!*). These elements alone make this spot a perennial guest favorite.

Adding to the appeal is the menu, which is packed with "comfort foods." For openers there's a choice of homemade chicken noodle soup or onion rings. Specialties of the house include meat loaf, served with mashed potatoes and vegetables; fried chicken; and old-fashioned pot roast. There are also Caesar salads and sandwiches. Milk shakes, ice cream sodas, and root beer floats are filling accompaniments. And when you've finished everything on your plate, "Mom" will ask if you'd like dessert. Standouts include s'mores, a graham cracker topped with chocolate and toasted marshmallows (you'll feel like you're back at summer camp); sundaes; seasonal cobbler, and angel food cake with whipped cream. Kids love this place. Grown-ups tend to enjoy the not-so-subtle reminders to eat their vegetables, too. A full bar is available. Reservations are suggested. **L D** **$$–$$$** ♥

HOLLYWOOD & VINE: The distinctive Art Deco facade ushers guests into a contemporary version of a 1950s diner—all stainless steel with pink accents. An elaborate 42-by-8-foot wall mural depicts notable Hollywood landmarks, including the Disney Studios, Columbia Ranch, and Warner Brothers (back when they were the only film studios in the San Fernando Valley). At the center of the mural is the Carthay Circle Theatre, where *Snow White and the Seven Dwarfs* premiered in 1937.

The buffet breakfast and lunch, known as Playhouse Disney's Play 'N Dine, are character affairs featuring Jo Jo and Goliath from Jo Jo's Circus and Leo from The Little Einsteins. The morning meal includes Mickey waffles, frittatas, fresh fruits, and house-made pastries. Lunch may offer items such as herb-crusted baked salmon with citrus butter, multigrain pasta with plum tomotoes and mushrooms, and salads. Dinner, which is character-free, also features carved meats, peel-and-eat shrimp, and mussels. Some soft drinks are included. Beer and wine are served at an extra cost.

The dinner buffet costs about $24 for adults and $12 for kids. Reservations are suggested. **B L D** **$$–$$$** ♥

HOLLYWOOD BROWN DERBY: The home of the famous Cobb salad is alive and well. This re-creation of the former Vine Street mainstay is quite faithful, right down to the caricatures (reproduced from the original Derby collection) that cover the walls. Arch gossip queen rivals Louella Parsons and Hedda Hopper (portrayed by convincing actresses) may still be spotted dining here, just as they did in the heyday of the real Brown Derby. The place is decorated predominantly

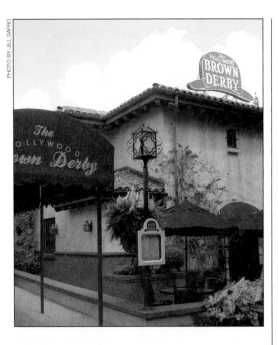

drive-in theater speakers are mounted beside each car. All the tables face a large screen, where a 45-minute compilation of the best (and worst) of science-fiction trailers and cartoons plays in a continuous loop.

in teak and mahogany, and the elegant chandeliers and perimeter lamps (shaped like miniature derbies) are reminiscent of those in the original eatery.

The menu features the famed Cobb salad, created by owner Bob Cobb in the 1930s. It's a mixture of ever-so-finely chopped fresh salad greens, tomato, bacon, turkey, egg, blue cheese, and avocado, served with french dressing. The salad is available with sesame-seared Ahi tuna or chicken. Desserts are tempting—particularly the grapefruit cake, a Brown Derby institution. The slightly formal atmosphere is not likely to enchant most kids. Reservations are suggested. **L D** **$$$**

MAMA MELROSE'S RISTORANTE ITALIANO:

This quirky Italian restaurant (with a California twist) is located in a warehouse that has been converted into a dining room. Appetizer flatbreads are prepared in a wood-burning oven. The menu also features risotto, chicken, pasta, and vegetarian options. More creative dishes include spaghetti with clams, mussels, and calamari in a spicy marinara sauce; and veal osso buco. Note that this restaurant may undergo a name and/or a theme change. Reservations are suggested. **L D** **$$-$$$**

SCI-FI DINE-IN THEATER:

This 250-seat eatery re-creates a 1950s drive-in theater. The tables are actually flashy, 1950s-era cars, complete with fins and whitewalls. Fiber-optic stars twinkle overhead in the "night sky," and real

The restaurant is also notable for its huge hot and cold sandwiches. Selections include ham sandwiches, smoked turkey sandwiches, barbecue ribs, and flame-broiled hamburgers. There's also a slate of tempting desserts, including cheesecake, milk shakes, and hot fudge sundaes. Reservations are suggested. **L D** **$$-$$$**

Fast Food & Snacks

ABC COMMISSARY: This restaurant, located near the Chinese Theater, features international cuisine: Cuban sandwiches, vegetable noodle stir-fry, fish-and-chips, tabbouleh, black bean salad, chicken curry, burgers, chocolate mousse, macadamia turtle tart, and strawberry parfait. There is ample seating, though diners are subjected to never-ending ads for ABC shows. **L D S** **$**

BACKLOT EXPRESS: Designed to resemble the old crafts shops on studio backlots, this spot seems rather authentic. There's a paint shop, stunt hall, sculpture shop, and model shop. The paint shop has paint-speckled floors, chairs, and tables; the prop shop is decked out in car engines, bumpers, and fan belts. There is indoor and outdoor seating. The menu includes burgers, hot dogs, salads, turkey sandwiches, vegetable paninis, and chili. For dessert, there's double chocolate bundt cake, chocolate marshmallow mousse, and peach tarts. Beer is available. **L D S** **$**

PHOTO BY JILL SAFRO

MIN AND BILL'S DOCKSIDE DINER: A waterside snack spot offering sumptuous thick shakes (chocolate and vanilla), as well as stuffed pretzels, coffee, soft drinks, and beer. **S** **S**

STARRING ROLLS CAFE: Baked rolls, pastries, muffins, croissants, and sugar-free desserts are sold at this sweet-smelling shop. Freshly roasted coffee, tea, and soft drinks are also served, making this a good place for an eat-and-run breakfast. Wine is served, too. **B** **S** **S–$$** ✸

STUDIO CATERING CO.: Situated next to the Honey, I Shrunk the Kids Movie Set Adventure, the eatery offers a Mediterranean-inspired menu. They have fresh grilled wraps, Greek salad, chicken stew, and fresh-baked desserts. Attached to a full-service bar, it's possible to order just about any refreshing libation under the sun. **S** **S–$$** ✸

SUNSET RANCH MARKET: Several well-stocked food stands on Sunset Boulevard offer snacking opportunities and quick bites. Blue umbrellas dot the outdoor seating area. *Rosie's All-American Cafe* specializes in cheeseburgers, chicken strips, and soups.

PHOTO BY JILL SAFRO

Catalina Eddie's offers plain and pepperoni pizzas, plus salads, chocolate cake and apple pie. Fresh fruit and vegetables, fruit juices, and soft drinks are available at *Anaheim Produce*. The turkey-leg cart also offers foot-long chilli dogs and and soft pretzels. **L D S** **S** ✸

Hot Tip!

Hollywood Brown Derby, Mama Melrose's Ristorante Italiano, and Hollywood and Vine offer a "dinner and a show" deal. Special seating for the evening's performance of Fantasmic! is included with the meal at no extra cost (though tax, gratuities, and beverages carry an additional charge). It's worth considering if you plan on eating dinner at the Disney-MGM Studios and would rather not wait on line (sometimes for more than an hour) for Fantasmic! To make arrangements, call 407-939-3463 and request the Fantasmic! dinner package.

TOY STORY PIZZA PLANET: This arcade is located near the Muppets attraction. The centerpiece is a Space Crane, complete with aliens and mechanical grabber. Games line the walls (pay as you play). A good spot for children with endless energy and parents who need to rest their feet. The limited menu includes (kid-friendly) pizzas, salads, desserts, and juice. **L D S** **S–$$** ✸

Studios Mealtime Tips

- To avoid traffic jams at fast food spots, consider eating at one of the restaurants that offer advance reservations—Hollywood Brown Derby, 50's Prime Time Cafe, Sci-Fi Dine-In Theater, Hollywood & Vine (dinner only), or Mama Melrose's Ristorante Italiano. To arrange for reservations in advance, call 407-WDW-DINE (939-3463). To obtain same-day seating, go to the kiosk at Hollywood Junction (on the corner of Hollywood and Sunset), before 1 P.M. or to the restaurant itself.
- The many indoor and outdoor nooks within the Backlot Express seating area are nicely removed from the beaten path; relative quiet can frequently be enjoyed here even during prime mealtimes.

B breakfast **L** lunch **D** dinner **S** snacks $ *under $15* $$ *$15–$29* $$$ *$30–$50* $$$$ *$51 and up*

In Animal Kingdom

Whether you eat like a bird or more like a horse, you'll have no trouble finding something to sink your teeth into at one of Animal Kingdom's eateries. The emphasis at this theme park is on fast food, with Rainforest Cafe as the only traditional table-service establishment (at least for the time being). The quick-service options cater to carnivores and herbivores alike, featuring everything from freshly tossed Caesar salad to chicken roasted in a 16-foot "wall of flames." Beer, including Safari Amber specialty brew, and wine are served at most restaurants.

Table Service

RAINFOREST CAFE: Like The Oasis, the region of Animal Kingdom that it borders, this cafe is a lush, soothing tropical jungle. Unlike The Oasis, any quiet moment here is merely a calm before the storm—as brief, dramatic thunderstorms occur throughout the day *inside* the restaurant. Gushing waterfalls, twisting tree trunks, and colorful fish add to the ambience. The environmentally conscious cuisine includes items like Planet Earth Pasta and the Plant Sandwich. (The Calypso Dip—fresh salmon, artichoke hearts, onions, spices, and cheese served with warm pita—is an especially tantalizing appetizer.) There's no net-caught fish on the menu, nor beef from countries that destroy rain forest land to raise cattle.

Note: The restaurant and bar are accessible from inside and outside Animal Kingdom, so admission to the park isn't necessary to enter. It is located to the left side of Animal Kingdom's entrance plaza. Reservations are suggested for breakfast, lunch, and dinner. **B L D S** $$-$$$

Fast Food & Snacks

ANANDAPUR ICE CREAM: Cool off with a soft-serve from Asia's local ice cream truck. The refreshing snack is available by the cone, cup, or in a soda float. **S** S

ROYAL ANANDAPUR TEA COMPANY: This hut dispenses hot and iced Asian teas in the village of Serka Zong. Light snack items round out the menu. **S** S

DINO BITES: In DinoLand U.S.A., on the far side of Chester and Hester's DinoRama!, is a a small wagon that offers desserts throughout the day. **S** S ☷

FLAME TREE BARBECUE: This fast-food spot serves up a selection of barbecued sandwiches and platters, all wood roasted. Sample the mild, tomato-based barbecue sauce or the spicy, mustard-based Carolina-style sauce with your smoked beef brisket, St. Louis ribs, and pulled pork. There's seating along the river. Located on Discovery Island, near DinoLand. Open seasonally. **L D S** S–$$ ☷

HARAMBE FRUIT MARKET: A healthy choice for snacking at Disney's Animal Kingdom is this fruit stand near the entrance to Kilimanjaro Safaris. **S** S

KUSAFIRI COFFEE SHOP & BAKERY: The bakery inside Tusker House provides a steady stream of fresh-from-the-oven breakfast treats and assorted desserts, plus cappuccino and espresso. **B S** S

PIZZAFARI: Individual pizzas are available plain, and with pepperoni. (The pizza is on the bland side, but will do in a pinch. Kids like it.) In addition to the cheese-laden bill of fare, the options here include Caesar salad with grilled chicken, and hot Italian-style sandwiches. Colorful animal murals decorate this counter-service restaurant, located on Discovery Island, near the bridge to Camp Minnie-Mickey. **L D S** S–$$ ☷

RESTAURANTOSAURUS: Located deep in the heart of DinoLand U.S.A., this spot is themed as a campsite for student paleontologists. It's filled with fossils, bones, and such; class notes line the walls. This eatery offers fast food at lunch and dinner: burgers, chicken salad, hot dogs—plus chicken nuggets, and Happy Meals. Breakfast is an all-you-can-eat, character-hosted buffet, called Donald's Prehistoric Breakfastosaurus. It's an entertaining meal, powered by the antics of resident students, who wait tables between classes. Cost is about $19 for adults; $11 for kids ages 3 through 9. Reservations are suggested for the breakfast buffet. Book early. **B L D S** $-$$

TAMU TAMU REFRESHMENTS: Got a hankering for something cool and creamy? Stop by this spot in Africa's Harambe (across from Tusker House). Here you can indulge in soft-serve ice-cream cones, floats, and sundaes. There's seating next door. **S** $

TUSKER HOUSE: Harambe village sets the stage for a dining adventure at this top-notch fast-food restaurant. Seating inside is quite civilized, with cherry-wood-colored tables and carved chair backs; there's also outdoor seating under the thatched roof. The menu—which happens to be one of the best in the park—features rotisserie chicken. Other highlights include grilled salmon, chicken salad, vegetarian sandwiches served with fruit, fried chicken sandwiches, and turkey wraps with corn chowder. Side dishes such as fresh vegetables, and mashed potatoes round out the creative options. **L D S** $-$$

PHOTO BY JILL SAFRO

Animal Kingdom Mealtime Tips

- Restaurantosaurus and Rainforest Cafe are the only restaurants to offer full breakfasts; a handful of stands, including the Safari Coffee Cart, supply light options.

- At press time, the only restaurant that offered reservations for all meals was Rainforest Cafe. To arrange for reservations in advance, available up to 90 days ahead for all meals, call 407-WDW-DINE (939-3463). To obtain same-day seating, go straight to the restaurant. We recommend making reservations. Rainforest Cafe may keep longer hours than the Animal Kingdom park.

- The many seating pavilions along the river near Flame Tree Barbecue provide waterside dining that's nicely removed from the hubbub of Discovery Island; it may be relatively calm here, even during prime mealtimes.

- A great place to meet Donald and pals such as Mickey, Pluto, and Goofy is at Restaurantosaurus during the daily character breakfast. (Characters appearing at the breakfast are subject to change—though Donald is always in attendance.) Don't forget to make reservations.

In Downtown Disney

The region known as Downtown Disney encompasses the Marketplace, Pleasure Island, and the West Side. An admission fee applies for many Pleasure Island venues. (There is never a fee to roam the West Side or Marketplace.) On average, Downtown Disney restaurants operate from 11 A.M. to midnight; most of the snack spots are open from 11 A.M. to 2 A.M. For details, call 407-939-4636. It's worth noting that while the restaurants really hop at dinnertime, they are not terribly crowded at lunch (except, possibly, on the weekend).

BONGOS CUBAN CAFE (West Side): This creation of Gloria Estefan spices up the Disney dining repertoire with a menu driven by Cuban and Latin American flavors. Its slate of traditional and nouvelle Cuban dishes, such as black bean soup, plantains, steak topped with onions, and flan, tempts taste buds. Indoors, the elaborate mosaic mural and palm-leaf railings set the scene; the patio for outdoor seating wraps around a three-story pineapple. A take-out window provides snacks on the go. Reservations are not available. **L D S** $$-$$$

CAP'N JACK'S RESTAURANT (Marketplace): This pier house juts right out over Lake Buena Vista, providing water views. The appetizer menu is so tempting—crab cakes and clam chowder—that it's as good for lunch or dinner as it is for a snack. Entrées extend to king crab legs, lobster, mahimahi, and "landlubber" specials. There is a variety of wines, beers, and other cocktails—and the house's special frozen margaritas are tasty. Cap'n Jack's is a lovely place to chill out, especially in late afternoon, as the sun streams through the blinds and glints on the polished tables and the copper above the bar. Reservations are not available here. **L D S** $$-$$$ 🐭

CHEESECAKE FACTORY EXPRESS (West Side): Located on the top two floors of Disney-Quest, this fast-food restaurant serves much more than the sweets it is famous for. Offerings are prepared fresh from the four main counters. Highlights include warm spinach and artichoke dip served with chips and salsa, grilled portobello mushroom sandwiches, barbecue chicken pizza, and lasagne in a chicken Bolognese sauce. Also available is a selection of hearty soups and salads, tasty sandwiches, and several specialty burgers and hot dogs. Temptations abound at the dessert counter—they come in the form of frozen mud pie, hot fudge brownie sundaes, cookies, cakes, and of course, cheesecake. Note that DisneyQuest admission is required for access. **L D S** $-$$

EARL OF SANDWICH: (Marketplace): The decor of this dining spot reflects the history of the sandwich and the family that is credited with its creation. It specializes in deli cuisine, with hot and cold freshly prepared sandwiches with original sauces and spreads. Breakfast sandwiches are available, too. Snacks such as ice cream sandwiches, cookies, brownies, and scones are an option. Soft drink selections include sodas, smoothies, juices, teas, beer, and lemonade. **B L D S** $-$$ 🐭

FULTON'S CRAB HOUSE (Between Pleasure Island and Marketplace): This traditional seafood house, operated by Levy Restaurants, occupies the three-deck riverboat formerly known as the *Empress Lilly*. Permanently docked on the western edge of Lake Buena Vista, it is a tribute to Robert Fulton, who invented the steamboat. The place is so serious about seafood that it has hooked up with fishermen worldwide to ensure that the fish and shellfish arriving daily are at their freshest.

The menu changes each day to reflect new arrivals, but is always filled with several types of crabs, oysters, and fish, plus lobster, steaks, grilled chicken, grilled vegetables, and combo platters. Signature dishes include cioppino, a

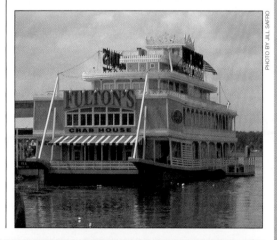

PHOTO BY JILL SAFRO

savory seafood stew with a tomato broth base. Accompaniments extend to corn-whipped potatoes and grilled asparagus. Desserts, coffee, and specialty drinks are also served.

Fulton's interior is awash in nautical knick-knacks and nostalgia. Seating on the deck is sometimes available. The adjoining Stone Crab lounge has an excellent raw bar—the perfect place for lunch. Reservations are suggested for lunch and dinner at Fulton's. **L D S** $$$-$$$$

GHIRARDELLI SODA FOUNTAIN AND CHOCOLATE SHOP (Marketplace): San Francisco's famous sweet-maker finally comes east with a soda fountain extraordinaire. Stop in for a chocolaty treat, root beer float, or refreshing malt. Antique chocolate-making equipment demonstrates how the famous Ghirardelli chocolate got its start. There's no better place to please a sweet tooth. (And there's always the possibility of a free sample.) The coffee is tops, too. **S** $-$$

HOUSE OF BLUES (West Side): The nightclub that Blues Brother Dan Aykroyd helped launch doubles as a Mississippi Delta–inspired dining spot. House of Blues gives Downtown Disney a culinary boost from the bayou—namely, home-style Cajun and Creole cooking. Finally, WDW has a haven for diners desperately seeking their fill of such savory things as jambalaya, étouffée, and homemade bread pudding. A gospel brunch is presented on Sundays. Reservations are suggested. **L D S** $$-$$$

McDONALD'S (Marketplace): The Golden Arches and all of its McSpecialties (plus pizza) are on hand until the wee hours in this installation of the familiar fast-food establishment, located on the western edge of the Marketplace. **B L D S** **S**

PLANET HOLLYWOOD (West Side): This branch of the famed restaurant chain is a standout for its spherical silhouette. Built on three levels, this colossal globe is packed with classic movie and television memorabilia.

The creative, wide-ranging menu features first-rate salads, sandwiches, pasta dishes,

PHOTO BY JILL SAFRO

burgers, appetizer pizzas, fajitas, and dessert specialties. Be sure to consider sampling the blackened shrimp, Far East chicken salad, vegetable burger, or pasta primavera. Cap off the meal with a piece of butter rum cake. Reservations are suggested. **L D S** $$-$$$

> ## Hot Tip!
> The wait for Planet Hollywood is usually shortest between 1 P.M. and 5 P.M.

PORTOBELLO YACHT CLUB (Pleasure Island): The inviting, Bermuda-style house combines high gables and beamed ceilings, bright Mediterranean colors and earthy tones. The pleasant establishment is divided into several informal dining rooms, each of which displays an interesting collection of maritime memorabilia.

The bustling open kitchen turns out grilled meat and fish and small gourmet pizzas baked in a wood-burning oven. Try the *quattro formaggi*, a four-cheese pie that's a true taste treat and a great appetizer or snack. Pasta offerings include *spaghettini alla Portobello* (pasta with shrimp, scallops, clams, mussels, crab legs, tomatoes, garlic, olive oil, wine, and herbs) and *penne all'arrabiata* (long pasta tubes with plum tomatoes, mushrooms, pancetta, garlic, onions, and fresh herbs). Be sure to save room for desserts such as *crema brucciata*, white chocolate custard with a caramelized sugar glaze; or *cioccolato paradiso*, a layer cake with chocolate ganache frosting, chocolate toffee crunch filling, and warm caramel sauce. Portobello also offers a selection of specialty coffees and an impressive wine list. Reservations are suggested. `D` `$$$`

RAINFOREST CAFE (Downtown Disney Marketplace): There's no mistaking the environmental orientation of this Amazon-emulating eatery. The atmospheric dining environs transport guests to a makeshift rain forest, complete with banyan trees, tropical fish, gushing waterfalls, and a friendly population of hand-raised parrots. A talking tree offers a constant stream of ecological insights, and animal experts are on hand to field questions.

Sophisticated special effects envelop guests in tropical storms, complete with lightning and thunder. Menu items include Planet Earth Pasta, Island Hopper Chicken, and the Plant Sandwich (portobello mushrooms, zucchini, roasted red peppers, and fresh spinach). A merchandise shop stocks logo clothing. Reservations are not available at this location.

Note that there is another Rainforest Cafe located at Disney's Animal Kingdom (reservations *are* accepted there). `B` `L` `D` `S` `$$-$$$`

RAGLAN ROAD (Pleasure Island): As authentically Irish as you can get on this side of Emerald Isle, this warm and lively establishment blends fresh ingredients to create traditional Irish fare with a modern flair. The menu comes courtesy of Kevin Dundon, one of Ireland's best-known chefs. His selections are perfectly complemented by the welcoming atmosphere, complete with antiques and bric-a-brac, free-flowing spirits, and live entertainment. `L` `D` `S` `$$-$$$`

WOLFGANG PUCK CAFE (West Side): Wolfgang Puck's choice of Walt Disney World for his Florida debut is sure to spur a surge in cravings for his trademark California cuisine. Among his specialties are gourmet pizzas, Thai chicken satay pastas with fresh vegetables, Chinois Chicken Salad, and rotisserie chicken. The menu is equal parts sophisticated and straightforward—and ever so fresh. There's also an excellent sushi bar. Colorful mosaics decorate his restaurants. Reservations are strongly recommended. `L` `D` `S` `$$$`

WOLFGANG PUCK CAFE—THE DINING ROOM (West Side): The formal upstairs area in the cafe is devoted to the more elaborate of Wolfgang Puck's cuisine. Consider sampling the baby vegetable risotto and grilled chicken with squash ravioli in a sage brown butter sauce. Reservations are required. `D` `$$$-$$$$`

WOLFGANG PUCK EXPRESS (Marketplace and West Side): Renowned chef Wolfgang Puck turns his talents to fast service and signature treats, including gourmet wood-fired pizzas, rotisserie chicken, seasonal soups, focaccia sandwiches, and fresh salads—including his famous Chinois Chicken Salad. `L` `D` `S` `$-$$`

WETZEL'S PRETZELS (Marketplace and West Side): Whether you prefer pretzels on the salty or sweet side, Wetzel's has something to satisfy. Ambitious snackers enjoy the Mexicali, the Sinful Cinnamon, and the Three-Cheese varieties. Ice cream is available, too. `S` `$`

Crossroads of Lake Buena Vista

WDW visitors can get everything from soup to McNuggets at the Crossroads of Lake Buena Vista shopping center, near the resorts on Hotel Plaza Boulevard. Choices include Pebbles (the best bet for adults), Perkins (popular with families), T.G.I. Friday's, Red Lobster, McDonald's, Taco Bell, Jungle Jim's, Pacino's, Chevy's Mexican Restaurant, and Pizzeria Uno.

In the WDW Resorts

Among the more pleasant surprises at Walt Disney World is the elaborate theming of the Disney hotels. Each resort sports a fanciful setting quite foreign to Central Florida, reminiscent of such places as the Pacific Northwest; the more regional-minded offer a tasty sampling of the native cuisine to complete the picture. Whereas the deluxe properties provide a variety of dining options, including at least one full-service restaurant, moderate resorts feature a food court plus an informal dining room, and the value-oriented All-Star resorts keep guests' appetites in check with food courts.

Reservations are an important part of the full-service dining circuit (call 407-WDW-DINE). Character meals are an option for breakfast, Sunday brunch, lunch, and dinner (see page 252).

All-Star Resorts

Each of these resorts features a food court. The *End Zone* food court in Stadium Hall at the All-Star Sports resort, the *Intermission* food court in Melody Hall at the All-Star Music resort, and the *World Premiere* food court in Cinema Hall at the All-Star Movies resort have similar offerings. The selections include pasta, pizza, burgers, hot dogs, sandwiches, salads, ice cream, a variety of breakfast and baked goods, plus a "grab and go" section. **B L D S** $-$$

Animal Kingdom Lodge

BOMA—FLAVORS OF AFRICA: Big and bustling, this eatery, designed to resemble an African marketplace, has exceptional buffet fare from more than 50 African countries. Reservations are strongly suggested. **B D** $$$

JIKO—THE COOKING PLACE: This sophisticated spot, which is awash in colors of a sunset, features excellent, familiar food with an African touch—seafood, steak, chicken, and vegetarian offerings infused with the vibrant flavors and fragrant spices of Africa. The wine list is comprised of South African vintages. Reservations are suggested. **D** $$-$$$

THE MARA: An enormous fast-food restaurant that has something for just about everyone—including a "grab and go" section for those in a hurry. **B L D S** $-$$

BoardWalk

BELLE VUE ROOM: This cozy cocktail lounge, located on the resort's second floor, offers continental breakfast each morning. **B S**

BIG RIVER GRILLE & BREWING WORKS: Guests observe (and later sample) as the brewmaster creates three flagship ales and two seasonal brews at this working brew pub. The menu features a selection of sandwiches and salads, plus variations on pub favorites, such as veal meat loaf with Tilt Pale Ale sauce and lobster pot-pie. **L D S** $$-$$$

BOARDWALK BAKERY: The aromas wafting from Spoodles' next-door neighbor on the boardwalk reveal the fresh-baked goods therein. Display windows allow guests to watch bakers at work. **B S** **S**

ESPN CLUB: A sports bar/family restaurant one-two punch, ESPN Club surrounds guests with no fewer than 80 TV monitors, so no one misses a play. The standard, reliable fare includes wings, burgers, sandwiches, salads, and assorted entrées. **L D S** $$-$$$

FLYING FISH CAFE: This eatery delivers creative seasonal menus with an obvious emphasis on seafood options. As an example of the entrées created in the open "onstage" kitchen, consider the potato-wrapped yellowtail snapper. While seafood is the specialty, steaks are also served. Save room for a homemade dessert. Reservations are suggested. Seating is available at the chef's counter—handy for solo diners. **D** $$$-$$$$

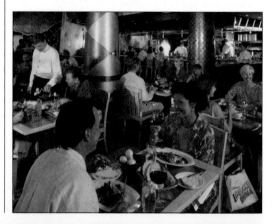

SEASHORE SWEETS': Located next to the Flying Fish Cafe, this old-fashioned spot sates sweet tooths with candies, saltwater taffy, and ice cream and frozen yogurt. Specialty coffees are also offered. **S** **S**

SPOODLES: This family restaurant with butcher-block tables and Mediterranean tastes is between Seashore Sweets' and the BoardWalk Bakery. Dinner menus highlight specialties from Greece, Spain, Northern Africa, and Italy, and encourage diners to share dishes and try new foods. Offerings range from pizza to braised lamb shank with a creamy herb polenta. The breakfast menu features eggs, meats, fish, cereal, and French toast. A take-out window allows passersby to pick up pizza by the slice. Reservations are suggested. **B D** **$$-$$$**

Caribbean Beach

OLD PORT ROYALE: The food court in Old Port Royale features a large dining area and the following fast-food eateries: *Grab N Go Market* serves croissants, freshly baked rolls, pastries, ice cream, and other treats. Italian specialties are the order at the *Royale Pizza and Pasta Shop.* Soups, salads, and hot and cold sandwiches make up the selections at *Montego's Deli.* Burgers and grilled chicken sandwiches are among the offerings at *Old Port Royale Hamburger Shop.* **B L D S** **$-$$**

SHUTTERS AT OLD PORT ROYALE: Prime rib, lamb chops, and pork loin are among the items on the menu at this cozy restaurant within Old Port Royale. Reservations are strongly suggested. **D S** **$$-$$$**

Contemporary

CALIFORNIA GRILL: Perched on the hotel's 15th floor, with terrific views of sunsets and Magic Kingdom fireworks, this acclaimed restaurant offers the best in West Coast cuisine in a stylish, relaxing atmosphere. (It has been named "restaurant of choice" by *Orlando Magazine*.) The ever-changing menu is defined by sophisticated use of fresh produce. Wood-fired California pizzas, beef filet with tamarind barbecue sauce, goat cheese ravioli, sushi, and warm Valrhona chocolate lava cake—all spectacular—are made to order in an open kitchen. Grilled pork tenderloin with polenta and balsamic-vinegar-smothered cremini mushrooms suggest the chef's culinary prowess. There's even a vegetarian zone on the menu. The wine list is updated daily. Reservations strongly suggested. All guests must check in on the resort's second floor. **D** **$$$-$$$$**

CHEF MICKEY'S: Chef Mickey and his pals host this buffet-style feast, with dramatic views of the monorail passing above. Colorful life-size illustrations of Disney characters decorate the room. The changing menu takes advantage of seasonal offerings; a sundae bar provides a sweet finish. This is a popular eatery with a loyal following. Be prepared to drop your fork and swing your napkin on a moment's notice. Reservations are suggested. **B D** **$$-$$$**

SNACK BAR: After leaving its first floor home of 35 years, the Contemporary resort snack bar has moved up in the World—all the way to the fourth floor, beside Chef Mickey's. This spot serves light fare around the clock (though there is usually a bigger selection by day). `BLDS` `$-$$` 🔱

Coronado Springs

MAYA GRILL: The only full-service restaurant at this resort, it features steak and seafood with a Latin American flair. Many items are cooked over an open-pit, wood-fired grill. Breakfast is presented as an all-you-can-eat buffet. Reservations are suggested. `BD` `$$$` 🔱

PEPPER MARKET: This colorful food court has a large seating area and lots of stands where vendors sell pizza, sandwiches, salads, burgers, stir-fry, Mexican specialties, baked goods, margaritas, and more. Note that a 10 percent gratuity is added to the bill whether you eat in the dining area or not. `BLDS` `$-$$` 🔱

Disney's Old Key West

GOOD'S FOOD TO GO: Hamburgers, cheeseburgers, deli sandwiches, salads, ice cream, and snacks are among the offerings. `BLDS` `$` 🔱

OLIVIA'S CAFE: An assortment of Key West favorites, including tasty shrimp dishes and conch fritters, are featured alongside contemporary Southern fare. `LD` `$$-$$$` 🔱

Fort Wilderness

Most people cook their own meals here. Some supplies are available at both the Meadow Trading Post and the Settlement Trading Post (open from 8 A.M. to 10 P.M., in winter, to 11 P.M. in summer).

TRAIL'S END RESTAURANT: It's a little off the beaten path for anyone but Fort Wilderness guests, but for many it's well worth the trip. The informal log-walled restaurant offers a relatively inexpensive, all-you-can-eat breakfast (one of the biggest bargains on property), including grits, biscuits, gravy, and a tasty "breakfast pizza." Lunches feature chicken, pizza, soup, and chili. For dinner, expect smoked pork ribs, peel-n-eat shrimp, fried chicken, carved meats, a salad bar, plus a variety of side dishes and desserts. There are sandwiches and a taco bar at lunch. Pizza is served nightly from 4 P.M. until 10 P.M. (until midnight on weekends). Beer and wine are served by the glass or by the pitcher. `BLDS` `$-$$` 🔱

Grand Floridian

CÍTRICOS: The most recent addition to the Grand Floridian's impressive restaurant lineup specializes in market-fresh European cooking. The fare varies seasonally but may include items such as sautéed tiger shrimp with ziti, artichokes, bell peppers, and roasted garlic in a spicy wine sauce.

The menu suggests a wine from the extensive international list for each appetizer, entrée, and dessert; for $25 the waiter will bring one for each of three courses. The stunning view of the Seven Seas Lagoon is a year-round staple. A private dining room is available for parties of up to 12 people. Reservations are suggested. Closed Monday and Tuesday. `D` `$$$-$$$$` 🔱

GASPARILLA GRILL & GAMES: Grilled chicken, burgers, pizza, hot dogs, and soft-serve ice cream are the mainstays at this 24-hour take-out restaurant near the marina. There is indoor and outdoor seating. Continental breakfast is also available. `BLDS` `$-$$` 🔱

GRAND FLORIDIAN CAFE: Traditional American cooking is the specialty at this picturesque spot. Although the menu varies, selections have included pastries, sandwiches, burgers, ice cream, and vegetarian offerings. There are also salads and an assortment of more traditional entrées. Reservations are available. `BL` `$$$` 🔱

NARCOOSSEE'S: The partially open kitchen is the focal point at this casual, airy octagonal dining spot on the shores of the Grand Floridian beach. Specialties of the house, which vary seasonally, may include Maine lobster, grilled lamb chops, or pepper-seared jumbo scallops. House staples include charbroiled meats, seafood, and vegetarian options. It's also possible to enjoy a cocktail on the veranda overlooking the Seven Seas Lagoon. Reservations are suggested. `D` `$$$-$$$$` 🔱

1900 PARK FARE: A sophisticated buffet menu and subtle decor make this the most elegant character restaurant on-property. Big Bertha, a band organ built in Paris nearly a century ago, sits 15 feet above the floor in a proscenium. Mary Poppins and friends (characters vary) mingle with guests during breakfast. Cinderella and her storybook friends visit the dining room during the dinner hours.

Keep in mind that the lineup of characters does change from time to time. Dinner features seafood, salads, pastas, vegetables, breads, and prime rib. The offerings change weekly. Reservations are suggested. **B D** $$$ ☻

VICTORIA & ALBERT'S: The intimate dining room seats only 60, and elegant touches have included Royal Doulton china, Christofle silver, and Riedel crystal. The menu is customized daily. Each night there are fish, fowl, red meat, veal, and lamb selections, which depend on the best ingredients in the market and are described in detail by your waiter. The chef may even make a personal appearance to say hello or to accommodate special requests from patrons, or guests may choose to dine at the chef's table in the kitchen (for an additional charge).

There are also choices of two soups, two salads, and desserts, including specialty soufflés of fresh berries, chocolate, or Grand Marnier. There is an extensive wine list, and wine pairings are available (for an additional $55).

Once guests have made their selections, they are presented with a personalized menu as a souvenir of the event. A harpist provides background music. At the completion of the

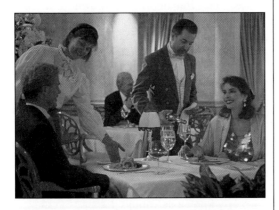

meal, women receive a long-stemmed rose. Jackets are required. One oddity of note: Every host and hostess at the restaurant is named Victoria or Albert (or at least claims to be). Reservations are necessary. **D** $$$$

Polynesian

CAPTAIN COOK'S SNACK COMPANY: A good spot for a light breakfast, hamburgers, fruit, salad, sandwiches, and snacks; cans of beer and bottles of wine are available. Open 24 hours a day. *At press time, this spot was undergoing refurbishment.* **B L D S** $-$$ ☻

KONA CAFE: Located on the second floor of the Great Ceremonial House, just around the corner from 'Ohana, this casual restaurant features a South Seas decor and an exotic menu. Lunch and dinner menus have Asian-influenced entrées. Possibilities include noodle bowls, and macadamia-dusted mahimahi. A variety of desserts are among the offerings. Adjoining the cafe is a coffee counter that's perfect for a quick bite en route to the monorail. The coffee is exceptionally good. Reservations are suggested for all meals. **B L D S** $$-$$$ ☻

'OHANA: On the second floor of the resort's Great Ceremonial House, this restaurant features a dramatic, 16-foot-long open fire pit. Dinner choices in the all-you-can-eat, family-style feast include poultry, pork, and beef, all roasted on skewers up to three feet long. Meats are marinated in original combinations of soy, ginger, lemongrass, or garlic, and are served family style with an assortment of vegetables, salads, and potatoes au gratin.

The meal ends with pineapple-coconut bread pudding served a la mode with bananas Foster sauce, or additional dessert offerings (for an extra charge) such as banana tarts. Polynesian singers entertain at dinner, while periodic hula hoop and coconut-rolling contests amuse young children.

There's no menu from which to order. Servers simply deliver course after course. By all means, sample everything that comes your way.

The dining room itself is large and open and offers fine views across the Seven Seas Lagoon all the way to Cinderella Castle in the Magic Kingdom. Lilo, Stitch, and their good friends Mickey and Pluto host a character breakfast each morning. Breakfast fare is basic and presented family style. Reservations strongly suggested. **B D** $$$-$$$$ ☻

Par for the Course

The pleasant *Sand Trap Bar & Grill* in the Bonnet Creek Golf Club is a convenient dining option for golfers playing the adjacent Eagle Pines and Osprey Ridge courses. It's also close to the Magic Kingdom resorts. In addition to the traditional breakfast items, Sand Trap serves appetizers, burgers, soups, and sandwiches. There is a full bar; ice cream and milk shakes are available. **B L D S** $$ ☻

Pop Century

EVERYTHING POP!: Guests of this resort dine in the food court in Classic Hall. The selection includes pasta, pizza, chicken, burgers, hot dogs, sandwiches, salads, breakfast items, and baked goods. **BLDS** $-$$ 🐭

Port Orleans French Quarter

SASSAGOULA FLOATWORKS & FOOD FACTORY: The stands at this festive food court feature pizza, pasta, gumbo, burgers, sandwiches, soups, salads, spit-roasted chicken, barbecued ribs, ice cream, and a full selection of fresh bakery products, including tempting beignets. **BLDS** $-$$ 🐭

Port Orleans Riverside

BOATWRIGHT'S DINING HALL: Be sure to notice the boat that's being built in this table-service eatery. Specialties include Southern dishes as well as American home-style favorites. Reservations are suggested. **BD** $$-$$$ 🐭

RIVERSIDE MILL: This high-ceilinged food court styled in the image of a working cotton mill offers half a dozen food counters and a sprawling seating area. Collectively, the stands offer pizza; pasta; fried, grilled, and roast chicken; burgers; barbecued ribs; salads; sandwiches; and fresh baked goods.

For guests on the go, the food court's deli does double duty as a convenience store, stocking sandwiches, juices, beer, wine, snack items, and prepared salads. **BLDS** $-$$ 🐭

Saratoga Springs

THE ARTIST'S PALETTE: Fresh pizza, salads, sandwiches, and desserts are among the selections at this artsy establishment. **BLDS** $-$$ 🐭

THE TURF CLUB: A cozy lounge offering, in addition to a pool table and TV, fare such as burgers, BLTs, and grilled salmon. **LDS** $-$$

Swan & Dolphin

CABANA BAR & GRILL: Burgers, grilled chicken sandwiches, fruit, and yogurt are served at this full-service poolside eatery. **LS** $

DOLPHIN FOUNTAIN: A soda fountain with grown-up appeal, this is an ideal spot for a sweet snack or a light meal. Homemade ice cream is the specialty of the house. Burgers, sandwiches, and salads may also be available. **LDS** $-$$

FRESH MEDITERRANEAN MARKET: The Dolphin's sun-drenched restaurant offers salads, sandwiches, and Mediterranean-inspired dishes. The coffee is Starbucks. Reservations are suggested. **BL** $$-$$$

GARDEN GROVE CAFE: Situated in a greenhouse, this Swan spot offers a full breakfast menu and fresh fish and shellfish at lunch. At dinner, the restaurant is transformed into Gulliver's Grill, where buffets and family-style platters are presented and a magician entertains.

Desserts are baked fresh daily in an open pastry kitchen. As you approach the restaurant, take a look through the glass windows to see the chefs at work. Breakfasts (Saturdays and Sundays only) and dinners (every day) featuring Disney characters are held here. Reservations are suggested for dinner and for character breakfasts. **BLD** $$-$$$

PALIO: This Italian bistro is known for its bruschetta, focaccia, pasta, and pizza. Other specialties include veal and fish dishes. Strolling musicians may add to the ambience. Reservations are suggested. Located at the Swan. **D** $$$

PICABU: This Dolphin cafeteria is a bit above the norm. The food is usually fresh, and the lines are seldom very long. The convenience store (which is, conveniently, open 24 hours) offers snacks and sundries. Note that this recently refurbished spot was formerly known as Tubbi's. **BLDS** $-$$

SHULA'S STEAK HOUSE: Like the original Shula's in Miami, this Dolphin dining spot specializes in generous portions of certified Angus beef, in addition to chicken and fresh fish dishes. The eatery pays tribute to the 1972 Miami Dolphins—the year legendary coach Don Shula led his team to a perfect NFL season. Photos and souvenirs abound, and the menu comes on an autographed football (yours to keep for about $350). Reservations recommended. There is no children's menu (child care may be arranged). Business casual is the preferred attire. **D** $$$-$$$$

SPLASH GRILL: Burgers and other grilled fare join ice cream on the menu at this Swan poolside spot. Drinks are served. `L` `S` `S`

TODD ENGLISH'S BLUEZOO: A sophisticated addition to the Walt Disney World dining scene, this Dolphin eatery is the brainchild of celebrity chef Todd English. The menu features an innovative selection of fresh seafood, including a tempting raw bar. The pan-seared jumbo sea scallops take top honors in the appetizer category. All of the entrées are tempting, as well: from crisp filo-baked salmon to spit roasted swordfish to bluezoo's dancing fish. Landlubbers can indulge in oven-roasted filet of beef (with wild mushroom-short rib ragout and bacon-wrapped asparagus) and roasted breast of chicken. Choose from a famed medley of desserts. Reservations are suggested. Note that it's possible to get food service at the bar. Ask for the café menu. `D` `S` `$$$-$$$$`

Wilderness Lodge

ARTIST POINT: Housed in a cavernous dining room decorated with artwork representing painters who first chronicled the Northwest landscape, this fine dining spot offers a creative menu that incorporates buffalo and venison, in addition to more traditional items such as beef and chicken, plus salmon and more. The solid wine list spotlights wines from the Pacific Northwest with custom wine flights and half bottle suggestions. Reservations are suggested. `D` `$$$-$$$$` 🐭

ROARING FORK SNACKS: Salads, burgers, fries, sandwiches, yogurt, chili, and snacks are available at this stone-walled nook near the main pool. `B` `L` `D` `S` `S` 🐭

WHISPERING CANYON CAFE: This family-friendly restaurant serves hearty all-you-can-eat fare such as smoked barbecued meats with a variety of sides and salads, plus homemade desserts (for an extra charge). Assorted sandwiches and entrées are available à la carte at lunch and dinner. Reservations are suggested. `B` `L` `D` `$$$` 🐭

Yacht & Beach Club

BEACH CLUB MARKETPLACE: Inside the Beach Club, this spot serves hot and cold breakfast items, salads, sandwiches, and desserts (including homemade gelato). It has some groceries and "grab and go" items. `B` `L` `D` `S` `$-$$`

BEACHES & CREAM SODA SHOP: This small restaurant is on the Yacht Club side of the resorts. It offers sundaes, cones, floats, shakes, and sodas. Breakfast items are available, as are burgers and fries. `B` `L` `D` `S` `$-$$` 🐭

CAPE MAY CAFE: A wonderful all-you-can-eat beachside clambake is held each evening at the Beach Club. Favorite menu items include clams, mussels, chicken, shrimp, red-skin potatoes, and chowder. There is a character breakfast buffet each morning. Reservations are suggested. Though the price has gone up a bit, this is still a great WDW value. `B` `D` `$$$` 🐭

HURRICANE HANNA'S GRILL: Located in the Stormalong Bay area. Hot dogs, burgers, sandwiches, salads and ice cream are on the menu. There is also a full bar. `L` `S` `S` 🐭

YACHT CLUB GALLEY: Vivid ceramic-tile tabletops emphasize the nautical theme at the Yacht Club. Breakfast features a buffet and a full menu; lunch and dinner are à la carte only. Reservations are suggested. `B` `L` `D` `$$-$$$` 🐭

YACHTSMAN STEAKHOUSE: As its name implies, beef is the house specialty. Guests may watch the butcher choose cuts of meat in the glassed-in shop. The filet mignon is exceptional. Be sure to order the side of mushrooms. Seafood and chicken are available. Located at the Yacht Club. Reservations are suggested. `D` `$$$-$$$$` 🐭

GOOD MEALS, GREAT TIMES

Name/Location	Meals	Style*	Price**	Characters	Theme
Cinderella's Royal Table Magic Kingdom (page 227)	Breakfast	Family style	B: $32/22 L: $34/23 D: $40/25	Cinderella and friends like Snow White and Belle	Medieval banquet
Liberty Tree Tavern Magic Kingdom (page 227)	Dinner	Family-style	D: $28/13	Minnie, Goofy, Pluto, Chip, and Dale	Traditional Thanksgiving dinner
Crystal Palace Magic Kingdom (page 228)	Breakfast Lunch Dinner	Buffet	B: $19/11 L: $21/12 D: $28/13	Pooh, Eeyore, Tigger, and Piglet	Sunlit conservatory
Garden Grill Epcot (page 231)	Lunch Dinner	Family style	L: $21/12 D: $28/13	Mickey, Pluto, Chip, and Dale	Home-style country cooking
Restaurantosaurus Disney's Animal Kingdom (page 241)	Breakfast	Buffet	B: $19/11	Donald, Pluto, and Goofy	Paleontologist hangout
Chef Mickey's Contemporary Resort (page 247)	Breakfast Dinner	Buffet	B: $19/11 D: $28/13	Mickey, Minnie (at breakfast), Goofy, Donald (at lunch), Pluto, Chip, and Dale	A celebration
1900 Park Fare Grand Floridian Resort (page 248)	Breakfast Dinner	Buffet	B: $19/11 D: $29/14	B: Stars like Mary Poppins D: Cinderella and friends	Turn-of-the-century circus
'Ohana Polynesian Resort (page 249)	Breakfast	Family style	B: $19/11	Lilo, Stitch, Pluto, and Mickey	Tropical hut
Akershus Norway Pavilion, Epcot (page 232)	Breakfast Lunch Dinner	Buffet	B: $23/13 L: $25/14 D: $29/14	Belle, Jasmine, Snow White, Sleeping Beauty, and Mulan	14th-century Norwegian castle
Cape May Cafe Yacht and Beach Club Resorts (page 251)	Breakfast	Buffet	B: $19/11	Goofy, Minnie, Chip, and Dale	Seaside picnic

* Family-style and buffet meals are all-you-can-eat dining experiences. Family-style features a set menu and table service; buffet-style meals usually present more dining options and are self-serve.
** Adult prices are followed by children's prices (diners ages 3 through 9)

CHARACTER DINING

Featured Items	For Dessert	Tip	Wins the . . .
B: French toast, eggs, bacon, fruit	Danish	Book the first seating and request a table by the window for a prime view.	**Best Setting** (in Cinderella Castle)
Turkey, flank steak, ham, stuffing, mashed potatoes, vegetables, Stouffer's mac and cheese	Not included with the meal, but available for an additional charge: fruit pie	Though the fare, which is served family style, isn't exactly gourmet, it tends to please picky, young eaters.	**Heartiest Fare** (Most guests feel stuffed after dinner—much like they do on Thanksgiving.)
B: French toast, eggs, cereal, frittata, fruit L/D: Shrimp, carved meats, pasta, veggies, pizza, salad	B: Sticky buns L/D: Cakes, pies, make-your-own-sundaes, cookies	Don't be put off by this restaurant's size—the characters make the rounds surprisingly quickly.	**Best Theme Park Buffet** (Lovely setting, convenient location, and an appetizing menu.)
B: Eggs, potatoes, sausage L/D: Catfish, beef, chicken, veggies, potatoes, stuffing, (mac and cheese for kids)	B: Bakery basket L/D: Strawberry shortcake or fruit cobbler à la mode	Expect to pay an additional $3 per table for salad at lunchtime.	**Best for Vegetarians** (Ask for the vegetarian meal—it's a tasty ravioli primavera.)
Pancakes, French toast, eggs, quiche, breakfast potatoes, sausage, grits, cereal, fresh fruit	Danish, muffins	Beware of prankster waiters!	**Best Place to Find Donald Duck** (As the host, he makes the rounds all morning long.)
B: Eggs, pancakes, Mickey waffles, fruit, cereal D: Carved meats, seafood, pasta, veggies, pizza, salads	Make-your-own sundaes, cheesecake, pies, cookies	A celebration happens every 30 minutes. Be sure to stick around for at least one little party.	**Best All-Around Character Meal** (It has a fun and festive setting and a kid-pleasing menu.)
B: Pancakes, eggs, waffles D: Prime rib, pasta, seafood	B: Sticky buns, muffins, Danish D: Key lime pie, cheesecake, bread pudding	Breakfast here is a nice way to start a Magic Kingdom day. The park is just one monorail stop away.	**Fanciest Foods** (The quality is superior to the other buffets, and there's still plenty to please the kids.)
Mickey waffles, eggs, biscuits, fruit, bacon	Sweet baked goods	Don't forget your autograph book and camera. The characters spend a good amount of quality time at each table.	**Speediest Service** (This restaurant is rarely packed, which makes for faster service.)
B: Scrambled eggs, potato casseroles, French toast sticks, bacon, sausage, fruit L/D: Norwegian fare and kid-friendly selections	Danish, pastries	This is the only place to have breakfast at Epcot's World Showcase. (And it's the only table-service breakfast option in the whole park.)	**It's not Cinderella's Castle, but it's still pretty cool.** (It's much easier to score reservations here, too.)
Eggs, French toast sticks, Mickey waffles, sausage, fruit, cereal, grits	Cheese crepes	For guests staying in the Epcot area, Cape May is one of the best breakfast options.	**Best Chance of Getting a Table Without Reservations** (But make the arrangements, anyway!)

All characters, menu items, and prices are subject to change. Prices are rounded to the nearest dollar.
Call 407-WDW-DINE for current details or to make reservations. This listing is not comprehensive.

RESTAURANT ROUNDUP

Dining Disney style is one of the most enjoyable aspects of the vacation for many visitors. But with so many different restaurants to choose from, it can be difficult to select the spots that will best suit your family. Regulars to WDW are quick to recommend their favorites to newcomers. We, of course, are no exception to the rule. What follows is a rundown of the restaurants that we always try to include in our trips to the World and wholeheartedly recommend to those who are planning a visit. To pick these Birnbaum's Bests, we considered such factors as food quality, restaurant atmosphere, location, and overall value.

TOP WDW RESTAURANTS FOR FAMILIES WITH KIDS

TABLE SERVICE

Biergarten . . . . Epcot (p. 232)
Boma—Flavors of Africa . . . . Animal Kingdom Lodge resort (p. 246)
Cape May Cafe . . . . Beach Club resort (p. 251)
Chef Mickey's . . . . Contemporary resort (p. 247)
Cinderella's Royal Table . . . . Magic Kingdom (p. 227)
Crystal Palace . . . . Magic Kingdom (p. 228)
50's Prime Time Cafe . . . . Disney-MGM Studios (p. 238)
Garden Grill . . . . Epcot (p. 231)
Rainforest Cafe . . . . Animal Kingdom and Downtown Disney (pp. 241, 245)
Sci-Fi Dine-In Theater . . . . Disney-MGM Studios (p. 239)

FAST FOOD

Columbia Harbour House . . . . Magic Kingdom (p. 228)
Everything Pop! . . . . Pop Century resort (p. 250)
Liberty Inn . . . . Epcot (p. 236)
Pecos Bill Cafe . . . . Magic Kingdom (p. 227)
Pinocchio Village Haus . . . . Magic Kingdom (p. 227)
Sunset Ranch Market . . . . Disney-MGM Studios (p. 240)
Sunshine Seasons . . . . Epcot (p. 231)
Tusker House . . . . Animal Kingdom (p. 242)

BEST KIDS' MEAL PRESENTATION

Old Port Royale . . . . Caribbean Beach resort (p. 247)
The meal comes in a sand bucket with a shovel.

BEST PLACE TO CELEBRATE A CHILD'S BIRTHDAY

Chef Mickey's. . . . . Contemporary resort (p. 247)

RUNNER-UP

Mickey's Backyard Barbecue. . . . . Fort Wilderness (p. 260)

BEST FIREWORKS VIEW

California Grill . . . . Contemporary resort (p. 247)

BEST VEGETARIAN MEALS

Jiko—The Cooking Place
Animal Kingdom Lodge resort
(p. 246)

BEST SPLURGE FOR GROWN-UPS

California Grill . . . . .Contemporary resort (p. 247)

RUNNERS-UP

Artist Point. . . . . .Wilderness Lodge resort (p. 251)
Jiko—The Cooking Place. . . . . . . Animal Kingdom Lodge resort (p. 246)
Les Chefs de France . . . . Epcot (p. 233)
Stone Crab Lounge (inside Fulton's) . . . . Downtown Disney (p. 243)
Victoria & Albert's . . . . .Grand Floridian resort (p. 249)
Wolfgang Puck Cafe. . . . . Downtown Disney (p. 245)

BEST DINNER SHOW

Hoop-Dee-Doo Musical Revue: This crowd-pleasing saloon hall show has been going like gangbusters since 1974. Kids enjoy the silly humor, while adults eat up the bottomless buckets of ribs, fried chicken, and other down-home dishes. Presented at Fort Wilderness (p. 260).

RUNNER-UP

Mickey's Backyard Barbecue: If it were offered year-round, this would be our number-one choice. It's more of a big, informal party than a show, complete with a kickin' country band, games for the kids, and line dancing with Disney characters. The self-serve, all-you-can-eat barbecue fare is varied and plentiful. Presented at Fort Wilderness (p. 260).

GOOD MEALS, GREAT TIMES

255

BEST PIZZA FOR GROWN-UPS

Portobello Yacht Club ...... Downtown Disney, Pleasure Island (p. 244)
California Grill (flatbread) .... Contemporary resort (p. 247)

BEST PIZZA FOR KIDS

Toy Story Pizza Planet .... Disney-MGM Studios (p. 240)

BEST FIXIN'S BAR

Pecos Bill Cafe .... Magic Kingdom (p. 227)

BEST BUY

Trail's End Restaurant
Pioneer Hall, Fort Wilderness (p. 248)

BEST ITALIAN FARE

Portobello Yacht Club ...... Downtown Disney, Pleasure Island (p.2 44)

RUNNER-UP
L'Originale Alfredo di Roma Ristorante .... Epcot (p. 234)

BEST ROOM SERVICE

Yacht and Beach Club .... (p. 251)

BEST THEME

50's Prime Time Cafe .... Disney-MGM Studios (p. 238)
RUNNER-UP
Sci-Fi Dine-In Theater .... Disney-MGM Studios (p. 239)

BEST OUTDOOR CAFE

Big River Grille & Brewing Works .... BoardWalk resort (p. 246)

BEST SEAFOOD

Coral Reef . . . . Epcot (p. 231)

RUNNERS-UP

Flying Fish Cafe . . . . BoardWalk resort (p. 246)
Todd English's bluezoo . . . . Dolphin resort (p. 251)

BEST CRAB CAKES

Stone Crab Lounge . . . . Fulton's Crab House,
Downtown Disney, Marketplace (p. 243)

BEST BLOODY MARY

Stone Crab Lounge . . . . Fulton's Crab House,
Downtown Disney, Marketplace (p. 243)

BEST CHICKEN WINGS

ESPN Club
BoardWalk resort (p. 246)

BEST ICE CREAM

The Plaza . . . . Magic Kingdom (p. 229)
**Ghirardelli Soda Fountain and
Chocolate Shop** . . . . Downtown Disney, Marketplace (p. 244)

BEST STEAK

Yachtsman Steakhouse . . . . Yacht Club resort (p. 251)

RUNNER-UP

Shula's Steak House . . . . Dolphin resort (p. 250)

BEST SUSHI

Wolfgang Puck Cafe . . . . . Downtown Disney, West Side (p. 245)

RUNNER-UP

California Grill . . . . Contemporary resort (p. 247)

Reservations Explained

Disney's reservation system, formerly known as "priority seating," covers most full-service restaurants on Walt Disney World property. The name may have changed, but the procedure is the same. It was designed to provide the assurance of a reservation without delays caused by no-shows and latecomers. Here's how it works: You call ahead to request a seating time; you arrive five minutes before the assigned time and check in at the podium; you receive the next available table that can accommodate your party. The system works like traditional reservations, so you will always be seated before any walk-ins.

We recommend making advance arrangements. Seating times can be secured up to 180 days ahead* by calling 407-WDW-DINE (939-3463). One notable exception to that rule is Epcot's Bistro de Paris which accepts reservations up to 30 days in advance. Hours are Sunday through Saturday from 7 A.M. to 10 P.M. The number of tables available in advance varies. If you are unable to book ahead of time, try to make same-day arrangements.

Most WDW resorts have at least one phone in the main lobby that provides direct contact with the "Dine Line." Simply touch 55—the call is free. From other locations, dial 407-WDW-DINE. Once at the theme parks, dining reservations can be made at the restaurant itself; at City Hall in the Magic Kingdom; in Epcot at Guest Relations in Innoventions Plaza; by Hollywood Junction in the Disney-MGM Studios; and at Guest Relations in Animal Kingdom. Bookings can also be made at Guest Services in Downtown Disney Marketplace and at the West Side.

*For Disney Resort Guests *Only*

Do you have a confirmed reservation at a Disney-owned-and-operated resort? If so, you are entitled to a very special perk: Call 180 days prior to the first day of your hotel reservation and you can make dining reservations for up to 10 days of your stay. That's like getting a 1-to-10-day jump on everyone else! (Stays longer than 10 days will require a second call. Inquire when you make your first set of dining reservations.) Have your confirmation number handy when you call WDW-DINE.

Advance Planning

While some WDW restaurants always seem to have an available table (like the Marrakesh in Epcot's World Showcase), others are booked far in advance. The restaurants for which careful planning is essential include Cinderella's Royal Table in the Magic Kingdom (call 180 days ahead and keep your fingers crossed!); Les Chefs de France in Epcot; Donald's Prehistoric Breakfastosaurus in Animal Kingdom; and California Grill in the Contemporary resort.

While the Walt Disney World reservation system is often successful, there are times when the wait for a table can be unexpectedly long. This is most likely to occur during peak mealtimes at restaurants that offer buffets or family-style meals, where patrons will often opt for seconds (or thirds). For this reason, be sure to check in at the restaurant particularly early for all character-hosted meals.

Hot Tip!

At most WDW restaurants, reservations are scheduled in five- or ten-minute intervals. If they don't have a 6 P.M. availability, ask about a 6:05 P.M.

Reservations are necessary for all dinner shows—the Hoop-Dee-Doo Musical Revue, Mickey's Backyard Barbecue, and the Polynesian Luau; they can be made by calling 407-WDW-DINE (939-3463). Dinner show reservations can be booked up to 180 days in advance. If you can't get a table for an early performance, consider a later one (they are usually less heavily booked).

Keep in mind that, with the exception of dinner shows, a WDW dining reservation is not a traditional reservation. Don't be surprised if you have to wait a bit when you arrive at your assigned time. Your party will be given the first table that opens up.

Note: Because the dining scene at Walt Disney World is ever-evolving, we advise calling 407-WDW-DINE (939-3463) to confirm current reservation policies.

Dinner Shows

The fact that Disney is expert in family entertainment is nowhere more readily apparent than amid the whooping and hollering troupe of singers and dancers who race toward the stage at Fort Wilderness resort's Pioneer Hall. As guests plow through ribs, fried chicken, and strawberry shortcake, beer, wine, and soft drinks, these enthusiastic performers sing, dance, and joke up a storm.

The gags are groaners, but the audience eats 'em up. It's all in the course of an evening at the ***Hoop-Dee-Doo Musical Revue,*** presented nightly at 5 P.M., 7:15 P.M., and 9:30 P.M. Cost is $50.22 per adult and $25.43 for children (ages 3 through 9).

Note that the dining room in Pioneer Hall can be chilly year-round. Bring a sweater to combat the sometimes intense air-conditioning.

PHOTO BY JILL SAFRO

> ## Hot Tip!
> The Hoop-Dee-Doo Musical Revue is a tremendously popular show. Make your reservations as far in advance as possible.

Also presented at Fort Wilderness is ***Mickey's Backyard Barbecue.*** A country band gets guests out on the floor to kick up their heels (the line-dance lessons help, too), and Disney characters join in the fun.

Dinner consists of plenty of picnic favorites: barbecued ribs and chicken, corn-on-the-cob, and baked beans. The seasonal dinner show costs about $39 per adult and $25 for kids. Tickets are required, so book ahead.

Disney's Polynesian Luau show is called ***Spirit of Aloha.*** Set in the beachfront backyard of a Hawaiian house (at the Polynesian resort), the show invites guests to join in a musical celebration.

The luau experience combines traditional music as well as more contemporary ditties from the animated Disney film *Lilo and Stitch.* The performers' dancing is some of the most authentic this side of Hawaii. *The Spirit of Aloha* is presented in an open-air dining theater in Luau Cove, adjacent to the Seven Seas Lagoon.

The all-you-can-eat feast is influenced by the flavors of Polynesia and includes draft beer, wine, soft drinks, and dessert. Menu items include roasted chicken (made with a new

recipe), wild rice, and vegetables. The kids' menu features peanut butter and jelly sandwiches, mac and cheese, chicken nuggets, and hot dogs. Cost is $50.22 for adults and $25.43 for kids.

Plan to arrive at least 30 minutes before showtime, and allow extra time for transportation and parking. (Note that prices include tax and gratuity and are subject to change.) The show may be canceled due to inclement weather (though tables are sheltered).

Reservations: Arrangements for dinner shows may be made up to 180 days in advance by calling 407-WDW-DINE (939-3463). Groups of eight or more should call 407-939-7707.

A credit card number is required for all dinner show reservations. Full payment is required upon booking. It's also possible to redeem Disney Dining Plan credits for dinner shows. At press time all Disney dinner shows were participating in the dining plan. They are considered "signature meals" and cost two table-service meals per person. *Note that cancellations for any dinner shows must be made at least 48 hours prior to showtime to avoid paying full price.*

Lounges of WDW

No one ever said the Magic Kingdom's no-liquor policy means that everyone in the World is a teetotaler. Actually, some of WDW's tastiest offerings are liquid (and spirited), and some of its most entertaining places are its bars and lounges—many of which serve things to chew as well as sip.

Hours vary depending on the locale, but generally, watering holes at Epcot, Disney-MGM Studios, and Animal Kingdom shut their doors at park closing. Pool bars at the resorts keep daytime pool hours. Last call at lounges in the resorts is anywhere from 10 P.M. to midnight. Downtown Disney Marketplace spots stay open until the shops close, usually 11 P.M. Pleasure Island and the West Side may keep things going until about 2 A.M.

All-Star Movies, All-Star Music, & All-Star Sports
Silver Screen Spirits at All-Star Movies, **Singing Spirits** at All-Star Music, and **Team Spirits** at All-Star Sports serve beer, wine, and specialty drinks by the pool.

Animal Kingdom
DAWA BAR: Enjoy Safari Amber beer and African music under the thatched roof.

RAINFOREST CAFE: The diminutive Magic Mushroom bar serves, among other things, fruit blends and specialty drinks.

Animal Kingdom Lodge
CAPE TOWN LOUNGE AND WINE BAR: Sip African wines at this tiny spot near Jiko—The Cooking Place. It has the largest selection of African wines in the United States.

UZIMA SPRINGS: The poolside bar serves cocktails and snacks during pool hours.

VICTORIA FALLS: On the mezzanine level, this lounge offers coffee, tea, wine, and other spirits.

BoardWalk
ATLANTIC DANCE: This dance hall showcases music videos, a deejay, and a full bar.

BELLE VUE ROOM: Snacks and a full bar accompany old-time tunes from antique radios in this lobby cocktail lounge. ♥

BIG RIVER GRILLE & BREWING WORKS: A working brewpub where patrons may order appetizers at the bar and sample the brew master's flagship ales and specialty beers. ♥

ESPN CLUB: The ultimate sports bar provides live radio and television broadcasts along with a menu of ballpark favorites. ♥

JELLYROLLS: Dueling pianos and lively sing-alongs are the draw at this unique club, serving beer and other drinks.

LEAPING HORSE LIBATIONS: The pool bar offers cocktails, tuna sandwiches, fruit salad, and garden salads in a carnival setting.

Bonnet Creek Golf Club
SAND TRAP BAR & GRILL: Appetizers and sandwiches supplement the libations here. ♥

Caribbean Beach
BANANA CABANA: Refreshing drinks and snack items are served at this poolside bar.

Contemporary
CALIFORNIA GRILL LOUNGE: Prime 15th-story digs, eye level to the Magic Kingdom fireworks. A selection of California wine, all manner of other drinks, and items from the restaurant menu (including sushi) are offered in this tiny space within the California Grill restaurant. ♥

OUTER RIM: This lounge overlooking Bay Lake screens sporting events and serves cocktails and appetizers after 4 P.M.

SAND BAR: A full bar is offered poolside, weather permitting. Fast food is available at the adjacent counter area.

Coronado Springs

FRANCISCO'S: Located in the main building, this lounge serves specialty drinks, beer, wine, and light Mexican snacks.

SIESTA'S: Swimmers can take time out for burgers, sandwiches, tacos, and cocktails at this spot near the pool in the Dig Site area. ❤

Disney-MGM Studios

TUNE-IN LOUNGE: A sitcom living room setting, with comfy couches and chairs, characterizes this lounge next to the 50's Prime Time Cafe. Waiters play the roles of sitcom "Dads," and old TV sets play scenes from beloved sitcoms (all of which feature food). Appetizers, mixed drinks, beer, and wine are served.

Disney's Old Key West

GURGLING SUITCASE: This pocket-size lounge on the Turtle Krawl boardwalk serves an assortment of Key West specialties along with traditional cocktails, beer, and wine.

TURTLE SHACK: Refreshments at this poolside spot include cocktails and fast-food items.

Downtown Disney

All clubs have bars serving specialty drinks, beer, wine, and cocktails. The excellent *Stone Crab* lounge inside *Fulton's Crab House* (located between Pleasure Island and the Marketplace) and *Bongos Cuban Cafe* (West Side) are notable for exotic cocktails and scenic outdoor seating. Pleasure Island's *Portobello Yacht Club* also has a pleasant lounge. The *Rainforest Cafe* (Marketplace) is the site of the *Magic Mushroom* bar.

CAP'N JACK'S RESTAURANT (Marketplace): Agleam with copper and right on the water, this bar's specialty is its delicious strawberry margaritas. The nibbles of garlic oysters, clam chowder, and shrimp on the appetizer menu are great for a snack or a meal. ❤

Hot Tip!
For a late-night cocktail, head to Downtown Disney. The resort lounges tend to have last call before midnight.

Epcot

All restaurants, including some fast-food spots, serve alcoholic beverages. Some have a small lounge at which patrons may wait for tables. A few other Epcot locales actually specialize in liquid refreshments:

MATSU NO MA: In addition to exotic sake-based specialty drinks, this Japan pavilion establishment offers a fine panoramic view of World Showcase Lagoon, with Spaceship Earth as a backdrop—one of the best vistas of the property available. Japanese beer, green tea, and sushi are also served.

ROSE & CROWN PUB: This watering hole—a veritable symphony of polished woods, brass, and etched glass—adjoins the Rose & Crown Dining Room in the United Kingdom pavilion. British, Scottish, and Irish beers are available, along with a score of specialty drinks and appetizing snacks imported from the other side of the Atlantic. On special occasions, there may be live (and lively) piano music. ❤

SOMMERFEST: Just outside the Biergarten restaurant in Germany, there's a small shaded terrace where soft pretzels, bratwurst, Black Forest cake, beer, and wine are available. ❤

Fort Wilderness

CROCKETT'S TAVERN: Cocktails, beer, wine, appetizers, and light sandwiches are served in a rustic setting. ❤

Grand Floridian

MIZNER'S: Named after the eccentric architect who defined much of the flavor of Florida's Gold Coast, this handsome retreat serves ports, brandies, and appetizers.

NARCOOSSEE'S: This lagoonside bar-within-a-restaurant offers cocktails and a list of international wines. ❤

❤ Disney Dining Plan participant at press time

POOL BAR: This bar stands by with beer, frozen drinks, and fast-food items.

Polynesian

BAREFOOT BAR: This oasis next to the swimming pool lagoon serves beer, frozen tropical drinks, and fast food. Seasonal.

TAMBU: Adjoining 'Ohana restaurant, this bar offers Polynesian-style appetizers and specialty drinks in a tropical setting.

Pop Century

PETALS: This poolside watering hole serves beer, wine, and cocktails.

Port Orleans French Quarter

MARDI GROGS: Beer, specialty drinks, and snacks are among the offerings at this poolside spot.

Port Orleans Riverside

MUDDY RIVERS: The poolside bar serves beer, specialty concoctions, and snack items.

RIVER ROOST: Situated in a room designed as a cotton exchange, this lounge features specialty drinks, as well as light hors d'oeuvres.

Saratoga Springs

THE TURF CLUB: This charming corner of the resort serves all manner of spirits. There's a pool table, too!

Swan & Dolphin

CABANA BAR & GRILL: Beer, frozen drinks, and fast-food selections are the main offerings at this Dolphin poolside spot.

KIMONOS: This Swan spot, attractively decorated in Japanese style, has a full bar, as well as sushi and other tasty treats.

LOBBY COURT: The winding corridors of the Swan lobby have comfortable couches and chairs, punctuated by piano music. A special menu with international wines, ports, cognacs, and cigars is offered.

ON THE ROCKS: Specialty drinks, beer, wine, and snack selections are offered at this pool bar.

SHULA'S STEAK HOUSE LOUNGE: This cozy cigar bar adjoining Shula's Steak House features rich wood tones and leather chairs—

Hot Tip!
At many Walt Disney World lounges, you may order food from a neighboring or nearby restaurant's menu.

the perfect place to sip a cocktail and puff a stogie while playing armchair quarterback.

SPLASH GRILL: Beer, frozen drinks, and fast food are served at this Swan poolside cafe.

TODD ENGLISH'S BLUEZOO BAR: Awash in blue hues, this spot within Todd English's bluezoo restaurant offers a variety of drinks, including the "Zooberry Cocktail."

Wilderness Lodge

TERRITORY: Located between Artist Point and Whispering Canyon Cafe, this homage to the explorers of the Great West is a nice spot for a predinner treat. Appetizers, beer, wine, and specialty drinks are served.

TROUT PASS: This poolside bar serves beer, frozen drinks, and snacks.

Yacht & Beach Club

ALE AND COMPASS: The cozy lobby watering hole proffers appetizers and a specialty drink menu complete with specialty coffee (espresso, cappuccino, etc.) and ale. It's small, but still one of the more inviting lounges on WDW property. 🔴

CREW'S CUP: Styled after a traditional New England waterfront pub, this lounge has a seafaring feel to it. It's next door to the Yachtsman Steakhouse (with a view of the choice cuts that are about to become dinner!), has almost 40 beers, and is a charming spot for a drink before dinner. There is also a tempting appetizer menu. This is one of our favorite places to relax after a long day in the parks.

HURRICANE HANNA'S GRILL: This poolside spot offers specialty beverages, frozen drinks, and beer, plus fast-food items. Alcohol-free concoctions are available, too. 🔴

MARTHA'S VINEYARD: While a full bar is available, a small-but-satisfying selection of wines from Martha's Vineyard (and other areas) is this spot's specialty. Appetizers and snacks are served.

INDEX

15% OFF Lunch or Dinner

for up to 8 guests in the HOB Restaurant (excludes alcohol)

Enjoy distinctive Southern-inspired cuisine in an enjoyable atmosphere filled with creative folk art. Opens daily at 11 A.M. For reservations, call 407-934-2623.

Subject to terms and conditions on reverse side

15% OFF Admission to the BEHIND THE SEEDS

Tour at The Land
for up to 10 guests

Bring the entire family backstage for a one-hour, interactive tour of the greenhouses and fish farm at The Land.

For same-day reservations, present coupon at the Tour Desk next to the entrance of Soarin'. Or call ahead to 407-WDW-TOUR (939-8687) and mention *Birnbaum Offer*.

Subject to terms and conditions on reverse side

Up to 20% OFF Accommodations

- Receive 10% off the non-discounted rate most nights 2/1/07–2/15/07; 2/20/07–3/24/07.

- Receive 20% off the non-discounted rate most nights 1/1/07–1/31/07; 4/15/07–5/25/07; 5/29/07–6/28/07; 7/5/07–8/30/07; 9/4/07–11/21/07; 11/26/07–12/19/07.

The number of rooms available for these offers is limited with a minimum of 20 rooms available most nights for the dates listed above. For reservations, call 407-939-7540 and ask for package code BPQ or the Birnbaum Offer.

Subject to terms and conditions on reverse side

15% OFF Behind-the-Scenes Tours

at Disney's Animal Kingdom
Choose your adventure: Trek behind the scenes for a revealing look at the way specialists care for the animals on the *Backstage Safari Tour*,

or discover how designers combined art, architecture, and storytelling to create the park's exotic locale on the *Wild by Design Tour*. For more information on the tours, see pages 212–213 of this book. Call 407-939-8687 for reservations.

Subject to terms and conditions on reverse side

15% OFF EPCOT® Dive Quest admission

Epcot® Dive Quest is a scuba-diving adventure open to all certified scuba divers ages 10 and up.

Call (407) 939-8687 for reservations.

Subject to terms and conditions on reverse side

15% OFF DISNEY'S DOLPHINS IN DEPTH admission

for up to 4 guests

Disney's Dolphins in Depth is an educational dolphin interaction program open to all guests ages 13 and up.

Call (407) 939-8687 for reservations.

Subject to terms and conditions on reverse side

DISNEY'S HILTON HEAD ISLAND RESORT

Up to 20% OFF Accommodations

- Receive 10% off the non-discounted rate most nights 5/3/07–5/25/07; 5/29/07–5/30/07
- Receive 20% off the non-discounted rate most nights 1/1/07–2/15/07; 2/20/07–2/28/07; 3/1/07–3/28/07; 4/15/07– 5/2/07; 8/26/07–8/30/07; 9/4/07–11/21/07; 11/26/07–12/31/07.

The number of rooms available for these offers is limited with a minimum of 20 rooms available most nights for the dates listed above. For reservations, call 407-939-7540 and ask for package code BPR or the Birnbaum Offer.

Subject to terms and conditions on reverse side

10% OFF admission for up to 4 guests

Before 4 P.M. at
Disney's Fantasia Gardens or Disney's Winter Summerland
Miniature Golf Course.

Subject to terms and conditions on reverse side

10% OFF*
Food and Non-alcoholic Beverages

at *Disney's Wide World of Sports*® Complex

Subject to terms and conditions on reverse side

$10 OFF Purchase of $50 or More

at the **LEGO Imagination Center**®
at DOWNTOWN DISNEY® Marketplace

Subject to terms and conditions on reverse side

10% OFF SEGWAY™ EXPERIENCE

for up to four guests

Guests can experience the thrill of learning to ride a Segway™ while discovering *Epcot*®.

For additional information and reservations, call 407-WDW-TOUR (939-8687) and mention the *Birnbaum Offer*.

Subject to terms and conditions on reverse side

Disney Rewards® Visa® Card

Earn *Disney Rewards*^SM2
No Annual Fee
No Block-out Dates

FREE $50 *Disney Gift Card*^*1

APPLY TODAY!

Call 1-888-729-1401 or visit
Disneyworld50gift.com
and mention key code 6JR303

You must apply for the card, be approved and use your card to receive your free gift.

Subject to terms and conditions on reverse side.

Offer is valid for 10% off one round of miniature golf before 4 P.M. Limit four Guests per coupon. Not valid with any other discounts or offers. No photocopies accepted. Offer is subject to availability. Restrictions apply.

© Disney

Expires 12/31/07

Excludes Grand Villas. Minimum length-of-stay requirements may apply. All prices and other terms are subject to change without notice. Offer does not apply to group rates or any other discounted rates. Advance reservations required. This coupon may not be redeemed for cash in whole or in part.

© Disney

Expires 12/31/07

Qualifying amount applies to merchandise only. Limit one coupon per transaction. Coupon must be redeemed at time of purchase. Not valid toward prior purchase or gift certificates. Coupon cannot be redeemed for cash or replaced if lost or stolen. May not be combined with any other offer or coupon. Offer not valid at other LEGO stores or *www.lego.com*. Valid only at the LEGO Store in DOWNTOWN DISNEY® Marketplace.

Coupon code: 999132

Expires 12/30/07

Please present this coupon to your server before ordering. Not valid with any other offers or discounts. Limit one coupon per party per visit. Valid only at the Official All Star Café®. Valid for dine-in experience only. Coupon is nontransferable and holds no cash value. No reproductions accepted. *Walt Disney World*® employees are ineligible to receive coupon discount. Tax and gratuity not included.

Not valid on Atlanta Braves spring training game dates.

Valid 10/1/06–12/31/07

Offer is valid for a 10% discount on all *Epcot*® Segway™ guest programs. Limit of four (4) guests per coupon. Offer is subject to availability. Not valid with any other discounts or offers. Reproductions of coupon are not accepted. Coupon may not be redeemed for cash in whole or in part. Park admission is required. Age and rider restrictions apply.

© Disney

Expires 12/31/07